Religious Experience and Religious Belief

George Wall

University Press of America, Inc.
Lanham • New York • London

In memory of Amelia --
who knew God

Copyright © 1995 by
University Press of America,® Inc.
4720 Boston Way
Lanham, Maryland 20706

3 Henrietta Street
London, WC2E 8LU England

All rights reserved
Printed in the United States of America
British Cataloging in Publication Information Available

Library of Congress Cataloging-in-Publication Data

Wall, George B.
Religious experience and religious belief / George Wall.
p. cm.
Includes bibliographical references.
1. Experience (Religion)   2. Belief and doubt.   3. Psychology, Religious.
I. Title.
BL53.W25   1995
291.4'2--dc20   94-25225

ISBN 0-8191-9832-3 (cloth: alk paper)
ISBN 0-8191-9833-1 (pbk: alk paper)

⊖™ The paper used in this publication meets the minimum
requirements of American National Standard for Information
Sciences—Permanence of Paper for Printed Library Materials,
ANSI Z39.48–1984

Contents

Acknowledgments	vii
Chapter One	1
Preliminary Considerations	
Criticism of Naturalisic Explanations of Religious Experience	
Chapter Two	37
The Explanation from Background Influences	
Chapter Three	89
The Explanation from Desire and from Unconscious Motivation	
Chapter Four	143
The Explanation from Desire and Unconscious Motivation: Three Special Cases	
Chapter Five	175
The Explanation from Desire and Unconscious Motivation: Eastern Forms of Experience	
Chapter Six	205
The Notion of the Unconscious Criticism of Other Possible General Defeaters of Religious Experience	
Chapter Seven	253
The Effects of Religious Experience	
Chapter Eight	265
The Religious Overrider System	
Chapter Nine	295
Two Conflicts in Religious Beliefs	
Conclusion	337
Bibliography	339

Acknowledgments

I wish to thank all those who were willing to be interviewed by me, as well as the leaders of the various religious communities who made the interviews possible. I also wish to thank the Alister Hardy Research Centre for kindly permitting me to go through their files on religious experience. Polly Wheway was of special assistance in helping me find my way around the Centre.

I owe a debt of gratitude to my colleagues who read over an original draft of the book. Bruce Nerenberg, a friend of many years, provided helpful criticisms on the psychological portions of the manuscript. Bruce has a PhD in philosophy and was Professor of Philosophy at Shimer College. He is now a practicing clinical psychologist. Larry Lacy, Chairman and Professor of Philosophy at Rhodes College, and William Alston, Professor of Philosophy at Syracuse University, also provided very helpful criticisms. This book, whatever its deficiencies, is much improved because of the criticisms of these people. More importantly, I have been enriched by their frank critiques and by the personal care and support they offered me.

Finally, I note that the project of this book has been the most fulfilling academic enterprise of my life. Although very demanding, it was great fun, not to mention a source of personal growth.

Chapter One

Preliminary Considerations

1. The Nature of Religious Experience

The term 'religious experience' is anything but clear-cut and well-defined; moreover, it is not without undesirable connections. However, I do not think that a precise definition is possible or necessary, and no other term that I can think of is without undesirable connections. Actually, whatever the undesirable connections of 'religious experience', it had, in my opinion, a redeeming connection in our century by way of the writings of William James. *Varieties of Religious Experience* served to enhance the status of the term, giving it blue-blood connections, with the result that it became widely employed in the writings of philosophers of religion, theologians, and, to a degree, in popular parlance. Therefore, not being a fighter by nature, I shall join the crowd.

James says that "in the distinctively religious sphere of experience, many persons . . . possess the objects of their belief, not in the form of mere conceptions which their intellect accepts as true, but rather in the form of quasi-sensible realities directly apprehended." (*Varieties*, 63) The phrase 'quasi-sensible realities' is less than felicitous for the religious Object, but what James seems to want to emphasize is that the direct apprehension of the Object is along the lines of the direct apprehension of physical objects in perception.

James's concept of religious experience is spelled out more specifically in his description of what he calls "salvation," something which he sees as the "common nucleus" among the various religions. His description is of salvation as experienced by "those more developed minds," exemplified by his various cases in *Varieties*. (498-99) For these minds, says James, salvation is an experience in which the individual

> becomes conscious that this higher part [of him, that is, the part seeking salvation] is conterminous and continuous with a MORE of the same quality, which is operative in the universe outside of him, and which he can keep in working touch with, and in a fashion get on board of and save himself when all his lower being has gone to pieces in the wreck. (498-99)

Since James is considering a select form of religious experience, his description excludes a whole range of religious experience. The description focuses on union (a term James repeats several times in the context following the statement quoted) with a MORE, a higher Consciousness. Union is one form of religious experience but hardly exhausts the range of religious experience. Moses' experience at the burning bush was certainly a religious experience, yet Moses did not seem to experience union with Yahweh. Moses was simply aware of Yahweh's presence. Likewise with Paul in his conversion: He was aware of Christ's presence but did not seem to sense union with Christ.

Yet James' description captures what I see as an essential aspect of religious experience—individual consciousness meeting a MORE, a higher Consciousness. I am more inclined to traditional language, in which we would speak of spirit meeting Spirit; however, I shall stay with the language of James. Thus, putting the notion of higher Consciousness together with what James said earlier about direct apprehension (I shall use 'direct apprehension' interchangeably with 'direct awareness'), I shall say that religious experience is the direct awareness of a divine Consciousness, with the awareness taking any of a variety of forms—awareness of a Presence or awareness of union, with union having many degrees.

The Sense of 'Direct Awareness'

Whatever James thought about the relation between religious experience and sensory perception, I think that the two are best thought of as cousins, with religious experience being a more direct form of awareness than sensory perception. Why more direct?

In thinking of religious experience along Jamesian lines, as consciousness meeting Consciousness, we may stake out an ontological position which provides for a more direct awareness of the Divine than of the objects of sensory perception, such as computers, cars, cats, and catwalks. This greater directness is illustrated by the terminology often employed by people having religious experience: "I was in God"; "I was catapulted into this huge Reality of a different dimension"; "I was absorbed into something wondrous, what I felt as LOVE"; "I communed, just as— well, like Moses on the Mount"; "I was at rest, as in a great peaceful Ocean"; and so on. The language here conveys much more than directness, but it is the language of participation or union, and participation indicates a high level of directness. Introspection is, I should say, as high a level of directness as we can get, and we could use the language of participation for introspection—the objects of consciousness are wholly within consciousness. Normally, in religious experience the participation is in the reverse from introspection; that is, we sense ourselves as in the Divine, not *vice versa*, although many times we hear people saying, "I was wholly within God, and God was wholly within me." Even if we said that God was wholly within us, we would not mean, as in the case of introspection, that the Divine is strictly an aspect of our consciousness.

We must remember, of course, that union (participation) is only one form of religious experience. Yet even in cases of being aware of the presence of the Divine, we are, as it were, face to face with the Divine— there is a directness, absent in the case of physical objects. If we took an idealistic approach to physical objects, whether it were that of Berkeley or Bradley, we could get a directness similar to what I am saying is present in religious experience. If physical objects, at least as perceived entities, are conscious realities, then as perceived entities they participate in us. (The story here needs much enlargement, but I must refrain from enlargement.) However, I am taking a realistic approach to physical objects. Taking this approach, I shall refer to the sort of direct awareness present in religious experience as "direct-awareness-R."

I note that the ontology of religious experience I have staked out is, as far as I can tell, logically possible. More on this below. Of course, it is not the only possible ontology, although I shall refrain from elaborating other possibilities. I shall note another possibility toward the end of this chapter.

Perhaps I can provide some further clarity to the notion of direct-awareness-R by relating it to William Alston's notions of absolute immediacy and mediated immediacy. Absolute immediacy is a state in which one is "aware of X but not through anything else, even a state of consciousness." (1991, 21) Introspection is a case of absolute immediacy, for in being aware, say, "of feeling excited, there is not a conscious state of being aware of my feeling that is distinguishable from the feeling." (21) Mediated immediacy is a state in which "one is aware of X through a state of consciousness that is distinguishable from X, and can be made an object of absolutely immediate awareness, but is not perceived." (22) The phrase 'but is not perceived' indicates that we are not to think of states of consciousness as perceived; or in Alston's words, "I am thinking of perception as involving at least as much mediation as we have in [mediated immediacy]." (22) Mediated immediacy is the sort of awareness we have in the case of physical objects. When I see my neighbor's cat pounce on a jay under my feeder, I am directly perceiving this situation. I distinguish what is happening here—direct perception—from seeing a similar situation on television, or even seeing it reflected in a mirror (cases of indirect perception).

Direct-awareness-R is clearly not a case of absolute immediacy, for in religious experience one is aware of X (Consciousness) through one's state of consciousness. Instead, direct-awareness-R is a case of mediated immediacy, for Consciousness (X) is present to consciousness (the subject), but the subject's state of consciousness is distinguishable from X. All the same, there is a higher level of immediacy in the awareness of Consciousness (X) than in the perception of physical objects.

One point that I would stress is that our focus is awareness, not belief. Belief is very different from awareness, although belief may very well accompany awareness. In being aware of the squirrel in my front yard, I believe that the squirrel is there; indeed, I know that the squirrel is there. However, I have many beliefs, as well as items of knowledge, unaccompanied by awareness and not derived from direct awareness. E.g., I know that there is a Mt. Everest in the Himalayas, although I have never been there. What I especially wish to stress is that religious experience is awareness of, not belief that. It is not inference of a divine Reality, any more than seeing a squirrel in my yard is an inference from some other perception or set of perceptions or beliefs. Inferring the Divine from the awareness of something else, such as the starry sky above or a felt need within, is very different from being aware of the Divine (e.g., "I was in God").

I could add further words about direct awareness R, but I do not think that I would provide further clarification. If someone thinks that the notion is too vague or that it is objectionable on other grounds, I shall simply stick with Alston's notion of mediated immediacy, saying that direct awareness R is a form of mediated immediacy, and thus at least as immediate as the perception of physical objects.

Direct Awareness of Divine Consciousness

Religious experience, as I am considering it and as I think James considers it, is the experience of a MORE, a higher Consciousness. Thus, hearing a voice, as in the case of Moses and St. Paul, is in itself not necessarily a religious experience. In both cases, though, I take the voice to be an aspect of a whole experience which came through as divine Presence. I add that in the majority of cases I have studied, a Voice is usually explicitly recognized as internal and as an aspect of a total experience of divine Presence. People will say something which may be put briefly: "God met me and said such and so; but it wasn't anything audible. It was internal, from within." They also often go on to say that the speaking was not like a thought coming into consciousness. It was unique. When people speak like this about God, I shall take the experience to be a direct awareness of a communicating Consciousness. If one's experience is just words, disassociated from any sense of divine Presence, I shall not consider the experience religious. Words imply some sort of speaker, but I am considering religious experience as direct awareness of the Divine. Inferring some presence or other from words or a voice will not count as direct awareness.

I treat visual material (for example, a vision of Jesus) the same way as auditory material, for I place both within the general category of visions. In the cases I have looked at, having a vision of a divine Being is usually associated with a sense of Presence. Yet the association need not be present. One might have a vision, say, of the suffering Christ, seeing blood flowing from His wounds. Because of the vision one might feel grief, compunction for sin, or gratitude, but one need not sense the presence of Christ. Thus, I shall not consider a vision of a divine Being as a religious experience, unless there is a sense of Presence associated with it. Certainly, a vision resulting in, say, gratitude to Christ, constitutes a religious experience in a very important sense but not the sense which is germane to the purpose of this book. I might say that I am working with a technical or quasi-technical sense of 'religious experience'.

The Exteriority of the Divine Consciousness

In religious experience we are aware, says James, of a MORE that comes with the "appearance of exteriority." The term 'exteriority' is not easy to clarify, a fact which does not in the least affect the sense of exteriority, a sense which is, e.g., not present with our daydreams but is with our perception of a rose. Generally, lack of conceptual or causal clarity has nothing to do with things appearing in a certain way or being as they are perceived. When a child, I had not heard of the term 'exteriority' or of any criteria for determining exteriority; yet I still correctly distinguished things external from things internal. I perceived the rocky shoreline at Laguna Beach as external and recognized my imaginary playmates as strictly fabrications of me.

Yet we may, I think, provide some clarification for the term 'exteriority'. A conscious object (or process) having exteriority has at least two characteristics. First, it is given (a term with a hoary tradition, and a term also needing clarification), presented to consciousness—it just shows up, whatever we may be thinking or willing. Second, it is clearly different from us, not to be identified with or reduced to our conscious life. I am performing Bach's C Minor Fugue when an obsessive idea flies onto my conscious screen, the result being that I forget the rest of the fugue, to my consternation and the consternation of my audience. I may say that the obsessive idea, the idea which ruined my delicate performance of the fugue, was given—it came on my conscious screen, independently of what I was thinking or willing, for I was concentrating on Bach's fugue and willing that I give a knock-down performance. Yet the idea lacks exteriority, for I identify it as strictly an aspect of me. And, I might add, I identified unwilled thoughts as aspects of me before I knew anything about unconscious processes. Rocks and trees, though, I identify—and identified from my earliest memories—as realities different from me. They are both given and different from me, and thus have exteriority.

As a clarifying footnote on 'exteriority', James offers the following quotation from the French author, Recejac: "'When mystical activity is at its height, we find consciousness possessed by the sense of a being.'" (499, footnote two) Saying that our consciousness is possessed by the sense of a being seems to be very much like saying that a being different from us is given, presented to consciousness.

Perhaps the best clarification James gives is in the words 'operative in the universe outside of him'. The MORE is not identical with the individual self or some aspect of it. The MORE transcends the individual self, both conscious and unconscious.

The Possibility of Direct Awareness of Another Consciousness

And now I return to my promissory note. I shall say a few words about the logical possibility of Consciousness meeting consciousness.

Someone might ask how we can apprehend or be directly aware of another consciousness and its attributes. A full, adequate answer to this question is clearly beyond the scope of this book and at this stage also beyond my capabilities. All the same, I shall make a few responses.

First, the fact is that religious experience seems to present us with the reality of another Consciousness, so we either go with experience or deny the possibility on theoretical grounds. However, no theoretical ground which I am conversant with seems in any sense decisive or as decisive as what experience presents. More precisely, I do not know of any decisive argument showing the logical impossibility of a direct awareness of another consciousness, Divine or human.

Second, we seem to accept the possibility of direct communication between separate consciousnesses. Some people claim that they can communicate telepathically, a controversial claim, of course. Suppose that we simply focus on the telepathic ability of "reading another's mind," of becoming aware of the thoughts and feelings of another. In mind reading one consciousness is targeting another and becoming aware of the contents of the other consciousness. The evidence for mind reading seems strong enough to keep us investigating the issue or waiting for the results of investigations. Obviously, if we think that mind-reading can be investigated, we do not think that it is logically impossible—we do not, for example, look for round-squares. Moreover, the usual argument against telepathy in all its forms is not that it logically cannot occur but that it just, in fact, does not occur—the evidence is not there, or has been cooked, or something of the like. Again, we do not even mention evidence if we think that something is logically impossible.

Third, if awareness of another consciousness is a problem, then awareness of many other items is also a problem. How do we determine that some thoughts are of the past, are not imaginary, but are of events which occurred? Pastness does not come as a tag or as a color-marking on certain conscious material. We just apprehend that some things are of the past—they are not now occurring or happening, are not imaginations or dreams or hopes, but are what occurred, what happened. We can pile on further words, yet we shall, I think, end up saying something of the sort, "It just is a memory, just is of the past. Period!"

Additionally, we could note that the same must be said even in the case of sensory material. We might say that sensory material can be distinguished because it is obviously different—blue is not red, red is not the sound Middle-C, and so on. Yet how do we perceive the difference between red and Middle-C? What is there to distinguish the two? Only the difference between red and Middle-C! In short, I think that again we are reduced to saying very simply, "We are just aware of the difference. Period!" I believe that we must say the same for the difference between dreams and waking experience. Thus, I do not see any reason for not taking the same approach for the awareness of another consciousness. If someone maintains that distinctions between memory and imagination or between colors and sounds or between dreaming and waking experience are more obvious and more secure than the distinction between consciousnesses, then, apart from further arguments, I shall be inclined to claim bias.

Fourth, one reason why awareness of another consciousness may be considered a problem is that consciousness is not of a sensory nature. Yet much of our conscious life is neither sensory perception nor of sensory content, yet we are at least as confident epistemically of the non-sensory as we are of sensory perception. I am hoping to visit my friends next month in Washington D.C.; also, I am feeling elation as I recall celebrating Father's Day yesterday with my daughters. I am at least as confident epistemically of my hope and of my feeling of elation as I am of the cup of coffee at my left hand. Or put otherwise, if my hope and my feeling of elation are epistemically problematic, so is the perception of the coffee cup. The point here is not that religious experience is of the nature of feelings; rather, the point is that awareness of non-sensory items is often epistemically very secure, and that this may be the case with the awareness of other consciousnesses. Fifth, the awareness of another consciousness is a problem we meet every day; or better, it is not a problem for us every day, even though we are not clear about what is going on. The fact is that we perceive other persons—embodied persons, to be sure. How do we do it? How do we recognize them as persons, as conscious beings—by inference, direct awareness, some combination of the two, or what? The answer to this question is anything but settled in philosophy, yet its failure to be settled has no impact whatsoever on our confidence that we are dealing with persons, that, for example, my friend John is drinking coffee with me. The basic moral of the story here is not that becoming aware of an embodied consciousness is exactly like becoming aware of a disembodied consciousness. Rather, the moral is one that we have already come across: Lack of knowledge of how we do something does not in the least affect the fact that we are doing it.

The upshot is that I do not see any special problem in being directly aware of another consciousness—in particular, a divine Consciousness.

Direct Consciousness of the Divine

I hope that all my remarks so far are in reasonable order, but whether they are or not, I must press on, for I still have a distance to go before reaching my working notion of religious experience. I have talked much about the Divine and have noted James's reference to a MORE, without saying anything about the MORE (or any divinity of whatever name or title), other than what James says, namely, that It is a higher Consciousness. For starters that will do, except that I shall underline what I think James accepts, namely, that the Consciousness may be impersonal. Certainly, in *Varieties* he includes examples of contact with an impersonal Consciousness. In short, I wish to include under the canopy of religious experience all the experiences, both from East and West, in which the Divine is experienced, in the words of the Chandogya Upanishad, as the "unspeaking, the unconcerned." (Third, Prapathaka, Fourteenth Kanda) Although many experience the Divine as "the unspeaking, the unconcerned," they (or at least many among the many) still recognize the impersonal Reality as essentially mind-like or of the nature of consciousness. S. Radhakrishnan, referring to Brahman, says, "All being is consciousness, and all consciousness being" (Radhakrishnan, 1957, 617).

Whatever our positive concepts of mind or consciousness, we can at least say that it transcends the strictly spatio-temporal, the world of electrons, magnetic forces, computer chips, brain states, baseballs, cabbages, sealing wax, and other like realities. However, Plato's Ideals also transcend this world. Are they Divine? I am ready to seriously consider the Good as having the status of divinity, largely because Plato characterizes It as "not only the author of knowledge to all things known, but of their being and essence, and yet the good is not essence, but far exceeds essence in dignity and power." (*Republic*, 509) Yet I should not want to give divine status to the ideals of justice, beauty, perfect equality, and so on because they do not seem to partake of consciousness at all. They are more idea-like than mind-like (if talking about ideas separate from mind makes sense). Be this as it may, I should wish to say that mind or consciousness, in addition to transcending this world in the sense of being non-corporeal, has some of the following qualities: knowledge, intention, purpose, thought, bliss, peace, creative power, or moral perfection. None of these applies to Plato's ideals (the ideal of justice, e.g., is an ideal *of* moral perfection; it does not *have* moral perfection), and perhaps none of them applies to every form of recognized religious Object East and West. Some expressions of Buddhism and Hinduism, e.g., would probably not be comfortable with any of the terms listed, although perhaps I could ease some of the discomfort by saying that purpose and intention need not be explicitly conscious but may be similar to unconscious processes. (We must always be careful not to go so far as to reduce purpose and intention to impulses or forces which we could not distinguish from some kind of strictly spatio-temporal impulse or force, such as an electromagnetic impulse.)

Thus, I shall say that the Divine is of the order of mind or consciousness, transcending the strictly spatio-temporal order, and having certain positive characteristics, such as knowledge, intention, purpose, thought, bliss, peace, creative power, or moral perfection. The Divine also significantly transcends the human order in reality, power, or perfection. An extraterrestrial being with higher intellectual powers than a human would not be a divinity, whereas Zeus, the Unmoved Mover, Yahweh, Allah, Brahman, and the MORE would be. In the case of the MORE we have a reality which is clearly more knowledgeable and powerful than humans but seems to be distinguished mainly as the locus of the highest values. James says of the MORE that on its "hither" side it is "the subconscious continuation of our conscious life." (502) On its "farther" side it is an ideal region, a mystical or supernatural region of "an altogether other dimension of existence from the sensible and merely 'understandable world." (506) But it is not merely an ideal region, constituted by forms similar to the Platonic forms of justice and beauty, for it is both a region with which we may commune and a region producing effects on us. The natural appellation for this region, according to James, is "God." Thus, to be accurate, we should say that only the farther side of the MORE is God. However, I shall use the term 'MORE' as equivalent to this farther side.

Our Working Notion of Religious Experience

Where have we come, then, in our short journey into religious experience? We have arrived at the following position: Religious experience is direct awareness of or encounter with a divine Being of the sort characterized above. This approach to religious experience permits us to make the following judgments. If a person senses a unity with Nature but senses nature as strictly physical, nothing more than a space-time reality, the experience is not religious because we do not have a divinity. Or if a person has an experience of peace, serenity, and ecstasy while listening to Beethoven's "Sixth Symphony," the experience is not religious but aesthetic, for to have feelings of peace, serenity, and ecstasy is not to have a direct awareness of divine Presence or Reality. Or if a mother senses that her seven year old son will not live to be eight, a date five months hence, and he dies in a bicycle accident the next month, or if a father senses at three-thirty one afternoon that his son has just escaped from great danger, and the father later discovers that the son at exactly three-thirty had barely missed being hit by a train, neither the mother nor the father had a religious experience because neither had a direct awareness of divine Presence. The experiences of both fall in the category of psi-phenomena, not religious experience.

I shall not claim that my characterization of religious experience provides for clear-cut judgments of every experience served up as religious. Indeed, I grant that my characterization is far too vague for such a task. I do not wish, though, to take upon myself the task of working out precisely the notion of religious experience, for my aim is not to develop a precise classificatory criterion (if one could be developed—something I seriously doubt, especially if the criterion is to draw wide, if not universal, agreement). In a sense my approach is simply to stipulate: I stipulate that the experiences I present are religious. But if I am simply stipulating, why did I not just start out doing so and save myself time and trouble? Because I wanted to give some sense of the kind of game I am playing. Instead of merely shouting "Safe!" or "Out!", without any apparent rhyme or reason, I wanted to give some sense of the reasons for my calls. At any rate, I do not consider my stipulating to be arbitrary, for I think that most people would agree that the experiences I appeal to fall in the class of religious experience, whatever other additional sorts of experience might also fall in the class. We must, I think, begin with our crucial examples, working out our definitions from them. As Alvin Plantinga says, "We must give examples and hope for the best." (1974, 1)

What I want to do, then, is see what tentative conclusions we can come up with by looking at examples of experiences in which people sense divine Reality. My study may not include what some people would include under religious experience, or, for that matter, my study may include more than some people would include. Our differences over what is to be included or excluded should not affect the conclusions we draw on the basis of my sample.

2. Religious Experience As Justification for Religious Belief

The time has now come to work toward a statement of my general objective in this book. To begin with, I shall accept the thesis that religious experience is a rational ground for religious belief. This thesis has at least two interpretations. The first has been developed recently by several people, including William Alston, Alvin Plantinga, and Richard Swinburne. They maintain that religious experience provides *prima facie* justification for religious belief; that is, a religious belief grounded in religious experience is justified, unless it can be defeated or overridden; or in common parlance, the belief has a presumption of innocence, is innocent unless proved guilty. (Alston, 1991; Plantinga, 1983; Swinburne, 1979) I shall use the phrases 'the *prima facie* status of religious experience' or 'the presumptive status of religious experience' as shorthand for 'religious experience is *prima facie* justification for religious belief'.

The second interpretation is represented by William James. According to him, religious experience does not provide *prima facie* justification for religious belief but provides data which must be explained by some hypothesis or other. The God hypothesis is one hypothesis to explain the experience, the best hypothesis from James's viewpoint.

I shall adopt the approach of Alston, Plantinga, and Swinburne, focusing especially on the expressions of this position in Swineburne and Alston. I shall not, however, neglect the Jamesian position, for I shall see how it fares on the basis of the evidence and arguments I present.

3. The Principle of Credulity

Swinburne introduces what he calls the "Principle of Credulity" (PC).

I suggest that it is a principle of rationality that (in the absence of special considerations) if it seems (epistemically) to a subject that x is present, then probably x is present; what one seems to perceive is probably so. How things seem to be is good grounds for a belief about how things are. From this it would follow that, in the absence of special considerations, all religious experiences ought to be taken by their subjects as genuine, and hence as substantial grounds for belief in the existence of their apparent object—God, or Mary, or Ultimate Reality, or Poseidon. (1979, 254)

I take the second sentence of this quotation to be Swinburne's best expression of PC. Whereas the use of the letter 'x' in the first sentence may lead us to think exclusively of objects, 'things' gives us a broader perspective, so that we immediately understand that we may be talking about processes and states of affairs, as well as objects. More importantly, though, using the term 'perceive' in the first sentence is misleading, for Swinburne wishes to include memory, for example, under PC ("that we seem to *have had* such and such experiences is in itself good grounds for believing that we had" [italics mine], 256), but memory would not normally be considered a form of perception. Further, the case for religious experience does not rest on its being closely parallel to perception; indeed, I have noted that sensory perception is not a very good parallel for religious experience. Thus, even if there are significant differences between sensory perception and the "perception" of religious experience, religious experience may still be a good ground for religious belief. This certainly seems to be Swinburne's position. Thus, the term 'perceive' is better dropped.

Using Swinburne's words, we could restate PC as: In the absence of special considerations, how things seem to be (epistemically) is good grounds for a belief about how things are. A more felicitous expression is provided, I believe, by Caroline Franks Davis, who suggests the following: "'What seems (epistemically) to a subject to be the case probably is the case, unless there are defeating conditions.'" (1989, 97)

Two further points about PC need to be stressed. First, 'seems' is used in an epistemic, not a comparative, sense, a distinction introduced by Chisholm and accepted by Swinburne. To use 'seems' (or similar appearance words) in an epistemic sense "is to describe what the subject is inclined to believe on the basis of his present sensory experience." (Swinburne, 245-246) If I say, "The bird seems to be a red-headed woodpecker," what I am saying is that I am inclined to believe, on the basis of my present sensory experience, that the bird is a red-headed woodpecker. To use 'seems' in a comparative sense is "to compare the way an object looks with the way other objects normally look." (246) If I say, "The bird seems from here to have a red head," what I am saying is that from here the bird's head looks the way red things normally look. I may not be inclined to believe that the bird's head is red because from my position, with the rays of the sunrise shining on the bird's head, it does look red; but it really is not because the bird has a sparrow's shape.

Second, 'seems' is being used in a technical sense. Obviously, I would never say, looking out my back window, "That seems to be a red-headed woodpecker going up my oak tree." If a friend were in the room, the friend would likely say, "Seems? Is there something wrong with your eyes?" If the bird were half a block away, then I might say, "That seems to be a red-headed woodpecker down the block there on the magnolia tree." Swinburne is taking a certain epistemological viewpoint, making a distinction between how we take things, as opposed to how things are. Thus, we could use other terms or phrases, such as, 'I take myself to perceive' or 'it appears to me that', or 'the putative object of my perception is' and so on. At any rate, the term 'seems' (and its cognates, along with alternative terms or phrases) is being used in a technical sense, so that for clarity I should probably put the term in quotes, but I shall simply rely on our memories.

The main point of PC is that seemings justify belief. My seeming to remember the recent birthday celebration for my younger daughter is all that I need to justify the belief, 'We celebrated Susan's last birthday with a big hamburger fry in the park'. Similarly, my seeing (seeming to see) a squirrel running on my lawn is all I need to justify the belief, 'A squirrel is running on my lawn.' Clearly, my memory and perceptual beliefs are not groundless, in the sense of just appearing in my consciousness as beliefs; rather, they are grounded in my experience of certain happenings. Nevertheless, the beliefs are not inferred from other beliefs but rest strictly on my experience. As Plantinga says, "upon having experience of a certain sort, I believe that I am perceiving a tree. In the typical case I do not hold this belief on the basis of other beliefs; it is nonetheless not groundless." (1983, 79) What I shall say, then, is that my belief about remembering or seeing is non-inferentially justified by what I seem to remember or seem to see. Swinburne adopts this approach, I think. At least he emphasizes that induction (inference) is not the justification for believing that something—for example, a table—is as we see it. Neither is it the justification for memory. (255-56)

If I am correctly interpreting PC, then PC is saying that we do and may stop for justification purposes with what seems to be the case. In doing so, we are assuming a number of other things to be in order—for example, in sense perception we are normally assuming an understanding of color terms. Coherentists could say that assuming proper color classification leaves the perceptual story incomplete because we have not made reference to other experiences with which our perception must cohere (a concept, by the way, which is anything but clear) in order for our perceptual belief to be justified. Suppose that we just grant coherentists their point—following PC does leave the perceptual story a bit incomplete. Yet coherentists will have to end their story somewhere by appealing to seeming, at least at the point where they say that certain items just do or do not seem to cohere—or more accurately, that the seeming coherence of the items is *prima facie* justification for believing that they actually do cohere. We might say that the story PC tells ends at an earlier point of seeming than does the story of coherentism, although the allowance for defeaters in PC really makes the two stories end very close together, so that the two stories may be different only in the words they use. I shall not pursue this line of thought any further, but will simply record my opinion that the story PC tells ends at a proper point of seeming. In simply recording my opinion, I emphasize that this is not a book in which I systematically develop and defend an epistemological position. I am, in effect, identifying with an epistemological position defended by others, adding a few remarks here or there where I deem them necessary or useful. I do not view myself as resolving, or even contributing to the resolving, of tangled, controversial epistemological issues.

I have noted that PC is a principle about the *prima facie* justification of beliefs. In seeming to apprehend something we do not have decisive evidence for what we seem to apprehend, but only *prima facie* evidence, evidence which can be defeated or overridden by "special considerations," but evidence which, if it cannot be defeated or overridden, unqualifiedly justifies belief in what we seem to apprehend.

4. *Incomplete or Imprecise Descriptions*

But now I wish to raise a question which requires an extended excursion but will receive only a brief excursion because this is not a book about everything. However, the question is important for an understanding of PC and for a later section of this book. (Chapter Nine) The question I have in mind is one we have already come across: What about cases in which we do not or cannot characterize what we apprehend with a degree of exactness or precision? Or put differently, What if we characterize something vaguely or inexactly? How does this affect belief and its justification?

The beginning question is, What is it to characterize something exactly or precisely? If I merely say that the woodpecker has a red-head and do not specify the exact color of red, have I characterized the head of the woodpecker exactly or precisely? I think not. However, if my belief is only that the head is red, my experience is a ground for believing this and lack of precision does not seem to be relevant.

However, what if my friend Jerry says, "I saw this very striking rock formation when I was hiking in the Andes. The combination of the colors was extraordinary and the way the rocks were arranged—well, in a way they looked as if someone had put them there, but not really. And of all things, I had left my camera back in camp. The next day when I returned, the whole formation had slid down the mountain. That, too, was extraordinary. Looked very stable to me the day before." Now suppose that Jerry does not draw well, is always the worst player at "Pictionary," is, in fact, always the source of great amusement when he plays the game. Moreover, as others try to draw the formation, trying to get the right colors and the right shape and formation of the rocks, Jerry always says either, "That's not even close," or "Well, that's better than Joe's attempt, but it's still not what I saw." Jerry, then, saw a specific kind of rock formation, which he describes as striking. The belief that he has could be articulated in any number of ways, but suppose that when Joe questions whether he really saw the rock formation, Jerry says: "Listen, Joe! That rock formation was there, and there just as I saw it." Actually, at the time of seeing it Jerry could have said, "That's the strangest rock formation I've ever seen, but there it is." In other words, he believes it exists just as he sees it, a belief justified by his seeing it, a belief that would be no more justified if he could describe what he sees in exact, complete detail.

We could, I think, apply in every case of belief-justification the formula just stated; that is, we could say, "What I see exists just as I see it." Even in the case of the woodpecker I could say, "The head is a specific kind of red, not like your sweater but brighter—well, it's just the way it is. There, take a look!" Or I could say more generally, "There's a woodpecker with a distinctively colored head." Or I could get so broad as to say merely, "I see something." Suppose, then, that we speak in very general terms, such as, "I see something, and I believe that it exists just the way I see it." Not describing more specifically the something I see may not be helpful to other people, but the justification of my belief certainly does not depend on whether I have stated the belief in a helpful manner for other people.

I might even say, "I see something, but I don't know what it is." The first time I saw a gorilla I was sitting on my father's shoulders, enjoying a ride through the San Diego Zoo, a ride which quickly turned traumatic, for as we came to the gorilla cage, two very boisterous gorillas were bellowing and beating on their chests. I was frightened as never before, my father's assurances having absolutely no calming effect. I outscreamed the bellowing gorillas, thinking that at the batting of an eye they would be through the heavy wire-mesh fence and upon the whole crowd of people, including me. As for what I was seeing, I could have said something like this: "I see something, but I don't know what it is. But it sure is just the way I see it—so let's get out of here!" Now the justification of my belief that the gorillas were there, doing what I saw them doing, would not in the least have been diminished by my inability to classify the creatures as gorillas. Obviously, saying in this case that I see something, I knew not what, is not like saying, "I see something down there in the last cage, but I don't know what it is. I can't quite make it out."

Now the reason I touch on these matters is twofold. First, the justification of my belief that things are as I see them does not seem to be a function of describing in detail, describing fully, or even describing accurately what I see. Of course, I never did pursue either the question of exactly what a detailed, full, or accurate description is or whether we can get such a description, usually or ever. I shall leave these questions for others to attend to.

Second, people having religious experience often say something along the lines of "It defies description" or "It was like this, but not exactly." Now some very ordinary experiences also defy description, experiences philosophers call "primitive," experiences such as colors, sounds, pleasures, pains, and so on. For example, someone without pain receptors might say, "Tell me what experiencing pain is really like. What does it really feel like?" The answer to that question is: "Experiencing pain isn't like anything—not like colors, sounds, or anything else. A pain is a pain—nothing else. You have to feel a pain yourself in order to get the answer to your question." Thus, inability to describe an experience may just reveal its primitive nature, not that someone is unclear about the experience or that the experience is not a suitable ground for belief about reality, viz., that reality is as experience presented it. The experience of God may in many respects be primitive. Often, I should say, it is more like Jerry's experience. We can give some description of it. "Well, you know what it's like to perceive another person? Sensing a divine Presence is like that, only nothing physical is there—and by 'there' I obviously don't mean 'spatially there'. What happens is that you experience this Reality—and you know you're experiencing It as clearly as you know that I'm talking to you now." Calls for added descriptive details may or may not bring forth more information. However, our belief that there was a Presence such as we experienced (a suchness we cannot fill in very well) seems as justified as Jerry's belief that there was a striking rock formation such as he perceived (a suchness he cannot fill in very well). In short, a halting description of religious experience does not, I should say, weaken the justification for belief in the Object experienced.

5. *PC and Alston's Doxastic Practices*

Returning now to PC, I note Swinburne's view that PC is a principle followed by people generally or at least by those proceeding rationally. PC is a principle of rationality; that is, rational people do form beliefs on the basis of what seems to be the case. Moreover, Swinburne mentions several different sources for forming beliefs, among them, sensory perception, memory, and inference. Additionally, he talks about defeaters, the assumption being, I should say, that we have systems of defeaters, with one system not necessarily applying to every way of forming beliefs (for example, we do not employ sensory defeaters to test inference). Thus, Swinburne has not, perhaps, worked himself all the way to what Alston refers to as a doxastic practice, but I should say that he has come fairly close. For Alston a doxastic practice

> can be thought of as a system or constellation of dispositions or habits ... each of which yields a belief as output that is related in a certain way to an 'input'. SP [the practice of forming perceptual beliefs], for example, is a constellation of habits of forming beliefs in certain ways on the basis of inputs that consist of sense experiences. (1991, 153)

Specifying each way of forming beliefs and considering each way as a doxastic practice is, in my opinion, more accurate and complete than lumping everything together in the principle I refer to as PC. Thus, whatever Swinburne intended, I shall take PC to include implicitly the full array of doxastic practices, many of which are specifically noted by Alston. This full array of practices, each taking a certain class of experience (e.g., sensory experience) as prima facie justification for belief based on the experience, is, using Swinburne's terms, rational. Alston says as much.

6. PC and Skepticism

As I said, my task is not to provide a defense of PC. Thus, I shall rely mainly on the defenses made by Swinburne and others, especially Alston. I shall, however, follow up briefly on one remark by Swinburne. He maintains that if we do not accept PC, we shall land in a skeptical bog. (254, f. 1) By 'accept' here Swinburne seems to mean 'accept as a principle of rationality'. As for what he means by 'skeptical bog', I cannot say for certain because he does not elaborate. I shall simply make several observations.

To begin with, in accepting PC we are, in effect, accepting it as a basic justifying principle, basic in the sense that it is not derived from any other proposition. Swinburne says that PC is a principle of rationality but offers no support for PC in the way of deriving it from another proposition. Or more exactly, he says that "it seems to me, and I hope to my readers, intuitively right in most ordinary cases such as those to which I have just been referring, to take the way things seem to be as the way they are." (254) I take Swinburne to be using 'intuitive' in a common philosophic sense, namely, 'self-evident'. He is saying, in effect, that we just grasp PC to be a rational principle; we just evaluate it positively, period. He does consider objections to using the principle for religious experience (255-60), but that is an indication, I think, that the scope of PC is debatable. However, he does not derive the principle from some other proposition. Saying that "it seems intuitively right" is not, I should say, an appeal to another proposition justifying PC. It is an appeal to the experience of grasping the positive epistemic status of PC and noting that PC "stands on its own two feet," is OK just by itself, apart from some other proposition from which it might be derived. Moreover, his appeal to intuition is, I think, a way of indicating that invariably we are going to end up with some proposition (or propositions) as basic. Someone may demur on the issue of basic propositions, saying, for example, that coherence is the way to justify any proposition or principle (or doxastic practice). If one takes this approach, then apart from any criticism of coherence itself (such as that it is a vague concept or that we might have a number of equally coherent, yet incompatible, systems), we should have to say that at least the proposition about coherence in the previous sentence seems to function as basic, for it is certainly not a proposition to be justified by coherence or some other proposition; or if it is, then it will suffer either from circularity or infinite regress. If my interpretation of Swinburne is incorrect on the import of appealing to intuition, then what I have just said may be taken as what I believe. Put in the language of doxastic practices this would go as: We just grasp our doxastic practices as rational. There is nothing to add in the way of deriving the practices from some proposition or other or grounding them in some other practice. They are simply rational, period.

Several points are worth noting. Intuition itself is a form of seeming; therefore, someone might say that intuition is a part of PC, which would mean that we are using PC to support PC. Saying this is incorrect if, as I said above, the appeal to intuition is not an appeal to a proposition justifying PC. Again, saying that PC is intuitive is, I maintain, just saying that we give it a positive epistemic evaluation without appealing to anything else. Any further attempt to justify PC will quickly land us in circularity or an infinite regress. Of course, a major point of Alston is that attempts to justify epistemic practices invariably land us in circularity. (Chapter Three of Alston) Suppose, for example, that we wish to justify SP, the doxastic practice of forming beliefs according to sense perception and its related overrider system. Our justification will invariably have to appeal to sense perceptions, the very material which is in question. One might say, e.g., that SP is justified because by using it we can successfully predict. Yet apart from sensory perceptions we cannot determine successful prediction. Thus, either we engage in circularity or we simply say that SP is intuitive.

Now in saying that PC (or some doxastic practice) is intuitive we do not, I think, commit ourselves to the incorrigibility or infallibility of PC. We might think that some judgments are incorrigible or infallible, say, introspective judgments, but that does not mean that we would take our judgment about PC to be incorrigible or infallible. In effect, we go with PC because "it seems intuitively right," but that does not mean that we would never give up on PC or certain applications of it, for we may discover that a contrary principle (perhaps a principle far more qualified than PC) seems intuitively right also, so that we have "intuitively right" against "intuitively right," a problem not unknown in the history of philosophy, and one which is not beyond resolution, for after further consideration one position may seem to be "more intuitively right," an expression which may be less than ideal but which indicates what I view as epistemic reality, viz., that there are degrees of epistemic worth or status or whatever similar term we wish to use. Alston takes a similar view, noting that some doxastic practices are superior to others—e.g., he sees SP as epistemically superior to CMP, the Christian doxastic practice. (236)

Suppose, though, that instead of accepting PC as a rational principle, we just let ourselves sink in the skeptical bog, perhaps going all the way to the bottom, or to what we conceive as the bottom, viz., to a Cartesian kind of demon proposition. I am of the opinion that this proposition is self-defeating at best and incoherent at worst, but obviously I cannot spell out my opinion. To do so would require at least another book. I shall simply say concerning radical skepticisms that they end up assuming many truths, often the very truths which are at issue. I shall note this point below. Or perhaps the more forceful thing to say is that our discussions, philosophical and otherwise, are for those who have decided that we can achieve some true beliefs. Clearly, we would not discuss anything with a person withholding all belief, and we would not discuss anything with persons who thought that they were deceived about our presence.

What we may say, then, is that in the end have to go with the only show in town—or the only show where there is any action. Our task is, in effect, to discover what the show is— that is, what the principles, methods, and practices of rational judgment are. Swinburne, for example, seems to offer PC not as some innovative, newly discovered principle but as a principle which we do, in fact, employ. He is calling something to our attention. The same goes for Alston and his doxastic practices. Alston is worth quoting at some length on this point.

> We cannot look into any issue whatever without employing some way of forming and evaluating beliefs; that applies as much to issues concerning the reliability of doxastic practices as to any issue. Hence what alternative is there to employing the practices we find ourselves using, to which we find ourselves firmly committed, and which we could abandon or replace only with extreme difficulty if at all? The classical sceptical alternative of withholding belief altogether is not a serious possibility. . . . If we could adopt some basic way of forming beliefs about the physical environment other than SP, or some basic way of forming beliefs about the past other than memory . . . why should we? What possible rationale could there be for such a substitution? It is not as if we would be in a better position to provide a non-epistemically circular support for the reliability of these newcomers. . . . We cannot take a step in intellectual endeavors without engaging in some doxastic practice(s) or other, and what reasonable alternative is there to practicing the ones with which we are intimately familiar? (149-50)

Can we then, prove or defend the rationality of our doxastic practices? Only by using them and thus proceeding circularly. However, if our practices prove themselves (circularly), then at least we have consistency. Of course, achieving consistency is itself a rational goal, requiring the use of certain rational practices, so that again we have not avoided circularity. All that this shows, I think, is that we cannot provide a non-circular defense for our practices, not that our practices are non-rational or unreliable. Moreover, as I noted, the problem with any wholesale skepticism is that the skeptics must either keep silent or employ the practices (at least many of the crucial ones) they are questioning, a situation which I consider to be as close to the vindication of our practices—of their rationality, as well as their reliability—as we shall ever get.

7. *Practical Rationality vs. Reliability*

Alston argues that the sort of considerations he presents in defense of our doxastic practices leave us only with what he calls a "practical rationality." (149-50) We are *prima facie* rational in pursuing our accepted doxastic practices, but the rationality is practical in the sense that it is not the rationality attached "to a doxastic practice if sufficient reasons were given for regarding it as reliable," that is, as likely to achieve the truth. However, he goes on to argue that it is rational to judge our established doxastic practices to be reliable. More specifically, he shows that in judging a practice to be rational (he uses as an example SP) we commit ourselves to judging that the practice is reliable; i.e., we can make the first judgment and fail to make the second only on pain of incoherence (178-9). Having said this, though, he notes that he still has not shown "that it is at least probably true that SP is reliable." (180) Any such showing would involve circularity, which, of course, does not mean that SP is not reliable. Alston has more to say, but I think that the strongest point to make is that either we end up with him or with one of the various levels of skepticism, none of which carries attractive epistemic credentials. Indeed, my remarks on skepticism were designed to show that either skepticism ends up assuming what it is skeptical about (i.e., it goes over, in effect, to Alston's camp) or it refrains from all belief, including belief in skepticism.

8. Evaluating Doxastic Practices

The First Two Tests

Having argued that, in the end, our doxastic practices can be defended only circularly, Alston does not regard just any practice as acceptable. He suggests three tests for doxastic practices. The first test is internal, the second external. We may test a doxastic practice internally by whether or not it leads to massive, persistent contradictions— e.g., SP would be unacceptable if it led to massive, persistent contradictions in perceptual beliefs. We may test a practice externally by whether or not it leads to massive, persistent conflicts with other established practices—for example, if SP conflicted regularly with deductive reasoning, both could not be acceptable practices. (170-73) The internal and external criteria may be referred to respectively as internal and external consistency.

Parsimony

I am inclined to think that integral to many of our doxastic practices is the Law of Parsimony, which may be stated as: Choose the explanation or hypothesis which is at least as simple as any other. The law is also referred to as Occam's Razor, which may be stated as: Do not multiply entities beyond necessity. Whatever the deficiencies in spelling out the exact nature of parsimony for all circumstances, we seem to use parsimony as a criterion in major portions of our reasoning. Certainly, we us it in scientific theorizing. E.g., the ether is eliminated from relativity physics not because it cannot be made consistent with the observational data but because it is unnecessary. More generally, we could today have a consistent classical theory accounting for every observation of relativity physics, but it would be a fixed-up theory, i.e., a theory with numerous *ad hoc* hypotheses, and thus a less simple theory than relativity theory. Simplicity is also a criterion in ordinary judgments about the world— e.g., judgments about the continuity of objects. Simplicity is also a criterion in the sphere of religion. E.g., the idea of a committee of gods creating and sustaining the universe does not seem necessarily inconsistent; in fact, today the social theory of the Trinity, in which the Trinity is conceived as a society of three gods, has some strong advocates. The problem with any multiplication of deities is not inconsistency but simplicity. Actually, if we think of God as creator and sustainer of all natural causes, we could introduce angelic intermediaries between God and the processes of natural causation—as many intermediaries as we wish. The main reason for not doing so, I think, is again simplicity.

In the case of a doxastic practice we could rid ourselves of many internal and external inconsistencies by introducing *ad hoc* (non-parsimonious) explanations. If we think that consulting the liver is an adequate practice for predicting the course of physical objects, we may iron out any conflict between prediction and what actually happens by way of *ad hoc* hypotheses. If, say, we are using the practice to predict the course of the space shuttle Atlantis, we shall find massive predictive failure (with a chance success every now and then); yet by tacking on *ad hoc* hypotheses we can explain the failure; moreover, in the future when the same prediction is at issue, our *ad hoc* hypotheses will permit us to make the predictions—consulting the liver will work. Consulting the liver simply fails at making new predictions, predictions of events not yet observed (e.g., we send Atlantis on a new path with a new mission). This failure— the failure to make correct predictions of the as yet unobserved—may in itself be taken as a test of a procedure for prediction. My approach will be to view parsimony as integral to many of our doxastic practices, including a religious doxastic practice.

Swinburne clearly gives parsimony a fundamental role, even if he would not include it within PC. He says the following.

> *Simplex sigillum veri* ('The simple is the sign of the true') is a dominant theme of this book.... All that I have been concerned to show here is the crucial influence of the criterion of simplicity within science. If we are to adopt in our investigations into religion the criteria of rational inquiry which are used in science and ordinary life, we must use this criterion there. (56)

The Third Test

Returning now to Alston's evaluative tests for a doxastic practice, we may say that a doxastic practice exhibiting both internal and external consistency would have warded off two significant overriders, so that its claims to rationality could be seen as strong. Alston also introduces a third test for evaluation of a doxastic practice, self-support: The practice delivers what it promises. (173-75) Does SP promise successful prediction? Well, it delivers. Of course, it delivers by its own criteria— sense perception—but that is no mean feat, for at least the practice exhibits consistency. Consulting the liver for successful prediction does not deliver, except by consistently adding *ad hoc* hypotheses, and thus that practice lacks self-support. For Alston, self-support does not provide evidence for reliability, that is, for the likelihood that a practice is truth-achieving; rather it functions "as a way of strengthening the prima facie claim of a doxastic practice to a kind of practical rationality." (174)

9. The Religious Application of PC

The essential question for my study concerns the status of PC in its religious application, i.e., the status of a religious doxastic practice. The first question, then, is whether or not a religious doxastic practice enjoys the *prima facie* rationality of our other accepted doxastic practices. Already I have noted Alston's admission that some practices have a higher epistemic status, are more reliable than, others—e.g., SP is superior to, or more reliable than, the Christian doxastic practice (CMP), the reason being that SP has fewer inconsistent outputs than CMP. However, the fact that one practice is superior to another does not mean that the other practice loses its *prima facie* status of rationality. The question is whether the inconsistencies in the output of a practice are so many and persistent that they overcome its *prima facie* status of rationality. Alston does not think so for CMP (238) or for other religious practices. Swineburne, for his part, does not see any strong reason for rejecting PC in its religious application. (255-60)

10. A Universal Religious Doxastic Practice (URP)

I shall not narrow attention to CMP or any other doxastic practice of a particular religion, simply because I want to see what happens when we look at religious experience from a universal perspective. I think that there is a kind of URP. At least there is in the sense that many, including a sizable number in the Christian community, employ methods or criteria they consider valid for anyone; moreover, they reason with and try to persuade people from other religions, showing thereby that they think of the others as employing methods or criteria similar to theirs, often discovering in the process that they and the others do, indeed, employ similar methods or criteria. In fact, I am inclined to say that what I would place in URP (for example, the methodological criterion that any reasoning must meet the canons of logic) I would also place in CMP and that anything further does not really belong in CMP. In taking this approach, I may not be in harmony with everybody, or even the majority, in the Christian community, but I think that I would find myself with numerous allies. Thus, from now on my remarks concerning the ingredients of URP may also be considered remarks about the ingredients of the CMP that a number of people, including me, work with. As for the ingredients of URP, I shall spell them out in some detail in chapters Eight and Nine.

Problems with CMP, the Christian Doxastic Practice

A major problem with CMP is specifying what it is. Alston states that "CMP takes the Bible, the ecumenical councils of the undivided church, Christian experience through the ages, Christian thought, and more generally the Christian tradition as normative sources of its overrider system." (193) Obviously, CMP does not incorporate everything from each of these sources, so that we have to decide which elements from the various sources are to function in CMP—hardly an easy task and one not carried out by Alston in anything but sketchy form. We can gather some of the elements of CMP from what he says, but we have nothing in the way of a systematic, fairly complete listing of the elements.

Because of the vagueness of CMP we have difficulty in determining which groups to include in the CMP camp and which to exclude. Different denominations and subgroups of them, not to mention sectarian groups, interpret and use the different sources in highly varied ways, some rejecting (at least in word) an entire source, such as Christian tradition. Alston's approach is to count a group in the CMP camp as long as it does not depart from the sources in such a way as to "make a mockery of them," an approach which leaves us exactly where we were, namely, in vagueness. If we are not clear about the elements of CMP, we certainly will not be clear about when somebody makes a mockery of them.

Alston tries to ameliorate the denominational-sectarian problem by noting two things. 1) Christian groups (including Christian sects, I presume) which differ in their use of the sources often work together on common projects. 2) Groups differing in their doctrines may use the same tests for perceptions of the divine. (193-94) I think that both points hold no less in the interreligious sphere than in the intraChristian sphere. Thus, Christians and Hindus, Christians and Buddhists, Christians and Muslims, and so on function together in common religious projects. Perhaps Alston has some more specific project in mind, but certainly he will admit that Christians participate with other religious groups in enterprises from peace marches to panels aimed at raising religious consciousness. As for using common tests for perceptions of the divine (religious experience), many Muslims and Hindus, for example, would be no less ready to recognize the authenticity of Christian religious experience than would Christians from different denominational groups. Indeed, I can think of Christian groups that are reluctant to recognize the authenticity of religious experience in other Christian groups.

The upshot is, I just do not think that Alston has specified CMP precisely enough to get us out of the denominational-sectarian morass. I think that we are left largely just to stipulate who is in the CMP camp and who is out. Moreover, as I mentioned above, any attempt to be more precise must focus on methodology, not belief. What is of first importance is, for example, not whether trinitarian doctrine is in CMP but why it is included or excluded. Thus, methodology (or in different language, the criteria for judging experience and belief) seems to be of central significance. Moreover, to repeat what I said above, I believe that specifying methodology will lead us to some form of URP.

A Reason for Developing URP

I have stated my belief that we do have URP—perhaps informal and imprecise but certainly no more so than CMP. Moreover, I think that we have reason to work with URP, rather than CMP or any other particularistic practice. The reason is as follows.

Supposing that the doxastic practice of each major world religion, along with numerous sects thereof, are equally adequate—each is internally and externally consistent, and each is self-supportive—we certainly should want to look for a reduction of practices, if not a complete elimination of all but one. Some practices have outputs inconsistent with the outputs of others; we know that practices with inconsistent outputs cannot both be reliable (that is, likely to get us to the truth); yet we cannot choose between the practices. This situation does not mean that no practice is reliable, only that we are not able to pick the one which is, if there is one. The result is a weakening of confidence in the reliability of any particular practice, as well as a weakening in the rationality of engaging in any practice, a point which Alston admits. "It can hardly be denied that the fact of religious diversity reduces the rationality of engaging in CMP (for one who is aware of the diversity) below what it would be if this problem did not exist." (275). Religious diversity also reduces our confidence in the reliability of our particular religious practice. The reason seems to be one of simple probability: If we have competing (incompatible) practices, each of which is as likely as any other to be reliable, then the probability that any single one is reliable is a function of how many others there are. E.g., if there are ten competing practices, then the probability that any one is reliable is one-tenth. Moreover, I do not believe that Alston has, as he claims, taken the sting out of this consideration. He maintains, that "we have no idea what noncircular proof of the reliability of CMP would look like, *even if it is as reliable as you please.* Hence why should we take the absence of such a proof to nullify, or even sharply diminish, the justification I have for my Christian M-beliefs [beliefs based on religious experience]?" (272) However, the absence of noncircular proof is not the problem; rather, the problem is the presence of competing practices to CMP, practices which have an equal claim to reliability. We may be rational in engaging in one or other because each meets the conditions of a rational doxastic practice (internal and external consistency, and self-support), yet even the rationality of engaging in any particular practice is reduced, as we have noted. I agree with Alston that the reduction is not such as to make engaging in some practice, say, CMP, irrational; yet our confidence in the rationality of the practice is reduced. If we could eliminate diversity in practices, we could be in a better position rationally. (We would not necessarily be in a better position, for other problems might arise with a single practice. See below.) Is there any way to lighten this burden of abundance?

One way would be to consider the practices incommensurable—each practice is designed for a different Reality. I shall eschew this course. Another way would be to engage in a detailed comparison of the practices. They may not all be equally adequate, one practice having, e.g., more internal or external inconsistency than another, or less self-support. I do not know that anyone has shown that this is not the case. Thus, I do not think that we need to say straight off that one practice is as likely to be reliable as any other practice. However, a major way of bringing unity among the various religious practices is to develop URP, which, as I have suggested, will consist essentially of methodology. I use the term 'methodology', noting that Alston says that a practice is "essentially the exercise of a family of belief-forming mechanisms." (165) Alston has his reasons for going with 'belief-forming mechanisms', and I shall not say that the phrase is equivalent to what I call "methodology." However, I think that we are talking about much the same thing. My main point is that instead of concentrating on the beliefs or doctrines in the overrider system, we should look at the methodologies or mechanisms by which the beliefs got there. In doing so, we may find common methodologies or mechanisms in the various religions, or at least far more commonness in method than in specific beliefs or doctrines. In short, perhaps we already have URP, and it is essentially methodological.

An Objection to URP

Although I have chosen to go for URP, I am aware of a major reason for not doing so: The broader the religious practice, the more inconsistent outputs we get. The question is whether URP ends up with inconsistencies so great that the practice loses its *prima facie* rationality. I shall let this question rest until chapters eight and nine, assuming until then that our religious doxastic practice (URP) is *prima facie* rational. Obviously, we could artificially narrow a practice to eliminate all inconsistency. E.g., in the case of SP, we could narrow the practice to exclude eyewitness testimony of accidents, testimony which often ends up in unresolvable conflict. I have the sense that this sort of narrowing is of the same genre as narrowing a religious doxastic practice to a particular religion or sectarian expression thereof. If so, we purchase greater consistency at the price of arbitrary stipulation. I have just employed some pejorative terms, engaged in a bit of rhetoric— which I shall just leave as is. More helpful, I think, will be my attempts to show that we (many people) do employ a kind of URP.

I do not know exactly where Swinburne would stand on the issue of religious doxastic practices. He does not restrict PC in its religious application to a particular religion; thus, I am inclined to think that he sees PC in its religious application as resorting to considerations universal in nature.

11. Epistemic Conditions for Overriders and Counters

Overriders

Given any doxastic practice—URP, CMP, SP or another—what are the requirements for something to function as an overrider? I should think that anything functioning as an overrider (I shall equate an overrider with a defeater) needs stronger epistemic credentials than what it overrides—in our present discussion, religious experience. In the perceptual sphere, our overriders are usually other perceptions, or theories solidly based on perceptions. If I say, "My, those are beautiful chrysanthemums," and my sister-in-law says, "Look more closely, George; those are daisies, not chrysanthemums," she is appealing to more careful perception, which will count for more than my initial superficial perception. Or in the case of memory, I may say to my brother, "Remember that fourth of July when we were fishing down past the Checkobee estate, and we caught a batch of corbina?" and my brother says, "No, George, we weren't fishing down there; we were fishing over by what we called 'Fisherman's rock'"; and I say, "Oh yes, you're right; now I remember." My memory is corrected, jogged by my brother's remark. Again, for whatever reason, I take my second memory as having higher status. The main point is not that perception must be corrected (overridden, defeated) by another perception or memory by another memory but that the correction must be by something of higher epistemic status or greater epistemic weight. Of course, I believe that we have degrees of epistemic weight, so that we have a range of defeaters, from weak to strong.

Counters

Both Swineburne and Alston speak only of defeaters; however, I believe that we need another class of items, viz., what I shall call "counters." I could say to my brother, "That's not the way I remember it," but his remarks have put some doubts in my mind. His memory serves as a counter to mine; at least I cannot think of why I should count his memory as worse than mine. In short, we have not only overriding material but countering material, material which does not have enough epistemic weight to override but which has enough weight to give us pause or reason to doubt, material which weakens the *prima facie* justification of our belief. Counters range from weak to strong, as do defeaters.

The general message for the evaluative system of a religious doxastic practice is this: Anything which is to override beliefs based on religious experience must have higher epistemic status than those beliefs; anything which is to counter beliefs based on religious experience must be roughly equivalent in epistemic strength to the beliefs. The mildly attentive reader will note that I have just stated a methodological criterion, universal in scope, and thus a criterion suitable for URP. The requirement is present, I think, in various religious communities, although it is not adhered to consistently, so that numerous epistemically weak beliefs, some of which are only logically possible, drift into overrider systems.

12. The Objective of This Book

The time has come for me to state the objective of this book. I intend to consider some proposed general objections to (I shall refer to them as proposed general defeaters of) religious experience as *prima facie* justification for religious belief. If there are compelling objections to (general defeaters of) PC in its application to religious experience—defeaters of all religious experience, not just some experience or other—then religious experience is not *prima facie* justification for religious belief. We simply would not be rational to accept the application of PC in the sphere of religious experience—not rational to accept any religious doxastic practice.

What I wish to concentrate on first of all are some proposed general defeaters which are commonly introduced as naturalistic explanations of religious experience. A few comments on naturalistic explanations are in order.

Swinburne on Naturalistic Defeaters

Swinburne notes four general sorts of defeaters for the claim that one has experienced an object, for our purposes, a religious Object. The fourth form of defeater is the one in which naturalistic explanations would fit. The defeater is along the following lines: "Whether or not x was there, x was probably not a cause of the experience of its seeming to me that x was there. One obvious way in which this can be done (without casting any doubt on other of my perceptual claims) is by showing that (probably) something else caused my experience." (263-64) The general naturalistic defeater goes, then, like this: Whether or not God exists, God does not cause religious experience because there are strictly natural causes of the experience. Swinburne does not think much of this defeater, for

> if there is a God, he is omnipresent and all causal processes only operate because he sustains them. Hence any causal processes at all which bring about my experience will have God among their causes; and any experience of him will be of him as present at a place where he is. And so if there is a God, any experience which seems to be of God, will be genuine—will be of God. He may bring about that experience either by intervening in the operation of natural laws (producing an event other than natural laws would ordinarily produce) or by sustaining their normal operation [so that] . . . natural laws are such as to bring about religious experiences. (p. 270)

The crucial phrase here is 'if there is a God that is the sustainer of all causal processes'. For the sake of the argument I shall assume that the existence of this sort of God is a question mark; in short, whatever the strength of the actual reasons we have to believe in God, considered as the sustainer of all causal processes (and the reasons may be strong enough to make the existence of this God as probable as Swinburne thinks), I am supposing that we have no more reason to believe than not to believe. I am making this assumption for two reasons. First, I think that it helps us isolate the strength of naturalistic explanations *vis a vis* the presumptive status of religious experience. Second, many people do not think it more likely than not that there is a God and that this God is the sustainer of all causal processes.

Given my assumption, then, we proceed as follows. We have religious experience; given PC, we have reason to believe in the Object of the experience. However, we discover that the experience is accounted for by natural causes. Now God may be the sustainer of all natural causes, but according to our assumption we have no more reason to believe this than not to believe it. We have, though, parsimony, which Swinburne clearly accepts. A naturalistic explanation of religious experience is more parsimonious than a theistic explanation, for in the theistic explanation we introduce God in addition to the naturalistic explanation. (In reasoning that covers the full range of human experience we may find, as does Swineburne, that resorting to God is overall more parsimonious.) Yet does the naturalistic explanation defeat in this case—

does it override the *prima facie* status of religious experience; does it prove guilt? I think not. Instead, it functions as a counter, a strong counter which significantly weakens the presumptive status of religious experience.

Swineburne does not consider counters and does not proceed on my assumption. As a result, he ends up saying that a naturalistic explanation will not override "unless it can be shown on other grounds significantly more probable than not that God does not exist." (270) This statement would be acceptable to me if the term 'significantly' were dropped, as I think it should be.

In the above quotation Swinburne says that "any experience which seems to be of God, will be genuine—will be of God." If this were so, then we could not override any experience seeming to be of God, such as an experience seeming to be of God commanding us to take revenge on some enemy; in short, no experience seeming to be of God would be bogus. Yet Swinburne definitely believes that some religious experience is bogus. The fact that God is among the causes of religious experience does not guarantee that the experience is genuine, any more than the fact that God is among the causes of hallucinations (God sustains the causal process) guarantees that the perceptual seeming of a flying purple dinosaur will genuinely be of a flying purple dinosaur. The problem seems to be that Swineburne is trading on an ambiguity in 'experience of God', shifting from experience of God as a direct apprehension to experience of God as an indirect apprehension, that is, apprehension by way of tracing God through natural causes. He is saying something similar to the following: We perceive the sun when looking at a bush in the moonlight. Since the sun is ultimately the cause of the bush's color, growth, and existence, not to mention the cause of moonlight, we could say that we are perceiving the sun— perceiving it, of course, very indirectly.

Swineburne is correct, though, in saying that God may employ natural causal circumstances to bring about religious experience. Of course God may also not employ natural causal circumstances. I do not think that mental events are necessarily causally dependent on natural causes, such as brain activity. In other words, at some later date of far more advanced brain theory and technology than now, we may discover that certain mental events, such as telepathy, out-of-body experiences, and religious experience, occur without any brain activity which might cause the events; for example, we may discover that while religious experience is occurring, the brain activity is strictly that of normal sensing. The theory of the paranormal (theory which no one has decisively shown to be incoherent) is that mental events function at times outside of the parameters of natural law; thus, why not outside any causal activity of the brain? Similarly, theistic theory of religious experience at least includes the possibility that divine Consciousness intersects with human consciousness, without any brain activity being the cause of the experience; or if there is brain activity related to the experience, it is causally induced by the experience. (The experience, for example, may leave memory traces in the brain.) A naturalistic explanation would, of course, rule out the possibility that religious experience is not associated with a distinct set of natural causal circumstances, such as a special kind of brain activity.

Yet even if we have a naturalistic explanation involving a special kind of brain activity, this explanation does not rule out God, for God may use natural causes to bring about religious experience. Swineburne suggests two possibilities. a) The natural events necessary and sufficient for religious experience are disconnected from the regular functioning of natural law, with God "producing an event [for example, brain activity of a certain sort] other than natural laws would ordinarily produce." (270) The experience produced by the brain activity is genuinely of God. Coming up with a naturalistic explanation would be a matter of showing that the brain activity producing the experience was not really disconnected from natural law, and thus we would immediately find ourselves with the next possibility. (I note that we cannot consider explanations from brain activity, for there are not any, at least in terms of specific brain activity; and there will not be any until both brain theory and technology vastly improve.)

b) Natural laws are "such as to bring about religious experiences" (270), i.e., natural laws (e.g., laws of learning) are such as to bring about an event (say, brain activity) producing an experience which, again, is genuinely of God. Showing that there is not a naturalistic explanation will be a matter of showing that this second possibility does not hold. My criticisms of naturalistic explanations are designed to show just this. More precisely, I choose what I view as the strongest naturalistic explanations of religious experience, my purpose being to show that the explanations are not adequate.

We must remember, of course, that a strictly naturalistic explanation of religious experience is more simple than a theistic explanation, its greater simplicity giving it a countering force. If it is probable that there is a God and that this God sustains all natural causes, then the countering force will be weak. However, taking my restrictive assumption, the countering force will be fairly strong. If my criticisms of naturalistic explanations are on target, then naturalistic explanations, at least the ones I consider, will not have any countering force.

Chapter Two

Background Influences

1. Procedure

My first aim, as I have said, is to consider some common naturalistic explanations of religious experience. According to my account in the last chapter, naturalistic explanations function at best as general counters to, not general defeaters of, religious experience as *prima facie* justification of religious belief. Whatever the function of naturalistic explanations—whether as general counters or general defeaters— my procedure will be to measure each naturalistic proposal against the material on religious experience which I have examined, a portion of which I have gathered myself. More exactly, I shall use the method of counterexample, citing specific cases as counterexamples to each proposal. Since the material I have is anecdotal, not statistical, I am following the only method which seems reasonable, a method, moreover, which is very powerful, resting on reasoning of the general form:

> If thesis x is true, then we should find y.
> We do not find y.
> Therefore, thesis x is not true.

A specific example of this general form of reasoning would be:

> If religious experience is strictly a result of culture, then at least the essential features of the experience should incorporate the values and ideas of the subject's culture.

Religious experience often does not incorporate the values and ideas of the subject's culture.
Therefore, religious experience is not strictly a result of culture.

As for resorting to anecdotal material, we are, according to theistic theory, restricted to this approach; that is, divine Reality is not manipulable, the occasion of encounter not being determined by us. We wait for the occasions and then report them. In obtaining case reports we can, of course, require as exacting a method as possible, developing all the relevant information we can. I do not claim to have met this requirement because for the most part I have simply used the material available, material which was not developed under an exacting method. As for the material I gathered, it also is weak methodologically. I add that I am unaware of material of consistently better quality than what I consider.

I do not wish to suggest by my previous remarks about divine Reality that nothing in the broad category of controlled experiments can be employed for investigating the phenomena of religious experience. Of course, one element will always stand outside of rigorous scientific control and analysis, namely, the religious experience itself. We cannot observe the experience but can only observe (listen to, record, and so on) reports of the experience. Be this as it may, we might, for example, test to determine whether the necessary and sufficient condition for the report of religious experience is sensory deprivation or some substance, such as peyote. The material I have raises questions about both these possibilities, although I do not discuss either possibility systematically or in depth. Of course, if both sensory deprivation and peyote were sufficient conditions for the report of a religious experience, they would not rule out religious experience as a genuine encounter with God, for both might unalterably place us in the proper state for receiving the divine Presence; or both might be non-veridical parallels of true religious experience, the same as hallucinations are non-veridical parallels of true sensory experience. The first alternative I would tend to dismiss on grounds of parsimony. The second alternative would require a systematic comparison of religious experience with the other two sorts of experience. I do not make this comparison.

2. The Nature of the Data

As for the material on religious experience which I have, some I have gathered myself, recording most of it on audio tapes, but recording some in the form of detailed notes written down while interviewing the subjects. I did not use a questionnaire to discover background information about the subjects, information such as level of education or economic status. I have information of this sort in a number of cases, but I did not systematically attempt to get it. What I was mainly interested in was the religious background of the person, an account of what led up to the religious experience, the setting in which the experience occurred, the description of the experience, and an account of its effects on the life of the person. I assumed in each case the honesty of the person, unless I had evidence to indicate otherwise. Many of the people within the Christian faith were recommended by clergymen who saw the people as extremely serious about their religious lives. The Hare Krishna people I interviewed were certainly serious enough to have made a countercultural move, many to the extent of adopting an Eastern form of dress. Of course, the Christians were also countercultural to a substantial extent, that is, in the way of value orientation, but not in the way of dress and not to the extent of adopting a non-Western religion. The point is that people who are serious enough to take these countercultural routes are not likely to engage in systematic deception. In fact, they were in communities which would discipline them, withdraw recognition, or simply drum them out if they were discovered to be leading deceptive lives. My impression of the people was that they were serious, committed to the basic moral precepts of their faith, aware of the high demands of their faith, with many of them readily confessing their imperfections and their falling away, on occasion, from their own commitments.

Most of the material I examined was obtained from the Alister Hardy Research Centre in Oxford, England. (In the text this material may be recognized by the number in the parentheses following the name starting each case. The name in these cases is fictitious.) The material at the Centre is in the form of letters written in response to invitations for people to write about their religious experience, the invitations having been published in newspapers, periodicals, magazines, and so on. A number of letters were followed up with a questionnaire asking for various details about the persons and their backgrounds. I do not consider letters, together with questionnaires, to be of the quality of interviews. Too many questions are left unanswered by the written approach. At least I had many questions about the interpretation of simple statements, questions which can easily be cleared up in an interview. I do not mean to indicate that my interviews eliminated all questions, but I find the interviews to be more complete.

The people who wrote in to the Centre conveyed to me the same impression of honesty as the people I interviewed, many of them stating that they had kept their experience to themselves for fear of being considered "cracked." Others stated that in no case was anyone to see what they said other than investigators at the Centre, and some said that they did not want anything they said published. Many welcomed further investigation, which did occur in some cases by way of follow-up questionnaires.

Having said all this about the honesty of the people writing in, I should not be in the least surprised to have some respond to my use of their accounts: "Oh, my writing in was a big joke. How funny that all these scholarly people would swallow my story." And I would laugh with them, commending them for adding a few smiles to the world. Of course, a few accounts which are jokes do not make every account a joke.

Aside from the question of honesty, there is the question of accuracy of reporting. Reporting may be distorted for a variety of reasons, not the least of which is memory. Neither I nor the Alister Hardy Research Centre checked for the accuracy of memory. In some cases people mention keeping diaries, but only rarely. I am going on an innocent-unless-proved-guilty approach. If a person had a religious family, for example, one which systematically attended religious services, I hardly think that this fact would be forgotten or seriously distorted. The same would go for persons not having a religious family, or having only one parent who was religious. As for religious experience, remembering the details, such as the date, time, or specific items of the setting, might be difficult, although many times people said that the memory of the experience was as fresh as the day they had the experience; in any case, the basic features of the experience (whether God was perceived as loving or powerful) or what the feelings were (whether peace, anxiety, grief, joy, ecstasy, or something else) would seem to be readily within the recall of normal persons. Of course, the closer people were to the experience the more confidence we would have in their memories, although distant experiences, particularly of a life-changing nature, are likely to remain fixed in memory. A life-changing experience is one which people reflect on again and again, recalling and reviewing what took place, perhaps doing so orally, so that the experience remains fresh, taking on, perhaps, a certain fixed form, with details added or subtracted but with the basic structure remaining the same. In sum, I think that taking the recall of the people as generally reliable is a reasonable course. In a court of law we can stump most witnesses on details of memory, but we have not for that reason ruled out all witnesses from the courtroom.

3. *The Cultural Explanation*

Pascal remarked that "faith in baptism is more received among Christians than among Turks." (Pensees, # 252) One way to explain religious experience would be to say that it is a result of general cultural influences. The term 'explain' may be given several meanings, so that we may have different explanations according to the meaning we have in mind.

First of all, we could explain in the sense of providing a necessary condition. Thus, the cultural thesis could go along the following lines: The religious ideas and values of culture are a necessary condition for the occurrence and content of religious experience. I shall say that a naturalistic explanation providing a necessary condition for religious experience is a weak explanation in the sense that it does not defeat or override religious experience as justification for religious belief, but it may weaken the presumption that religious experience justifies religious belief. I say "may weaken" because the necessary condition may have no effect. For example, we might suppose that, contrary to reality, we cannot have a positive attitude toward the Divine apart from positive cultural influences, and we cannot have a religious experience apart from a positive attitude toward the Divine. Yet even if this supposition were true, we should hardly think that a positive attitude toward the Divine, conditioned by our culture, somehow vitiates, even marginally, the validity of religious experience. Major religions consistently try to get people to feel positive, very positive, about the Divine (as is witnessed by the images of God as Light, Water, Divine Food, and so on, along with the encouragements to seek, be open, pursue, thirst for, and so on), but do not think that thereby the validity of religious experience is in any way negatively affected. Thus, I do not think that a naturalistic necessary condition automatically weakens the *prima facie* status of religious experience, that is, weakens the presumption that religious experience justifies religious belief.

Second, we could explain in the sense of providing a sufficient condition. I believe that a naturalistic explanation providing a sufficient condition for religious experience is far stronger than an explanation providing a necessary condition, and thus has a far greater weakening effect on religious experience, although not an overriding effect and not necessarily an effect great enough to completely wipe out the *prima facie* status of religious experience. For example, we might suppose, contrary to reality, that sincere prayer always results in religious experience. Yet even if this supposition were true, we could think of sincere prayer as similar to opening our eyes in the light—doing so is sufficient for seeing the objects of the world, but it certainly does not mean that the objects are not there or that they are necessarily distorted in our perception of them. However, given considerations of parsimony, I am inclined to say that a naturalistic sufficient condition weakens the *prima facie* status of religious experience—it weakens but does not override.

Third, we could explain in the sense of providing a necessary and sufficient condition. I shall say that a naturalistic explanation providing a necessary and sufficient condition for religious experience is a strong explanation in the sense that it is strong enough to counter the *prima facie* status of religious experience or to override religious experience altogether. The strength of the explanation rests, I believe, on considerations of parsimony. I am unsure about automatic overriding effects. For example, we might suppose, contrary to reality, that fasting and sincere prayer are the necessary and sufficient conditions for religious experience. I do not think that this supposition provides an overrider because prayer and fasting could well be the means by which we open ourselves sufficiently to Divine action. However, employing another example, we might suppose that stimulating the brain in a particular area of the frontal lobe is the necessary and sufficient condition for religious experience. That strikes me as something more like an overrider. I do not know that there is a difference in principle between my examples. Perhaps I make a distinction because the former example is associated with religion and with positive assumptions about the encounter with God, whereas the latter example is not. I shall leave the judgment on this matter to the reader.

Returning now to Pascal, I am not certain that he offered his remark about culture as a weak explanation (a necessary condition). I think that his remark was more along the lines of the following thesis: Culture generally shapes a person's religion. This thesis could be developed in a number of ways, but one way would be: The religion generally practiced in a culture tends to be the religion adopted by those newly taking up religion, say, children and adults who convert to religion. A statistical study could determine the exact extent to which people newly taking up religion adopt the generally practiced religion of their culture. I have little quarrel with this form of thesis, which I shall call a "tendency thesis." It is, however, not a thesis relevant to my study because practicing a religion is not equivalent to having a religious experience, and my study is about religious experience. I shall make this point many times because it is crucial for a proper evaluation of my central thesis.

We could change the cultural thesis to be relevant to religious experience by saying the following: People tend to have religious experience within the framework of the dominant cultural religion. This thesis is relevant, especially if it is offered as part of an attempt to account for religious experience independently of an appeal to God. We could sharpen the thesis as follows: Religious experience is largely the product of culture. Since a religious experience largely a product of culture edges God into a very small corner, the cultural thesis, if true, would stand as at least a fairly strong counter to the justification of religious belief by religious experience. If the cultural thesis were supplemented with other naturalistic theses filling the gaps (theses about psychological state, social circumstances, special family influences, genes, and so on), then God is edged into an ever smaller and smaller corner, with the result that our naturalistic account, if true, takes on the form of a defeater or a serious weakener.

As I noted, my objective is to consider suggested defeaters which attempt to give a naturalistic account or explanation of religious experience. I do not think that a cultural explanation could be meant as a strong explanation, for cultural experience is clearly not a sufficient condition for religious experience. A cultural account aims at best, I think, to be a weak account, an account of a necessary condition.

4. Stating the Explanation from Religious Background

Actually, the cultural thesis stated above—religious experience is a product of culture—is too vague to be useful. One specific form the thesis might take would be: A necessary condition for the content of a religious experience is that the content be present within the cultural experience of the subject. This thesis would be falsified by finding a person within the standard Christian setting who experiences God along

Hindu lines. Finding such a person is not difficult, and I shall cite a number in Chapter Five when I consider experiences of an Eastern cast. Thus, I shall leave the cultural thesis just stated and go on to a more plausible form of the cultural thesis.

A very common form of the cultural explanation is that religious experience results from religious influences, particularly those in early life; i.e., consistent exposure to religion, especially exposure in the home but also in institutions such as church or synagogue, is the explanation for religious experience. This thesis about the influence of religious background is usually stated in the general way I have just stated it. However, the thesis needs to be spelled out more precisely.

I do not think that the explanation in terms of religious background is meant as a strong explanation, i.e., as a statement of the necessary and sufficient conditions for having a religious experience. We can find numerous people who have had strong, positive religious backgrounds but who have not had religious experience in the sense of awareness of divine Presence. The people may be committed and active in their religious life, but that is in no way equivalent to having religious experience. I think immediately of an older student, about forty, who recently told me that she simply has not experienced a sense of Presence, even though she is committed and active in her church—indeed, deeply desires an experience of Presence. Any number of people with strong, positive religious backgrounds have not only failed to have a religious experience but have given up entirely on religion, having become agnostics or atheists. Thus, an explanation in terms of religious background is probably not designed to state a sufficient condition and thus is not meant to be a strong explanation. Instead, I think that the explanation is meant to state no more than a necessary condition. I say "no more than" because the explanation is often in the form of a tendency statement along the lines: People having religious experience tend to come from religious families. This sort of statement obviously could not function as a defeater or even as much of a weakener, and would thus be little threat to religious experience as justification for religious belief. I shall, then, look at the explanation from religious background as stating a necessary condition and will spell out the explanation in the form of three theses.

To say that religious background accounts for religious experience is, I think, to say first of all that a necessary condition for the content of religious experience—that is, what one perceives God to be (a spiritual Force, a loving Presence, and so on) or to be doing (energizing with power, flooding with love, and so on)—is that the content be explicitly present in previous religious teaching. I shall call this claim "Thesis C." Since Thesis C explains only the content of religious experience, not the occurrence of the experience, Thesis C must, I should say, be supplemented by Thesis O: A necessary condition for the occurrence of religious experience is religious teaching about the desirability and value of having a religious experience of the general sort one has (say, of Jesus Christ or Allah). Yet Thesis O seems to be deficient by itself. At least one other thesis seems to be required, namely, that a necessary condition for the occurrence of religious experience is a generally positive attitude toward religion. I should think that the positive attitude would have to be fairly strong, strong enough to nurture an openness toward, if not a desire for, religious experience. Moreover, for the positive attitude to work as part of a general explanation in terms of religious background, the positive attitude would have to result from (in a weak or strong sense, that is, with religious influences being either a necessary or sufficient condition) influences in home or society. I shall call this thesis "Thesis P."

I do not know whether or not Theses C, O, and P are implicit in the thinking of those who claim that religious experience is a function of religious background, but I should think that some form of the theses would be implicit—at least if the explanation from religious background is to weaken the justification of religious belief by religious experience.

I note that Theses C, O, and P are stated in vague form; for example, Thesis O requires that the positive experience of religion be "fairly strong." Perhaps more precision can be achieved, and I shall certainly not deny that it can, but I shall certainly deny that putting numbers to something necessarily adds precision—e.g., putting strength of attitude on a scale of one to ten. I think that we can do no better than follow the insight of Aristotle to the effect that we should never try to achieve more precision than the subject permits. His exact words are:

> Our discussion will be adequate if it has as much clearness as the subject-matter admits of, for precision is not to be sought for alike in all discussions, any more than in all the products of the crafts. . . . We must be content, then, in speaking of such subjects [politics and ethics] and with such premises to indicate the truth roughly and in outline, and in speaking about things which are only for the most part true and with premises of the same kind to reach conclusions that are no better. In the same spirit, therefore, should each type of statement be received; for it is the mark of an educated man to look for precision in each class

of things just so far as the nature of the subject admits. (*Nicomachean Ethics*, Book I, 1094b:10-25)

I think that Aristotle is entirely on target. As a result, I shall adopt his approach throughout my discussion. I.e., first of all, I shall not try to get any more precision for concepts than the present state of the subject-matter allows. Second, my overall aim will be nothing more than truth which is rough and in outline form, at conclusions which are only for the most part true.

The main point now, though, concerns precision in measuring psychological states, such as attitude. Specifically, I wish to maintain that if we are talking about the conscious state of attitude-toward-religion, then we should simply admit that this attitude (or any other attitude) is not quantifiable in any strong form; i.e., it cannot be broken down into units which are measurable in some physical way and which are invariable from individual to individual or in the same individual over time. I grant that we probably could work out some form of quantifiable psychological test for religious attitude, inasmuch as we already have a range of tests for a variety of psychological or personality states. In other words, we might have an MMPI measuring religious attitude alone. We would have quantified results, just as we now have quantified results with the MMPI. We still might not consider ourselves to have advanced much further than characterizations of attitude as strong, weak, or in-between, although I have no objections to saying that we would have gained some precision. However, we would not have the precision of the natural sciences, what I have referred to as a strong form of quantification. Theoretically, attitude might be reducible to something physical, say, a set of brain processes, so that strong quantification would be possible in principle. Yet this possibility would be of no consequence to us now because we have not identified the brain processes and therefore could not monitor them.

In the rest of this chapter and the next I shall cite counterexamples to the explanation from religious background, which I have reduced to the theses C, O, and P. These theses together constitute no more than a necessary condition for religious experience.

5. *General Counterexamples*

Sheila (2155)

Sheila reports that her parents were peripherally attached to the Quakers but were basically humanists. She was studying with some friends the decline of Rome and became interested in Plotinus.

> One day at noon I was sitting in the autumn sunshine and using my brain harder than I have ever done, trying to understand Inge's account of Plotinus' One. 'The One, losing nothing from itself, overflows.' I concentrated upon this statement and suddenly the meaning of the words supplied itself. I simply saw that it was so—lo and behold. Did I experience what Plotinus (via Inge) calls 'superconsciousness'?
>
> The only bodily symptoms were tears of joy (to which anyhow I am rather prone). The sun seemed to become a luminous cloud and shed an almost palpable radiance on me. I was aware of a sort of cosmic gesture towards the earth in which I seemed to be included. . . . It seemed for a moment as though I stood 'in the great hand of God.'
>
> As in a dream, the laws of time and space seemed to be suspended. I do not mean that anything 'supernatural' happened, but it would not have seemed inconsistent if it had.
>
> Similarly the sequence of cause and effect was in abeyance; and one felt outside grammar. Any distinction of subject and object, active and passive, noun and verb was lost.
>
> Thought and emotion fused too. Perhaps this accounts for the impression of significance I had, and heightened awareness. In these respects my state resembled mild intoxication.
>
> That it was not an hallucination is, however, the most abiding conviction that I have. The verb 'to know' took on new depth that day making all previous knowing seem mere 'knowing about.'

Yet having made this statement about knowing, she goes on to say, in a skeptical vein:

> My aim at present is to steer clear of any unwarranted assumptions about the nature of my experience. I don't know whether anything outside me was involved; I have no evidence to exclude an explanation on physiological, psychological, astrophysical, spiritual or divine grounds.

I am inclined to say that Sheila apparently forgot what she had previously said about knowing. Or perhaps she could spell out what she knew so that it would be consistent with saying that the explanation of her experience was, say, physiological or psychological. However, since she denies that the experience was a hallucination, and since she would undoubtedly view hallucinations as having strictly physiological or psychological causes, her remarks are puzzling. Perhaps she meant to say something like: "I don't have any evidence that the experience wasn't caused by something physiological or psychological, but I still know that I experienced exactly what I said—the One, a fusing of subject and object, etc." Here we meet, as we continually shall, the inadequacy of the written material I have examined. A few questions to Sheila could have cleared up what she meant, but nobody asked her the questions, so that we must either speculate or simply move on. I shall move on, noting before I do that her experience did not cause any lapse of her critical faculties, something that we shall see in many of the individuals we shall consider. One very deep prejudice among some non-religious people is that people having religious experience are just a gullible sort. Some religious people are, unquestionably; but then, so are some non-religious people. At any rate, all that I wish to say is that very often people having religious experience, certainly many among those I studied, are anything but gullible—indeed, are just the opposite. We shall have occasion to note this many times as we proceed.

Sheila's experience was essentially an experience of oneness, and yet it was also an experience which she describes as a "sort of cosmic gesture towards the earth," an experience, we might say, of the overflow of the One. She was experiencing what she took to be objective Reality, Its objectivity being along the lines of a physical object—the physical object is there with its characteristics, and the subject just perceives the object with its characteristics.

What prepared Sheila for the experience, if anything prepared her, was her study of Plotinus. Yet we shall find people who have not studied Plotinus or the mystical writings of others who, all the same, have an experience of oneness. Moreover, we can be certain that not everyone who studies Plotinus intensely has the experience of oneness. I imagine, e.g., that few deep Plotinus scholars have ever had the experience they write about. Thus, intense study of Plotinus is neither a necessary nor a sufficient condition for the experience of oneness.

As for our theses, I should say that Theses C is falsified because the words of Inge concerning Plotinus were far too weak to convey the meaning of oneness Sheila experienced—her "brain" couldn't figure the words out. "The meaning of the words supplied itself" only in her experience. She goes on to describe the experience in terms familiar in descriptions of oneness or merger: The laws of time and space were suspended; the distinction between subject and object, active and passive, noun and verb was lost; thought and emotion fused. She apparently knew all this language before the experience, but the experience supplied the meaning. The words were, according to her account, just that—words. They carried little, if any, meaning to her; or whatever meaning the words carried, it was not in the least comparable to the meaning conveyed by her experience. It is almost as if her study of Plotinus provided her with a warehouse, a mere shell, which was without any wares. Her experience provided the wares.

Yet her experience seems to break out of the Plotinian mold, for she speaks of a cosmic gesture and of standing in the great hand of God, phrases which seem to convey some sort of personal Reality, phrases, moreover, which are not standard within conventional Western religion. Again, the content for her experience seems to be supplied from the experience itself, not some form of past conditioning, at least any conditioning that we can locate.

As for Thesis O, since Plotinus, and Inge, too, present the mystical experience as desirable, certainly the highest state a human can achieve, the thesis is not falsified. As for Thesis P, the evidence is too thin to make a firm judgment. Sheila's objective clearly seems to have been understanding, intellectual understanding, of mystical experience. She could have been antagonistic toward the experience itself, desiring simply to understand; or she could have had a fairly strong positive attitude toward it; or she could have been neutral toward it.

We may also note that Sheila was not in anything like a crisis situation. She was in pleasant surroundings, and although she was making a full-scale effort to understand Plotinus, she was engaged in something which gives no impression of being unpleasant—just the opposite. Her participation in the study group reveals that she enjoyed using her brain.

Mark (554)

Mark writes as follows concerning an experience which lasted over nine months.

> The experience included a sublime consciousness of a personalized sustaining power which defies description. I recall wondering whether I had found God or had God found me. I was infinitely more concerned with and aware of people and my environment. Mental perception and originality of thought were heightened. Living reached undreamed of levels of sheer joy.
>
> Recognizing this as a religious experience I was at first surprised to discover little correlation between my experience and the Church's beliefs and behavior.

The main point to note here is that Mark sees his experience as outside the teachings of the church. He does not specify how it is outside; merely that it is. I suggest that it could be considered outside the teaching of the church at least in the following ways. To begin with, although Mark's description of God as "a personalized sustaining power which defies description" is consistent with Biblical or church doctrine, it does not employ the usual language of the church and does not express the usual emphasis of the church. The emphasis of the prayer book of the Church of England (C/E), the church Mark was familiar with, is of God as divine authority-figure and judge, with considerable emphasis being placed on God as wrathful Judge. In addition, Mark speaks of his state of consciousness as sublime, a term which is not common within the traditional church setting. One would at least expect the term 'joy', a term which he does employ later on. Further, Mark says nothing about forgiveness of sin but does speak about heightened perception and thought.

Whether or not I have accurately located what Mark took to be the major differences between his experience and the teaching and beliefs of the church, the main point is that he was keenly conscious of the difference. Thus, we may say that the content of Mark's experience was not the content of the teachings he was familiar with from the church; at least, the content of his experience was not the content of the standard teachings of the church. I shall simply not say that never did Mark come across the phrase 'a personalized sustaining power'. However, I am of the opinion that people who try to explain religious experience by religious background have in mind that the teachings to which a person was *regularly* subjected, not just words or phrases here or there, play a role in that person's religious experience. Thus, words or phrases which people may have heard but were not part of any consistent teaching, words or phrases, moreover, which people give no evidence of having latched on to prior to their experience, will not fulfill the conditions of

Thesis C, or will do so only weakly. In Mark's case, then, I shall say that Thesis C, if not falsified, is only weakly fulfilled. Obviously the beliefs Mark was taught were also not a sufficient condition for the content of his religious experience; otherwise, the church's standard beliefs would have shown up as the content of his experience. As for Thesis O, I think that Mark is fairly clearly saying, "I had an experience which was far from anything the church said I should seek or have." His experience was outside the standard representation of what is desirable or valuable. Thus, Thesis O is falsified. We do not have enough information to make a judgment about Thesis P.

On Reducing Religious Experience to Feeling

Before leaving Mark I wish to focus on his description of God as a personalized sustaining power. Some people try to reduce religious experience to feelings, i.e., to a conscious state consisting entirely of feelings. Thus, they would say something along the following lines: "Consciousness of a personalized power is strictly a feeling of a powerful presence." I note, however, the oddness of talking about a "feeling of a powerful presence." What sort of feeling is that? We feel bored, tired, anxious, peaceful, joyful, angry, happy, and so on, states clearly distinguishable from apprehending something like a jet streaking through the sky, a squirrel, a camelia—or a personalized power. (I note that I can do no better in characterizing feelings than merely give examples. All the same, I can clearly distinguish between feelings and thoughts, feelings and physical objects, etc.) As I now think about a powerful presence, my object of thought is not strictly or mainly feelings, so I do not know why it should be (or necessarily is) in religious experience. We clearly seem to be talking not about some feeling or combination of feelings but about awareness or apprehension of an Object, as in the apprehension of a physical object. Indeed, we could also talk about a feeling of the presence of a physical object—a tree, a flowing stream, a house. Only this is very odd language, and we do not use it—for good reason. We take ourselves to be apprehending something, something which is not a feeling. Likewise with consciousness of a personalized power: It does not seem to reduce to a feeling any more than does consciousness of my brother sitting in the rocking chair across from me.

Suppose, though, that consciousness of a personalized power (or any other religious Object) is nothing but a feeling or a set of feelings. We should still have to marshal an array of further arguments in order to show that the feeling state constituting religious experience cannot be the means for us to become aware of the Divine directly, in the sense of direct-awareness-R. If we grant that sensory perception provides for the direct awareness of physical objects, why should we not say the same about feelings, or at least certain feelings? Why should the awareness of a brown, oblong object flying through the air be considered the direct awareness of a football in motion, or if our perception includes a sizeable chunk of the playing field, the direct awareness of a forward pass? In other words, why should visual items, and not feelings, be considered direct awareness of external realities? The former makes no more *a priori* sense than the latter, at least as far as I can tell.

Moreover, if we are in the business of reducing consciousness of a divine Object to feelings, we might as well go wholesale and include other objects, including sensory and memory objects, in our business. In other words, we could say, e.g., that the sense of givenness in the case of a sensory object is just a feeling. But the reply to this is, "So what?" What we call the sense of givenness really does not matter in a way (other than that our language may be odd and confusing), as long as we keep our eyes on the issue of substance, viz., the epistemic significance of givenness. The fact is that the sense of givenness (assumed here to be a feeling) characterizes sensory perception and is crucial for the claim that what we perceive is distinct from us and has the character we are aware of it having. Nothing has changed by considering givenness to be a feeling. The same would apply to givenness in the case of religious experience.

What about memory? A memory of my daughter's birthday celebration is different from what I imagine the surface of Venus to be. What makes something a memory and something an imagination? A feeling? Certainly not anything I normally classify as a feeling. I just seem to apprehend something as being about what happened, and something else as being imaginary. Yet the suggestion might be that what distinguishes memory material is the sense of pastness associated with it, the sense of pastness really being a feeling of pastness. I shall first of all demur strongly about any such feeling. Secondly, I shall note that if it is a toss-up between introducing a feeling of pastness in association with certain items of thought and simply going with an apprehension that certain items of thought are about the past, parsimony would decide for the latter. (The same consideration would apply in the case of givenness.) Finally, I shall say, as in the case of givenness, nothing seems to change by introducing the feeling of pastness. The items considered to be memory items remain so, and the epistemic weight of the items remains the same—that is, there is no a priori reason that I know of why a so-called feeling of pastness may not be the means for accurately flagging memory items.

The upshot is that I shall not reduce religious experience to any kind of feeling state. I have attempted to show that doing so need not be of any epistemic significance, except that it introduces odd and confusing language. Therefore, I shall not consider Mark's consciousness of "a personalized sustaining power" to be essentially a feelings state but essentially a state of direct awareness of a personalized sustaining power— no less of a direct awareness of an object than the direct awareness of a sparrow.

Juan

When Juan was a youth, his mother took him to a Methodist church, "off and on," he says, with the on days being days he regularly ditched Sunday School. After high school he ditched the religious scene altogether. However, while he was in his 30's, his marriage began to come apart, with the result that one afternoon he began to search for help, his early touch with the church reminding him that perhaps help could be found in a church. He tried several churches, without finding a minister at hand, finally deciding to return home with the message for his wife that a divorce was the only solution to their problems. While driving home, he passed a shopping center with a building having a rainbow on it, "a rainbow," he says, "which was just like the one on my place of business. So I turned in, and found that the shopping center was really a church. I decided to go in and see the minister, my thoughts being that he would surely agree with me that I should get a divorce." The minister was not at hand here either, but Juan did not leave, going instead into the sanctuary, where, he says, "my life was replayed before me. I saw my failure as a husband and father, and felt guilt. That was my main feeling. And I started weeping." After spending some time in the sanctuary, he walked out, immediately meeting a woman, who saw that he was very troubled. Her first words were, "Jesus can change your life," his reply being, "There's just too much water gone under the bridge." Yet the woman persisted, asking him if he would say a prayer after her. Juan says, "I felt it was pretty impossible to repair my marriage, but I said to myself, 'I'll try anything; it's not going to hurt me.'" He repeated after her a prayer confessing his sins and inviting Christ into his life. Instantly, he says,

I felt this inner peace, a tremendous sense of peace—that I'd never felt before . . . and an almost inexplicable answer that everything was going to be all right. I felt hope. And there was a feeling of love—I felt I was being loved by Somebody, by Jesus. Intellectually and rationally I couldn't figure it out. It was totally irrational.

Juan went home determined to save his marriage. His wife was thoroughly skeptical of his new religious commitment, but within a month she committed herself to follow Christ, with the result that not only did Juan and his wife not divorce but at the time I write this (nine years after the interview) he reports that their marriage "is on an altogether different level. We have become close."

Although Juan had a weak religious background, we may suppose that the content of his experience is at least consistent with what he garnered from his early contact with the Methodist church. This supposition may be incorrect, but it does seem reasonable. Thus, Thesis C is not falsified. However, both Theses O and P are falsified. The religious background of Juan was far too weak either to teach the value of having a religious experience or to give him a generally positive attitude toward religion. His regular ditching of Sunday School and his abandonment of religion after high school indicate that his attitude toward religion was anything but positive. Moreover, his contact with the woman who led him in prayer was far too brief to create the conditions specified by these theses. In fact, as far as Thesis P goes, Juan explicitly says that his attitude was, "I'll try anything"—not the most positive of attitudes.

Since Juan experienced God in a crisis situation, we might introduce the thesis that crisis explains his experience. However, we can immediately write off crisis as a necessary condition for a religious experience, for Sheila was not in a crisis. Of course, crisis is not a sufficient condition, for many people in crisis simply abandon God altogether.

An Explanation of Juan's Experience: The Set Thesis

One way to get around what I have just said—in fact, to get around my counterexamples generally—is to say that crisis was a necessary condition for *Juan*. In short, although some specific natural factor may not be necessary or sufficient for all religious experience, some set (perhaps a set of one) or other of natural factors is necessary or sufficient for each religious experience. I shall call this the "Set Thesis." Thus, crisis, for example, may not be necessary for all religious experience, but it may have been for Juan's religious experience. In other words, we would say something along the following lines: Juan's personality type (susceptible to guilt, for example) and religious background (weak) were such that the severe crisis of his divorce was the triggering condition for his religious experience. Crisis was the necessary condition which, when added to the other conditions, made them sufficient to produce the experience in Juan. In saying this, we are really saying, I think, that the combination of factors would be a sufficient condition in anybody. To get a more plausible set of conditions, we may add that people must, like Juan, turn to God through prayer or some similar religious activity. We may, and probably would, have to add something else (perhaps much else), but for now we have four factors: specific personality type; weak religious background; severe crisis; and turning to God. I shall call all these factors in combination C1. The set C1, then, is, according to hypothesis, a sufficient condition for religious experience, a condition which will be fulfilled only in certain persons, such as Juan. For other persons we may find other combinations of factors functioning as sufficient conditions, say, C2 or C3 . . . Cn. I am not averse to the Set Thesis, as long as it stays on this kind of track. However, if the Thesis gets on another track, I am averse to it.

The track which the Thesis really needs to stay off of is the one where we end up saying, e.g., that crisis was a condition for religious experience in Juan, but not necessarily for anybody else. The problem here is essentially methodological: How would we confirm a thesis concerning causation in a single individual? If crisis is not a general condition for religious experience, or if crisis in combination with other factors is not a general condition for religious experience, then why should we think that it was a condition for Juan? By the mere fact that crisis preceded the experience?

If we go for an explanation in terms of the unique state of a person, then we can give up trying to find causal conditions. We may write Juan's history, in the sense of describing him and the events of his life, but we may not write anything causal about his religious experience. Or if we do, it will certainly not be testable. For example, we could say that what was unique for Juan in C1 was the particular sort of guilt syndrome he had. Yet how shall we test for the causal nature of this syndrome? If the syndrome is unique, a consequence of his particular history, we could never duplicate the unique conditions forming the syndrome in order to see whether or not the syndrome is doing what we say it is. Even if we could clone individuals, we could not pull off the test because we would need one group with Juan's history, the history which brought about his unique guilt syndrome, and at least one other group with a history similar in all respects, except in those respects which brought about the unique guilt syndrome of Juan. (I am assuming here that guilt syndromes are not genetic or entirely genetic.) Aside from the improbability of a history affecting only one characteristic (guilt) without affecting many others, I say that the test is just not possible, even in principle, at least if 'in principle' means 'something that actual humans would or could carry off anytime in the foreseeable future'. Thus, I think that we may dismiss the Set Thesis insofar as it appeals to the unique—such an appeal is simply beyond testing and presents a mere possibility, a possibility which is hardly strong enough to affect the *prima facie* status of religious experience.

Before concluding this fairly lengthy excursion into the Set Thesis, I wish to enter the reminder that I never promised to cover all naturalistic possibilities. I set myself the task of considering what I see as some major naturalistic counters to religious experience. Moreover, I have done little in the way of considering combinations of factors, largely because combinations are not discussed in the literature, or at least the literature I am familiar with. If I have failed to consider a strong overriding possibility, then that is my failure. In fact, I can think of sets which might override and will mention some later on. I note, however, that we do not have the evidence at present to make a decision concerning the sets I mention.

Ron

Ron stated that he never went to church and that his father wanted absolutely nothing to do with religion, often pulling out a dollar bill and saying, "This is God." What Ron picked up about God he picked up from friends and from literature on the streets. At the age of thirty nine he found himself in a failing marriage, largely, he says, because of his approach to life. "I had been in Vietnam, assigned to an assassination squad. Human life didn't mean much to me. I'd gone through life figuring I'd do what I had to to get along—step on toes or whatever." After six years of marriage he discovered one day that his wife was through having her toes stepped on. The marriage was finished. Not knowing what to do, he drove up on a hill and said, "OK God. I've heard of you. If you are God, you're listening. If not, I'm talking to myself. For thirty nine years my life has been one complete screw-up. I'll give my life to you." He sat on the hill from one until six in the morning, thinking not only about God but also about the possibility of driving right off the hill to his death. By six he was saying to himself, "Well, now I talked to myself, and nothing happened." He drove down the hill, came to an intersection, and sensed something telling him to turn left into a driveway. He turned left and found himself in the parking lot of what looked like a shopping center but which was in reality church buildings—a church had bought the shopping center. Several weeks later, after having attended the church and having begun to read the Bible, he was sitting in a Bible class one Sunday morning, saying to himself, "Christ, I want you in my life." He describes the results as follows. "I could feel a power coming in me—a warm, loving feeling. I could feel arms go around me. I opened my eyes. I felt that God was there. I felt God's love." Two weeks later at his baptism he says that his loneliness and guilt left him.

I do not think that a firm judgment is possible on Thesis C. Ron had attended the church long enough to gather substantial information about Christ. He even may have heard some people talk about feeling God's arms around them. The church was one in which people regularly gave their "testimonies." As for Thesis O, it is falsified because what was presented as desirable to Ron was accepting Christ into his life, not having an experience of surging power or arms of love about him. He may have heard people describe experiences generally similar to his, yet the descriptions only presented some possible outcomes of accepting Christ, not that which was to be sought or that which was considered standard. Thesis P is not falsified—Ron's experience in the church created a positive attitude in him toward religion and probably toward religious experience. The particular church was one in which religious experience was fairly common and one in which, as I said, the experiences were commonly reported.

We may note that Ron, as Juan, was in crisis. Also Ron desired God's reality, yet God did not, as it were, come for the desire and asking. I shall discuss in detail the argument from desire in Chapter Three, but shall make a few remarks here concerning the role of desire in Ron's experience.

When Ron drove up to the hill, he clearly wanted something to happen—apparently, some evidence of God's reality; yet he drove down, keenly aware that nothing had happened. Driving along, he did, indeed, experience what he took to be guidance to the church but nothing in the way of a full sense of God's presence. That did not occur until several weeks later, while he was sitting in a Bible class. Therefore, the notion that desire for religious experience is a sufficient condition for the experience—that somehow religious experience is a result of our own desires and wishes, that it comes at our beck and call—is falsified by Ron's experience on the hill. The notion that desire for a religious experience is a necessary condition for the experience is falsified by Ron's experience in the Bible class, for although he was desirous of finding God, that desire at the time did not necessarily translate into a desire for a religious experience and, in any case, did not translate into a desire for the specific form his experience took. The specific form of the experience came as from the outside, as a gift, a surprise, something which took hold of him. Admittedly, he had asked Christ into his life, but that act is something which evangelical Christians believe may occur without any special feelings at all, not to mention religious experience. As I noted previously, accepting Christ is not presented as necessarily resulting in an experience of a certain form, an experience which one may or should seek and expect.

Feelings and Ron's Experience

I also wish to focus on the feelings present in Ron's experience in the Bible class. He says, "I could feel a power coming in me—a warm, loving feeling. I could feel arms go around me." Ron does not say, "I felt as if a power were coming into me." In short, Ron experienced a power coming into him. The phrase "a warm, loving feeling" cannot be taken as identical with his sense of a power coming in because a warm, loving feeling is not necessarily a feeling of power. However, the essential point is that Ron stresses the feeling aspects of the experience. Moreover, he says that arms went around him—again, he does not say that it was as if arms went around him, but "I could feel arms around me." And that, I think, is why he opened his eyes. He needed to double-check on whether arms were really around him.

Ron also describes the loving power as "coming in me"—the power has a sense of exteriority to it, as if something is coming in from the outside. A runner might say, "I really felt strong during the last quarter of that 10K—almost as if I had a surge of power." But really feeling strong and feeling "almost as if I had a surge of power" is not the same as feeling "a power coming in me." The former is clearly what we might call "the language of internality," language strictly about one's own feelings; the latter is the language of externality, more like saying, "You bet I felt a shock. What's wrong with that switch?" The shock is clearly from without, nothing like the feeling of strength during the race. Thus, Ron identifies the power as coming in him.

In addition, he says, "I felt that God was there. I felt God's love." Ron's language here mirrors the sloppiness of contemporary usage, something that I shall comment on at greater length in Chapter Three. However, briefly I emphasize the following: We do not feel *that*; we feel love, hate, anger, joy, and so on; we believe, think, or sense *that*. Thus, I tidy-up Ron's statement to say: "I was aware of God being there. I felt God's love." Or it could read: "I was aware that God was there and loving me."

Returning to Ron's words that he felt God's love, I wish to comment further on the notion of externality, which I have already mentioned. A fundamental point to remember is that loving feelings do not just float about unattached—they are moored to persons. Love is not an abstraction, not a one-place predicate. We do not say, "Ron loves," but, "Ron loves Rhonda." Ron is being loved, and being loved means the involvement of another person. The base experience of being loved is, I should say, the experience of other persons being present with us, perhaps putting their arms around us, stroking our face when we are sick, playing baseball with us. I think about how my dad loved me; I remember his love; I say, "Dad really loved me"; but I do not feel him loving me now, for he is dead. I shall certainly not deny that Henry might say, "I felt the love of Harriett," his dead spouse; but if Henry's feeling is not inspired by memory of some specific occasion or occasions, then I would guess that he believes in the afterlife and in interaction with persons in the afterlife. At any rate, the main point is that the paradigm of love for us humans involves the presence of another person.

Just as important to remember is that our being loved by another does not reduce to our feelings. The love of another may stimulate a range of feelings in us or may stimulate our love in return, a love which will likely involve some feelings, perhaps very strong ones. Yet our feelings are obviously not the love which the other person has for us. We may, in fact, perceive the love of the other—however we do—independently of any feelings. Indeed, we may be an ice-cube, totally unresponsive, and yet we can say with utter certainty, "I don't know why, but John loves me, loves me unconditionally."

Similarly with God. We may perceive God as loving without experiencing any feelings. We shall come across many subjects who did not have feelings or sensations, or at least did not describe any. Some said something along the lines of: "I sensed a Benevolence," an almost impersonal Reality. The Benevolence did not seem personally involved with the individual—was just sort of there, apprehended as external to the individual, infusing all reality, much the same as sunshine infuses the space of a cloudless day. Ron, though, had feelings—warm feelings. We might say that he had feelings similar to those he had when someone loved him. And Someone was loving him. "God was there." The warm feeling and the sensation of arms around him were associated with God being there, yet neither the feeling nor the sensation has any necessary relation to the awareness of God's loving presence. E.g., we could sense acceptance without feeling accepted. I see nothing illogical about saying, "I sensed her as tremendously accepting, but dammit, I just can't feel accepted!" Indeed, I think that this experience is fairly common in our experience with other humans. It is also common in our experience with God. The main point concerns not the commonness of the experience but the fact that love and acceptance do not reduce to feelings, so that we may sense both from God without necessarily having any feelings.

Now the final point takes up on the last one: Persons are not—any more than their characteristics, such as love—reducible to feelings, so that whatever the feelings Ron had, they simply do not constitute the reality of the Person he apprehended, the Person he calls "God." We might suppose that he identifies the Person as God because of the great power and love he experiences. Yet there is a problem here. Why does he go from the power or love he feels to God? Is the power or love he feels so immense, so far beyond anything that he ever felt, that he immediately thinks of God? He does not say anything of the sort, although we shall come across others who do. Indeed, he and many others do not represent their feelings of love, power, and so on as immense—greater, e.g., than any love or power they ever experienced or could experience in the world. They do not say something along the lines of, "I had a gigantic burst of power in me, as if an atomic bomb had gone off." Certainly, the feeling of arms around him was not some feeling more powerful than the feeling of human arms around him. I think that what we must say is this: Many people perceive the power or love of the Divine as great, whatever the level of their feelings—almost like seeing a distant mountain, seeing it as small, yet knowing that it is immense. The reason is, I believe, that people generally do not go inferentially from great power or love to the Divine but experience everything as a package; that is, the experience is a Gestalt of a powerful, loving Presence. That we can apprehend another consciousness with its attributes is a matter I already considered in Chapter One and shall not add anything here. We may be wrong about the claims we make for our experience; perhaps our particular experience is not really an experience of a loving Presence, but that is a different matter from what we are aware of, of what appears to us. My present point is that persons, and God in particular, do not reduce to our feelings. The sum of the matter is that God does not reduce for Ron to any feeling or set of feelings.

I note, finally, that Ron's experience is not unusual, for many have feelings or physical sensations associated with the experience of God.

Mike

Mike was brought up as an agnostic. His mother was a Protestant, his father a Jew from Warsaw, who, because of the Holocaust, had largely abandoned his religious beliefs. The most both parents did to provide religious training for Mike was to help him understand the cultural significance of religion. Yet while in college Mike became a serious devotee of the Hare Krishna movement. He relates several experiences of Krishna's presence.

> I experienced joy. Internally I felt a flooding, a warm flooding, where all stress melted. I had an awareness of Krishna's presence, not like you might feel every day. It's not like there's another person in the room monitoring your conversation. Yet I felt Krishna's presence as if in the room.

> Other times I've felt zapped or flooded by mercy coming from Krishna. It's manifested as a warm, flooding sensation, and peace; all anxiety goes away, melts—sort of like being immersed in a spiritual Jacuzzi. All this is the mercy of Krishna.

Mike mentioned that these experiences would usually come while he was chanting or perhaps serving in the temple, although they might come on other occasions.

Mike's experiences do not fit the content of his early religious training (or lack of it); instead, they fall within the general framework of Hare Krishna teaching. Yet the specific form of the experience was not present in the Hare Krishna teaching Mike was familiar with. He strongly asserted, "I didn't manufacture the experiences to fit the Scriptures," going on to observe that in a number of cases he found the Scriptural descriptions of the experiences after he had the experiences.

Thus, Thesis C is falsified, as well as Thesis O. Thesis P is not falsified, for Mike had come to have a positive attitude toward religion and religious experience by way of the Hare Krishna community.

One point to note about Mike's experience is that it does not seem to be directly related to religious practice or ritual. Mike mentioned that his experiences would often come while chanting or while serving in the temple, but not always. Thus, religious practice or ritual is not a necessary condition for religious experience. In Mike's case it was also not a sufficient condition. In short, sometimes while not chanting he would experience Krishna's presence, and sometimes while chanting he would not experience Krishna's presence.

A question which naturally arises with Mike concerns what we are going to do about the specific references to Krishna. The same question arises concerning the specific references to Christ in other people. I could say that what Mike calls "Krishna" others call Christ. More on this in Chapter Nine.

6. Experiences of Childhood and Early Youth

Some of the strongest counterexamples to the thesis that religious experience is a function of religious training or background are provided by the experiences of children and pre-teen youth, experiences which simply burst the mold of home or church training. I shall consider a number of cases, but a far more complete and systematic account is found in Edward Robinson's *The Original Vision* (New York: The Seabury Press, 1983).

Socrates

One of the most noteworthy of childhood experiences is that of Socrates. In the "Apology" Socrates relates that when he was a child, he began to hear a Voice. He does not tell us how young he was, and he does not tell us exactly how he "heard" this Voice, that is, whether it was audible or whether it was interior, from within. He does tell us, though, that the Voice was a divinity, functioning strictly as a restraining Voice, never telling him what to do but what not to do. ("Apology," #31) I shall take Socrates' words that the Voice was a divinity to mean that the Voice came to him as a divinity—came not as mere words, which he infers to have a divine origin, but as a divinity speaking. I cannot demonstrate that this interpretation is correct, but I take it to be as plausible as any other.

The basic point to note is that hearing a Voice was anomalous in the society of Socrates, a fact underscored by the inability of the Athenians to take him seriously on the matter of his Voice. Greek society was definitely not Hebrew society, in which a person could appear on the scene, announcing that the word of the Lord had come to him, with nobody considering him particularly odd; but for a Greek to claim guidance by a Voice, a divine Voice, was an eyebrow-raiser. The Pythoness at Delphi may be moved by the gods, but she was an institutionalized oracle, recognized throughout Greek society. Also there were other prophets who had a kind of semi-official status, along the lines of Teiresias in "Oedipus the King." All the same, for someone to come on the scene, having no institutional or official credentials, yet claiming personal guidance from God, was uncommon, to say the least. Socrates was just something of a cultural oddity; and since he mentions nothing of family influence—for example, that father or mother experienced divine guidance—we may suppose that he simply came to the experience naive.

If what I have said about Socrates and his society is true, Theses C, O, and P are falsified. C is falsified because the notion of a Voice, although present in Greek society by way, e.g., of the Pythoness, took an unusual turn with Socrates; that is, it spoke only to forbid, and it spoke for personal guidance. O is falsified because having a Voice for personal guidance was not held up as an ideal for Athenian youth. P is falsified because Socrates gives the impression that the Voice came uninvited, as something of a surprise, not something he had been thinking about, desiring, feeling positive about.

We should also note that Socrates did not just accept the Voice without critical evaluation. He notes in the "Apology" that the Voice consistently led him to do what was right, a statement which probably means 'right' not only in a moral sense but in the sense of 'not leading astray' or 'leading in a prudent or wise way'. Thus, Socrates used rational criteria to evaluate the Voice, a course which is followed by many of the people who report religious experience. Their minds are not inactive, but are inquiring, questioning, and doubtful. E.g., when Ron did not experience anything while sitting on the hill between one and six in the morning, he said, "Well, now I just talked to myself." Sheila also was very definite that her experience of the One was not a hallucination or a dream.

Cindy

Cindy states that her parents never went to church and she also never went to church. All the same, as a child she felt God as a secret Friend to whom she spoke, a God "of everything and behind everything." God was the kind of friend she could talk to not only about the pleasant things of her life but also about her guilt, about things she had done wrong. She frankly states, "I don't know where I got my concept of God." Cindy was an only child, and hence we might suppose that she was lonely, although she did not say she was. Some people I came across specifically mention that they felt lonely as children, but most do not mention being lonely, a number mentioning, instead, a pleasant childhood with friends, siblings, and loving parents. Thus, loneliness is not a necessary condition for a religious experience, and it is certainly not a sufficient condition, for many lonely people never have a religious experience. I take this to be common knowledge.

The main question, though, is how Cindy came up with the idea of a friendly God that is at the same time a God of everything and behind everything, a God, moreover, that could relieve guilt. Her ideas of God seem fairly standard, i.e., fully within the Christian religion, for her God is the loving Creator. Yet she does not recall being taught these ideas and says that she never went to church. If these statements are correct, then how she arrived at her notion of God is puzzling, especially the notion of God as Friend. In some churches a person might pick up the notion of God as a friend, but Cindy says that she did not go to church. Thus, it looks as if Thesis C is falsified. However, the lack of systematic teaching fairly clearly falsifies Theses O and P. She was clearly not subjected in any systematic sense to teaching which placed a value on religious experience of the sort she had or would create a positive attitude toward religion in her. If she simply experienced the ideas floating about in her particular cultural milieu, I assume that she would have come across as many negative, frightening ideas about God as positive, friendly ideas. The religious atmosphere of her childhood does not seem to have been negative, but it also does not seem to have been positive. I should term the atmosphere "religiously neutral."

One suggestion might be that Cindy's experience of God was a kind of projection based on her need of a friend. (We could introduce a similar explanation for Socrates' Voice. How plausible does that seem in his case?) If so, then the question is why she did not simply create an imaginary friend, as do many other children. Why the turn to God, especially without strong, consistent teaching concerning God as loving, friendly, and forgiving? Why a child would turn to God rather than a more "flesh and blood" imaginary playmate (God was not a playmate!) is in itself puzzling, I think. Moreover, why the child would find forgiveness in this divine Friend, when guilt and forgiveness were apparently not big issues in the home, is even more puzzling. I say "puzzling," not to indicate that these questions cannot be answered satisfactorily. Further investigation of childhood experiences of God and of imaginary playmates might produce some very plausible answers. Perhaps considerable research has already been done, although I do not know of it. A further point is that Cindy, as an adult, took seriously the friendly God of her childhood. I do not know of any adults who take seriously the imaginary playmates of their childhood.

Meg
(unnumbered, although from the Alister Hardy Research Centre)

Meg attended C/E Sunday school each week, not especially because she wanted to but because she was expected to. She relates an experience which she had at age eleven during a children's service in church.

She says that she had learned to shut out sermons, which "didn't exactly enthrall me," by entering a private world of daydreams. On the day of her experience she had entered her imaginary world, but something extraordinary happened. She had, in her words, a "mind explosion," a totally new level of awareness.

> The change took place so swiftly and the new level of consciousness proved so superior that my mind was immediately stilled with the wonder and awe produced by the beautiful 'something' going on.
>
> This 'new world' existed entirely in an inner-realm and couldn't be compared with the normal earthly one because it had nothing to do with the functions of our ordinary five senses. I couldn't *see* any change, only *feel* it in the same way we can feel the emotions we create. It was a new kind of awareness of an inner reality.
>
> I seemed to merge with such a colossal amount of love that its proportions remain beyond the limits of human description; I'll simply refer to it as love with a capital L, the power of which proved so immense that it felt as if someone had plugged me into a power-point.

It filled my senses with a great vitality and created the amazing feeling of inner-brightness; so real was this brightness that I became convinced that I'd turned into a beacon of glowing, radiating light. I was existing at a brilliantly-supreme level of consciousness which proved welcoming and homely, yet resplendent and magnificent at the same time. I felt ALIVE for the first time in my life and I wanted to stay that way!

I saw, with a level of wisdom far beyond my eleven years, that the ritual taking place around me was meaningless repetition and had nothing to do with the self-expression I was experiencing; and I knew, long before the service was over that *their* kind of 'religion' definitely wasn't for me.

In adult life Meg had further experiences which played on the same theme of being immersed in LOVE.

To begin with, I shall note that although Meg says that she did not see any change in her, she could only feel it, the feeling ends up being "a new kind of awareness of an inner reality." The awareness is essentially of a colossal amount of Love, a Love with which she merges. The Love is a reality just sort of there, like the ocean, in which we may immerse ourselves. Yet she felt the power of this Love, her feelings being of immense proportions, as if she had been plugged into a powerpoint, thereby becoming like a giant light bulb. In this respect her experience differs from that of Ron, whom we met in the last chapter, and who apparently sensed the power of God's love apart from feelings like those of Meg.

As for the influences of background, we immediately note that her experience leaps beyond the customary beliefs and expectations of the church. To be sure, the God of the church is said to be love, power, and light, but this God is represented just as much, particularly within the C/E (note the prayer book), as the judging Monarch. Besides, the notion of merging with a colossal amount of love is not standard within the C/E, especially in children's instruction and worship. One may hear people speak of union with Christ or God but speaking of merger with a vast LOVE is at least uncommon. Finally, the actual sense of merging with this LOVE is not something usually talked about in the church, a point underscored by Meg's awareness that what was going on in the church had little to do with the reality she experienced.

I should say, then, that Thesis C is falsified because of the sense of merger with Love—this would not be an idea Meg would likely come across. Theses O and P are likewise falsified, a point underscored by what Meg takes as the formalistic religion of the church, a religion failing to emphasize encounter with God, a religion she clearly did not and does not feel positive about. The fact that she went to church essentially because she had to points up further a less than positive attitude to the business of religion.

I might also note that Meg does not mention being in any sort of crisis situation. She was simply in church as she regularly was. She was not enthralled by preaching, but she had learned to block it out fairly effectively. Her state was probably comparable to my state at age eleven— I would either read or draw pictures during the sermon, knowing that preaching was going on but not having the slightest idea of what was being said, feeling all the while mild satisfaction or enjoyment in my reading or drawing, as well as in the awareness that I was with my parents. Thus, the notion that religious experience arises out of a crisis situation certainly is not supported: Crisis is neither a necessary nor a sufficient condition for religious experience, not sufficient, obviously, because some people turn entirely away from a religious life because of some crisis.

I would note further that Meg did not seem to want any kind of experience such as she had. The experience seems to come to her unexpectedly, as a surprise.

Karen (1050)

As a contrast to Meg, I note the experience of Karen. Meg, we have seen, comes to her experience, feeling religion to be something of a burden and a bore. Her attitude was generally negative, yet she had a life-changing religious experience. Karen, too, had a negative attitude toward religion, finding Sunday School a meaningless bore; yet Karen, in contrast to Meg, jettisoned all her religious beliefs at age ten. The point I wish to make is that having or not having a religious experience does not seem to be related to early attitudes toward religion in any regular way. There may be tendencies one way or another (appropriate data on this have yet to be developed) but nothing in the way of a necessary or sufficient condition. One person (Meg) may have a negative attitude toward religion yet have a religious experience; another (Karen) may have a negative attitude and go on to jettison religion; another may have a positive attitude and go on to have a religious experience; still another may have a positive attitude and yet jettison religion. Cindy, for example, after her positive childhood experiences, abandoned religion during her early adult life, finally returning only after having drifted into the occult and alcoholism.

Pam (206)

At age eleven Pam had an experience of unity with all of nature. She reports that in the experience "I knew that, in some strange way I, the essential 'me', was a part of the trees, of the sunshine, and the rivers, that we all belonged to some great unity." I assume that Pam is thinking of the essential "me" as something other than her physical nature, namely, as something psychological or spiritual. Thus, she is sensing some sort of spiritual Unity encompassing all of reality, a sort of pantheistic Reality, a kind of Reality that is definitely not part of the standard teaching of church or home.

Pam mentions that she went first to a Baptist Sunday School and then to a C/E Sunday School, both of which she disliked. About six months before her experience she switched to a Congregational Sunday School, which, she says, was great fun. Since Pam says nothing to the contrary, we may suppose that the teaching in each Sunday School was traditional for that setting; in short, we may suppose that she did not hear anything about a pantheistic sort of deity. Supposing this, we may say that Thesis C is falsified. Moreover, supposing that her religious training did not include instruction about the value or desirability of having a pantheistic sort of experience, Thesis O is also falsified. In other words, any teaching in the Christian community concerning the value or desirability of religious experience would be teaching about religious experience with the Christian God or Jesus Christ. By having a pantheistic experience, one automatically will be having an experience which is not explained by early religious training in Christianity. As for Thesis P, we do not have enough information to make a definite judgment. Although Pam had fairly lengthy negative experiences in Sunday School, her experience at the time of sensing a spiritual Unity was positive, at least positive about Sunday School, which is definitely not the same as being positive about religious experience.

I might note that Pam was not in any crisis situation but apparently was enjoying life as a normal eleven year old. In addition, she, in contrast to most others I studied, did absolutely nothing as a result of the experience; i.e., the experience had no effect on her life. Reflecting back on the experience, she says that she views childhood life as on a different plane from adult life, and in adult life she never had an experience like that of her childhood.

Bea (2366)

Bea, when a "young girl," had, like Pam, an experience of heightened perception and a sense of unity with all. She emphasizes that in the experience "I was still myself (I didn't *merge*) in the sense that I still saw all this from a consciousness." Bea says that she had contact with several people in childhood with fairly broad ideas but none who thought of God in terms of a Unity encompassing all. Her memories of God at this time were of a distant, awesome being. As in the case of Pam, I shall say that Theses C and O are falsified. Not enough data are available to make a definite judgment on Thesis P, although her childhood view of God as a distant, awesome being would not seem to be very supportive of a positive attitude toward encounter with this Being.

Dick (201)

Dick says that starting in childhood he had a kind of experience which he cannot name or describe in words. He is, though, very clear about his perceptual state whenever the experience occurred.

> This is always a *fully conscious* experience: Whatever is going on around me still goes on, whatever sounds there are are still heard (indeed any sound that occurs seems, in some strange way, to *accentuate* the silence)—but the experience seems to belong to a separate realm, so that I am conscious at once of externals *and* of the experience.

Dick then goes on to describe the experience.

> A phrase I have come across which goes some little way toward naming the experience is: 'A Roaring silence.' This is a silence which exists *in spite of* any sounds which are going on, and which feels totally dominant and authoritative, even though it does not in any way blot out any circumambient sounds: Stronger than any perception, it still does not obstruct any perceptions, and yet it establishes itself as—for the time being—commanding.

> It is a silence which is like *an enormous statement*, even though I have never been able to put into words (or even to formulate in some nonverbal way) whatever it is that is being stated.

> As a child, I experienced it as rather menacing, almost as a kind of unseen and unspoken analogue of mockery, as though—still speaking purely analogically—someone were nodding their head at me knowingly, as much as to say, 'Ah, *we* know, and *you* don't.'
>
> All these phrases seem to diminish the total *otherness* of the experience I actually had: It was utterly unlike anything I experienced in ordinary life. After my childhood, the rather menacing quality which I had felt in the experience, ceased: In all other respects, it still occurred. It continued to be totally unforeseen: One moment, everything was as usual; the next moment, it was there.... It has never been possible to evoke it.... It has never occurred when I was praying, or consciously relaxing. It is *totally unlike* any of the experiences of great calm and stillness which I do sometimes have in prayer, or in deep relaxation. It only occurs when I am at my most 'ordinary'—and not often then!

Dick goes on to list a few of the ordinary occasions: sitting at table in a resthouse; walking across a college campus while in a very angry mood; alone in his room, while visiting his two daughters.

As for what the experience means, Dick says the following. These experiences leave me with no new knowledge (and yet they *feel* as if they are supremely important)—and I can find no "meaning" in them. They cause no change in my life or disposition, as far as I can see, except that I remember that they occurred, and could at any time occur again.

> All I can say of them is that they are something enormous that occurs at odd times in my life, and which is a *highly tangible* encounter with something which feels *totally other*. None of all this conveys the *feel*, the quality of the experience: It is like a break-through from another dimension.

The notion of a roaring silence is not the kind of notion one would pick up in standard—or offbeat—religious circles, and not the kind of notion one would expect a child to have. In fact, from what Dick says he apparently hit on the term 'roaring silence' after childhood, a fact which indicates that no terminology during his childhood seemed to be sufficient for the experience. The experience clearly broke the molds of his childhood language and experience. In fact, Dick as an adult is still at a loss to describe the experience adequately, saying that it is "totally unlike anything I experienced in ordinary life." Thus both Theses C and O are falsified. Dick does not say enough about his early childhood for us to make a judgment about his attitude toward religion or religious experience.

Dick says that in childhood the silence had a menacing quality, as if someone were mocking him with a knowing nod, saying, "Ah, we know; you don't." Why an authoritative silence should convey a menacing message to Dick is unclear. Perhaps silences were menacing in his home or elsewhere. We do not have information on this point. However, we might hypothesize that the silence is somehow a projection of his early experience with his parents. More specifically, we might hypothesize that the experience arose from guilt, with the silence and knowing nod representing parental responses to his misbehavior. In other words, the silence was a projection of parental disapproval, conveying also parental intentions to punish in some unknown way. The fact that the experience lost its menacing nature when Dick became an adult may mean that in adulthood Dick resolved the childhood conflicts with his parents.

Although this explanation has a degree of plausibility, it has three major flaws. First of all, the idea of a knowing nod, indicating "we know; you don't," is a strange way to refer to guilt about some misbehavior, for the person who has misbehaved knows that he has. We should expect a statement along the lines, "Aha! we know. Don't think you can hide anything from us." The statement we have seems to convey the sense of lacking experience or knowledge of something important. The second flaw in the explanation is that even if it accounts for the experience in childhood, it does not account for the continuation of the experience in Dick's adult life. The absence of the menacing quality would indicate that problems of guilt with parents were resolved; however, Dick says nothing about resolving anything with his parents at the time when the menacing experiences ceased. The third flaw is that the experiences were presumably not just menacing in childhood. Although Dick says that nothing seems to happen because of the experiences (they "leave me with no new knowledge and "cause no change in my life or disposition"), they seem to be positive to him—they are "supremely important," something "enormous," a contact with a Totally Other, leaving him, as he says in another place, "very happy," even though he cannot say why. Perhaps all these qualities of the experience showed up only after childhood, yet Dick does not say so. Thus, we may presume that even in childhood the experiences had the positive qualities of being supremely important and enormous.

Actually, the real puzzle about Dick is why he, an obviously very intelligent man, should be puzzled about the meaning of his experiences. He seems to reveal an almost naive literalism of mind, almost an obtuseness—not to mention a neglect of Biblical data. The notion of silence is found regularly in Scripture, is a common element of Christian worship, and carries with it the idea of communication from God (in short, authoritative communication). I simply mention one Biblical instance, namely, the Elijah story, according to which the mighty God comes to Elijah not in earthquake, wind, or fire but in a still, small voice. Moreover, the notion of God communicating in contentless silence is, I should say, clearly conveyed in the Scripture "Be still and know that I am God," a Scripture read in worship about as regularly as any other Scripture. Further, the notion of a Silence clearly conveys the sense of mystery, the sense that the Divine is beyond words, beyond description, a notion which may have been behind Dick's sense of the Silence as communicating, "We know; you don't."

As for a modern statement about the awareness and meaning of a contentless Silence, I mention a few lines from a poem by the present pope (John Paul), a poem titled, "The Shores of Silence."

> The distant shores of silence begin at the door.
> You cannot fly there like a bird.
> You must stop, look deeper, still deeper, until
> nothing deflects the soul from the deepmost deep.
>
> Meanwhile you always step aside for Someone from beyond,
> Who closes the door of your small room.
> His coming softens with each step
> and with this silence strikes
> the target of the depths.
>
> You are the Calm, the great Silence,
> free me then from the voice.
> In the tremor of Your being let me shiver
> with the wind. (Wojytla, 1979, 5, 16)

Admittedly, neither this poem nor Scripture conveys the notion of a roaring silence. However, I am not trying to say that the notion of a roaring silence can be derived from Scripture; only that Scripture offers profound insight into the meaning of silence. The same would go for Scriptures from other world religions.

Yvonne (1263)

Yvonne was brought up in a home in which her mother was only vaguely Anglican, her father totally uninterested in religion. There was no religious instruction at home except "for stray remarks by a not very inspiring governess." Regular religious instruction did not begin for her until age eleven, when she went to a boarding school. She was between eight and ten years old when she had the following experience.

> I was in the garden, muddling about alone. A cuckoo flew over, calling. Suddenly, I experienced a sensation that I can only describe as an effect that might follow the rotating of a kaleidoscope. It was a feeling of timelessness, not only that time stood still, that duration had ceased, but that I was myself outside time altogether. Somehow I knew that I was part of eternity. And there was also a feeling of spacelessness. I lost all awareness of my surroundings. With this detachment I felt the intensest joy I had ever known, and yet with so great a longing—for what I did not know—that it was scarcely distinguishable from suffering.

Yvonne's experience may not seem unambiguously religious, for it was simply an experience of eternity. Since Yvonne does not elaborate on this experience, we cannot be certain what she takes eternity to be; however, eternity is clearly another dimension outside duration, a dimension associated with spacelessness. We could, then, capitalize the 'e', taking Eternity to be just another name for God. Yvonne certainly views her experience as religious, connecting it in further writing with another childhood experience, "a good while after the first," when she "quite suddenly felt convinced of the existence of God," again feeling herself in a different dimension and experiencing an intense joy and "incredible longing." At the very least we could call her first experience pre-religious, an experience opening her to another dimension, a spiritual— timeless, spaceless—dimension of reality. Moreover, the important point is that the experience does not fit her early religious training, or lack of it; i.e., her early life did not prepare her—provide the concepts, the values or the feelings— for an experience of the sort that she had. All the theses—A, O, and P—are falsified.

An additional point to note is that Yvonne was not in any kind of crisis situation. She remarks that she had an insecure childhood, "which might have been unhappy but for the intense joy I derived from nature and solitude"; yet an insecure childhood hardly equates with crisis. Moreover, the regular joy of her nature experiences is not equivalent to the joy of the two experiences she relates, experiences which she classes as the most vivid experiences of several in which she was "seized by a strange, unaccountable joy." Thus, we may say that she was not seeking the sort of experiences she had—she was seized by them, and the joy was strange and unaccountable. She says that the experiences were always triggered "by certain conditions: country surroundings, a warm, sunny, still day mostly with birdsong, especially the cuckoo, and in perfect solitude." If we are going to look for any necessary or sufficient conditions, we shall have to consider not only the conditions just listed but also Yvonne's insecurity as a child, along with perhaps other conditions. Given the variety of conditions in which children and adults experience the Divine, the conditions listed by Yvonne are hardly necessary. That they are sufficient is also highly doubtful, for many an insecure person has been in nature without experiencing any kind of divine Reality. Perhaps an insecure person in nature must hear a cuckoo for the experience to take place. Obviously, I do not have data to strike this suggestion, but I am highly doubtful about it and certainly welcome any test on the subject.

Clark (489)

Clark writes that as far back as he can remember, he felt a Presence, a sweet, cold Presence, "a dazzling Darkness," which was in everything. He says that he did not sense it as personal, but he did sense it as love.

The images here are definitely not the images common to church or home. Perhaps Clark is reading back these terms into his experience. That may be true to some extent for all the people I am considering in this section. The real question, though, is whether the terms Clark uses describe his experience with some accuracy. 'Dazzling darkness' certainly is not an expression of a child, yet the only question is whether the expression accurately captures his experience as a child. The church regularly speaks of God as light, yet Clark speaks of God under a different image, that of darkness, the image used in the church for sin and ignorance. Since Clark's image is clearly meant to be positive, it could be an image for the mystery of God. In addition, Clark experienced the Presence as cold, an image contrasting with the usual phrase 'warmth of God's love'. What this image meant for Clark is anything but certain, but it may be associated with the distance of the Presence, its distance in the sense of level of Reality. Thus, the stars, of which we know very little, are far from us, existing in the cold darkness of outer space. Whether or not Clark is making this sort of allusion, I cannot say for certain. The main points I wish to make are that 1) his experience was outside the mold of his social world, and 2) if there is supposed to be some problem for Clark of reading his adult terminology back into his childhood experience, then it is a problem for anyone describing any childhood experience.

On point two the real issue is, as I have noted, whether Clark is accurately describing his childhood experience, and that is essentially a problem of memory. None of the subjects I am considering remarks about keeping a diary or relating the experience to adults. In fact, many explicitly say that they avoided speaking to adults, to mother or father or people in the church, for fear of being reprimanded—a clear indication that as children these people saw their experiences standing outside the accepted mold of church and home. Be this as it may, I should say the following concerning the memory of childhood events: We may have at least as much confidence in the recall of religious experiences in childhood as we do in the recall of other, more ordinary, experiences; indeed, since the religious experiences of the people I am considering stand out for them as extraordinary, we may have at least as much confidence in the recall of the experiences as in the recall of other extraordinary experiences in childhood.

Assuming, then, that Clark's description of his childhood experience is on target, we must say that Thesis C is falsified; likewise, Thesis O. No judgment can be made on Thesis P.

James (1050)

James notes that at age nine he experienced union with God, an experience which totally convinced him that God is "not the God of hell," a belief which obviously conflicted with his religious training. Thesis C is falsified, as is Thesis O—O because James was not likely taught to value experiences of a God different from the God of church and home. In fact, I have my doubts that union with God is a notion familiar to a nine year old.

Alice (770)

Alice writes that although she was brought up in the C/E, her religious ideas were influenced little by the church or her family. She found church a bore and her school years dull and miserable. The main contribution of her parents was that they were very loving. At age ten she began having an experience of the following sort.

> A most over-powering sense of beauty . . . generates in me at the time I am seeing [beautiful scenery] an emotion different to any other, when I feel without any doubt a sense of vast timeless benevolence—that all is well, that everything and everyone are part of the same plan; that there is no need to feel afraid or worried.

To begin with, I note that although Alice talks about an emotion and of feeling something ("I feel a sense of vast timeless benevolence") she does not seem to be just having emotions but seems to be apprehending a timeless Benevolence. Saying that she "feels a sense of" is at the very least a strange way to speak of simply having an emotion.

The notion of a vast timeless benevolence is certainly not the sort of notion one would gather from regular attendance at the C/E or at religious schools. The God of Christianity is strongly represented as personal, whereas Alice's experience, although logically requiring a personal being, is cast in more impersonal terms and is, at any rate, cast in terms unfamiliar within the C/E. Moreover, the exclusive emphasis on benevolence is again not part of the tradition of the church, where, as I noted previously, one hears as much about God's judgment as about God's love. Thus, I should say that Thesis C is falsified, as are Theses O and P—P because Alice was anything but positive about the religion she was experiencing.

One possible explanation for Alice's experience is the love she experienced in her home. Yet a loving home does not seem to be a necessary condition for having a religious experience of a loving Presence. Terri, a person I shall consider in Chapter Four, experienced union with God (a loving Being for her), even though she grew up in a broken home in which she was neglected, regularly going from parent to this or that relative and then back. One relative was supportive and loving, but the experience with the relative was not constant and was countered by the other experiences of neglect and lack of care. Numerous people experiencing a loving Presence come from fractured homes, homes in which conflict or neglect is on the daily menu of events. Of course, a loving home is also not a sufficient condition for having an experiencing of a loving Presence, for many loving homes result in children who are agnostics or atheists.

Obviously, a sense of beauty, even an overpowering sense of beauty, is also not a necessary or sufficient condition for a religious experience, even though Alice's experience took place in association with an overpowering sense of beauty. When studying Platonic writings concerning the Good, the True, and the Beautiful, I often give my students an assignment to go to a place of natural beauty and open themselves to and mediate on the beauty there. Only a few report something close to a religious experience, although many convey that the beauty inspired peace, calm, or other positive feelings. Thus, beauty is not a sufficient condition for religious experience. Beauty is also not a necessary condition, for many people, most whom I have studied, do not have their experience in association with any sense of beauty.

Angelique (4051)

Angelique, a person who is now a psychiatrist, states that

> as far back as I can remember I 'knew' of the existence of God: Whatever gradually developing sense I had of myself as an entity was accompanied by a sense of someone other, invisible and infinitely greater than any other 'person' and different to them, a kind of all-powerful, pervasive force within the world but far from being impersonal was loving and beneficent with a real interest in me. No doubt the good loving attributes owed something to my knowledge of my loving parents, but was someone quite definitely other than them. I never used any word for this person—after all I never needed to—but other people's use of the word 'God' or 'Creator' seemed to fit pretty well. I never saw or heard anything that I recall but the knowledge was as certain as the knowledge that other people continued to exist when they left the room.

As for her home background, Angelique says the following. I came from a long line of deeply religious freechurch people on my mother's side, but as my parents were both agnostic and anti-church I don't remember religion ever being a topic of conversation at home. Apart from a few brief flirtations with Sunday Schools I did not attend church until at 13 years old I went to boarding school.

Angeligue was baptized at age sixteen and continued to have religious experiences later in life. Whatever may be the case for her later experiences her early childhood experiences seem to falsify all the Theses, C, O, and P, the main reason being that her parents were agnostic, with religion hardly "ever being a topic of conversation at home." I would note especially Angelique's statement that she did not use the term 'God' for the Someone Other she experienced but came to see that people's use of the term—not her use—seemed to fit what she was experiencing. In short, she apparently did not have enough background in the use of the term 'God' to apply it automatically to The Someone Other she experienced; instead, she plagiarized the term from others after she listened to how they used it. As for Thesis P, it is falsified because there does not seem to be a positive attitude prior to the start of her experiences; rather, her positive feelings about religion seem to arise from her experiences.

Angeligue makes several comments about her experiences, both in childhood and later, comments which go beyond the topic of this chapter, yet comments which I shall introduce at this point in order to complete her account.

She claims that the experiences, unlike most other experiences, are beyond evaluation

> because they have the quality of being not only self-authenticating but being the ground or standard by which everything else in my subjective experience can be, and is judged. This phenomenon itself is not unknown in abnormal states of delusion and hallucination but is not as common in them as might be supposed and in my experience invariably leads to progressive mental deterioration, pain, and eventually psychological and social disintegration, whereas the only objective test of spiritual experiences is that they show fruit in enhanced sensitivity and maturity, and lead to growth in all areas of the personality.

Angelique here reflects critically on her experiences, classifying them as self-authenticating, aware as she does this that some people in delusional states also take their experiences as self-authenticating. She then introduces an additional test for her experiences, viz., the effects in her life. Or perhaps we may take her to be offering a defeater to the suggestion that she might have been in a delusional state when she had her experiences. In that case her experiences would not be exactly self-authenticating, although perhaps so. If I believed in self-authenticating experiences, I can well imagine myself saying: "Look, I know what I know. But as long as you need convincing, let me say this: Delusional people etc." In Chapter Eight I shall consider the evaluation of religious experience by way of its effects, taking up, among other things, the specific effects mentioned by Angelique.

Angelique also mentions that although her experiences have presented her with a personal Reality, she on occasion becomes so absorbed in the Reality, the experience is so Other-directed, that she has total loss of a sense of self, a fact which for her does not take away from the personal nature of the experience. Actually, having an other-directed experience which is still personal is very common in ordinary experience, not just religious experience. I may become absorbed in a thunderstorm, engrossed in and fascinated by the streaking lightning, not in the least aware of self; yet after the storm I am well aware that self was present, acutely aware and perceptive. The recession of self-consciousness into the background does not in the least mean that some sort of impersonal union has taken place.

> Finally, Angelique mentions two items of major importance. There is also the paradox that although on the one hand these are the most significant things in my life and probably the most enduring in that they do not seem to fade like memories of ordinary experiences—yet I know that in my Christian life they are somehow the least important— one of the means by which the spirit calls my attention and then works on me, one contribution I make to the corporate body of the church, but certainly not more valuable than my simple presence at worship on Sunday or the least Christian service I give to others.

She notes the imprint of the experiences on memory—they are the most enduring of her experiences; in addition, she notes that they are really not more significant than more ordinary experiences, a point noted by a number of other persons reporting on their religious experience. Here Angelique is speaking about significance in her religious development and in the religious community. Others will speak of epistemological significance— i.e., they will assert that although the experiences are unusual, they do not have more significance in terms of authenticating the reality of God than the ordinary, daily sense of God's presence.

Marie (3866)

Marie is now in retirement, having had a career as a professional psychologist. She reports that she had the following experience at age ten.

> Without any warning, I was afflicted with a sickness of the spirit. Life became dark and burdensome. I was filled with a feeling of guilt. I was without hope and I felt doomed. I suppose in an adult this condition would be diagnosed as pathological depression. I never thought of seeking help from adults because, in some obscure way, it was all my fault and I was being punished for something I did not quite know what. I have no idea how long this lasted, maybe a few weeks, maybe

a few days. Each day was like a deadly weight which I dragged around. . . . Then one night, when I was considering that I was too miserable to go on living and too bad to die because I would have to go before the Judgment Seat, I suddenly heard a voice (not a real voice, rather an audible thought). The exact words were: 'Though thy sins are as scarlet, they shall be white as snow.' I did not know or recognise the origin of these words. All that I knew was that it had something to do with religion, and that it was a promise. So I immediately claimed that promise, saying that if the promise were not fulfilled, I would have proof that the church was telling lies and I would resist all further contact with religion. Then I fell asleep immediately.

Next morning I awoke and knew that a miracle had happened. My burden had fallen away, I was free, I was new-born. Everything was sparkling and full of light. For the next few days I walked around in wonderment. My heart full with gratitude. Then quite suddenly the voice spoke again. This time I think it was day-time and I was walking along the street. The exact words this time were: 'You are no longer your own, I am God and you belong to me, and you must consult me about every major decision you make in life. I have a PLAN. I need you and I will guide you.'

I did not tell other people about my 'experience.' My instinct was to keep it private. I did try to tell my parents about it because I wanted them to share my joy, but I was only ten years old, and I think they were rather scared. I knew that they did not fully understand, so from that date I have shared my secret with nobody. It is only in recent years that I have been able to adopt an objective attitude to the whole experience, which proved to be the mainspring to the whole of the rest of my life. Sixty years have passed since then, and I have remained deeply committed to God and to the idea of steadily unfolding Purpose in my life. Incidentally, I am not deeply committed to any Christian Church, although I am more at home in the Scottish Presbyterian church, which I know best. I do not feel it is important.

Marie could not figure the reason for her guilt, even after decades of reflection, as a psychologist. Obviously, she did not see anything special occasioning the experience, either within her home or within her behavior. We may speculate that the general environment of a Scottish Presbyterian home and church was custom-designed to enhance guilt, yet there did not seem to be anything unusual at age ten to trigger Marie's state of severe guilt.

As for Theses C, O, and P, I shall say that Thesis C is not falsified, my assumption being that either in home or church she likely would have picked up the notion of a Voice speaking, as well as the Scripture passage from Isaiah (even though she did not remember hearing it), along with the notions of belonging to God and of God having a plan for her life. However, neither home nor church provided a model for her experience, i.e., held up the sort of experience she had as desirable or to be pursued. Her parents did not understand her experience, exhibiting, as she thought, fear. They did not seem to grasp what had happened and therefore could not have been presenting the experience as something to be pursued. She did not even tell anyone in church, so she certainly could not have been receiving any positive images there of the kind of experience she had. Thus, I shall say that Thesis O is falsified. Thesis P also seems to be falsified. Marie says little about her feelings concerning religion at an early age, but her guilt experience and the feelings surrounding it—doom, fear, loss of hope, punishment— certainly do not indicate a positive feeling toward God and religion or a positive feeling about religious experience. Who would want much to do with this God of the Judgment Seat? Moreover, her willingness to abandon the whole project of religion if "the promise were not fulfilled" seems to indicate a less than positive attitude toward religion. I shall say, then, that Thesis P is also falsified.

Since Marie was ready to abandon the project of religion after the first Voice experience, I am inclined to think that the experience was not imbedded in a sense of Presence but was strictly an experience of an "audible thought." The second experience of the Voice seems to be clearly of a Presence communicating.

Calvin (3451)

Calvin was brought up in a Christian setting. At age twelve he began to have questions about the meaning of life, questions which distilled into "a doubt of the reality of my own, or anything else's, existence." The doubt led to the following experience.

> I began to grasp for the first time, exactly what God was; at one level, he was a human being (not of my own age, neither aged, but a young man of 20 to 30); at another level, an all pervading Energy which encompassed, and was part of, the whole universe, of every living

thing, including myself; and also, the Creator of the Universe. It was so amazing that I was communicating with this all-pervading Energy force as an equal—and in doing so, I too was encompassing the universe, becoming a part of everything around me. I found myself liberated from the confines of my body; no longer bound by skin, I saw things so much clearer than before—colours, everything was so vivid, I felt so ecstatic—I soared way up into the blue sky, beyond.

The experience was repeated throughout the summer. Calvin says, "My bliss was so total, that the smallest fraction of time seemed an Eternity of happiness—Eternal life had become a reality." Temporal reality remained, however, for when Calvin returned to school, he experienced the hard earthly reality of peers who did not understand him. Adult reality was no better, for although he spoke in Methodist chapels, he apparently received anything but a warm, sympathetic hearing. He says that since his experience the constant message he has received from Christian people is, "Renounce your experience," the result being progressive alienation from Christianity.

I would first of all remark on Calvin's sense that God was a young man of age 20-30, a thought which at first glance may seem bizarre but at second glance seems very appropriate. Why? Because age 20-30 may be viewed as a prime time of life, and the term 'Life' may be written in capitals over Calvin's whole experience: God is experienced as the Energy of life and creation. Thus, the idea of a young man 20-30 fits well. Obviously, I do not know the interpretation Calvin placed on his experience of God as a young man of 20-30; indeed, I would say that even if he found this aspect of his experience puzzling, it is subject to the interpretation I have given it, and, if so, makes sense within the context of his total experience. Subjects of religious experience may very well fail to find reasonable interpretations for aspects of their experience. Already I have made this point in the case of Dick and would introduce the reminder that even the writers of Scripture often did not fully understand the significance of the messages they were announcing (1 Pet. 1:10-12). Second, I note that Calvin had a sense of merger with God and the universe, although in the merger he seemed to maintain a strong sense of self.

In Calvin's case we easily see that Theses C and O are falsified. Thesis C is falsified, for Calvin did not come from a setting in which the ideas of his experience were current, a fact underscored by the lack of understanding from his peers and by the demand of adults to renounce his experience. Thesis O is also falsified in that the type of experience he had was not held up as something to be pursued—underscored especially by the demand to renounce the experience. Calvin says nothing directly about his attitude toward religion at the time of his experience, but he does say that he was filled with doubt about the meaning of life and the nature of reality. These doubts would at least seem to indicate that he had serious reservations about the teachings of Christianity he had received. Therefore, I shall say that Thesis P is also falsified.

An interesting addendum to his experience is that about ten years after he had it, having read accounts of LSD experiences which made them look very much like his experience, he decided to see for himself about LSD experiences. He says that he took the "drug a large number of times," coming to the following conclusion.

> The LSD experience could in no way be regarded as equal to the true mystical experience; it lacks the perfect inner peace and the verbal communion with God which are essential to a true religious experience. Also, it is of necessity a very passive experience, since one is not in complete control of one's faculties, a thing which could not be said of the true religious experience as I know it.

I do not accept Calvin's remarks that verbal communion is essential to religious experience. Calvin had verbal communion (we pick that up from his remarks about the LSD experience, not from the description of his original religious experiences) but is not for that reason justified in generalizing. I also note his remark that in his religious experiences he was in complete control of his faculties, meaning, I take it, that his critical capacities were alive and active. I suppose that the main point is very simply: Calvin sees the two experiences as different, however he describes the difference.

I cite Calvin's remarks about LSD not because I think that they may be generalized but simply because they represent one person's comparison of his religious experiences with his LSD experiences. I do not know of a careful, complete, systematic study of the two kinds of experience. At any rate, what Calvin says is enough to falsify a thesis to the effect that LSD is a sufficient or necessary condition for religious experience, for it was neither in his case. Calvin does say: "I would not preclude the possibility that some people may have had a true mystical experience during the course of an acid trip." I would not preclude the possibility either. What I would preclude is the thesis that LSD, or any other chemical substance known to us now, is a necessary or sufficient condition for religious experience. Obviously, I have not cited any evidence against other substances. I simply assume common knowledge, LSD being illustrative of what could be said of other psychoactive substances.

Barbara (861)

I end the account of childhood and early youth experiences with an experience which is not a religious experience but which is instructive, especially for later purposes. (Chapter Eight) At age nine Barbara, kneeling to pray, hears a question, as if from the outside, "Is there anyone to pray to?" The answer comes, "No!" She concludes from her experience that there is no God and feels, as a result, a great sense of relief.

What we may conclude is that if the voice really came from the outside, then there is some sort of transcendent being, i.e., a being outside the plane of our normal experience, perhaps God. If the being is God, then perhaps God is being playful, speaking ironically. Clearly, if the voice is not that of God, it might be the voice of a deceptive being and thus would not be worthy of belief. One resolution of the whole situation would be to say that the voice is Barbara's, i.e., it is some sort of projection of her desires. The sense of relief seems to indicate that her view of God made her uncomfortable. Since she says nothing about her view of God, I can only speculate on this matter. Yet if my speculation were to be confirmed, we should, I think, have a reason to suspect the authenticity of the experience. Yet I am not certain that this explanation of the experience is really any stronger than the explanation in terms of an ironic statement from God. I shall not attempt to decide between the explanations.

As for God being playful, I see no reason not to take this suggestion seriously. C. S. Lewis does, coming up with the idea that heaven is essentially a place of play. Peter Kreeft in his book *Heaven* builds delightfully on the notions of Lewis. (1980, 93, 196-97) Of most weight, I think, are the words of Jesus that unless we turn and become like children, we shall not enter the kingdom of God. (Mtt. 18:3) Although I have never heard a clergyman develop this passage in terms of the theme of playfulness, I do not know what characterizes children more than playfulness, and thus am of the opinion that playfulness, a kind of divine playfulness, is an essential characteristic of the children of the kingdom. I also cite Abraham Maslow's notion that amusement is a godlike quality, although he notes that amusement is "strangely lacking in most gods." (Maslow, 1968, 93)

That people often meet the Divine as playful or amusing is clear from the investigations I have made. I shall cite two cases.

Sandy (1292)

Sandy was at a church committee meeting, which was dealing essentially with trivialities or, at least, matters which had little to do with the core mission of the church, matters such as repairs to the church roof. There was much bickering and dissension, and then, according to Sandy, the people on the committee felt the Spirit of God come upon them, the result being that they ended up roaring with laughter and taking actions with unanimity and good humor. It certainly escapes me why a God of love would not inspire the good feelings of laughter in people, and why this God would not help people to see and laugh at the utter absurdity of their actions. Also what is noteworthy in Sandy's account is that a number of people had the same religious experience at the same time, an especially strong indication of objectivity.

Patricia (2961)

Patricia, at eighteen, was confused, wanting understanding. She recounts what happened when she cried out to God. She cried, "'Oh God, if you exist, speak to me now,' and a man's well-spoken voice said quietly, 'Hullo, Patricia.' I laughed, and He laughed with me." My friend John, who has waded through some difficult theological thought, once wrote the following line of poetry: "If God has a sense of humor, we're OK." A philosophical defense of the humor and playfulness of God does not at this time seem especially difficult to me, although such a defense, at least from my hand, will have to wait a future time. At any rate, what we may say about Patricia's experience is that it certainly does not fit ordinary forms of teaching about God because the God of ordinary religion is anything but a God of laughter, as Maslow notes. Perhaps she was confused at this stage of her life because of problems with men; she does not say. If she was, we might expect a man's voice; but a man's voice taking the humorous turn that Patricia experienced—that is extraordinary.

I also note that in Patricia's case, as well as Sandy's, we have a falsification of Theses C and O. As I just noted, the God of ordinary religion is anything but a God of laughter. In Patricia's case we also seem to have a falsification of Thesis P because Patricia seems to cry to God not out of a positive attitude toward God and religion but out of a sense of desperation, not even firmly believing that God exists.

Summary

All the theses we began with, as well as any combination of them, have been falsified by the cases of the last two chapters. Thus, we can say generally that religious background does not explain religious experience in the sense of being a necessary condition.

As we have looked at the theses, we have also considered other suggestions, none of which seemed adequate. Loneliness might be viewed as a necessary condition for a religious experience. Cindy, for example, may have been lonely; likewise Ron, with his disintegrating marriage. Yet Alice and Angeligue, with their loving parents, were probably not lonely. Actually, none of the people considered, not even Cindy, mentions loneliness; thus, loneliness, if present, was not considered from the adult viewpoint (when the experiences were related) as a significant feeling within the context of the religious experience.

In addition to loneliness, we saw that crisis might be suggested as a necessary condition for religious experience, yet many of the people we considered were not in a crisis situation. A still further suggestion was that a strong sense of beauty is a necessary condition; however, this suggestion fared no better than the others. Religious ritual or practice of one form or another was also seen as not offering much hope.

A still further possibility we considered is that a necessary condition for religious experience is wanting, desiring, or expecting the experience, a thesis which is really just a strengthened form of Thesis O. A reasonable hypothesis is that religious teaching has effect because it creates a desire for or expectation of religious experience. Yet in numerous cases we found no connection between desires or expectations and religious experience. Ron's experience on the hill and Dick's statement that his experience of the "roaring silence" was unpredictable and uncontrollable are typical of the subjects we have considered. If the explanation from desire (as I shall call it) is going to be saved, it will have to move to the level of the unconscious, a move I shall consider in the next chapter.

Thus, what I wish to do now is look at the explanation from desire a bit more systematically, considering both the appeal to conscious and unconscious desire. I shall focus on people who were non-religious at the time of their experience.

Chapter Three

The Explanation From Desire and From Unconscious Motivation

"People have a religious experience because they want it."

This is perhaps the most common explanation for religious experience to be found both among scholarly and lay people. The explanation is, I should say, assumed by the explanation from religious background. A religious background is supposed to influence a person favorably for religious experience; i.e., somehow it creates a desire for the experience, or it creates a favorable attitude towards religion, an attitude which, in times of crisis or other life situations, develops into a desire for religious experience. Apart from desire religious background would be without effect. Thus, the explanation from religious background will not go without the explanation from desire—or so it seems to me. However, even if I am incorrect on this point, neither my evaluation of the explanation from religious background nor my evaluation of the explanation from desire depends on any connection between the two.

1. Analysis of the Explanation

I am not certain how the explanation from desire is intended, whether as a full causal explanation, as an explanation stating strictly a necessary condition, or as an explanation stating strictly a sufficient condition. It is likely intended in different ways by different people. The fact seems to be that sometimes the object of our desire appears for no other reason than that we desire it; i.e., desire by itself sometimes seems sufficient to create an experience of what we take to be the object of desire, a phenomenon that occurs even in the sphere of sensory perception, as the following account shows.

Writing in the February, 1990, "Newsletter" of the Alister Hardy Research Centre for Religious Experience, Michael Jackson, one of the researchers at the Centre, reports on his trip to Medjugorje, Yugoslavia, a village which became in the 1980's a magnet for pilgrims and tourists because of visions of the Virgin Mary received by six children beginning in 1981. Many of the visitors to Medjugorje have given accounts of seeing a variety of spectacular (miraculous!) phenomena. Mr. Jackson's account is as follows.

> The most widely reported phenomena seemed to be solar—each evening I watched the most spectacular sunsets over the mountains, to learn afterwards that other people had seen the sun spinning or pulsating while I had simply seen it set, albeit gloriously. Similarly the stars were seen to flash on and off, or to move in formation; the clouds made shapes or words; and the cross on top of the hill had been observed to spin, or to become a shining white figure. Finally (at least amongst the people that I met), rosaries were observed to turn into gold, especially when taken up the hill of the cross. Unfortunately, my experience of this paralleled the sunsets—I encountered one group on top of the hill, gathered round and exclaiming over their transfigured rosary, but alas, it looked disappointingly normal to me.

Assuming the accuracy of Mr. Jackson's perception, we may say that many people at Medjugorje have seen what they wanted to see. If this sort of thing happens in the case of sense perception, then certainly it can happen in the case of religious experience.

However, what is clear is that not everybody who desired to see unusual phenomena at Medjugorje did so. Mr. Jackson does not report on this fact, but I imagine that a survey of visitors going to Medjugorje in order to see the miraculous would reveal that a sizable portion of them saw nothing. Surveys aside, I have several friends who made the journey, desirous of seeing all the spectacular phenomena that others have reported, but seeing nothing; or sometimes they saw what others said they saw (for example, a pulsating sun), whereas other times they did not, without any noticeable difference in their desire—any slackening of it or any dilution of their sincerity. Thus, desire by itself, be it intense desire, does not seem to be a sufficient condition for perceiving what we desire.

Since this is common knowledge and also applies, I presume, in the sphere of religious experience, I doubt that the explanation from desire is usually meant to state a sufficient condition. Some additional conditions are normally assumed or explicitly spelled out. E.g., in the case of Medjugorgje we might say that people will see the unusual celestial phenomena as long as their intense desire is accompanied by a pure and devout heart. Of course, we have to say that this explanation is false, given any common measures of a pure and devout heart. The main point, though, is that the explanation sees intense desire as bringing about the perception of its object only in conjunction with some other condition(s), and thus intense desire is only a necessary condition at best.

I shall not try to decide what people usually have in mind by the explanation from desire because neither I nor anybody else has adequate evidence for making the decision. What I shall do is simply consider the explanation from desire to state either a necessary or sufficient condition—i.e., I shall simply cover the possibilities that desire is a necessary condition, a sufficient condition, or both.

I shall state the explanation from desire in the following way: Consciously having a fairly intense desire to experience a religious Object is a necessary or sufficient condition for our experiencing that Object. 'Experiencing that Object', a phrase in which the Object may be named (such as Jesus, Krishna), is a locution for 'having an experience in which we take ourselves to encounter that Object'. Also, I introduce the vague phrase 'fairly intensely' because I think that a low level desire, say, a desire expressed as "Yes, I wouldn't mind that," or "Yes, I'd kind of like that," would be unlikely to bring about an experience in which we experienced the object of our desire.

I wish to emphasize that the explanation from desire, as I have stated it, takes the view that desire shapes experience, so that the Object we experience (take ourselves to experience) is like the Object we desire. Desiring a religious Object fairly intensely is the condition (necessary or sufficient) for experiencing *the* Object, that is, the Object desired. For example, the desire to experience Christ is the condition for experiencing Christ, not Allah. Logically, any desire—for example, a desire for a trip to Guam or a desire not to have a religious experience—could be related as a necessary or sufficient condition to religious experience. However, the explanation from desire accepts the view that the Object experienced is like the Object desired. Indeed, to experience an Object unlike that which we desire is just to say that we did not experience the Object we desired, and it is, of course, also to say that desiring the Object was not a sufficient condition for experiencing the Object.

Perhaps, though, what is really functioning as the necessary or sufficient condition for religious experience is a desire simply for Something beyond us, a MORE (to use the terminology of William James), and thus a desire which can be fulfilled by a wide variety of divine beings. To begin with, I note that the variety of divine beings cannot be unlimited because the MORE would at least have to be within the conceptual repertoire of a person. E.g., if a person were unfamiliar with Eastern ideas of God, we should not expect those ideas to show up in that person's religious experience. Only ideas entertained by the person, ideas in that person's experience, could be expected to show up. One cannot desire what one has no ideas for. Further, if a person desires, say, an experience with Christ, that person is not desiring an experience with just any sort of MORE but with a specific MORE, namely, Christ. The fact that we can put the desire for Christ into the conceptual category of a desire for a MORE does not at all mean that the person is desiring a MORE of whatever sort. In fact, many people consider notions alternative to their common religious notions deficient or even heretical. They shun, not desire, an experience of a Being different from what they believe in or are accustomed to, and thus they are definitely not desiring a MORE that can take a variety of forms. E.g., most people who desire an experience with Christ do not desire an experience with Allah, for they consider Allah deficient in some way and may even see belief in Allah as heretical. As a consequence, we must deny that basic to the desire for a religious experience is the desire to experience a MORE, a desire which could be fulfilled by a variety of religious objects. Granting that the religious Object people desire can be included in the concept of a MORE, we may not go on to say that they desire a MORE of whatever sort, any more than the fact that Crescent Bay may be included in the general concept of bays means that my desire to swim in Crescent Bay is a desire to swim in any bay whatever.

Since the explanation from conscious desire is an explanation we have already found deficient, I shall mainly focus in this chapter on the natural extension of the explanation from conscious desire, viz., the extension to unconscious desire. Without examining the central issues relating to unconscious desire—such as the possibility, nature, and status of unconscious desire—I shall simply assume that an unconscious desire is similar to a conscious desire in certain essential respects: Although we are not aware of the desire, it is a desire for something (it, like a conscious desire, has an object), and it affects our behavior so that we move in the direction of the object of desire. E.g., a man may have an unconscious desire to marry a woman like his mother, with the result that he ends up doing so, although he never consciously had the desire to do so and may even deny that his wife is like his mother. An unconscious desire may also affect us or manifest itself in us in many other ways, such as through dreams, free association, projective tests, slips of the tongue, obsessive and compulsive behavior, and so on. In other words, unconscious desires do not dwell within us without leaving traces of their presence on conscious and semi-conscious levels—without leaving footprints, graffiti on the wall, empty bottles, and scraps of paper. To be sure, crucial evidence may not be available, particularly in situations from the past, inasmuch as, e.g., dreams were not reported or free association not employed. Most of the material I have lacks the sort of evidence which would be strongly relevant to determining the presence of unconscious desire (evidence from dreams, free association, and so on), with the result that the discussion of unconscious desire will be more speculative than I should like it to be.

As in the case of conscious desire, I shall say that an unconscious desire, to function as a necessary or sufficient condition for a religious experience, must be a fairly strong desire. The full explanation from desire will now be as follows: Consciously or unconsciously having a fairly intense desire to experience a religious Object is either a necessary or sufficient condition for experiencing the Object.

2. The Desire for Religious Experience in Western Society

At this point I wish to make some comments about the role that the desire for a religious experience has in Western society. The desire for a religious experience, the desire to encounter God, is not, I submit, very common in Western society. Alfred North Whitehead characterizes 20th century religion as "tending to degenerate into a decent formula wherewith to embellish a comfortable life." (Whitehead, 1961, 178) William James says something similar when he observes that for a few, religion is an acute fever, but for most, it is a dull habit. The religion of the dull habit, the religion of comfort, is hardly the religion of pursuing encounter with God. The religion of adventuring in the spirit (Whitehead), the religion of acute fever, is a religion of the few, of the minority, of the remnant. Therefore, we should not expect to find the desire for God widespread in society. Although Whitehead and James are referring to the conscious approach to religion, I see no reason for not extending their words to the unconscious. No one has ever shown that whereas people consciously pursue a comfortable, dull-habit religion, unconsciously they are desiring a serious, life-altering encounter with divine Reality. The evidence we have is, I think, strongly in the opposite direction. In fact, many people who are very religious, at least in the sense of being very active in institutional expressions of religion, practically run from the religion of divine encounter, although they would be the last to admit that they are running. I shall cite some evidence on this point in the next chapter.

To be sure, we could probably show that people of dull-habit religion are less than satisfied with their religion, but this dissatisfaction usually remains a kind of vague dissatisfaction which people do not pinpoint in the sense of understanding that it may arise from a superficial approach to religion. Moreover, the vague dissatisfaction over superficial religion is often incorporated into a larger and broader dissatisfaction or disease, arising essentially not from superficial religion but from inadequate fulfillment in career or marriage, or just general poor functioning in life. At any rate, we should not suppose that the desire to meet God experientially—whether we think of this desire as conscious or unconscious—is widespread in society. My approach will be to assume that the desire is not present unless there is evidence to show otherwise.

Further, if we narrow our attention to the small class of people who take religion seriously, I should say that most of them are thinking more in terms of belief in God than encounter with God. What they are desiring and struggling to do is move from unbelief to belief, from little faith to greater faith, from shallow ethical concern to deep ethical commitment, or perhaps from doubt and confusion to assurance; but all these desires or aims are a considerable distance from desiring an experience of God's reality, of God's presence. People generally do not, I should say, make any natural or necessary connection between having strong religious belief and encountering God; more precisely, they do not see that strong belief requires an encounter with God. And rightly so, for strong belief is related to a wide variety of things: an early family life in which religion was taken seriously and yet enjoyed, a strong argument for God, a radical change in oneself or another, a sense of peace, a sense of meaning and purpose—the list could go on indefinitely. The fact is that many people have strong belief in God without ever having had an experience of God's presence. Thus, I think that I am on firm ground in saying the following: The desire for faith is not equivalent to, does not reduce to, is not even usually, a desire to encounter or experience God.

A forceful illustration of this point is evangelical Christianity, an approach to Christian faith in which people are urged to accept Christ or surrender to Christ or commit themselves to Christ. Yet in evangelical Christianity the urging to accept Christ does not translate directly into "seek and expect to have an experience of Christ's presence," even though the experience of accepting Christ is sometimes represented as encountering or meeting God. Indeed, there is a very clear awareness that no experience of any sort may occur, so that one often hears words to the following effect: "Accepting Christ or surrendering to Christ is an act of will, having certain objective results (such as forgiveness, peace with God, and union with Christ), regardless of subjective feelings (such as feeling forgiven, feeling peace, feeling at one with Christ)." Moreover, even if most people within the arena of evangelical faith desire and expect to feel forgiveness, peace, and joy, none of these feelings, or all of them together, automatically translate into a desire for an experience of God's presence. I should say that what people usually desire or expect is action from God in the way of results, effects—like forgiveness, peace, joy, a sense of meaning—not the experience of God's presence. Encountering God means for them either experiencing the effects of God's action or of being confident that objectively their status before God is radically altered—they now stand forgiven, at peace with God, in union with Christ, and so on. Thus, even within evangelical Christianity, desiring to accept Christ does not necessarily or usually translate into the desire to experience God's presence; or so I should say on the basis of the evidence I have, evidence which is fairly extensive but not systematic, at least in the sense of being statistically developed. If what I have said about evangelical Christianity is true, then it is certainly also true for those forms of Christianity which are more formal and ritualistic, in which there is not the emphasis on a kind of decisive moment of accepting Christ.

I do not wish to pass over that small coterie of folk within and without the church who are questing for a sense of Presence, who are seeking, along the lines of Brother Lawrence, a life of practicing the presence of God. I also do not want to overlook those traditions, from Quakers to Pentecostals, in which the standard approach is to seek God's presence. The point, however, is that the coterie of people is relatively small—a remnant.

Although I have been speaking above of conscious desire, I again see no reason for altering my conclusions when moving to the unconscious level. I.e., if people explicitly state, e.g., that they would like to rise above their doubts to strong faith in God, I do not see any reason for getting this desire down on the unconscious level in any other form—in any other form than a desire for strong faith in God, which, as I have said, is not equivalent to the desire for a religious experience. If we are going to change the desire in moving to the unconscious level, we shall need specific evidence for doing so. The upshot is that even in the class of the seriously religious, we should not presume an unconscious desire for an experience of God's presence. We shall need specific evidence in order to make this claim.

But let us suppose that behind much religious struggle is a desire for assurance—perhaps, even, a desire to return to the simplicity and assurance of childhood belief. Admittedly, an encounter with God is a great assurance builder, although not always. Already we have noted Pam (p. 68), who wrote off her childhood experience of God as irrelevant to her adult life. We might also note in her case that there is no evidence and no reason to suppose that as a child she had some sort of crisis of faith, needing assurance. She was already in the stage of acceptance, belief, assurance—i.e., in the stage of childhood. Moreover, since her experience introduced her to a pantheistic God, a God unlike the received God of society, she was likely to receive some negative feedback, hardly the best way to enhance assurance. At any rate, the experience certainly did not bring her the kind of assurance that made faith a secure matter for her as an adult. In fact, she just sort of opted out of the life of faith. Below, we shall come across Elizabeth, whose experience left her aware of the riddle of the universe—hardly a state equivalent to assurance.

The main point I wish to make, though, is not that encounter does not always produce assurance but that encounter is only one way in a wide range of ways, including the acceptance of bad arguments, to produce assurance. Moreover, assuming that encounter is the best way to produce assurance, we have no evidence that this fact is recognized on the unconscious level. In any case, if we attribute to a person an unconscious desire to find the assurance of childhood, we should not translate that desire into a desire for religious experience, unless we have evidence for the translation.

Many of the remarks made above about unconscious desire also apply to unconscious guilt over abandoning faith, an explanation which will, of course, not be applicable to any number of the people we have considered and will consider, viz., those who either never had any faith to begin with or always had faith (i.e., as long as they can remember, they believed)—in short, those who never abandoned anything.

At this point I wish to collect into one principle all the above remarks on conscious and unconscious desire. My main point has been that the specific desire for encounter with God is infrequent, even among the serious seekers of faith. Given that this is so on the conscious level, I have argued that we should presume the same on the unconscious level. More specifically, I have said that we should not suppose unconscious desire for God to be different from conscious desire, unless we have specific evidence to the contrary. To think otherwise is to run afoul of at least two widely accepted rules of reason. The first is parsimony. Making an appeal to the unconscious without evidence for doing so is, in effect, to make an *ad hoc* appeal to the unconscious, an appeal which, of course, will be less parsimonious than not making the appeal. The second rule is a rule of equity in reasoning and may be stated in the nursery rhyme form: What's sauce for the goose is sauce for the gander. I think that I can make clear the point of this rule by way of a couple of examples. If someone is going to introduce an unconscious desire for God in those who encounter God but give no evidence of any desire for God, then I shall introduce an unconscious desire for God in those who do not encounter God (e.g., Bertrand Russell), thereby voiding desire for God as a sufficient condition for religious experience. Or I could introduce unconscious desire to avoid God in the case of people not giving evidence of any such desire, i.e., people having religious experience, and thus I would void unconscious desire for God as a necessary condition for religious experience. Of course, I would void only in the sense that my appeal (the possibility I suggest) would be as reasonable as an opposite appeal. A more reasonable course is, I think, the one I am taking, viz., introducing unconscious desire for God (or unconscious desire to avoid God) only in cases where there is evidence for it, presuming in the other cases that it tracks conscious desire. On grounds then of parsimony and the equity rule (there may be other grounds I have failed to mention), as well as the ground that the conscious desire for religious experience is infrequent, I introduce the following principle: There is a general presumption against conscious desire for an experience of God, and a general presumption against unconscious desire for God being different from conscious desire. I shall refer to this principle as *Socrates*, the italics serving to distinguish the principle from the person.

Given my statement of the explanation from desire, I shall briefly note here that neither form of the explanation—as necessary or as sufficient condition—is necessarily inconsistent with really perceiving God, i.e., inconsistent with the Object of desire really being present to a person, for desire might be the necessary or sufficient condition for genuinely encountering God. Some Scripture seems to say as much; e.g., "You will seek me and find me; when you seek me with all your heart." (Jer. 29:13) Assuming that seeking with all the heart involves desiring intensely, I should say that the verse views intense desire for God as a sufficient condition for finding God. The evidence I shall consider will test the religious form of the explanation from desire, as well as the naturalistic form. (In the end, I think that the religious explanation is a kind of naturalistic explanation. Seeking God is clearly a naturalistic form of behavior along the same lines as seeking to be honest or seeking to be a trumpet player of the quality of Al Hirt.)

3. Desire Not a Sufficient Condition

Now the question is: What does our case material show? Clearly, that desire is not a sufficient condition for religious experience, a fact poignantly pointed up by those people who seek God so hard and find so little that they are left disappointed, bewildered, depressed, traumatized— some to the extent that they just give up. Two accounts will suffice as illustrations.

Nina (2662)

Nina was going through a divorce, experiencing bouts of depression, when she had the following experience.

> One evening, sitting quietly alone, deep in thought as usual, I realized it was time to make ready for bed. I stood up to do so, and suddenly felt as though a great weight, burden, had been lifted from me—a great weight of worry and anxiety. I felt FREE. An indescribable JOY filled my whole being. I moved to the window and stood looking out at the darkness and became AWARE—not with my mind; I did not *think* it, I KNEW. I WAS. I felt part of the world, the universe. I BECAME (it is so difficult to describe). I knew there was a PLAN— and felt it to be MY PLAN, I was co-author, in league with it, had a

'hand' in it, in Sympathy with it (please excuse my trying to find the right way to describe it). I *knew* that EVERYTHING WAS MEANT TO BE—even the worst that could happen—it was all PART OF THE PLAN and NO MATTER WHAT HAPPENS—ALL IS WELL. The words, no, not the words—the AWARENESS that ALL IS WELL was outstanding.

She went to bed elated, "glorying in the knowledge that I had been granted the most wonderful peace of mind—and had doubtless been enabled to forgive myself. I fully expected to feel the same the next day—but I was wrong." In fact, she never felt the same again, soon afterward having a lengthy bout with mental depression, and undergoing treatment for it. At the time that she wrote her account, she said, "I feel that, whatever Divine Power had considered I was worth 'doing something' about, had now abandoned me as a hopeless case and not worth bothering about."

Here, then, is a woman who expected to "feel the same the next day." Whether she is referring just to the feelings of peace and forgiveness or to the feeling of being "part of the world, the universe" I cannot say for certain, although I am inclined to say, "Both." Since the feelings of peace and forgiveness came with the total experience and since she said that later she felt abandoned, she was most likely looking for a continuation or repeat of the total experience in which she felt part of the whole, a whole which included a plan. Further, we may presume that the natural reaction to loss of the feelings of peace and forgiveness, loss of a sense of a plan for her in this universe, loss of a sense of her being part of the universe, would be a desire for the renewal of the experience. Yet nothing!

At the time she had the experience she seemed to be on a religious quest, saying that "I became interested and absorbed in 'things spiritual'—I realised what 'seek and ye will find' meant." Thus, she may even have been seeking a religious experience, although certainly not the type she had, for her experience seems to come as something of a surprise and is beyond her capacity to describe. Having had the experience, she desired to have it again—apparently very much. Yet she did not have the experience. She illustrates, then, that the desire for a religious experience is *neither* a necessary nor a sufficient condition for the experience, although my main point for now is that her desire for a religious experience was not sufficient to bring about the experience.

Nina's case is one which naturally triggers some remarks about the unconscious. Suppose that we move desire to the unconscious level, saying something along the following lines: Unconsciously Nina really did not want God, really did not desire a repeat of the experience, indeed, feared a repeat. This explanation looks very implausible. Given the healthy, uplifting effects of the experience on her, as well as her strong, conscious desire of a repeat, an explanation in terms of the unconscious will have to offer more than the mere assertion that somehow, someway, she really did not want a repeat. Obviously, we should need evidence from other aspects of her life (dreams, e.g.) that she was unconsciously resistant to the experience. That sort of evidence is not available; however, the evidence we do have is sufficient to throw suspicion on the explanation from unconscious resistance. A fundamental question is why she had the initial experience. Did she initially want it unconsciously (as we have seen, there is no evidence of conscious desiring) and then immediately upon having the very positive experience reverse course? The explanation is, as I said, implausible, a kind of grasping for straws.

Or perhaps we could suppose a Freudian unconscious, with the experience indicating a resolution of guilt and childhood conflicts with parents. The question, then, is: What brought the resolution about and why did it not last or get repeated? If we suppose a non-Freudian unconscious with positive capabilities, an unconscious seeking to rebuild and reconstruct a damaged self, the question is: Why did the unconscious leave off rebuilding?

I would note that many other people have a one-time experience, like Nina, but the experience seems to do the trick for them, functioning as a kind of rock for their existence. They, too, desire a repeat, but it never comes; all the same, the one-time experience functions as a solid foundation for constructing a new and better life. Often the work of construction is carried on with others, in or out of religious institutions. Nina does not seem to have sought assistance from helping people or groups until she was forced to by a state of depression. In any case, her one-time experience was not a rock for the reconstruction of her life. The reason, I think, lies close at hand. Nina was going through a difficult divorce, feeling cut-off and abandoned, having deep doubts about her self-worth. These feelings and doubts were strong enough to divert her from the very positive nature of the experience.

Having criticized explanations from the unconscious, I do not mean to imply that an explanation in terms of the Divine is home free. If Nina's experience is supposed to be a genuine contact with the Divine, then the question is why a loving Divine (presumably the sort of Divine she encountered) did not repeat Its work. As an initial response, I note that religious explanations often include a strong appeal to self-reliance and autonomy. They stress that God does not just pass the magic wand over us, resolving our problems once for all, world without end. What many religious people find is that their faith provides them with some resource or other sufficient to cope with what they need to cope with. The resource may be a sense of Divine presence, an assurance of Divine purpose, a loving friend or supportive community—the list can go on. Nina certainly had received the assurance of Divine purpose in her life. She was part of a plan; indeed, she was co-author of the plan. In short, she seems to have received a very clear message that she was to be active in getting her life in order. Yet, incredibly, she says: "I wonder too, whether there was a meaning in the Experience—a message, perhaps, for me, and I am too 'dim' to see it—understand it." Having missed the message, which she herself clearly articulates, she fails to move into action, waiting instead for a renewal of the feelings. I do not wish to be insensitive on this matter, ignoring, as it were, how heavily the blow of her divorce may have fallen on her self-worth. I simply wish to note how heavily a religious explanation may rely on individual autonomy and self-growth. Moreover, I shall not claim that the religious explanation is adequate. All I shall claim for now is that it certainly is not less adequate than appeals to the unconscious.

Beverly (1276)

Another case is that of Beverly, who had been ill to the point of death. She had been reading some Christian literature which recommended that whatever our condition in life, we should give ourselves to the will of God. This she attempted to do, but

> to my horror I realized that I was not accepted. An unutterable loneliness and desolation came upon my very innermost spirit. I was rejected, with a great vacuum, a chasm of emptiness and loneliness and terror, gaping before me. As I write this I recognize that the memory can bring a wave of near panic into my mind. Nothing can describe it.

Beverly was clearly looking for greater closeness to God, believing that yielding herself to God would help her realize this goal. Previously, she had had three experiences of union with God, experiences which seemed very positive to her. Yet on this occasion—nothing! or rather, a feeling of rejection and loneliness.

Her experience is not uncommon within the community of those who have experienced union with God, the experience often being referred to as the "dark night of the soul." Beverly had not heard of the dark night of the soul and was simply terrified by the experience until her son told her that he had learned about such experiences in school. This proved to be a great relief to her, although she ended her account by saying,

> I hope never to have even a glimpse of that terrible thing again. Coward for physical pain that I am, I remember knowing in my mind soon after, that if I had the choice between physical torture or this spiritual agony of terror and rejection—I would not choose the latter.

Various religious explanations may be given for experiences which are of the dark-night-of-the-soul sort. Since the experiences are reported mainly by those who have been vouchsafed experiences of union with the Divine, one explanation would be that the dark night experiences serve to underscore heavily the incomparable value of union with God and the utter horror of separation from God. In short, the experiences provide for a deeper appreciation of union with God. In addition, since separation from God is, on almost all accounts, the essence of what it means to be in hell, the experiences serve to underscore the true state of most of the world, so that the experiences would certainly function as an incentive to those having them to move out among their fellow humans, calling them with renewed compassion to flee the misery of a hellish existence. Again, I shall not presume that this (or any other) religious explanation is adequate, but I do think that it beats explanations from the unconscious, as I shall now attempt to show.

One explanation from the unconscious could be along the following lines. Unconsciously Beverly really did not fully submit to God, unconsciously did not desire God with all her soul. Yet the reply to that is, "What of it?" We must remember Juan, who prayed a prayer of acceptance or submission, thinking, "What do I have to lose?" We must also remember Patricia, who cried out to God in desperation and unbelief, experiencing, as a result, God's humorous response, "Hullo, Patricia!" The approach of Juan and Patricia is typified by the event in the Gospels of the father whose son was demon possessed and whose desperate cry was, "I believe; help my unbelief!" Full or total surrender or desire, desire without reservation, just does not seem to be a condition for religious experience. In fact, Beverly notes that her previous three experiences of union with God came without any desire at all for the experiences. "I had not sought them, and at the time did not even know that it was a recognized occurrence." At any rate, in the present case Beverly does not indicate that her desire was in any way conditioned or with reservations. Moreover, given *Socrates*, we should presume the same for unconscious desire. Other explanations from the unconscious could be developed, but I do not think that they would fare any better than the one I have just gone through.

We see, then, in the case of Beverly, as in the case of Nina, that desire is not a sufficient condition for religious experience and also not a necessary condition.

4. *Desire Not a Necessary Condition*

In the rest of this chapter I shall concentrate on the question of whether or not desire for an experience with God functions as a necessary condition for an experience of God. I shall be looking at people who at the time of their experience were non-religious and therefore presumably not desiring a religious experience of any sort. In chapter four I shall consider three cases which do not lend themselves to the explanation from desire, three cases on which I have the best evidence of any cases I studied, and hence cases which permit a much fuller analysis. And then in chapter five I shall consider people who had experiences outside the mold of their presumed desires or concepts.

Viola (4581)

Viola, a clinical psychologist, writes as follows.

> My husband and I were discussing separation . . . perhaps even had already agreed to separate (which we did about two months later), so it was not an uneventful period of my life . . . but on the day of this experience I was under no particular stress and cannot recall having any emotion at all, or at least nothing approaching an 'emotional state.'

It was about mid-morning. I came from the kitchen into the bedroom, sat at my dressing table, opened a drawer and began to do something quite ordinary, I can't remember what, when I was suddenly overwhelmed by the presence of God. I was absolutely astounded. I hadn't known there was a God at all. Having rejected the Roman Catholicism of my childhood while still in my teens, I was pretty much an atheist or agnostic and had no interest in religion. . . . I was just shattered, shaken to the roots of my being. . . . I stumbled over to the bed, got in, and pulled the bedclothes up over me like a terrified child; it wasn't an attempt to escape—which would have been ridiculous as God was manifestly within me—it was more a gesture to hold together, absorb the shock, and not actually shatter. This was not a vision; no lights, no voices, but a much more immediate and definite kind of perception as it involves recognition and not just apprehension of something or someone. In other words, this was not the apprehension of some being of incredible power and beauty and majesty who-must-be-God, this was "our" God, awesome indeed in the majesty of his power, which I found personally to be absolutely breath-taking and could never have imagined, but "ours" nevertheless in the sense of being non-alien, almost familiar in some way, the one whom on some level or another we have always known and instantly recognize even if we are seeing Him for the first time. God was entirely within me, not just some "divine spark" or bit or whatever, but all of God; also, God was entirely without me, complete—I could lift my eyes to where He was—and this was one and the same God. This did not seem at all odd at the time, just natural, the way it was. Also, in case it needs saying, this was not an experience of some divine "force" or emanation or other impersonal manifestation.

To begin with, Viola's statement is something of a model of direct awareness of God. The givenness of the experience is unmistakable— God breaks into her existence, uninvited, as clearly as a tornadic wind would roar into her home. She is totally shattered. Moreover, there is a sense of exteriority— God is distinct from her, both entirely within her and entirely without her. Further, she experiences nothing of a sensory nature, and the feelings she mentions—she was overwhelmed, astounded, terrified, shattered, breathless, and awed—obviously apply to her, not God. We could say that each of these feelings has a counterpart in God, so that God is overwhelming, astonishing, awesome, and so on; but in saying this, we obviously do not reduce God to any feelings or set of feelings. Indeed, God was overwhelming, astonishing, and so on for Viola because God was present to her in the "majesty of his power." Further, she does not infer that the Reality intruding in her life is God because of the majesty, beauty, and power of the Reality; instead, she is simply aware of the majestic, powerful God being present in her existence and to her awareness.

The Explanation From Desire and From Unconscious Motivation 105

Viola observes that at the time of the experience she was without any conscious religious interest, the result being that the experience caught her totally unawares, startling her as much as would a stranger walking uninvited into her bedroom. Indeed, the experience was in an important sense just like a stranger walking in uninvited—the Stranger comes in regardless of her conscious desires or wants. Further, Viola could wish away an uninvited stranger, but that would be of little use, of as little use as her having attempted to wish away the sense of God's reality, the God that was entirely within her and entirely without her. An additional point is that her sense of being "shattered, shaken to the roots," indicates that she was not exactly overjoyed at having the experience—yet the experience did not go away.

In attempting some sort of non-religious explanation we might begin by supposing that the crisis of divorce made Viola more open to other possibilities in life; all the same, we should have to grant that she definitely was not consciously pursuing the possibility of religious encounter and transformation. Moreover, as she says, she was not at the time of the experience in any "emotional state," i.e., in a kind of desperate state in which she would reach for anything. In other words, there was nothing of the desperation of Juan, who was "willing to try anything."

Yet perhaps Viola had an unconscious desire for God. *Socrates* makes this unlikely. Or perhaps she felt unconscious guilt for having abandoned belief in God. I shall now introduce another principle, *Plato*, a principle expanding on a central idea of *Socrates*. *Plato* reads as follows: We may not presume unconscious guilt of a specific form without evidence for it. *Plato* makes the turn to unconscious guilt in Viola's case unwarranted. Certainly, I do not mean to deny that people often cover up their guilts, yet to say that they cover up is just to say that we have evidence for the cover-up. To presume, without evidence, a specific kind of cover-up seems to me thoroughly unwarranted. In the case of Viola we do not have any evidence of guilt over abandoning her religion. Again, I note the incompleteness of the reports I have, so that perhaps there is evidence Viola simply does not present to us. However, I also note that Viola is a clinical psychologist, and she had reflected on her experience. At the time she wrote her report, almost forty years after the experience, she said the following.

> I am as convinced now [of the reality of my experience] . . . as I was during those astonished days immediately following the experience. Indeed, I am still astonished sometimes. Why should there be a God? I can think of no convincing reasons. And a personal God at that! It all seems so unlikely! Then I am astonished all over again.

Clearly, Viola had tried to figure out her experience, without success. Moreover, she would be likely, I think, to be aware of evidence—particularly, strong evidence—of unconscious desire or guilt, would be aware, e.g., of dreams which revealed desire for God or the presence of guilt. I shall not claim that all clinical psychologists and psychiatrists know themselves and are honest about themselves, yet presumably they are far more capable of recognizing signs of the unconscious, whether in themselves or others, than the average lay person, and if they are reasonably healthy, I presume that they would not have a strong aversion to mentioning these signs, particularly if the accuracy of their statements required doing so. Viola comes through to me as a reasonably healthy person, yet she mentions nothing about signs of unconscious desire or guilt. I also note that neither Angelique nor Marie (one a psychiatrist, the other a professional psychologist, both of whom seem healthy—see, pp. 77 and 79), makes reference to dreams or other material which would indicate unconscious desire or guilt. Moreover, Angelique does mention several cases in which she sees unconscious factors as influencing her religious beliefs, but her experiences of God she sees as thoroughly genuine, saying, "I could more easily doubt my own existence than that of what I know as God."

Inez (4337)

Inez was relaxed, in a peaceful state of mind, listening to music, when she suddenly felt extremely elated and peaceful. She had the sensation of floating and then of rotating, followed by the sense of another presence.

> Throughout the experience I was totally unaware of my surroundings. I was only seeing what I was experiencing. I could hear something telling me that this was what death was like. I feel that it was this other presence talking to me; and I believe that this presence was another part of myself, but it also had part of everything else in it as well. During the whole experience something was saying don't be afraid of death, don't be afraid of life, everything would be alright. I also had a strong feeling that I was communicating with everything at the same time. I realized I was just a very small part of an enormous whole. I did not feel inferior; I felt equal. I was a part of this whole thing, a part of the Universe, and a part of something that is perhaps a form of God.

I've left the most important thing until last. The amount of love I felt radiating from this presence would be enough to warm the entire world.

I shall turn, first of all, to a matter on which I issued a promissory note in Chapter One. Inez, as so many others, is afflicted with what I see as the sloppy use of language. She uses the term 'feel' and its cognates indiscriminately, revealing thereby the way our language has been corrupted by psychology. What has happened, I believe, is that language from the clinical setting (more specifically, Rogerian reflective language, such as, "So you feel angry about the way your parents treated you?") got transferred to the popular level, with various distortions occurring, distortions accompanying any such transfer. Attributing the corrupting influence to psychology may be just a sheer prejudice of mine—an innocuous one, though, for I should think that psychologists would be flattered that I attribute such weighty influence to them. I cannot think of any similar influence of philosophers. At any rate, our language is in a state of corruption in many respects, but a major one is the way we use the term 'feel'—"I feel that Bill Clinton is doing a good job as President." The reply to talk of this sort is: "No, sorry, you don't feel that; you believe it or think it. Now let's keep that straight!" (Some of my philosophical colleagues disagree with all that I have said in this paragraph.)

Inez has fallen badly into the misuse of the term 'feel'. She says, "I feel that it was this other presence . . ."; "I also had a strong feeling that I was communicating. . . ." Then she uses the term properly: "I did not feel inferior; I felt equal." As for saying that she felt love, I do not think that her language in this case is appropriate, although we could debate the issue. If she were speaking about her love for someone, she could very well say, "I feel love." Yet she is talking about the love from Another. As I mentioned in Chapter Two, love from another may affect our feelings, but the love the other has (or that the Other is) is not our feeling but something we perceive in or about the other, however the perception takes place. In any case, we know that something is wrong in the use of the term 'feel' when it is followed by 'that'. I say all this so that we may be alert to the language of the people relating their religious experience. We must be aware of when they are talking about feelings and when they are not.

With these comments about the term 'feel' registered, I return to Inez. She attended a Presbyterian church as a child but states that prior to the experience she was an atheist, and "I remain that way now." The exact nature of her atheism is unclear, but apparently it amounts essentially to rejecting what she sees as the God of the Bible, for she says, "I still cannot accept God in the Biblical sense." When she wrote her account, she was a member of the Society of Friends. At any rate, the main point about Inez is that she was not consciously desiring the sort of experience she had. The focus of her attention at the time was not on religion, and apparently her focus had not been on religion—at least she fails to mention any serious questing for God on her part, an omission which would be odd if, indeed, she had been on some sort of spiritual quest. She well may have toyed with various notions of God, but that is very different from desiring an experience with the sort of reality she encountered. Thus, Inez seems to be without any conscious desire for an experience of the sort she had, and we find no evidence that she had an unconscious desire for the experience. The evidence is inadequate, to be sure, but given *Socrates* and her general disinterest in religion, we should not presume any unconscious desire for religious experience on her part. Moreover, we definitely may not say that the experience by itself is evidence of an unconscious desire, for that would be a resort to a question-begging argument along the following lines:

> She must have had an unconscious desire for religious experience.
> Why?
> Because she had a religious experience.
> But why is that evidence of an unconscious desire?
> Because anyone having a religious experience must have had an unconscious desire for the experience.

The appeal to evidence must be an appeal to evidence other than the experience itself, evidence which may be found in those locales in which the unconscious allegedly breaks through— dreams, free associations, obsessions, and so on.

I note two matters in conclusion. First, Inez's experience has a definite Eastern cast. She says: "I believe that this presence was another part of myself, but it also had part of everything else in it as well." Since she uses the term 'believe' in the first sentence, she seems to be interpreting rather than describing, although the second sentence indicates that she seems to be describing, i.e., describing her experience. In any case, she ends up saying: "I was a part of this whole thing, a part of the Universe, and a part of something that is perhaps a form of God." Given her general lack of interest in religion, as well as her Presbyterian background, the Eastern orientation of her experience comes as something of a surprise. Second, she was in a peaceful state of mind at the time of the experience. Now perhaps peace, in combination with other factors (beautiful music, the beauty of nature, and so on) may function in certain personalities as a sufficient condition for religious experience. Further investigation of this possibility would be useful. However, our study to this point has shown that a peaceful state of mind, along with listening to music, is not a necessary condition for religious experience. Usually, peace follows, does not precede, the experience. A peaceful state of mind is also not a sufficient condition. I take this as common knowledge—many people have a peaceful state of mind without having an experience of the Divine.

Janette (1251)

Janette states that the following experience is one she has not related to anyone "partly because I didn't think I could hope to describe it without making it seem obvious and banal and even silly."

> When not consciously thinking about Life with a capital L, its meaning or anything like that, I was quite suddenly seized with a conviction that all matter (myself and everything else) was part of a much greater whole and that, from the smallest to the largest, everything was constructed on the same pattern and that all of this was part of, for want of any less loaded word, god. That was the important thing—a sense of belonging to an immeasurably great whole which was itself conscious, perceptive.

First of all, we should note that if Janette's experience was just a conviction that everything is a part of a whole which may be termed God, then it was not a religious experience. However, the conviction apparently results from the experience of "a sense of belonging to an immeasurably great whole which was itself conscious, perceptive." Her sense of belonging to a Whole is the reason for saying that she had a religious experience.

Janette describes herself at the time of the experience as an agnostic. At the end of her correspondence she adds the note: "In view of my age (54) and in case this experience might be thought due to chemical or emotional imbalance, I must add that this occurred eight years before the onset of the menopause." This type of note is found throughout the cases I studied. Many of the individuals want to quash any suggestion that they are not of sound mind, that they are a bit balmy, that they are "cranks," or that they are slightly "crackers." Moreover, Janette, along with the overwhelming majority of the the people I studied, clearly is of sound mind. The fact that she kept her experience to herself because, among other things, she did not want it to appear silly is a sign of her grasp of reality, as is the fact that she functioned normally as a wife and mother. The broader point Janette is making is that her experience was in no sense "cooked"—either by the chemicals in her body or by her conscious or unconscious self. Her point seems to be well taken.

Jason (17)

Jason writes in much the same vein as Janette, saying that he has told very few people about his experience, doing so "only when I was sure they would, if not understand, at least accept the feasibility of such experiences."

He describes himself as an "atheist/agnostic" from his early teens,

> a leftist humanist. My attitude to religion has been sceptical, with the idea that a belief in a superior being or an after-life was self-delusion, wishful thinking—a comfort against the harsh realities of existence. Because of my scepticism and reliance on 'reason' in all things, I knew that if I had not had these experiences myself I should have been greatly suspicious of anyone who said they had, and probably thought them a bit cranky.

During his later teen years he became obsessed with searching for the meaning of his life, a search which left him thoroughly frustrated, so frustrated that he ended up with a nervous breakdown at about age twenty. He does not mention undergoing treatment, but I shall assume that he had treatment. When he was on the road to recovery he says that

> I used to wake up regularly in the night, always searching for an answer to my own and the world's problems. Always questioning the reason for existence—a typical example of anxiety neurosis. And then on this particular night I awoke. It is here I find the difficulty—how can I explain in words that which is unexplainable in words? The best I can do is to say that I awoke and felt a growing excitement. That something was happening to me. And this thing grew and took over my thoughts and my whole consciousness. (I realize the danger of over-dramatizing. I am trying to be factual.) I felt that I was

experiencing eternity. I didn't see anything or hear anything. No visions, no voices. It was just a sense of being taken over by something outside myself, filling me with a joy and ecstasy beyond anything I had ever imagined possible. I felt I was part of this ecstasy and yet at the same time that all my doubts and questions were being answered. Not answered in any way that I can explain, it was just that the questions became meaningless in the face of this overwhelming something that had taken me over.

Jason worked his way back to normalcy, "got married, served in the army throughout the war, had children, lived a normal life," but, in his words, "didn't become religious. . . . The kind of people whose reasoning processes I respect are those like . . . Bertrand Russell."

Jason tries to explain his experience in terms of his unhappiness, and then generalizes his explanation to say that unhappiness is probably the reason that anybody has a religious experience, a suggestion which, given the material already covered, we know is without merit.

What is noteworthy about Jason's experience is that he was, in a sense, taken over: "This thing grew and took over my thoughts and my whole consciousness." This fact does-in any explanation from conscious desire, for in saying that the "thing" took over his thoughts and consciousness, Jason is saying that it just came—his desires were irrelevant. Indeed, he had just waked from sleep, the whole impression being that if he was desiring anything at all, he definitely was not desiring what happened. In addition, the fact that the "thing" is very peculiar, not wearing the ordinary apparel of God but coming as Eternity and as Ecstasy, and, in the end, just being indescribable, is another indication that the "thing" was not on his conscious mind. This latter fact alone is also sufficient to do-in any appeal to unconscious desire, for why or how unconscious desire would or could project a kind of God unfamiliar to Jason is anything but clear. More on this in a moment.

Jason himself is aware of unconscious explanations, having the following to say.

> Looking back, the obvious 'rational' answer is that I was in a highly emotional state and that this was the unconscious mind's way of relieving the tension. But you see, this happened to *me*, the logical, sceptical me, and for once I can't accept my own rational explanation! After all these years [about 30] I am still convinced that some 'force' outside normal experience came into my consciousness. I was going to say and this force was totally good, but that is not the word because right, wrong, good, bad didn't enter into it—the essence was joy, ecstasy, wonder and awe all rolled into one.

I should like to look at Jason's explanation from the unconscious a little more closely. First of all, though, I need to discuss the notion of the unconscious.

5. *Models of the Unconscious*

Freud's Model

The most common model of the unconscious is the Freudian model or some form of it. In Chapter Six I shall consider the Freudian model in some detail, taking the position that the model just will not do. For now I shall point out three reasons why the model will not do in the case of Jason, and thus will not do as an all-encompassing model.

First, according to the Freudian model, which I shall term "a pathological model," the unconscious is the repository of impulses and feelings which we are not aware of, impulses and feelings pressing for expression in consciousness or behavior. The unconscious is not the site for the rational development of possibilities or of material, dream material or otherwise, which brings about or expresses the resolution of anxiety. Thus, the unconscious cannot be the source for the development of the Something that took over Jason. Freud's concept of the unconscious simply does not provide for an unconscious capable of functioning in this way.

Second, material remains in or goes into the unconscious because the material is in some sense noxious to consciousness. E.g., I feel sexual attraction toward my best friend's wife, find the feeling intolerable, and thus move it (I assume nothing here about whether the move is conscious, unconscious, or a combination of both) to the unconscious. When visiting my friend again, I find an insurance salesman present, making a pitch not only for his health insurance scheme but also—at least as I see it—for my friend's wife, the result being that I am enraged. In my case the feeling of attraction is down on the unconscious level, but it still is active, active in disguised form, in the form of projection. However, in Jason's case the feeling of anxiety over the meaning of life apparently was not noxious, at least not noxious enough to get shoved down into the unconscious. Moreover, and this is the main point, even if the anxiety over meaning had an unconscious source, the unconscious would not be the site for detoxifying the toxic material so that a resolution of the problem could be achieved.

Third, Freud's explicit explanation of religion, developed on the basis of his model of the unconscious, makes religion a regression to infantile dependency on a father-figure that is both a source of sustenance and of punishment. The regression is a "defensive retreat forced by the intolerability of one's helplessness in the world and, ultimately, by the unmastered terror of one's own death." (Erdelyi, 1985, p. 198) Freud's explanation of religion seems severely limited.

To begin with, the resort to God is not defensive or a retreat if the reality of God is a genuine rational option. Freud did not think so, but he did anything but present convincing arguments for his position. Thus, turning to God may very well proceed essentially from rational motives; moreover, if we see rational motives as essentially the source of health for the self, we may say that those who turn to God (a sustaining and even punishing—at least in some sense—God) out of rational motives, are opening themselves to growth and development. Perhaps those who are motivated, or dominantly motivated, by the rational impulse are a distinct minority, so that Freud's words have a wide application. Yet if there is this minority, Freud's words do not have the universal application he thought.

Next, I raise the question of how we get from actual father to father-figure. This cannot be the sole work of the unconscious, for, as I noted in point one, the unconscious is not the site of rational development. Going from actual father to father-figure takes some development. Since the ego is the source of rational development, we should at least have to suppose some ego work. I think that Freud does; otherwise, he could never get what he says we regularly find in dreams—the appearance of hidden motives in forms we do not immediately or readily recognize. At any rate, we may suppose that the naked unconscious desire for return to infantile dependence on our father might very well come dressed up in the more acceptable clothing of belief in a fatherlike god. What we must note, however, is that the God-clothing does not fit any actual father; i.e., God is an idealization. When we have a sexual dream, e.g., the dream may come as a direct sexual encounter or under the guise of symbols, symbols which represent our sexual desires and cannot be considered idealizations of them. The symbols may be drained of feeling or may not, but if they are, that is hardly an idealization of the sexual impulse. God, though, is an idealization, removed, to a greater or lesser extent, from any actual father. As a consequence, Freud would have been more accurate to say that God represents a wish. Whether or not turning to God is infantile depends on whether or not the Object of the wish is also the object of rational belief, or, I would add, on whether or not pursuing the Object of the wish achieves major life values. If my belief in an accepting God makes me an accepting person, then I see nothing infantile about the belief, particularly if it is not decisively ruled out on rational grounds. Even if the belief is not rationally justified, we still might commend it for its usefulness in achieving positive human relationships. In this case we might say that the believer who is accepting is less advanced than the unbeliever who is accepting, but saying that the believer has regressed to infancy is both off-the-mark and a bit extreme—or so I should say.

Finally, the Object of much religious belief is not any sort of father-figure but a being either tending toward the impersonal or strictly impersonal, as in Eastern religion. Already, in my selective accounts from mainly Western sources, we have met a number of people with experiences of an Eastern cast. Since the experiences of an impersonal deity are widespread, Freud's explanation of religion simply ignores a great slice of the evidence. And here we may return to Jason, noting that the "thing" taking him over is anything but a father-figure, since it is cast essentially in impersonal terms. Moreover, there is nothing of punishment but much of ecstasy and joy. In addition, the experience hardly smacks of regression but of growth and expansion. What happened to Jason is clearly healthy, whatever our difficulties in giving a precise definition to 'healthy'. Regression to an infantile state is not healthy on the Freudian model. Further, Jason's search for meaning might be an expression of his fear of death, but it also might be an expression essentially of his desire for meaning! Fear of death certainly does not seem to be a preoccupation of his mind.

Freud's model of the unconscious and his view of religion do not, then, seem to be adequate, with the consequence that I shall not restrict myself to Freud's approach. However, before going on I wish to focus further on Freud's interpretation of religion, an interpretation astonishing for its hostility to religion and for its exclusion, as I just noted, of a large slice of evidence. Alfred North Whitehead said: "It is easy enough to find a theory, logically harmonious and with important applications in the region of fact, provided that you are content to disregard half your evidence." (Whitehead, 1961, 177) Freud's disregard of half the evidence on religion may be seen very clearly in the following.

In remarking about what he intended to do in the *Future of an Illusion*, Freud says that he was primarily concerned with what the common man understands by religion,

with the system of doctrines and promises which on the one hand
explains to him the riddles of his world with enviable completeness,
and, on the other, assures him that a careful Providence will watch
over his life and will compensate him in a future existence for any
frustrations he suffers here. The common man cannot imagine this
Providence otherwise than in the figure of an enormously exalted
father. Only such a being can understand the needs of the children of
men and be softened by their prayers and placated by the signs of
their remorse. Freud, 1962, 21)

Unfortunately, what Freud represents here as the common man's view of religion disregards at least half the facts about the common man.

First of all, Freud disregards the common men and women in the Western world for whom religion is highly problematic, who do not see it as explaining the riddles of the world with anything close to "enviable completeness." Certainly, many common men and women have read and identified with the book of Job, or the psalms in which the psalmist is distressed with God, or the prophets, like Habakkuk, who could not figure out why God permitted the gross injustices of the world. Indeed, the writers of Biblical literature included many common men— unquestionably, many of the psalmists and also many of the prophets, such as Amos. One problem, of course, is that Freud provides no criteria for determining a common person. Was David a common person? Admittedly, he became a king, but he had shepherd origins. What about the prophetic writers, such as Isaiah? Isaiah spoke to kings but mentions nothing of noble or priestly origins. Yet perhaps a common person is simply one who does not take religion very seriously. If so, Freud has so obviously stacked the deck that the common person will always be the loser—will always be what Freud says he is. Second, Freud's remarks concerning the common man's views of the afterlife disregard the fact that ancient Judaism did not have a belief in the afterlife; in fact, at the time of Jesus Judaism was still divided on the question of the afterlife, some believing, some not believing. Today, numerous common people have a religion in which the afterlife, if it plays a role at all, plays only a minor role. Third, the notion that common people try to soften a fatherly Providence by prayer and placate the Providence with remorse disregards the host of common people—including most of those in my study—for whom prayer and remorse are understood essentially as means of turning to and becoming open to God's activity. The image, rooted in Scripture, is that of turning to the Light, which always shines—not of rubbing the lamp furiously in order to coax out the light genie. Fourth, Freud completely disregards all the common folk of East, as well West, who worship an All, an impersonal kind of deity, not a fatherly Providence. Fifth, even if Freud does not disregard half the facts concerning the religion of common people, he disregards the facts concerning the uncommon people, the assembly of folk including the likes of Moses, Jesus, Muhammad, St. Francis, St. Theresa of Avila, Gandhi, Schweitzer., and the contemporary Mother Theresa. He must explain the religion of these spiritual elite, yet no explanation is forthcoming other than the one offered for the common man, namely, that of regression to the infantile: The individual feels his helplessness before life and regresses to a fatherly figure that will protect and care for him. If this is Freud's explanation of religion, we can hardly be surprised by his summary statement about religion, namely, that "the whole thing [religion] is so patently infantile, so foreign to reality, that to anyone with a friendly attitude to humanity it is painful to think that the great majority of mortals will never be able to rise above this view of life." (Freud, 1962, 21)

I think that the easiest way to point up the error of Freud's ways is to introduce an *ad hominem* argument of the following sort.

Freud: The turn to religion is a defensive retreat to infantilism.
St. Thomas: You don't say. Personally, I think your interpretation of religion is a defensive retreat to the infantilism of simply dismissing my arguments for God.
Freud: How do you get that?
St. Thomas: Well, isn't it clear? Feeling the helplessness of coming up with decisive arguments against a divine Being—in particular, decisive refutations of my arguments—you resort to the childish ploy of name-calling, i.e., of calling other people what you really are—infantile... so I guess that you're also projecting. Yes, and if you wish, I'll give a sexual twist to your motivation.

Obviously, one person's *ad hominem* is no better than another's. The argument is fallacious, its only purpose here being to direct the argument into more useful channels. The fact is, of course, that Freud may have been a very dependent person, with his abandonment of any dependence on God being a reaction formation. His authoritarianism, if that is a correct reading of Freud, could be another form of reaction formation. In other words, we must be careful about impugning the motives of others, for as St. Paul says, "in passing judgment on another you condemn yourself." The more important point is that the truth of religion, as well as of science, history, or whatever, is not necessarily vitiated by motives. Einstein may have strongly wished to achieve international acclaim by scientific theorizing, but that has nothing to do with whether or not his theorizing comes close to the truth (or whatever good theories come close to).

Since the consolation argument has a tenacity far beyond its rational merit, I shall make one more remark about it, not thinking, of course, that anything I have said or shall say will necessarily weaken the hold of the argument. In pursuing the *ad hominem* route above, I did not mean to be focusing simply on Freud, as if what I said applied only to him. The general point is that consolation, security, or whatever we wish to call it, is a sword cutting all ways. If I want consolation, I may find it in God, a scientific theory, sex, atheism, or a list of things as long as we can imagine. Moreover, if the motive of consolation vitiates the truth of what I adopt, then atheism, good scientific theories, and so on, are out, as well as theism. Indeed, any appeal to motives is going to get us in trouble, except perhaps the appeal to the motive of achieving the truth. Thus, my motive may not necessarily be to gain consolation but fame or wealth or power or success or relief from boredom or whatever. If the motive of consolation vitiates truth, why not these motives? Moreover, what persons could say that their motive to achieve the truth was untouched by any other truth-vitiating motive?

Rejecting Freud's interpretation of religion, we may, just for the sake of argument, stay for the moment with a Freudian approach to Jason's religious experience, saying that Jason's anxiety about the meaning of life had its source in his sexual life. Describing his condition before the nervous breakdown, Jason says, "I was getting no self-expression from my work, I was without social or sexual contacts." Thus, Jason was something of a frustrated young man. A Freudian model would lead us to say that his fundamental frustration was sexual, although the evidence for this thesis certainly does not outweigh evidence for the thesis that frustration from lack of meaning in work (symbolic of a more general lack of meaning in life, in which we might fit even the lack of sexual expression) was more fundamental. Following the Freudian model, though, we are left with the question of why he should have his religious experience. Did the experience symbolize in some decisive way the resolution of his sexual frustration? If so how was his frustration resolved? He says nothing about a more active sex life. His marriage took place after his experience. We may also say that nothing in the way of transference occurred while he was under treatment for his nervous breakdown—at least if transference occurred, it did not resolve his continued questioning about the meaning of life, along with the associated anxiety. The acute anxiety had subsided, but not the chronic anxiety. We also have no evidence of sublimation, of immersion in some alternate, fulfilling type of activity. What we have is an experience with a "thing" that simply does the trick in the way of resolving his anxiety. How does this "thing" enter the picture? It does not seem to arise either from the conscious or from the unconscious, at least an unconscious conceived along Freudian lines. Where, then, does this "thing" come from, and why at this particular time, rather than earlier or later?

The Mixed Model

At the very least we need a revised model of the unconscious, not just a more positive model, as we find in a number of ego psychologies, or a model which is positive toward religion, as in the case of Jung, but a model in which the unconscious can engage in rational work similar to what takes place on the conscious level. The unconscious I am looking for must include at least the capabilities present in the theory of Jonathan Winson.

Winson maintains that "dreams may reflect a memory-processing mechanism inherited from lower species, in which information important for survival is reprocessed during REM sleep. This information may constitute the core of the unconscious." (Winson, 1990, 94) According to Winson,

> dreams reflect an individual's strategy for survival. The subjects of dreams are broad-ranging and complex, incorporating self-image, fears, insecurities, strengths, grandiose ideas, sexual orientation, desire, jealousy and love. (94)

He cites a study in which seventy individuals in crisis situations reveal the consistency of their dreams with the ways that they are consciously coping with their crises. His conclusion is as follows.

> The characteristics of the unconscious and associated processes of brain functioning are very different than Freud thought. Rather than being a cauldron of untamed passions and destructive wishes, I propose that the unconscious is a cohesive, continually active mental structure

that takes note of life's experiences and reacts according to its own scheme of interpretation. Dreams are not disguised as a consequence of repression. Their unusual character is a result of the complex hesitations that are culled from memory. (p. 96)

Thus, according to Winson, the unconscious takes note of the life processes of the individual, working in tandem, as it were, with the conscious to provide solutions to the problematic processes.

Winson does not spell out his full theory, but he apparently wants to depart completely from Freud's "cauldron of untamed passions and destructive wishes." I do not believe that this is possible, given what we find in the self of that which is destructive and unhealthy, such as obsessions, compulsions, hysterias, hallucinations, neuroses, psychoses, and even some dreams (nightmares which leave a person simply torn). Thus, I shall accept an unconscious which includes the following elements. First, there are pathological elements; i.e., some impulses of the unconscious, if expressed in unmodified form, would be counterproductive to the well-being of the self. Second, the unconscious is not reducible to any single impulse, such as the sexual (the term 'sexual' in Freudian theory has a use which is not equivalent to use in common parlance); rather the unconscious consists of a range of impulses and feelings, from fear to creativity, the strength of the impulse or feeling depending on the person—i.e., the genetic makeup of the person, the history of the person, the present circumstances of the person. In a given cultural setting, say, ours, we may find the sexual impulse tending to be in a salient position, but that is not necessarily the case. Third, the unconscious, as in Winson's theory, is on better terms with the conscious, so that the two may be cooperative, as well as adversarial. Fourth, the unconscious, again as in Winson's theory, is capable of rational activity, of developing rational solutions to issues present in conscious existence. In order to get as powerful an unconscious as possible, I shall go beyond Winson and say that the unconscious can provide solutions that were not in process on the conscious level.

I shall dub my model of the unconscious "the mixed model" or "the mixed unconscious." I consider the model conceptually possible and theoretically more challenging to the thesis of this book than any model currently in use. The mixed model is something of a collage, without a full integration of the various elements; however, I am not trying to develop and defend a new theory of the unconscious. Instead, I am trying to get as challenging a theory of the unconscious as I consider possible. If there is incoherency in my model, then I shall have to drop the incoherent element and with it drop some challenge to the thesis of this book.

In relying on a mixed model, or even in relying on Freud's model, we move beyond the limits of an explanation from desire. Unconscious dynamics are not restricted to desire. Thus, I broaden the explanation from desire to include an explanation from unconscious dynamics.

6. *Return to the Case Studies*

Let us assume that the mixed unconscious may function so as to relieve severe tension. The problem is that we do not have the slightest idea of why or how the unconscious relieved tension in Jason when it did; in short, the relief is as unpredictable as a roulette wheel, with the result that the explanation lacks the status of a lawful empirical hypothesis. I am of the opinion that we run into the same problem no matter who the individual is--but more of this in the chapter on the unconscious. Moreover, supposing that the unconscious sometimes, for reasons we cannot fathom, relieves tension, why should the relief be associated with some kind of divine Being? Why should the unconscious employ conscious perception of a divine Being? If the answer is that we must have something which satisfies the rational mind, we have mountains of evidence to the effect that the divine Reality perceived is often, if not usually, at least as much of a puzzle and challenge to the rational mind as it is a rational solution. The "thing" Jason perceives certainly does not seem to provide him with rational answers; indeed, the whole experience confronts him as something "unexplainable in words."

We are left, then, with the question of why there is the experience of a divine Being. We may consider the mixed unconscious to be as creative as we wish, as creative as our dreams, e.g., but the question still is why the unconscious should present us with the sense of the Divine. What is the function of that experience? In Jason's case, why should not the unconscious just relieve tension directly without the experience of the Divine? Moreover, why should there be such a strong sense of the reality of the Something, such a strong sense that the experience is truly cognitive? Jason recognizes that his experience may not fit "rational" explanations, but the reality of the experience is such that he simply cannot give up on it. And what is true of Jason is true of most of the people I have studied. For them the experience carries with it a sense of the reality of the Divine—they cannot doubt, they sense that nothing could be more real, or they hold that the experience is self-validating, not to be judged by any other. Thus, if we say that the experience is a creative product of the self, just like dreams, we should remember that the experience is very unlike dreams in its sense of reality. We have no trouble judging that dreams do not present us with a reality beyond ourselves. I may have dreamed of a birthday party at my brother's, but there was no party—nothing other than a representation in my dream consciousness of a party. Or at best, my dream may accurately represent what took place—it could be a memory dream; but the accuracy of the memory is always judged by me in my waking state. Or I may wake up saying, "That dream was as real as anything I've ever experienced"; only, as I sit on the side of my bed perceiving my room and thinking about the dream, I realize that I am now experiencing something far more real. However, in religious experience, contrary to dream experiences, people are first and foremost awake, conscious, and often more acutely and critically conscious than at other times. Further, they take their perception as of Something real, at least as real as anything in the physical world, and perhaps more real; moreover, the conviction of reality remains after critical reflection, sometimes after many years of critical reflection. Jason was convinced at the time of his experience, and also thirty years later after much critical evaluation, that a Force outside of him entered his consciousness. People may not be explicit about their standards of judgment in the case of religious experience, but they are no more explicit in the case of dreams; yet people easily, correctly, and consistently distinguish dreams from waking experience, what they see as subjective reality from objective reality. Why not suppose an equally adequate capacity for judgment in the case of religious experience? Why suppose that human judgment fails in the case of religious experience but not in the case of dreams? These questions are, of course, basic to our whole study. I raise them at this point simply as a reminder that automatically tossing religious experience into the subjective hamper is nothing short of a prejudice. At any rate, whatever one's answer to the epistemological questions, the point for now is that people who have religious experience are awake and have a sense that what they encountered was non-subjective reality, many of them explicitly remarking that they definitely were not dreaming, hallucinating, or anything of the like. If we appeal to dreams as a parallel, they simply are not a parallel. The unconscious acts in religious experience as it does not seem to act anywhere else. More on this later.

Granting that religious experience normally carries with it a sense of cognitive apprehension, we may still think of the experience essentially as the result of a creative unconscious. Although religious experience differs fundamentally from dreams, it may be like dreams with respect to content. Dreams express fears, frustrations, insecurities, desires, hopes—the gamut of our feeling and conative life—in ways that are innovative and varied. E.g., one night a frustration dream may take the form of my being unable to run faster than someone I can easily beat, whereas the next night it may take the form of my being unable to get to my class for the day's discourse on Plato. The dream material is creatively cut to clothe the basic feeling of frustration. In a sense, the content of the dream is irrelevant; or more accurately, it can be anything which will carry the feeling of frustration. I note that in saying this I move away from the Freudian view that dreams disguise unconscious reality because they incorporate unconscious material toxic to consciousness. Instead, I take an approach more like that of Winson. I may not know how to read my dreams, but they are not necessarily deceptive. In fact, I might say that my dreams at times do not present any sort of reality, and thus are just meaningless appearances, or are like inner videos, designed to amuse, puzzle, or stimulate me. At other times, perhaps most times, they are meaningful in that they signify something about my conscious or unconscious life, and they require that I learn to read them, just as I must learn to read any sign. If a child sees vapor trails in the atmosphere, it may read them as strange new clouds, failing to realize that they represent the past path of a jet plane. The trails are not deceptive in any sense; the child has simply not learned to read them.

The main point is that the content of religious experience may be, like dream content, irrelevant—irrelevant in the sense that any content will do as long as it carries the essential aim of the unconscious. In the case of Jason, the aim would be a resolution of his anxiety over the meaning of life, the content being the "thing" that came as eternity and ecstasy. Unquestionably, his experience relieves his anxiety, but it does so, according to him, because all his "questions became meaningless in the face of this overwhelming something" which had taken him over. The sense of the reality of this overwhelming Something seemed to be crucial to the relief of his doubts and anxieties. In short, if he had not sensed the "thing" as real, or had come to believe that it was not, that it was like a dream or hallucination, he likely would not have experienced any resolution of his anxiety. The sense of the "thing's" reality seems to be at least a necessary condition for the resolution of the anxiety. I would generalize this point and say that the content of religious experience will simply not do the trick (anxiety resolution or whatever) unless it comes with a sense of reality.

Perhaps, though, the sense of reality was without any causal efficacy. Perhaps what brought the sense of resolution was the direct action of the unconscious, with the conscious awareness of the "thing" being just a kind of epiphenomenon. If so, then why the epiphenomenon? It is without causal significance, otiose with respect to the feeling of resolution. What, then, would be the motive for the unconscious to produce it? Perhaps the unconscious is playful, coming up with content which just represents creativity. Why, then, the sense of reality? If we are left simply to say, "It happens, we know not why," then we have introduced an explanation which leaves us with at least as much mystery as we began with—not a very productive explanation, aside from the fact that it is also anything but empirically derived or empirically testable. Supposing, though, that the "thing" produced by the unconscious was causally efficacious in the sense that it was the means by which the unconscious resolved the tension in Jason, we are still left with the question of why the unconscious did not just follow the simpler course of directly producing the feeling of resolution.

A further question is how the unconscious hit on the approach it did in Jason's case. Had Jason been pondering the notions of eternity and ecstasy, working out the various possibilities of the notions? No evidence of that. Or did the unconscious just hit on the notions of eternity and ecstasy, filling them with new meaning, independently of what Jason was thinking about? Does the unconscious, apart from what is happening in consciousness, go its own way, working out the content to be employed in resolving anxiety or tension? Our dream content often is independent of what has occurred on the conscious level—the people and events may be entirely novel; therefore, perhaps the unconscious works in the same way. The more important question, though, is: Can the unconscious produce in experience that which has never been experienced before? The fact is that Jason's experience of eternity and ecstasy seems to be different from any understanding he had of eternity and ecstasy prior to the experience, for Jason says that he cannot explain his experience in words. Apparently, the experience broke the molds of the common meanings available for 'eternity' and 'ecstasy'. The notions in their familiar usage are relatively unproblematic. For example, the normal religious use of the term 'eternal', as in the phrase 'God is eternal', is that God is without beginning and end, a notion which is clear and comprehensible. We may also speak of the physical universe—or better, energy—in this way, saying, according to the First Law of Thermodynamics, that energy is eternal, meaning that it is neither created nor destroyed. The ancient Greek atomists expressed the same idea when they maintained that atoms have always been and will always be. This notion of eternity is thoroughly comprehensible and was likely a part of Jason's repertoire of concepts. Theologians go on to speak of God as timeless, outside of or above time, a concept which is more problematic, yet which is comprehensible in the sense that we can come up with examples of timeless realities, such as mathematical truths. Whether Jason had this concept of eternity, I cannot say. He was a young man and an atheist, so that if he had been reading theological literature, we should be a bit surprised. He definitely does not mention doing so. At any rate, I shall assume that the term 'eternity' also carried for him the meaning of 'timeless'. All the same, he cannot fit what he experienced into any previous concepts. The experience could not be expressed in words. He is clearly into something which is new to him and his thinking.

Again, the question is: Can the unconscious introduce experiential content which a person has not experienced? Theoretically, I think the answer has to be yes. We know that the brain can be stimulated so that people who have never perceived colors will have an experience of color. What other experiences can be produced by brain stimulation? I suppose that the answer is: An indefinite number and kind. We might suppose, then, that the unconscious is linked to the brain in such a way that it can be the first level of the self (as opposed to consciousness) to receive the experiences resulting from certain stimulations of the brain (where this stimulation might come from would have to be specified), passing on the experiences afterward to consciousness. Other possibilities could, I am certain, be listed.

However, whatever we may think of as possible, neither the conscious nor unconscious self seems to present us with novel sorts of experience. Dreams, for example, although immensely creative, do not seem to use material underived from conscious experience. I may populate my dreams with people and other beings I have never seen, but I do not employ sensory material from an unknown sense or use sensory material unfamiliar to me, such as colors I have never seen. Neither do dreams seem to present us with new concepts, such as a new concept of a triangle. If someone cites Friedrich Kekule and his dream of a benzene-ring as an example of novel concepts in dreams, then the person is not citing anything relevant. Kekule's dream, which came to him while he was riding on a bus, sunk in deep reverie, was a dream of chains of carbon atoms dancing before his eyes, with one chain coiling on itself, snakelike, in the form of a ring. He did not see anything new, certainly did not grasp any sort of new concept—a ring is not a new concept. Moreover, the exact development of the ring-concept, so that it would have empirical application in chemistry, required hard conscious work. In other words, the new conceptual work was done on the conscious level. Thus, as far as I know, the unconscious normally goes with concepts available to consciousness or experiential content within the repertoire of the person. As a consequence, I shall be very hesitant about admitting that some new form of experience, such as Jason's experience of eternity and ecstasy, had its origin in the unconscious. The presumption is against it, so that we should need to come up with specific evidence that it occurred.

Another question we face is why a mixed unconscious would hold off on the nature of the "thing" until the moment of the experience. The "thing" does not seem to be threatening in any way. Why not, then, engage the conscious self in working out and evaluating the nature of the "thing"? If we decide to go with a cooperative unconscious, we cannot abandon that notion at the first bend in the road.

But perhaps the unconscious would be hindered or slowed by cooperating with the conscious. If the idea here is that the unconscious is more creative than the conscious, I find no evidence showing that this is so. Assuming that night dreams are expressive of some level of unconscious activity, I see little evidence that night dreams are more creative than daydreams, fantasies, imagination, or hard conscious thinking (we may think, for example, of the theoretical physicist or the novelist). If we suppose that the unconscious is often more creative because it lacks the inhibitions of the conscious, we shall have to come up with the specific inhibitions. What, e.g., were the inhibitions to Jason's conscious development of a "thing" of the nature he conceived? Besides, nothing that I have said about the mixed model of the unconscious rules out the possibility of conscious inhibitions reaching into the unconscious, or even having their basis in the unconscious. I have explicitly stated that a mixed unconscious incorporates the pathological, so that it may well contain impulses and material which negatively affect the creative, health-seeking impulses of the unconscious.

From all the above criticisms of the appeal to the unconscious, two emerge as most weighty. The first concerns what I shall call parsimony and may be pointed up by the question: What could be the possible motive of the unconscious for developing the sense of a real divine Presence? If the problem is a relief of tension, then why not a simple feeling of relief or peace? If the problem is one of meaning in life—and perhaps that was not Jason's basic problem—why not a simple sense that life has meaning, even though the person could not say what it is? Actually, Jason ended up as much in the dark about the meaning of life after his experience as before. What he sensed was that the questions about meaning "became meaningless in the face of this overwhelming something that had taken me over." But why should the unconscious go to all the extra work of a sense of contact with an overwhelming Something, rather than a simple sense that the questions were meaningless, or a simple sense that they were answerable in some way? The sense of divine Presence seems totally unnecessary for what the unconscious needs to accomplish. It is something like an ornament—superfluous, excessive. Therefore, I shall dub the excessive work of presenting a divine Presence as real, "the ornamental effect."

The essential question now becomes: Where else in the working of the unconscious do we find something like the ornamental effect? E.g., we do not seem to find anything like the effect in transference. The patient begins feeling toward the therapist as, say, he felt toward his father. The patient has no illusions about his reality or the reality of the therapist, only illusions about the nature of his feelings, illusions which are dispelled in working through the transference--the therapist helps the patient see what the feelings are all about. We do not find the patient having some new experience which he takes to be of an independent reality and which functions to resolve the issues of transference. (The exception, of course, would be a patient who has a religious experience during transference—a most uncommon event, I daresay!) Moreover, in working with dreams, the patient knows that the dreams are dreams, although he does not see what they are revealing—say, hidden feelings about his father. There is nothing in this situation of a non-reality presented as real and functioning as the basis for the resolution of a deep childhood conflict with the father. The closest we come to religious experience in the sense of taking something as real is hallucination; yet aside from deeply psychotic people, patients will quickly recognize hallucinations as such, without any aid from a therapist. Moreover, hallucinations do not normally resolve anything; rather, they are expressions of a person's pathology and do not function to resolve that pathology.

Transference, then, does not present us with anything like the ornamental effect. The same goes for dreams and hallucinations. This is an important consideration because apart from evidence that the effect is present throughout the working of the unconscious, the hypothesis that it is present in the case of religious experience—in effect, that it is present only in the case of religious experience—seems *ad hoc* and thus non-parsimonious. To avoid the *ad hoc* we need to show that something like the ornamental effect is integral to the notion of the mixed unconscious—i.e., the effect shows up in a principled or lawful way in various expressions of the unconscious. Presently, I do not think that this can be shown.

The second criticism extends the first, asking the additional question: Why does the unconscious come up with a solution at one time rather than another? Why did Jason have the experience at the time he did—not one month earlier, not one month later? In other words, the appeal to a mixed unconscious seems to be an appeal to an explanation of the following form: It happens, I know not why. This sort of explanation is, in effect, a non-explanation. I note in passing that the questions I raise here apply essentially to any experience of a person, whether religious or non-religious. E.g., why did a person have a highly sexual dream last night rather than two nights ago? Generally, I do not think that a question of this sort receives an answer which can be considered scientific in any sense. If any explanation is offered, I suggest that it is much like the explanations economists provide for changes in the stock market. The inadequacy of these explanations from a scientific standpoint is revealed by the fact that they do not provide for accurate, systematic predictions. More on this in Chapter Six.

Another problem associated with the sense of divine Presence is that it often not only leaves people with as much mystery as when they began but it introduces new mysteries. Jason, along with many, if not most, other people having religious experience, is left speechless, stopped in his rational tracks. The "thing" he experienced is incomprehensible, beyond understanding, a mystery, a paradox, a riddle. Moreover, Jason, along with most of the people I have studied, are anything but comfortable with this situation. They would prefer rational resolution—Jason goes for thinkers like Bertrand Russell!—yet they are thoroughly knocked off balance rationally. In addition, many people, because of the transformation experienced in their encounter with the Reality, have a life which is more difficult, at least in the sense that they start having adjustment problems with a society which values the transient rather than the eternal. Further, many have the problem of facing others who think that they have left their senses. Thus, we have to suppose that the unconscious resolves one problem (anxiety over the meaning of life) while introducing others—puzzles for reason and new problems in society. Why does the unconscious work in such a way? This is a new mystery we did not have to begin with.

Finally, I introduce the reminder that some people, unlike Jason, have a religious experience apart from any anxiety, stress, or crisis—at least that we can locate. What is the unconscious explanation for their experience?

Ben (1001)

But now I turn from Jason to Ben. Ben had rejected God at about age fourteen, immediately after having been confirmed, persisting in a kind of unremitting unbelief until age twenty five, when, he says, a corner of his mind got opened by what he thought might have been an answer to prayer. Then at age thirty four he read a book which opened more of his mind, opened it to the extent that he began to consider the possibility of God's existence. One night he was "nicely tucked up in bed considering the possibilities," when he was arrested by a Presence.

> Anyone who has tried to catch and watch his own mental processes will know what is meant by the queer feeling when a new important thought is struggling to be born. There is a kind of stirring or heaving in the wings and away from whatever may be the temporary focus of interest. But at once all the arc lights of inner attention turn in the direction from which the newcomer is making his presence felt. Sometimes there is disappointment; whatever it was slips away without identification. But this time, that which started the disturbance strides into the middle of the arena, identifies itself quite clearly and is almost immediately clothed in words of the English language. When these words are put down on paper they seem almost derisively obvious and trite. they are:
>
>> 'And if this Good God exists, then you— yes, even you, you ignorant stuck-up fool— might be brought into some kind of co-cooperation with him.'
>
> But with that trite and obvious thought . . . what else? This is where language shows its weakness. Shall he say a swelling trumpet chord from all the orchestras of heaven? Shall he say 'a mighty rushing wind' not blowing over and around his body, but raging through all

the open spaces between the electrons and protons and neutrons of which his body is made? These are approximations. But several things are certain. The whole experience was precipitated without a single physical molecule in the room being deflected from its normal physical course. The experience, though no words adequately describe it, was utterly real. It was not imagined, dreamed up, or 'supposed' or confined within the mind. It was physical sensation experienced in the body. It was not self-created from the inside. It was given from 'the MORE which is operative in the universe outside.'

The last words in quotation are obviously from William James.

We see that Ben, although agnostic at the time of his experience, was definitely entertaining the possibility of God's existence. Yet entertaining the possibility of God's existence is not in the least equivalent to desiring an experience of God's reality. Further, coming to belief in God is not equivalent to experiencing God's reality. Perhaps Ben was saying to himself that he would not believe in God unless he experienced God. That thought, if in him, apparently was not dominant in his consciousness, for he does not mention it. Besides, many people articulate that thought without ever having a religious experience, so that the thought is not a sufficient condition for the experience. Moreover, since the thought apparently was not present to Ben, it does not seem to be a necessary condition for the experience.

If the suggestion is that desire was present on the unconscious level, we have no evidence for that, and given *Socrates* we should not presume the desire. On the conscious level Ben is opening up to the possibility of God's existence. Why should we presume anything more than that on the unconscious level? He does not seem seriously threatened by the possibility, for he toys with it, not repressing the impulse to consider it. Why, then, should anything be going on unconsciously other than supportive, complementary activities? In short, if we are going to overcome the presumption of *Socrates*, we need some fairly strong evidence that something else is going on unconsciously than is going on consciously.

Actually, Ben himself has something to say about one form of a Freudian explanation. What he says is both amusing and on target.

> It would be useless, for example, for every Freudian psycho-analyst in Europe to try to tell me that it [my experience] was all a by-product of Oedipal feelings aroused by my relationship with my terrifying father. Incidentally my father, unlike Freud's, was not very terrifying.

Ben might also have noted that his experience seems to have little to do with a father-figure of any sort, certainly not a judging, guilt-producing authority figure. The emphasis is on the goodness of God and on entering into "cooperation" with this God, as well as on the physical sensations which seem to dramatize the inrushing presence of this good Being.

If one wishes to pursue oedipal issues, then the question is why, at this particular time in Ben's life, feelings associated with the oedipal conflict should surface. Ben seems to be in a process of religious search. What does the search have to do with feelings of guilt associated with the oedipal conflict? A multiplicity of answers is available, yet none really seems persuasive. Does the religious search represent the attempt to resolve guilt and heal the breach with the father? Yet what triggered the attempt at this time in Ben's life? Besides, Ben says, in effect, that there was no breach with his father, at least no breach of any significance. If the reply is that the breach, with its accompanying guilt, was on the unconscious level, the next question is why we should make any move to the unconscious level. The move, apart from evidence requiring or strongly supporting it, is unwarranted, being a violation of *Plato*.

Elizabeth (1481)

Elizabeth writes that at the time of her experience she was "a convinced atheist." The experience came upon her

> in the form of a mood, growing in intensity until it took hold of me completely. Although fully aware that my consciousness was undergoing a considerable change I was, all the same, quite unable to control the situation.
>
> It was as though my mind broke bounds and went on expanding until it merged with the universe. Mind and universe became one within the other. Time ceased to exist.
>
> It was all one thing and in a state of infinity. It was as if, willy-nilly, I became directly exposed to an entity within myself and nature at large. . . .
>
> As an atheist and materialist my frame of reference did not provide for an occurrence such as this. I seriously wondered if I had taken leave of my senses. My mind was on fire with feelings, visions, thoughts and ideas which came with such speed and clarity . . . that, at first, I was bewildered and did not know how best to judge their validity. . . .

It was, and still is as a continuing influence, the most overwhelming thing that has ever happened to me.

To begin with, we may say that since the experience made Elizabeth think that she was leaving her senses, she clearly was not looking for or desiring the experience consciously. Given *Socrates*, we may also say that she was not desiring it unconsciously. In addition, the experience did not cause Elizabeth to become religious in any traditional sense, although she apparently gave up being a convinced atheist. She says that her experience "did pose a riddle, the kind of riddle one cannot even attempt to solve without becoming keenly aware of the ultimate mystery of creation." She sees herself as religious in that she is aware of the riddle and is attempting to pose solutions to it.

One explanation of Elizabeth's experience might be that it is what Freud referred to as an "oceanic feeling," a feeling which Freud describes in terms related to him by a friend. "It is a feeling which he [the friend] would like to call a sensation of 'eternity', a feeling as of something limitless, unbounded—as it were 'oceanic'." (Freud, 1962, 11) Freud first of all says that what his friend describes as a feeling seems more like an "intellectual perception, which is not, it is true, without an accompanying feeling-tone, but only such as would be present with any other act of thought of equal range." (12) I think that Freud is entirely on target here, for religious experience is, as I have noted, anything but sheer feeling; it is clearly of the order of perception or apprehension, accompanied by feeling. It is nice, if not surprising, to have Freud as an ally on this point. Freud turns hostile, though, when he tries to explain the oceanic perception. He maintains that it is a return to an infant phase, to the phase when no distinctions were made between ego and the rest of reality, for ego was not yet formed.

The question is whether we can return to an infant phase; i.e., whether there can be any memory of that phase. Freud is inclined to accept the principle "that in mental life nothing which has once been formed can perish—that everything is somehow preserved and that in suitable circumstances . . . it can once more be brought to light." (16) This principle is so sweeping that Freud later modifies it to read: "It is rather the rule than the exception for the past to be preserved in mental life." (19) Certainly, even the revised principle is highly debatable, particularly, I should say in the case of going back to the infant stage of life. The question is whether the infant can even be said to have a mental life, i.e., a mental life other than sheer perception, the flow of sensations, a blooming, buzzing confusion, as James says. Does anyone really remember this state? We certainly need evidence other than the oceanic feeling; otherwise, the argument is viciously circular. I do not know of the evidence, if there is any.

Whatever the evidence for memory of an ego-less state, such a state is simply not like the oceanic state described by Freud's friend, by Elizabeth, and by numerous others. To sense the limitless is not, at least not necessarily, to be in a non-ego state. Moreover, to say that one senses a merging with the rest of reality is again not necessarily to deny the self, the ego. Some people talk about the loss of a sense of self, but others do not. Elizabeth did not seem to lose the sense of self. Says she, "it was as if, willy-nilly, I became directly exposed to an entity within myself and nature at large." Her statement is filled with ego-language.

A further point is that the oceanic perception is not, as Freud suggests, always, or even commonly, a form of escape. He says that "the 'oneness with the universe' . . . sounds like a first attempt at a religious consolation, as though it were another way of disclaiming the danger which the ego recognizes as threatening it from the external world." (19) Here we return to the old saw of consolation. Freud apparently forgot that the infant stage of life can be as threatening, irritating, and unpleasant as any other stage of life—unless we are to maintain that all the crying, wailing, and screaming of the infant add up to sheer expressions of joy. In other words, if the oceanic feeling is a reversion to an infant stage, we must remember that the infant stage is anything but a stage of consolation. Freud also apparently did not pay attention to what his friend said, for the man claimed that the oceanic feeling brings with it "no assurance of personal immortality, but it is the source of . . . religious energy," which he sees as potentially very positive. (11) We should qualify his statement by saying that the oceanic perception does not necessarily bring with it any sense of assurance of personal immortality; it very well may. However, the main point is that the feeling may be associated with religious energy, energy which provides in numerous cases anything but consolation because it drives persons into a lifestyle radically incompatible with the style of society. In the case of Elizabeth the experience posed a riddle to her, a riddle for which which she continually sought solutions. No escape here; no disclaiming the dangers of the world; no clinging to a consolation. Rather, an affirmation of the mystery of existence, an affirmation which continually leaves one off-balance, unsure, questioning.

A final point is that Freud admits that in love (I assume that his primary reference is to sexual love) the boundaries between self and the other sometimes tend to melt. Thus, love, not infancy, may be the paradigm for the oceanic feeling, except that we have no evidence of a necessary or sufficient link between experiencing love and experiencing merger with the universe. Obviously, not everyone experiencing the merger of love experiences merger with the universe, and just as obviously not all those experiencing merger with the universe have experienced the merger of sexual love—e.g., children. In sum, Freud's explanation of the oceanic feeling seems to be a non-starter.

Going a step further than Freud, we might try to explain the experiences of unity with the universe as a kind of return to the womb. Obviously, the notion of remembering from the state of the womb is far more problematic than remembering from infancy. Besides, what evidence is there that existence in the womb always or usually comes across as secure (Does it come across as anything?) rather than distressing? We have every reason to suppose that existence in the womb may be at least as distressing as it is secure, being a function largely of the mother's mental and emotional state. In addition, what evidence is there that Elizabeth or the other people experiencing union had some sort of unconscious desire to return to the security of the womb? In Elizabeth's case, as well as in the case of other atheists and agnostics, the reply might be that adopting the stance of the agnostic or atheist creates so much distress and insecurity for people that they want to move back to a less disconcerting existence, to the stage of a kind of primitive security.

To begin with, we need to question the notion that atheists and agnostics generally, and Elizabeth in particular, are in a state of distress, at least a state of distress any worse than religious people. Elizabeth gave no signs of having been in distress over her atheism. The idea that atheists and agnostics are generally in distress over their unbelief is not supported by any evidence I know of, although the idea is most certainly a popular prejudice. A delightful tale concerns James Boswell, an ardent believer, who, upon learning that his friend David Hume had only a few days to live, quickly made his way to Hume's house in order to engage him in serious conversation about the afterlife and proper preparation for it. But Hume did not want to converse about the afterlife but about literature. Actually, Hume had already reflected on the afterlife—probably far more than Boswell—coming up skeptical. Since Boswell was not likely to present any new information or argument, anything Hume had not already heard, Hume preferred a pleasant conversation about literature. Boswell just could not grasp Hume's sense of equanimity—

and he was not the only one. The common story was that Hume faked his equanimity, faked it because an unbeliever just could not be peaceful in the face of death—a nice little case of begging the question.

However, supposing that atheists and agnostics are uncomfortable with their unbelief (If we were to make this supposition, then we could develop another *ad hominem* argument against Freud to the effect that his attacks on religion arose out of his helplessness in relieving the distress of his unbelief.), we may note that many people give up agnosticism or atheism without making a move back to the womb of life in the form of having an experience of unity with the universe. Indeed, many jettison their unbelief without ever having a religious experience. In other words, the problem of distress and insecurity over unbelief is often solved strictly by belief, which is also often—usually!—achieved apart from religious experience, not to mention a religious experience of unity with the universe. Of course, not all those having an experience of unity with the universe are atheists or agnostics or, as far as we can tell, people with insecurities, that is, insecurities intense enough to make them unconsciously desire a return to the womb or some other supposedly secure and peaceful state.

Linda (2115)

Linda writes that

> I married in my early twenties and for the next fifteen years would have described myself, if asked, as an agnostic or humanist. It seemed to me possible that there was some kind of creative spirit behind the universe, but if so it was unknowable, 'totally other' and, in view of the amount of suffering and injustice in the world, indifferent to the human predicament. My scepticism seemed complete when within a short space of time two close friends died of cancer at an early age, each leaving young dependent families.

About this time her teenage son became involved in a church choir, with Linda often attending choir performances

> much as one would go to a football match or school play, merely to support one's child. . . . I remained an outsider. For me it was all totally meaningless and it seemed sad that so much beauty and energy was being expended on a mere illusion.

> One evening the service seemed more than usually boring and empty and I had just decided not to waste any more time in going to church, even to please my son, when we reached the point in the service where the priest turns to the people and says, 'The Lord be with you.' And to my great astonishment I suddenly knew that He was. From then on it was as though I was hearing the familiar words of the Prayer Book for the first time; even the Lord's Prayer took on a completely new significance. All the old cliches had come true, the eyes of the blind were opened, the ears of the deaf unstopped.

Linda then went through a period of searching, trying to figure out what had happened. She wanted to talk to somebody but did not feel comfortable doing so, with the result that she "read avidly and haphazardly all the paperback theology I could lay hands on, starting with *Honest to God.*" She began to read the Gospels but found them, particularly the Synoptics, "full of contradictions and harsh teaching." One afternoon, about two years after her initial experience, she was reading one of the Synoptics and came to the conclusion that Jesus was a sincere man suffering from delusions of grandeur.

> As I was getting ready to fetch my youngest child from school I felt over-awed by a strong sense of a presence and the sentence came from somewhere in my sub-conscious (I certainly had not read it that afternoon), 'Behold I stand at the door and knock,' and I knew that I had to surrender. From then on everything I had heard or read fell into place and I was filled with a deep sense of blessing and joy which has been renewed countless times since.

Linda takes this experience as an acceptance of the divinity of Christ. Her actual description of the experience is ambiguous as to exactly what went on and as to the presence she sensed. Apparently the presence was that of Christ, the words being those of Christ found in the Book of Revelation.

Linda goes on to note that since the two experiences described above, she has had numerous other experiences. She makes the following observation concerning her experiences.

> To me the interesting thing is that both 'turning points'—return to belief in God and acceptance of the divinity of Christ—came at times when I was feeling at my most sceptical and on the verge of giving up even the attempt to search. And the other 'revelations,' with . . . one exception, came at times when I was preoccupied with household tasks and not even thinking about religion.

Thus, Linda was certainly not consciously desirous of the two turning-point experiences. She notes that she was in a skeptical frame of mind prior to both experiences and prior to the first experience was also utterly bored with religious ritual--a frame of mind and an attitude which, if not expressing hostility to God and religion, then certainly expressing a lack of interest. Since we obviously do not want to say that skepticism or boredom is a necessary condition for religious experience, we are going to have to move to the level of the unconscious if we wish to dig up a plausible necessary condition. *Socrates* is enough to do-in this move, but perhaps we can look at the more detailed explanation which may be given in the case of Linda.

Linda's first experience, in particular, just seems to come out of the blue—it is totally unexpected. Here is Linda, bored to the limit by the ritual of the church, yet the ritualistic statement "The Lord be with you" is the catalyst for feeling the

"Lord's" presence. Is there any indication that something is going on unconsciously—that, e.g., she really has a deep desire for the "Lord"? Her skepticism about God would indicate otherwise. Or perhaps she feels guilty about her skepticism and boredom, so that she overcomes them by feeling the sense of presence. *Plato* does-in this suggestion. In other words, there is no evidence of guilt over her skepticism and boredom, and thus no reason to journey down the guilt path. Besides, even if guilt were present, mere belief in God would do the trick of relieving guilt. Why, then, a sense of presence, a considerable overdose for the supposed affliction?

The second experience is no less difficult to account for either on the conscious or unconscious level. Linda has just concluded that Jesus was a man suffering from delusions of grandeur, a conclusion hardly likely to inspire faith in Jesus as Savior and Lord; yet she inexplicably feels "over-awed by a strong sense of a presence." Did she unconsciously desire to encounter this Jesus whom she considered deluded? We can certainly imagine Linda wishing that Jesus were other than "a man suffering from delusions of grandeur," wishing that he was, indeed, what the church proclaimed Him to be, divine Lord and Savior; in fact, Linda probably did wish this, for she says that her conclusion concerning Jesus was a "sad conclusion." Yet wishing that something is other than it is remains far removed from desiring to experience the something—far removed, I should say, both consciously and unconsciously. Certainly, we can continue to insist on an unconscious desire, but the insistence remains a hollow possibility apart from any evidence of unconscious desire. As I already mentioned, the appeal to the unconscious does not relieve us of the requirement to produce evidence, for if there is unconscious desire, we should expect to find evidence of it in some sphere or other (dreams, free association, slips of tongue, and so on). Linda's report is too incomplete to make a clear-cut judgment about the unconscious; moreover, not much can be done now to fill in the gaps, unless, e.g., she kept a diary of her dreams before and after her experiences. One area of investigation would be to probe the unconscious of people in the process of religious growth. At any rate, we do not have probes of Linda. We have a very truncated account, which, as it stands, provides no evidence of unconscious desire or guilt.

I also note that in both experiences Linda feels a sense of presence before she surrenders. Someone might suggest that surrender is a necessary condition of a religious experience, yet surrender for Linda (specifically mentioned in the account of the second experience) comes after the sense of Presence. A possible ploy is to say that Linda had really surrendered unconsciously before she surrendered consciously. I shall simply let the principle behind *Socrates* take care of this ploy, and if something further is desired, I shall note that the ploy is question-begging.

Will

Will, a graduate of Purdue University in electrical engineering and with an MS from UCLA, considered himself to be scientifically oriented and analytical of mind. He had dropped out of church when a teenager and had acquired the reputation of being an atheist. In his early twenties he met some Christians who were intent on bringing about his conversion and who succeeded in getting him to participate in a Bible study and, finally, to attend their church. Their efforts brought him to the point of entertaining the possibility of God's existence.

On an Easter Sunday morning he attended their church, leaving in a disturbed state, disturbed largely because he did not see himself getting anywhere by approaching religion intellectually. That evening he had his TV on, watching the movie "Jesus of Nazareth," when, seeing the scene of the soldiers nailing Jesus to the cross, he exclaimed, "My gosh, they're nailing my Lord to the cross." Immediately he felt a wave or rush of the presence of God. At the time, he was lying on the floor, his head propped on his elbows; however, the rush of God's presence knocked him flat. He felt the love of God, the reality of God. He sensed that God was a person and that he was in contact with God. He notes that the experience was very emotional, although, according to him, he is not an emotional person. Says he, "My lack of emotion just drives my wife up the wall." The result of the experience was, according to him, that he stopped living for himself—he accepted "God's morality," and received the motivation to start living up to it.

Will was obviously on a search, but he was just as obviously not desiring an experience of the sort he had. He was searching for answers, a state which is not the same as desiring an encounter with God. Moreover, many people who are searching for answers either do not get answers or simply come to a state of faith without experiencing the presence of God. Thus, searching is anything but a sufficient condition for a religious experience. It is also not a necessary condition: We have come across numerous people who were not searching.

We might suppose that Will had unconsciously accepted Christ before his experience, the reason being that his words, "They're nailing my Lord to the cross," are a sort of slip of the tongue. He was, in effect, expressing what he had already worked out on the unconscious level. The question, then, is why he did not have some kind of experience at the time he unconsciously worked things out. Or perhaps the unconscious working out was accomplished at the point that he said the words. We have no evidence that this was so, and it is more parsimonious just to suppose that everything happened strictly on the conscious level. His exclamation, "My gosh, they're nailing my Lord to the cross," represents the culmination of his conscious struggle. At any rate, the question is why he had the extraordinary experience of God's presence and love. Coming to belief or acceptance of Christ does not require an experience of God's presence that knocks one flat. Moreover, if the supposition about working things out unconsciously is to the effect that acceptance or surrender is either a sufficient or necessary condition for religious experience, enough material has already been presented to show otherwise.

In sum, then, Will did not seem to desire the experience. If he was contemplating accepting Christ, that is not equivalent to desiring an experience of Christ's presence. Interestingly enough, his experience was of God's presence, not Christ's presence.

Diane and Tricia (3690)

Diane and Tricia, both age sixteen, were out skiing one night when, standing before a clump of birch trees, they both at the same time ran up to the trees, hugged them, laughing all the time, aware as they hugged the trees of Something more deeply diffused in nature but not personal. They said of the experience: "It was the nearest you could get to wrapping your arms round the whole world and giving it a big hug." They had a sense of oneness with the world and felt that there was a Something from outside which "sort of let us know it was there." They felt that they were receiving a gift and that therefore the Something had to be personal in a sense. (The conclusion here looks more like a reflection on the experience afterward than of what was sensed at the time of the experience.)

Both girls were in college at the time they were interviewed and seemed to be fairly sophisticated young women. They reported that at the time of their experience they were both avowed atheists, as were their parents. At the time of their interview they were confident that they had encountered a Something, but they had not developed any interest in traditional religion and apparently did not have an interest in investigating or pursuing further the Something they had experienced.

Since both girls were atheists at the time of their experience, we may presume that they were not considering God, searching for God, interested in God, and certainly not desiring, either consciously or unconsciously, to encounter God. The fact that they were skiing, skiing at night, would be a further reason for thinking that they were not searching for God or desiring an experience with God—they were out having a good time, preoccupied with the joys of skiing, not the existence of God. Yet looking at a standard mountain scene, not even a scene described by them as beautiful (it may have been very beautiful, but their feelings were not of beauty, for they say nothing about beauty), triggered an awareness of a Something that was both "from outside" and diffused through all nature. The fact that at the time of reporting their experience they had not done much about it indicates that the experience was something of an anomaly in their lives. The experience had come out of the dark of night, had left them open-mouthed, had knocked the atheism out of them, but had not done much more. This fact alone seems to falsify any appeal to unconscious desire. If unconscious desire to encounter God had been present, we would presume that it was part of a larger desire to know and understand God or to resolve something on the unconscious level. The experience did not seem to be the catalyst for anything other than the abandonment of their atheism.

Of course, what is unusual about this experience is that both girls responded simultaneously in the same way. One explanation could be that either one girl was cueing on the other or the unconscious desire for God—for which the evidence is negative—operated in both in the same way at the same time. As for unconscious desire, I have already addressed that possibility, although I shall additionally call in *Socrates*. As for one girl cueing on the other, this would require very strong dependency of one on the other, something which was not reported by the interviewer but would likely have been obvious, I should think, in the interview. Moreover, my view is that the natural reaction of one friend to another's running up to and putting her arms around a tree, laughing all the while, would be a puzzled, astonished, "Have you lost your mind?" or something of the like— not imitation. What we seem to have here is two people experiencing a transcendent Something at the same time, just as we had a number of people at the church meeting sensing the Holy Spirit and becoming immensely amused. The idea that religious experience is strictly individualistic, the same content never occurring at the same time to people who are together, just does not seem to be true. Of course, we have numerous accounts in the Christian Scriptures of what we might call "group experiences," such as the coming of the Spirit to the disciples on the Day of Pentecost.

The failure of Diane and Tricia to do much with their experience reminds us of the others we have come across who did not respond to their religious experience—could not figure it out and did not integrate it into their lives. Behaving in such a manner seems to be a very forceful piece of evidence that the people were not desirous of the experience, consciously or unconsciously. If the reply is that the experience turned out to be different from what the persons desired and hence they did not accept it into their lives, then at least we have shown that the desire to experience a religious Object is not a sufficient condition for experiencing the Object. Moreover, if people stop trying after one failure, they reveal that their desire was rather weak.

Summary

In this chapter we have considered people who were agnostic or atheistic at the time of their experience, and therefore people who obviously did not consciously desire the experience they had. We have also seen that an appeal to the unconscious is without merit, even using the mixed model of the unconscious developed in this chapter.

Chapter Four

The Explanation From Desire and From Unconscious Motivation: Three Special Cases

In this chapter I shall continue to consider the explanation from desire, concentrating on three cases for which I have more and better information than for any other cases.

1. Tim

The first case concerns Tim, a California boy whose home was in Hemet, an avid surfer from age thirteen, and into drugs at age fourteen. He came from a very religious home, his father being a Pentecostal minister, who, naturally enough, required Tim to go to church each Sunday. Tim did not develop any enthusiasm for church, saying that it was "just a big drag," such a drag that at age fourteen he essentially broke from church. Actually, he had stopped attending church at age eleven because there was not a church of the family's particular persuasion in Hemet (Tim's father at this time had entered the field of evangelism, so that he was not a minister of a particular church); but the break in mind and spirit came at the later time, when he also started using drugs.

Tim began with marijuana, moving on fairly quickly to a whole range of other drugs—uppers, downers, LSD, STP, peyote. He especially went for the psychedelics because he believed that through them he could get beyond the natural, the rational—reach into the supernatural. He was looking for more than ordinary existence offered, for a trip to the golden shores of the trans-normal, to the shores where satisfaction and meaning would meet him, to the shores which consistently eluded him.

Within a short time he started shooting speed, and even heroin, although he used heroin very little because it affected him as a downer. Speed, however, he went for because it produced a high which changed his character, giving him confidence, even releasing him from a slight stuttering problem which he had experienced since childhood and still experiences.

By age seventeen, living strictly for the high of drugs, he dropped out of school, lost interest in surfing, and became physically debilitated, losing considerable weight and strength, so that he could not have surfed if he had wanted to. He overdosed numerous times, contracted hepatitis, was in and out of hospitals, and became more and more of a physical wreck. Yet he did not change because for him the meaning of life consisted entirely in being on a constant high. Even though a number of his friends died from drug overdoses, he continued to use drugs, regularly risking an overdose for that daily high.

Tim's parents tried to help him, not letting up, sometimes making things difficult for him because they would report to the police any information they picked up from Tim about drug parties and drug pushing, with the result that the drug pushers became very unfriendly with Tim.

First Experience

On August 22, 1969, at a farmers' fair in Hemet, Tim was given a pill by some people he had met only a couple of times. He was leery about the pill but was ready to take whatever he could get his hands on— he wanted that high. About sixty minutes after taking the pill he started on a trip, one which he definitely wished he were not on. He had been tripping out four to five times a week, with a few trips being "bummers"; but this was really a bummer, not like any he had experienced before. He started having difficulty breathing and swallowing, with the result that for the first time during the entire course of using drugs he became afraid, afraid that he was going to die.

With fear in his soul, sitting on a park bench, alone, Tim had an experience which completely changed his life.

> It was about midnight. I was out there all by myself. And this force or being or whatever, spoke to my heart—wasn't a voice that I heard with my ear, but it was down in my heart. And it spoke to me and said, 'This is me.' And I said, you know, I said to myself, 'Me who?' At first I thought that this was just part of the drug too, part of my trip; I'd

finally found what I'd been looking for. But the being spoke to my heart and said, 'This is me. My grace and my mercy have kept you these years. But this is it. This is the last call.' You know, I thought, 'Well, what am I supposed to do? Am I gonna die?' All this conversation was goin' on inside me. 'Am I gonna die, then? Am I goin' back to the hospital and I'm not gonna come out this time?' And it seemed like the Presence said, 'Yes, but you can turn to me. You know, I'm here.' So... I did!... This being, that I felt like was Go... I felt that he was communicating with me, I felt that he was giving me a call, he was having mercy on my life, he was reaching out to me. I wasn't reaching out to him at all; he was reaching out to me.

The Absence of Conscious Desire

The last words are directly to the point of this section. Tim was aware that he had not reached out to "this force or being or whatever," but that it had reached out to him. It intruded into his thoughts, his heart, his life, while he was on a bad trip, his thoughts focused on how bad the trip might get, on whether he was ever going to get off the trip or simply ride on out of this life. Although Tim initially thought that perhaps the "trip" was drug-related, he immediately rejected that notion. In another report he states that the "Force or Being or Whatever" intruded with such an overwhelming sense of reality that any thought of the experience being less than genuine simply was driven from his mind. He says that he did not even think of the possibility of hallucination because he knew he was in the presence of reality—testimony of some significance inasmuch as Tim had been on drug trips practically daily and had hallucinated many times. He was thoroughly convinced that this was neither a drug trip nor hallucinatory. Certainly, what went on was not hallucinatory in any strict sense, for Tim definitely did not have any visual or auditory experiences, the words being to his "heart."

Tim is insistent that he was not thinking about God, was not considering God as a way out of his terror, was not praying for God's help. He was just plainly frightened, wondering whether "this was it"; i.e., these were his thoughts until—until the Voice spoke from within. Tim, then, was clearly not consciously desiring any sort of religious experience, not to mention the one he had. He says that although he was raised in a church which emphasized experience with God and in which many people had experiences with God, the form of his experience, God coming to him with the words 'This is me', was not something he had ever come across.

An Explanation from the Unconscious

But perhaps the Voice from within was his unconscious. The following account seems reasonable at first glance. Tim was afraid of dying, the fear forcing him to the realization, at least unconsciously, that his drug life must—absolutely must—come to an end. He says, "I just knew that if I didn't do something that night, it was over for me. I knew that my number was up." But how do something? Where would he find the resources to reverse course? In God, of course. Thus, the unconscious surfaced in consciousness by way of a voice, the voice of God, a being that Tim would recognize as a source of power great enough to get him out of his drug dependency. I am assuming here, following the model of the mixed unconscious, an unconscious working in tandem with the conscious self. In Tim's case the unconscious took a form which Tim consciously would recognize and find useful, viz., the form of God. What was essential in Tim's experience was the recognition that he absolutely must change, the resolution to change taking the form of submission to God, a being powerful enough to effect the change.

We should observe, first of all, that the account just given is non-Freudian as it stands. We could make it Freudian by referring to life (eros) and death (thanatos) impulses, saying that the life impulse asserted itself over the death or destructive impulse. How it did so would remain to be explained; i.e., how on this occasion the life impulse won the struggle or how or why it should express itself as the voice of God is anything but clear. Indeed, how and when the life impulse asserts itself over the death impulse is not clear in Freudian theory generally.

However, since I am following the mixed model of the unconscious, a model which, as I noted, I consider far more powerful than the Freudian, I may move beyond the consideration of impulses, appealing instead to the unconscious as a locus for the rational development of solutions to problems of the self; thus, I need not stumble over the very logical, rational way in which the unconscious supposedly works out the dilemma facing Tim. I note that the explanation is not strictly an explanation from unconscious desire. We could say that Tim was unconsciously desiring to get off drugs, even though he was not conscious of the desire. Again, his preoccupation was fear—the fear of dying. However, Tim's unconscious desire on this account would obviously not be a desire for religious experience. As I said, though, explanations from the unconscious need not be limited to desire, and I shall not presume that they are.

The main problem with the explanation offered is that it does not explain why any move to the unconscious is necessary at all, for Tim had no reluctance to consider God and turn to God. Although Tim had little use for religion in his youth, he was not negative about God, at least at the time of his experience. He observes that about a month before his experience, while in the psychiatric ward of a hospital, a couple of young fellows from Teen Challenge, a Christian drug rehabilitation group, came to visit him at his mother's request. They talked to him and left a Bible with him. In spite of the fact that Tim was the son of a minister, he had never read the Bible. On this occasion he began to read the Gospel of John and says, "I really began to trip out on the first chapter of John, thinking, `This is really neat; this is heavy stuff. God! Wow!'" But when he got out of the ward, he went right back to his old trips, not thinking any more about the "neat," "heavy stuff" he had read. The main point, of course, is that Tim did not have an aversion to God. In addition, Tim had called on God before. E.g., one time he was in jail, prayed to get out, made all sorts of jail-house vows, and then promptly forgot every vow when he did get out of jail.

The question, then, is why Tim did not merely turn to God, surrender to God, throw himself on the mercy of God? Why should not everything take place on the conscious level? The fact is that Tim came to strong belief in God—but he came to strong belief by way of sensing a Presence that confronted him as real. We may certainly say concerning Tim—indeed, he would be the first to say it—that if he had thought his experience was like a dream (he did consider the possibility that it was a drug effect), he would have walked away from it, thinking, as do most people, that perhaps our dreams say something about us, about our thoughts, fears, hopes, and wishes, but they do not tell us what is happening in the world outside our individual consciousness. All of Tim's conscious decisions during and after the experience— e.g., the decision immediately after his experience to go to his parents and find the "this is Me" God, the decision to get off drugs, and the decision to live a life devoted to God—were a function of, were dependent in his mind, on the reality of his experience, on God having really confronted him, spoken to him. Perhaps his decisions were causally irrelevant—i.e., perhaps what was going on at the conscious level was something of an epiphenomenon of what was going on at the unconscious level, the causally significant level. This would leave his decisions causally irrelevant, a view which is not congenial even to many forms of determinism, forms in which decisions figure as links in the causal chain leading to action. In any case, we should have to specify the crucial causal processes going on at the level of the unconscious and produce the evidence for the processes.

I am going to take the following position: If a person says, "The reason I decided to change my life is that p." (p in Tim's case would be, "I sensed God's reality"), then the presumption is that p is at least a necessary condition for the decision to change. This presumption can be overridden only by specific evidence that p was not a necessary condition. What is especially important to note is that resorting to the unconscious does not necessarily rule out p as a necessary condition. In fact, saying that the sense of Presence is a consequence of the unconscious is not inconsistent with saying that sensing a Presence as real is a necessary condition for a decision to change—or at least was so in Tim's case. However, there are several objections to saying that the unconscious generates the sense of Presence. Already I have noted two major objections. I shall summarize them and then introduce a third objection.

Three Objections to an Explanation from the Unconscious

The first objection concerns what I have called the "ornamental effect," the unconscious doing more than is necessary by introducing a Presence as real. If conviction of God's reality were necessary for Tim to change, the question is why the unconscious did not simply bring about strong conviction, without producing a sense of Presence—an unconscious able to do the latter could certainly do the former. Of course, conviction of God's reality is generally not necessary for change—indeed, change probably takes place most commonly apart from strong conviction about God. Conviction of God's reality normally follows from, does not precede, change perceived as from God. Most alcoholics who follow the AA Twelve Steps program turn to a Higher Power in sheer desperation, not with strong conviction, with the conviction concerning the reality of the Higher Power growing as sobriety persists and personal growth takes place. Thus, conviction of God's reality is generally not necessary for change, and we do not have the slightest reason to think that Tim was an exception to this general rule. Yet the main point is that even if conviction of God's reality were necessary in Tim's case, conviction could be produced directly, without introducing a sense of Presence. Indeed, the unconscious could directly produce a strong resolution to change, God not even entering the picture by way of a sense of Presence or strong belief or weak belief. The conscious self would certainly welcome such a resolution, finding it a strong confidence-builder.

Yet perhaps the unconscious regularly ornaments. Already I have spoken to this possibility. I shall simply emphasize the following. What we need to avoid is a hypothesis saying that the unconscious ornaments in the case of God-consciousness alone. That sort of hypothesis is egregiously *ad hoc* and because *ad hoc* also non-parsimonious. But, as I have maintained, we do not seem to find anything like the ornamental effect outside of religious experience, or if we come close to the effect, as in hallucination, the hallucination is easily recognized as such and does not resolve dynamic issues or act to enhance life value. (I introduce the reminder that the Freudian unconscious cannot be considered capable of producing a sense of divine Reality, for the Freudian unconscious consists of basic impulses and repressed, i.e., toxic, material from consciousness. The Freudian unconscious is not in the business of getting impulses integrated into life or of detoxifying the toxic material.) Moreover, even if something like the ornamental effect occurs outside of God-consciousness, I do not know of any principled explanation of its occurrences, i.e., an explanation which unifies under a single principle the various expressions of the ornamental effect. We might suggest the principle that the unconscious is creative and inclined to variety, so that it chooses from any of a variety of creative alternatives likely to work in a person's life. I do not find support for a principle of this sort; moreover, the continuing problem is why, as nowhere else in the workings of the unconscious, the individual is left with a sense of the reality of the experienced Object, a sense which remains even after critical reflection.

The second objection concerns lack of explanation—mystery. I.e., if we cannot explain why the unconscious does what it does (e.g., ornaments), and why it does so at the time it does rather than earlier or later, then we have to say that it just does— somehow, someway. Why, e.g., did the unconscious wait until Tim's life was threatened? Why not an earlier presentation of a Presence, say, two years before? Without principled answers to these questions, answers which I do not think we have, we are left with as much mystery as we began with. In short, we have explained nothing, at least scientifically, or even quasi-scientifically.

Now I wish to develop a third objection, which really amounts to an additional twist to the first objection. If God-consciousness is strictly a product of the unconscious, then the unconscious is presenting as real that which is not real, and thus the unconscious is engaging in deception. But why suppose that the unconscious deceives—systematically deceives—in the case of God-consciousness? Indeed, if the unconscious deceives about God, why should it not deceive about a whole array of items, including theorizing about the unconscious? What confidence, then, could we have in our theories of the unconscious or in psychotherapy? An essential aspect of any therapy involving appeal to the unconscious is patient insight, which largely depends on therapist insight. We should never be able to trust the insights of either if the unconscious were prone to deception. Naturally, the fact that the therapist has been through therapy is useless, for the therapist's insight would be dependent on another therapist, who may have been deceived by his unconscious, and so on *ad infinitum*. Or why not suppose that the unconscious systematically deceives in the case of sensory perception? The reason for not supposing any of this is PC—more exactly, it is PC and the absence of any principle of equal rational weight countering PC (a principle to the effect, e.g., that the unconscious systematically deceives us in all spheres of cognition—shades of Descartes' demon!). But if we go with PC in its application to sensory perception (doxastic practice SP), then what reason do we have for not going with it in its application to religious experience? Certainly, not that the unconscious systematically deceives in the case of religious experience, for that is an *ad hoc* speculative possibility without the presumptive weight of PC as a general principle, a principle including application to religious experience.

Obviously, if we, without reason or evidence, say that the unconscious systematically deceives just in the case of God-consciousness, then we have an *ad hoc* hypothesis, a hypothesis accounting for the particular phenomenon of God-consciousness but nothing else. Being *ad hoc*, the hypothesis automatically complicates our overall theory of the unconscious, so that the theory becomes less parsimonious than otherwise. If we say that the unconscious deceives in other spheres besides God-consciousness, then we should need a principle connecting the spheres. E.g., assuming that the unconscious causes some deceptive sensory perceptions (some hallucinations), we do not hold that the unconscious systematically deceives with respect to all our sensory perceptions; otherwise, the epistemic status of all our sensory perceptions would be threatened. What psychological principle, then, connects the selective deception in sensory perception with the systematic deception of God-consciousness? I do not know of any principle. The reasonable parallel between hallucinations and religious experience seems to be the following: As hallucinations are selective deceptions within the total sphere of sensory perceptions, so certain sorts of religious experience (some criteria for them will be presented in Chapter Eight) are selective deceptions within the total sphere of religious experience. Thus, turning to hallucinations for a parallel to systematic deception in the sphere of religious experience is simply a wrong turn.

The upshot is this: The notion of an unconscious which does not deceive but works in harmony with the standards of the rational self leaves us with a far more simple, coherent view of the self than the notion of an unconscious which deceives and does not cooperate with the conscious self in the case of religious experience. Suppose that we focus on the sense of conviction that is present in most, if not practically all, religious experience. We have found many who emphasized that in their religious experience they knew as they knew nothing else, that they were definitely not hallucinating or dreaming, that they were not cooking their experience in any sense, that their experience was even self-validating. Why not view all the claims to assured cognitive apprehension as ways in which the unconscious underlines the propriety of taking the experience to be of the Real? Conscious and unconscious are in agreement. Certainly, we posit agreement in the case of dreams—I wake up and just know that I am not dreaming, am thoroughly convinced that the trip I took around the world never did really occur, and never get it in my mind that all this is just deception by the unconscious. Why not take the same approach in the case of religious experience? The total self agrees that an encounter with an objective Real is taking place; the total self affirms that whatever rational criteria are present at the deepest level are fully met. Why suppose that in the case of religious experience the unconscious is deceiving us and going to great lengths to do so, producing convictions stronger in many cases than what we have with respect to other items of our experience, including sense perception? In short, why abandon a coherent, simple view of the self for one which can be made coherent only by tacking on *ad hoc* hypotheses to explain why the unconscious arbitrarily goes off on a deceptive track in the case of religious experience? I cannot come up with a good reason.

I also enter the reminder of the experiments done by Winson on dreams, experiments which tend to support the view that the unconscious works in conjunction with the conscious to resolve life problems, not doing so in any sort of deceptive manner. And again I note that the sense of reality associated with religious experience is not anything like the symbolism of dreams. Even if dreams are deceptive, they are so only because we do not understand the symbolism. In the case of a sense of reality, a deep conviction of truth, we are not concerned with symbolism at all; or if in some attenuated sense we are, then the same applies to sensory perception, memory, and so on.

The sum of the matter is this: The explanation of religious experience by way of a deceptive unconscious spells nothing but trouble and would, I think, be better left on the shelf, not to be dusted off again.

Guilt

I return, then, to Tim's experience and other explanations from the unconscious. Perhaps we could try an explanation in terms of guilt—conscious guilt, first of all. In brief, Tim knew that he had "sinned"; moreover, sin in a Pentecostal setting is represented as having very dire consequences; Tim feared the consequences of his sin, especially since he thought he was dying; therefore, he turned to God.

Yet Tim's conscious problem was not with guilt but with fear of dying, a fear which hardly necessarily equates with guilt and fear of judgment. Many people who do not believe in an afterlife fear their death—they simply do not wish to leave this life, either because it is very good or because it is very bad (and they want further tries) or because it is somewhere inbetween. Similarly, many religious people who give every evidence of forgiveness and freedom from guilt still fear death, desiring, say, to remain with an existence they know something about. (We shall observe this in the case of Terri, below.) In Tim's case guilt just does not seem to have been present in his consciousness. Moreover, his experience concerns guilt only peripherally; i.e., the experience is not essentially an experience of forgiveness, of being cleansed. It is an experience of a merciful God that calls Tim to change. In the further experiences of the hours following the midnight experience, the same thing may be said: Forgiveness is at best on the periphery of the experience; what is central is Tim's overwhelming sense of God's love. Yes, Tim asks for forgiveness, but he then mentions nothing about feeling cleansed or released from guilt. It is as if asking forgiveness is part of the formula for repentance, a standard element of what the potential convert is expected to do in the religion Tim was familiar with. Besides—and I underscore this point—guilt may be resolved, forgiveness may be experienced, apart from a sense of Presence, and for most people this is how forgiveness is experienced. Thus, we again are back to asking: Why the sense of Presence?

Oedipal Guilt or Conflict

Suppose, however, that we take a Freudian tack, saying that Tim's guilt (we have, as noted above, no evidence for any special problem of guilt in Tim) was rooted in conflicts with his father, sexual conflicts going back to the oedipal stage. We shall see shortly that there was something of a resolution of conflict between Tim and his parents during an experience following the midnight experience. However, there is no evidence that the conflict was rooted in an oedipal conflict from childhood. First of all, we do not know that there even was such a conflict, and we may not say that there must have been because all males go through the oedipal stage and the conflicts associated therewith. That is a theoretical position which does not, according to what I have seen, find support either in cross-cultural studies or in evidence from Western culture. Tim may have had oedipal conflicts, and admittedly we do not have the kind of evidence from him which would come through psychoanalysis or other procedures which presumably get at oedipal issues. Our evidence is limited, and limited to conscious reports, a deficiency present in all the accounts I consider.

However, sticking with the evidence we have, I find difficulty in saying that Tim was even in conflict with his father. Tim says that his father was a fairly harsh, demanding person. Yet Tim says, "I didn't have all that much to do with my father. My father never spent a whole lot of time with me, but I don't know that it registered with me. I don't remember feeling the resentment that I felt later." After his religious experience, after he had his own family and began to relate to his own son, he began to feel strong resentment toward his father for the lack of attention in childhood, a lack of attention associated to some degree with his father's role as a minister— he was often away from home. However, in boyhood Tim apparently did not feel strong resentment. He sums up the situation in this way: "We didn't hate one another; we just didn't know one another."

Thus, if we are to say that Tim had conflict with his father, the conflict was mild at the most. In a way, Tim just sort of tuned out his family, especially as he entered his teen years. At home he conformed to the rules, but outside he went his own way, thereby living a kind of double life but thereby also avoiding any serious conflict. Perhaps the tuning out masked a deeper conflict, yet we have no evidence that it did. At any rate, Tim did not finally settle his feelings about his father until later when, in the first years of fatherhood, he began to feel strong resentment toward his father.

Now if we suppose that strong resentment had been buried in Tim through all the years, being a hangover from unresolved oedipal resentment in childhood, then we shall have to say that the midnight experience did not really resolve any of the oedipal conflicts and guilt in his life. Thus, the unconscious, in presenting Tim with a divine Presence, really was not accomplishing what it set out to accomplish. According to the explanation under consideration, guilt rooted in oedipal conflict was supposed to be the underlying dynamic of the midnight experience, with the presentation of a divine Presence being the means of resolving the guilt and the associated oedipal conflicts. The problem is, the explanation also takes an oedipal approach to Tim's later resentment, a tack which requires us to say that everything else got accomplished by the midnight experience—Tim got off of drugs and started a totally different kind of life—except the main thing the unconscious was trying to accomplish. Moreover, Tim's strong resentment arises when he becomes a father, not when his son is in the oedipal stage, a period which seems more likely to be the catalyst for deep unresolved oedipal issues in Tim. And then, as we shall see, the apparent resolution takes place without anything like the sense of divine Presence. Our explanation seems to be drifting further and further away from the plausible.

A more plausible explanation of the resentment—certainly more parsimonious—is that Tim never really realized how he was neglected until he became a father, at which time he realized the nature and extent of his father's neglect, and resented it. In any case, what finally happened, in Tim's words, is, "I just forgave him for not being what I thought a father should be. I just forgave him that, just accepted him." If this has anything to do with oedipal issues, then the trail of the issues has certainly become very faint—or so it seems to me. When a son resolves a conflict arising from jealousy of his father and rebellion against the father's demands, he hardly does so by forgiving the father, the person whose demands or commands were supposed to be followed and whose demands—many of them, certainly the demand against incest—remain consistent with the son's present morality. In other words, if the conflict has oedipal roots, I should think that the son would feel some sense of having done wrong, some sense of guilt, so that if forgiveness enters the picture, it should be the father forgiving the son, not *vice versa*. If we are going to save the explanation, then we shall have to go for something like a reaction formation. I see little need to comment on this move. At any rate, Tim says that he forgave his father; and apparently he did, for afterward he and his father got along well, and when his father died in

1987, Tim did not feel guilt or regret—just the opposite, for during the twelve hour drive to the family home, he said that he felt communion with his father, felt the presence of his father.

I note, as an aside, that Tim has not lived with resentment, letting it poison his family relationships. He has attempted to be a caring father and seems to genuinely enjoy being with his son. As a graduation present for his teenage son, he took him on a several week surfing journey up and down the Southern California coast.

Thus, we had better leave the attempt to explain explanation the midnight experience by way of oedipal dynamics. The evidence, as I have indicated, just is not favorable for such an explanation. We may tack the explanation on in spite of the absence of evidence, but one of the main points throughout this book is that we must be very leery of tack-on explanations.

I think we must say, then, that in the midnight experience nothing arises to indicate unconscious conflict with parents (oedipal or otherwise) or attempted resolution thereof. In fact, the experience was not an experience in which anything was resolved. Tim, indeed, resolved to turn to God, and that was something of a resolution of his relationship with God; but he was not certain how to finish what he started, leaving the park bench in order to seek help from his parents.

Whence the God of Tim's Experience?

What is obvious is that if Tim's experience was in some way a resolution of conflict with parents and a return to and submission to a parental figure, then the parental figure he returns to is very different from his parents—certainly from his distant, demanding father and also from his mother, who brooked no deviation from her religious norms. The God of Tim's experience came with courtesy, with the deferential introduction, "This is me," reminding Tim of His mercy, and then gently calling Tim to turn to Him, noting, however, that "This is it. This is the last call." We could read these last two statements as a threat, but I think that in the total context of the experience they come through more like the clarifying statements of a counselor: "Next time, Tim, you're going to kill yourself—so it's now or never." If there is harshness here, it is the harshness of reality.

Given the demanding, rigorous nature of Tim's parents, how did he end up with the kind of God he experienced? In fact, the God of his Pentecostal religion was a demanding God, a God that punished eternally in hell. Did Tim just end up with the kind of God he desired or wished for? We may assume that Tim wished for a God of total love. We may assume that most other people in our society wish the same. In both cases the wish is probably not very strong. Tim says that God was just not part of his thoughts, so his wish for a loving God could not have been very strong. The role of God for Tim was definitely not the role of God for William Blake, of whom Alfred Kazin says: "He did not believe in God; under all his artistic labors and intellectual heresies he seems to have thought of nothing else." (1970, 6) In contrast to Blake's preoccupation with God, Tim put God in a kind of box marked "Past"— Tim says that God was in a compartment in his past, a compartment which he gave little attention to. We have to say, then, that the wish for a loving God was not strong on the conscious level; therefore, without further evidence we have no reason to presume greater strength on the unconscious level. In short, we have no evidence to presume anything other than a wish, a weak wish, that God were loving.

The question is: How could this weak wish get translated into a powerful experience of a merciful God? How could a weak wish *that* God be loving get translated into a powerful, life-changing *experience of* a loving God? In most other people with a similar wish to Tim's the translation does not happen. Most people, I should say, are burdened by their harsh God, who is often nothing but a mirror of their harsh parents. Some escape the harsh deity by simply jettisoning religion altogether. Most, though, never seem to free themselves from the harsh, unbending deity, whether they are active in religion or not. They participate in the rituals of forgiveness, but the rituals just remind them of how wicked they are and of how much punishment they deserve. A simplistic turn to unconscious desire is not going to account for a religious experience of the sort Tim had, for such a turn to the unconscious glosses the realities just mentioned. In fact, given a weak wish and the ineffectiveness of weak wishes, we are left again with an unconscious which produces religious experience mysteriously—somehow, someway.

Second Experience

After his midnight experience Tim resolved to find this God that spoke to him. Since he did not know anybody who knew God better than his parents, he went home, told his parents what had happened, and spent the rest of the night in prayer and conversation with them. This was hardly a homecoming, a running to his parents to let them know

The Explanation From Desire and From Unconscious Motivation 157

that he was no longer alienated from them. It was, instead, an attempt to complete with God what had been started on the park bench.

Tim's account of the time with his parents is as follows.

> As we prayed, I surrendered my heart over to God. I called upon him for help, asked him to forgive me of my sins, come into my life. I felt God's reality—not the same strength, not the same intimacy [as on the park bench.] It was like—on the park bench it was like a face to face experience. Not that I saw anything. It was just like it was so real, and intimate. At home it was . . . there was like a sense of presence of God there in the room as we prayed. The real sense that came into that room as we prayed was a sense of love. For the first time in my life I felt like I experienced what love was. I saw my mother and father with eyes I'd never seen them with before. It's hard to explain what I felt. It was just love. It was like I was enveloped and baptized in love. I was just overwhelmed by this sense of love—that He loved me, that He is love, and that everything in the universe that has anything to do with real love is Him. The love of parents toward their children. I began to see my parents through the eyes of love, rather than being a restriction in my life, an authoritative figure. I had seen their attempts to help me get off drugs as an interference in my life. I saw them as continually interfering with me. . . . But that night as I felt the experience of love, I saw what they were doing as not out of any harm to me or restricting me in any way but because they loved me.

First of all I wish to note that in Tim's case, as in other cases we have looked at, surrender took place after his initial experience, so that the idea of surrender being a necessary condition for religious experience is simply without merit; and the idea that it is a sufficient condition has no more merit. I personally have been with numerous people who have surrendered themselves to God (some in anguish and desperation, and thus unquestionably with total conscious sincerity) without anything happening, the result for a number being that they just gave up on God.

The immediate question about Tim's experience in his home is why the unconscious should take the turn of love, baptizing him in love. What he needed was power to overcome his drug habit. Why not a sense of power, especially since the God of his early training was as much a God of power as of love? Tim's love even reached out to some drug dealers. He says,

> I had a real sense of love . . . even there was . . . I was in strife at that particular time with some other young men over dealings in drugs and stuff—it's an involved story involving some sales of drugs and

things; and I can vividly remember . . . wondering if I could see them because even the hatred in my heart for them was taken out; I didn't feel hate any more for those guys.

Most of the questions we may ask about Tim's second experience are repeat questions, and therefore I shall not ask them. I shall, however, focus on the fact that Tim's experience in his home was essentially of God's loving presence. If we resort to the the unconscious, then the unconscious is presenting as real that which is not real and that which does not seem necessary to resolve Tim's problem of drugs. That problem was resolved on the park bench. I repeat that nothing in psychotherapeutic theory or practice suggests that a false sense of Presence or false belief is likely to bring about theresolution of deep unconscious conflict. True insight into unconscious dynamics is the object in psychotherapy and is supposed to function as a necessary condition for resolution of unconscious issues. I make no different supposition for my mixed unconscious.

I also note that conflict resolution came after the experience of God's love—thoughts of love for parents certainly came after the park-bench experience, and in the home the feelings of love for parents and understanding of them came after the sense of being baptized in love. Moreover, I note that Tim's negative feelings about the interference of his parents do not seem disproportionate to the reality of Tim's life. Tim's parents had been interfering, had been making things difficult for him—indeed, their interference may have been the reason why Tim was given some bad "stuff." Thus, I do not think that we find here signs of some deep unconscious conflict—signs that we have also not found elsewhere in the experience. The main point, though, is that the conscious resolution of conflict did not precede, but followed, the experience of a loving God. Do we have any reason to suppose something different on the unconscious level? Do we have reason to suppose a reversal of the order? Not without evidence, which, in the present case, is not to be found. If we appeal to the Freudian unconscious, with its impulses independent of and often contrary to the conscious, we must still produce our evidence; in addition, we must remember that the Freudian unconscious is not even relevant at this point— we are talking about an unconscious capable of working out solutions to deep problems of the self.

Third Experience

Tim remained praying and talking with his parents until daybreak, and then he went out on the streets of Hemet, heading for the park where he had met God the night before.

I went back down to the park that morning, and it's like . . . I finally got on that trip I'd been looking for. I walked down the street of Hemet, Calif., at daybreak and watched the sun come up and watched the birds fly. It's like birds were flyin' around, and singin'—and I'm going, "Wow, I'm seeing for the first time." Something happened. I had this sense of companionship with the Creator who made all this. I was just communicating without even saying anything to this Power. I was at one with It for the first time in my life. I took this abstract God I'd been taught about in this sterile-type church setting and all of a sudden that morning I was introduced to Him out in creation . . . and I go, "Oh, this is the same God. This is You." And I looked around at the clouds and stuff, and it's just like everything was saying, "This is Me; I've introduced Myself to you, I love you. This is what you've been looking for all this time—is me." And I said, "But you're out here? you're not down there in the church building? this is you?" Religion for me was a compartment over here from my past that I just didn't deal with. As a Hippie and as a person using drugs I spent a lot of time in nature, enjoying nature as nature, but I didn't even put God into it. [But now in the park] . . . I did little dumb things like get down on the ground and pat the ground, pat the trees, and I said, "This is God." And I still carried with me the sense of love. . . . I just began to trip out on God from that moment on . . . and that's been twenty years ago. My whole life changed. From that moment on I didn't even go back and need any drugs. It was just like that, it was over. I just left them behind.

This daybreak experience is perhaps even more puzzling than Tim's midnight experience or the experience with his parents. If we suppose that Tim's fear of dying functioned as the catalyst for the midnight experience, what functioned as the catalyst for the morning experience? It seems to come serendipitously, a kind of delightful cadenza, capping off the earlier experience. Actually, Tim's very words were, "That was the cap on the whole thing for me." Was Tim desiring the experience? Not consciously. He seemed surprised at what happened, filled with wonder. He was meeting God in ways that simply shattered the old molds of thought. Indeed, the whole experience has a kind of pantheistic cast, with Tim saying things not commonly heard within the church— he pats the ground and trees and says, "This is God." His sense of God's immanence was far stronger than is normally expressed within Christian settings. Moreover—and this is the central point—the experience just came, rising in his consciousness as the sun rose in the morning sky, apart from his wishes or desires.

Yet perhaps the experience arose from the unconscious. But why? Why this addendum to the previous experiences? The experience was essentially confirmatory of the reality of a loving God. Yet the reality of God was strongly conveyed to Tim in the midnight experience. Getting up from the park bench, he had no doubt whatsoever about God's reality. He had been "face to face" with God. Why confirm what is not in the least subject to doubt? And what is the unconscious doing confirming the reality of God? Even supposing that the sense of God's reality represented the resolution of some unconscious problem, why a confirmatory experience? The fact is that Tim sensed God's reality so strongly on the park bench that neither of his other experiences compared to it. This would seem to indicate that the unconscious work had been done. Moreover, returning to what I view as the central problem, we must ask: Why disguise the real unconscious dynamics by means of a sense of God's presence? We should remember that in a Freudian interpretation disguising (as in dreams, slips of the tongue, and so on) serves to keep toxic material from conscious recognition and thus is not useful for detoxifying the material. But here we do not even have toxic material, for detoxification (of conflict, guilt, or whatever) has already taken place. Thus, why a sense of God's presence and companionship? And why would a mixed unconscious resort to this form of deception?

Supposing that Tim wanted a confirmatory experience, we have already seen that a desire of that sort is not in the least sufficient to produce the experience. We remember Nina, who desired confirmatory experiences very strongly but ended up with nothing. Further, the major work of change had taken place in the midnight experience and after it in prayer and conversation with his parents. As a consequence, we should not suppose a need for the experience or a desire beyond the desire to repeat a positive experience, so that need could not function as a necessary condition, and desire, if it were a necessary condition, would be very weak. A still further question is why the experience took on a pantheistic cast? What was behind that?

In sum, Tim's experiences from midnight through morning do not seem to be the result either of conscious or unconscious desire, guilt, parental conflict, or anything else of the sort.

2. Terri

I now move to the second case, that of a woman, Terri, who was in the latter stages of cancer, not expected to live more than a couple of weeks. For about three weeks she had been steadily becoming more and more incoherent, so that now she was almost constantly incoherent, making sense only on occasion. What was obvious, though, even in her incoherency, was her anger—anger at dying. The day after Christmas her husband, Walter, sat weeping by her side, as she lay on the sofa, her only response being a disgusted look and a few mumbled words to the effect, "Oh knock it off, Walter. Everything is all fucked up, and your crying isn't going to change anything." She had not been an angry woman--just the opposite; yet she was angry about dying. Life had been very good; she had found great happiness in her marriage to Walter; she wanted to grow old with him, her dominant vision of their old age being that of walking down the mall in the evening, arm in arm, looking in a shop here or there, sitting for awhile on a bench, conversing with one another, conversing with friends, and then capping off the evening with an absolutely wicked hot fudge Sunday. Although she was a woman of faith, the afterlife held little attraction for her because it was simply outside her experience. She knew this life; she had experienced it; it was good. She was angry about dying.

The next day in the evening she had gone to the table for dinner, starting to eat before anyone else had come to the table, behavior she would have abhorred in her normal state, for she was a woman of class. When the rest of the family members reached the table, they were not seated more than a moment before she threw up. Walter says that his sole remark was, "Oh boy!"

He took her to the bedroom, cleaned her up, and then made her comfortable, leaving the room when she seemed to be dozing off. He checked on her about every half hour, but she seemed to be in a deep sleep. About 10:15 he walked in to check again, this time turning on the light. Walter gives the following account of what he saw.

She was radiant, absolutely radiant. I immediately thought of the Scripture which spoke of Moses' face after he had come down from the mount, that his face shone— so brilliantly that he had to put on a veil. She was radiant—and I knew, absolutely knew, that she was coherent. Her eyes were focused; a smile was on her face. I said,

'Terri, Terri . . . what happened?'

And in a voice barely audible, as if she were off in another land—I know that I intruded on the experience—she said,

'Walter, I've been in God.'

'You've been in God? What do you mean?'

'I can't really say, Walter. I've just been in God. It's beyond description.'

Terri was a very articulate woman.

'But what were you doing? Were you praying or something?'

A very dumb question, since she had been incoherent.

'I don't know. I've just been in God. . . . You know, Walter, you have to go with the flow—not resist, just go with God.'

Terri was so elated with the experience that she called a number of friends, four of them coming over to share her joy.

That night she and I did not sleep a moment—we had far too much to share. And share we did—over at least the next six weeks. Not until shortly after Valentine's Day did Terri start to become incoherent again. As for her anger—the venom was drawn. A counselor had tried to do it over several months, without success, but her experience of God did the trick. She did not accept death any more than before, but her basic attitude was—I will not be alone; I shall be accompanied . . . by God.

The Absence of Conscious Desire

Since Terri was incoherent, we may presume that she was not desiring anything—or, if there was any desire underlying her confused state, it was the desire not to die. Whether the experience came upon her while she was asleep, awaking her, or whether she was awake when the experience came, Walter could not say because she could not say. All that she knew was that she had been in God, taken up into God, swept along, as in a mighty current. When Walter walked in, she was experiencing the afterglow of the experience, radiant, joyous, at peace. Walter says that he had, indeed, intruded, for she would have rung her bedside bell if the experience had been completed. But no bell, for she was lying joyous, awestruck at the breathtaking, indescribable Reality that had swept, powerfully, into her life. She had a sense of surrender—

but not to death. Her surrender was to God, and it came after, or with, her sense of being in God. In short, God swept her up in the current of His powerful Presence and love, and she just realized that she had to "go with the flow."

We may note that Terri's experience had something of an Eastern cast to it, further evidence that she was not desiring an experience of the sort she had. The metaphor of the great river, carrying all in its mighty flow, is not customary in Western thinking about God but is fairly common in the East. She was aware of the metaphor by way of reading literature with an Eastern flavor, but, according to Walter, she had never conversed about God along these lines. As a result, we may reasonably suppose that she did not have a desire for the kind of experience she had.

Explanations from the Unconscious

But was it likely that she had an unconscious desire for some kind of experience of God? Even though Terri was a deeply spiritual person, her most basic desire preceding the experience was to stay alive. She did not want to die and was visibly agitated at the prospects of death. Walter says that she seemed to have always known that she would not beat the cancer, that she would die, knowledge which never made the prospect of death any easier for her to accept. Indeed, she always hoped to hear that most beautiful of words for cancer patients, 'remission'—a hope never realized. At any rate, Walter says, "Clearly, clearly, in a hundred ways, she conveyed to me that, yes, she knew she would die." Really knowing, then, from the beginning that she would die, she had, all the same, felt the gift of peace, felt also the gift of happiness (the term 'gift' was hers), gifts which she explicitly recognized as coming from the "Source of every good and perfect gift." She had felt these gifts through many of the toughest times of her approximately four years of surgery and treatment. According to Walter, Terri was the prime example of Murphy's Law: If anything can go wrong, it will go wrong.

However, during the last year of her life the gifts of peace and happiness had largely slipped away, so that at the time of her experience she was agitated, lacking peace, lacking happiness. We can be fairly certain, then, that at some level of her being she desired a renewal of these gifts; yet to desire the gifts is not the same as to desire union with God. Further, if someone suggests that religious experience is usually a powerful source of peace and happiness, the reply is that religious experience is too powerful—i.e., it goes beyond what is needed. Terri had experienced peace and happiness previously without having a religious experience, without the peace and happiness being clearly associated with a sense of God's presence. Thus, we have no reason to suppose in Terri a desire for anything more than a restoration of the gifts of peace and happiness. To desire an experience of union with God would be to desire an additional gift, a gift hugely beyond the gifts of peace and happiness. Terri may have had the desire for that huge gift, but we have no reason to suppose so.

Guilt

But perhaps she was really angry with God, so that her experience is to be explained from the perspective of unconscious guilt. This supposition is highly suspect from the beginning because the experience had nothing to do with forgiveness, release from guilt, or cleansing. The experience could certainly be viewed as one of acceptance by God, yet acceptance is not necessarily related to guilt; moreover, the experience was more one of union with God than acceptance by. According to Walter, Terri never did report any feeling of acceptance.

As for anger toward God, Walter reports that yes, Terri was probably angry with God. She had expressed anger at God before, particularly during a period of intense suffering in the spring of the year. But the fact is that she expressed the anger and never thought anything about it because her view was that God is big enough to handle her, or anybody else's, anger. For her, says Walter, expressing anger at God was as normal and free from guilt as expressing anger at him. In other words, expressing anger at God simply indicated something very important about Terri's relationship with God—she remained as much herself in that relationship as she did in her relationships with other people. She did not acquire a new persona or a new language when she conversed with and about God. Walter reports that immediately after the experience, when they stayed up all night talking, she exclaimed, "God is going to have an awful lot of explaining to do." She had always been a questioning woman, unafraid of tough issues, unafraid of doubt, so why should questioning and doubt cease just because she had been in God? The experience had been an experience of God's presence, not an experience of answering her questions. The experience did not stop her mind; instead, it seemed to have stimulated it.

Thus, we do not have any evidence of problems with guilt. Walter says, "The woman was simply impossible to guilt-trip"; and she certainly could not be guilt-tripped about her exploration of the reality of God, an exploration which led her over the rough ground of questioning and doubt. Her doubt arose because she had a profound sense of God's love, and she just could not explain how many things that happened, including some of her suffering, were consistent with God's love. But all this questioning and doubting was for her very natural, a part of being human.

Walter says that he has never met a healthier soul. Perhaps he is idealizing his wife after her death, but checking with her friends substantiates the view that she was a very healthy, happy soul, not plagued by guilt or self-doubt, a person who was simply a joy to be around. Walter reports that friend after friend told him how Terri simply made them feel important, and that is why friends were always around the house, even as the smell of death became more and more recognizable.

Walter also reports that he and Terri often played dream games, usually at her initiation; i.e., she loved to talk about her dreams, trying to figure out what they meant. Walter, a person with more than an average lay knowledge of psychology, would interpret her dreams for her, usually without satisfying her. She always wanted more complicated interpretations than he offered. A simple frustration dream, arising, say, from frustration at work the day before, just had to have a deeper, more complicated meaning. At any rate, Walter says that he never found in her dreams anything indicating guilt. Walter is not a clinical psychologist or psychiatrist, yet his opinion at least bears mentioning.

One more item on the issue of guilt is worth looking at. Terri was not pleased about her treatment as a child. Her father and mother divorced when she was about six or seven, her father seeing her from then on only infrequently, her mother caring for her only intermittently, often shuttling her off to grandparents and sometimes other relatives. When Terri was with her mother, she would usually find herself home alone at night, her mother spending most nights on the bar circuit. According to Walter, Terri just did not want to have much to do with either parent, and hence we could say that she harbored some anger toward both. The anger certainly did not seem to be intense, for it manifested itself strictly as a lack of desire to maintain any close contact with either parent. Walter says that when she talked about them, she did not tense-up or go off on lengthy critical tirades. According to him, she simply did not feel any need to be around them, although she did visit with each occasionally, never, to Walter's memory, engaging in angry confrontations but just carrying on as usual.

Security

At any rate, the suggestion might be that Terri's anger towards God was an expression of her anger towards her father and that the experience of God's presence was both a resolution of her guilt over her anger towards her father and the achieving of the security of a fatherly relation. The problem with this suggestion is that it just flatly ignores the facts. Walter is insistent that Terri had no guilt about her feelings toward her father or mother. They botched their parental obligations, so that as far as she was concerned, she was perfectly justified in wanting to distance herself from them. They had never gone for closeness and would not understand any attempts at closeness in her adult life, so why should she try? At any rate, the whole explanation from guilt does not go, if for no other reason than that Terri did not feel forgiveness, and the God of her experience was not sensed as Father or Father-image. Again, the experience had almost an Eastern cast.

Further, assuming that, contrary to the facts, she had a fatherly security to achieve, she did not achieve that security, at least in a form she most needed at that time—security in the face of death. Death remained a fear for her, something she did not at all wish to go through. Her experience of God simply reminded her and assured her that she would not go through death alone. The lack of resolution of the issue of death was, says Walter, most clearly manifested in an event about two weeks before her death. One morning while one of her children was bathing her, she literally shouted, "I am not going to die! I am not going to die!" Walter says that those words, spoken while he was in the other end of the house, still ring in his ears. The point to note is that the unconscious—if it is offered as the explanation for Terri's experience—did not accomplish what she most deeply desired. Why not? The appeal to the unconscious is supposed to be an appeal to that which can accomplish what a person most deeply desires. Some people achieve security in the face of death—often apart from any religious experience. Why not Terri? Why on one occasion does the unconscious fulfill desire and on another not? We are left with an explanation which really does not explain, an explanation which leaves us with as much mystery as we began with.

Finally, we come again to the issue of ornamentation and deception, the unconscious resorting to a sense of God's presence and reality to resolve guilt (assuming, contrary to fact, that guilt was the problem) when belief in God's forgiveness would do that. The sum of the matter, then, is that an appeal to unconscious guilt is as much of a non-starter as the appeal to unconscious desire.

Reaction of Others to Her Experience

Walter reports that Terri was at first very motivated to tell the story of her experience, to share it with others. Very quickly, however, she reversed course, never talking about the experience except when asked to do so. The reason? She found that her Christian friends in particular responded to her story with stony silence, a silence which just astonished her. No questions, no probing, no signs of wonder, nothing. Terry was absolutely amazed; however, she was, says Walter, a very courteous woman, so that she quickly resolved to tell her story only to those who asked, usually people whom Walter describes as secular.

In the last chapter I observed that the desire for religious experience is not widespread in society, indeed, that there is really a general resistance to religious experience. The experience of Terri is indicative of the fact that the experience of God's reality is perceived by many, if not most, as a little too hot to handle. I use the last phrase intentionally. Pascal, the French mathematician, scientist, philosopher, writer, and much else, had an experience of God's reality one night at age thirty one, an experience which he never described in prose, although he was a man of words, his Provincial Letters having had a lasting effect on the style of French writing. All he did was write a few impressionistic words and phrases on a piece of paper, which he sewed into his cloak. One of the words was 'fire'.

Exactly what Pascal wanted to convey by the term 'fire' I cannot say. However, I offer a few thoughts about the notion of God as fire. Fire radically changes whatever it encounters, so that our first reaction is to distance ourselves from it, not remembering that the change may be in the form of energizing or purifying. W. H. Auden has said, "We would rather be ruined than changed." (Auden, 1946, 134) Even though a pedestrian religion leaves us bored and stunted in growth, we hang on to it because we do not know where the Fire will burn, or for how long, or with what result. More pointedly, we cannot control the Fire and hence are reluctant to let it in, even though Pascal and many others maintain that the name of the Fire is 'Love'.

Terri experienced resistance to the Fire, a resistance which was essentially on the unconscious level—i.e., if Terri had asked any of the religious folk who really did not wish to hear her story whether they were committed to God or whether they wished to grow spiritually, they would have strongly replied in the affirmative.

3. *Walter*

The story of Terri and Walter is not finished, though, because Walter, too, had an extraordinary experience of God's presence, God's loving, supporting presence.

About two years before Terri died both Terri and Walter went to a Christian conference center to participate in a half-week conference, led by a nationally-known minister. Terri was especially interested in going because she had read several books authored by the minister. Walter also was interested in going, mainly because Terri wanted to go and also because the conference center was in a beautiful setting.

The conference was conducted with considerable freedom, no pressure being placed on anyone to attend meetings. Walter, feeling the need for solitude, missed about half the meetings, taking hikes, fishing in the river, sitting alone by the water. On the last day of the conference Walter went to the scheduled morning meeting but says that he felt very distant. He says,

> I was happy—I mean, feeling OK—about what was going on, but I just didn't feel a part of it. I guess I was still in my solitude phase. I was observing everything but sort of thinking, 'That's for them, not for me.' And I felt OK about that; didn't feel left out at all.
>
> I guess things had been going on about a half hour when a verse of Scripture hit me, not any Scripture mentioned during the conference—'Rest in the Lord.' It seemed as if this Scripture was addressed directly to me. As I focused on the words, I had this sense of the total sufficiency of God—'sufficiency' is the word that came to mind and stuck in my mind throughout the experience. God is totally sufficient. I really didn't think of anything in particular that God was sufficient for—just that God was sufficient. And then all this sort of culminated in the sense of God's sufficiency, a sufficiency which seemed to roll over me like waves.

I had started weeping when the experience began, something that I had never done in a crowd before. I don't mean that I made any sounds—tears just started streaming down my face. I was totally overwhelmed with the sufficiency of God. Terri looked over at me but said nothing.

Throughout the experience I was asking myself what was going on. In fact, I said to myself, 'What the hell is happening? Nothing like this has ever happened before. I mean, I've never really experienced God or had anything that was a clear and definite sense of God's reality. And yet now this is happening to me. How come, particularly since I wasn't really into this meeting? Sure, I said some prayers for Terri, but what would that have to do with this experience?' So all these thoughts are going through my mind as I'm feelings waves of God's sufficiency.

I guess this experience lasted about a half hour—at least it was still going on when the meeting ended. Naturally, Terri wanted to know what had happened, and when I told her, the whole experience started over again, but with less intensity. The experience was repeated on a number of occasions throughout the next year, always with less intensity than the first time. I still can't figure out how it happened. But I'll tell you, it's been like a rock—no doubt in my mind about the sufficiency of God. During the remainder of Terri's illness and after her death—again and again I found God sufficient; I found the resources I needed.

Absence of Conscious Desire

Again we find that there is no conscious desire for the experience—Walter was not thinking about having an experience of God of God's sufficiency. His attention was focused on what was going on around him. Moreover, he emphasizes that he did not sense any great need of God's resources; or better, he knew that he needed divine strength to walk with Terri through her illness, but he was confident of that strength and believed that he had been receiving it. In fact, he and Terri had been managing—they attributed their "managing" to God's grace—to live well, to enjoy the present that was theirs, even though it often was in the hospital. Walter reports a very memorable day, a wedding anniversary in the hospital, two days after Terri had surgery. At the end of the day he and Terri looked at each other and said, practically simultaneously, "Wasn't this a beautiful anniversary?" They had also taken trips--one out of the country. Their friends were aware of how the flame of life burned brightly, not seeming to flicker at all. Thus, Walter maintains that he had no conscious sense that he needed some special divine shot-in-the-arm. But, he says, "I sure did get one. Oh yes I did!"

The Resort to the Unconscious

Given what Walter says, I find any appeal to the unconscious to be without merit. A major question is why the experience occurred at the conference. Walter felt a great sense of need when he first learned of the nature of Terri's cancer, its terminal nature. No experience then. During her last year, when the flame flickered, no experience then—just the memory of the experience at the conference—no longer even the mild repeats of the experience. If the unconscious responds to deep desires or needs, I should think that it would respond at the moments of greatest need or desire. We are left again with an unconscious the why's and wherefore's of which are a mystery. We simply jump from one mystery (Why the experience at the time it occurred?) to another (What principle does the unconscious follow?). In addition, we have the problems of ornamentation and deception.

Walter is very clear that he was open to religious experience; indeed, he classes himself as someone "in pursuit of God." "But long ago," he says, "I became aware that I wasn't going to produce any experience in myself, that I wasn't going to jerk any strings on God. So basically my mode was—well, to use Biblical language—that of waiting on God. But I'd been in that mode for years, decades, and nothing really happened." Thus, Walter was in a general mode of "waiting on God"; however, on the day of the experience, he certainly was not focused on waiting, was not praying for or consciously desiring at that time an experience of God's presence. We certainly do not want to say that a general state of openness to God is a necessary condition for religious experience, for the material on the agnostics has already falsified that thesis.

We may now summarize the conclusions from the three cases of this chapter. The cases provide strong falsification of the thesis that conscious or unconscious desire for a religious experience is a necessary condition for the experience. The cases also call into serious question other explanations of religious experience from unconscious motivation or work.

8. The Appeal to Need

The material of this chapter, along with material from the other chapters, also does-in, I should say, any thesis that religious experience is a function of need, conscious or unconscious. The need-thesis is, I should say, another form, a broader form, of the crisis-thesis, namely, that being in a crisis of some sort or other is a necessary condition for a religious experience. We have seen that numerous people have an experience apart from any crisis; and the same is true, I should say, for need. A major problem, of course, is to specify the notion of need, a problem pointed up by asking: What is a need, how do we determine when a person has a need, and how do we determine the intensity of a need? Focusing briefly on Walter will help us see some of the issues here, and perhaps a way to handle them.

Walter was consciously aware that he needed strength beyond himself to be Terri's companion in the struggle with cancer. In other words, he would say that he had a need for God, yet he felt that he had been experiencing divine strength and was not at the time of his experience feeling a great sense of powerlessness, anxiety, discomfort, or anything of the like. Exactly what, then, was the nature of Walter's need for God? It was not like the need for food or water in the sense that failure to meet the need would lead to death, for Walter could have lived his entire life without paying the slightest attention to God. All the same, the need for God may be as intense as our needs for food and water. The psalmist says: "My soul thirsts for You, my flesh faints for You, as in a dry and weary land where no water is." (Ps. 63:1)

We may say, then, that Walter had a need for God. He surely said that he needed God and devoted a considerable portion of time and energy to the pursuit of God. But others claim needs of various sorts: a need for a better job, a need to learn algebra, a need to take a vacation, a need to get married, a need for a new car, a need to contribute, a need for sex, and so on. How can we collect all these needs together under a single notion? or can we? I tend to doubt that we can and shall, in any case, not pursue the issue of needs any further. What I have attempted to indicate is that the notion of need is anything but clear and would, for that reason, be best avoided unless it is indispensable. However, I maintain that it is dispensable, meaning that the only kind of need which seems relevant to the discussion of religious experience is a need which creates or is likely to create a desire for God. A need which does not become focused in a desire for God does not seem to be a need which could have any effect on a person in the way of bringing about a religious experience. Thus, if we try to show anything about a need, we shall have to show that it somehow created, or was likely to create, a desire for religious experience. Perhaps Walter's need for God was a need of this sort.

To begin with, Walter did not, on the day of his experience, have any special sense of need for God. I shall assume that an argument appealing to need would say something as follows: An intensified need for God (conscious or unconscious) will create (be a sufficient condition for) an intensified desire for God, and thus will be more likely to bring about religious experience than a less intense sense of need; absence of intensified desire will, of course, indicate absence of intensified need.

Walter's sense of desire for God had not increased in intensity on the day of his experience. In fact, he was feeling positive and satisfied, having had a superb nature experience the night before. He describes that experience as follows.

> I was fishing for bass. As I fished, I watched a thunderstorm move in from the south. The thunder got louder and louder until it was almost on me. The wind began to whip up sand and pebbles about me, so I ran back to the conference center and motioned to Terri to come out of a meeting. She and I stood together and watched the storm break in all its fury. I had seen God in it all and was awed and exhilarated.

He says that the next morning the feelings of the thunderstorm experience were still with him, so that perhaps the reason he did not feel a part of the activities going on around him was that he had already had his peak experience. Everything at that time was just sort of level ground—only he soon discovered that there was a peak he had not yet reached, a peak far higher than the one he had experienced. At any rate, Walter did not seem to have an intensified desire for God at the time of his experience, so that we may not infer an intensified unconscious need for God. (He denies an intensified sense of conscious need.) If we wish to find the desire for God in some need other than the need for God, I do not think that the results will be any different. Thus, need does not seem to provide a helpful explanation of Walter's experience.

The same would go for Tim, who at the time of his sunrise experience had less of a need for God than when the evening began. Having experienced God "face to face," we should have to say that his need for God was fairly well taken care, not to mention a number of other psychological and spiritual needs. The evidence is that basic needs, conscious or unconscious, had been taken care of in the two experiences following the sunrise experience.

In addition, we have cited others whose experience did not arise out of need, especially some of the children considered in Chapter Two. We shall come across others in Chapter Five, the chapter to which I now turn.

Chapter Five

The Explanation From Desire and From Unconscious Motivation: Eastern Forms of Experience

According to my statement of the explanation from desire, desiring some sort of divine Object is supposed to be a necessary or sufficient condition for experiencing the Object desired, not some other Object—i.e., if I desire an experience of Christ, then I should experience Christ, not Allah or Vishnu or Brahman or some other religious Object. In this chapter I shall consider people who had experiences different from what we may suppose them to have desired or even to have had concepts for. More specifically, I shall concentrate on people from the West who had experiences of an Eastern cast. I shall also continue to consider explanations from the unconscious which are not limited to unconscious desire for the Divine.

Already we have met a number of people who had experiences of a generally Eastern cast, i.e., experiences of merger or union with the All. In Chapter One we learned of Sheila, who had a Plotinus-like merger experience. In Chapter Two Pam spoke of being a part of everything, of "some great unity." Bea had a similar experience. Calvin said that he was communicating with an all-encompassing Energy, and in doing so sensed that he was "encompassing the universe, becoming a part of everything around me." In Chapter Three we found Inez saying that she sensed herself to be "a very small part of an enormous whole." Janette also spoke "of belonging to an immeasurably great whole." Elizabeth wrote, "My mind broke bounds and went on expanding until it merged with the universe." And Diane and Tricia ran and put their arms around trees, aware of "Something more deeply diffused in nature but not personal." But now I turn to others.

Lorraine (1986)

Lorraine describes four experiences which she had over a period of several months. At the time of the first experience she was sitting at her typewriter. Suddenly, she says,

> I was impelled into another dimension: This dimension was a Void. It is indescribable. It is ecstasy, and when, two hours later, I emerged from this Void, I knew a joy so intense that no words I can find will express this coherently. Naturally, I commenced to learn more of this experience, and discovered that it is sought by people of the East . . . for it is considered to be the 'Ultimate Enlightenment.' Never having meditated in my life, nor belonged to any sect or creed or party, I could not understand why I was vouchsafed this incredible experience, for it took place on two consecutive days, and changed my life. I began to be happy.
>
> Some weeks later, and now better informed, I awakened one morning, on the instant, and saw my own soul. It was pure energy, living energy. Then the scene changed, and I saw the world inhabited by this living energy; saw how it moved before the forms which it inhabited. . . . I saw so much at this incredible moment that I cannot even begin to list here that which I learned, but this I will say: We are all inhabited by this energy; it moves before us in future time and can, and does assume the aspect of light. When I saw my soul I knew from whence it came for it was of the exactly same nature as the Void.
>
> Months passed, and I was again sitting before this typewriter when, without warning, I saw the true nature of time. . . . I learned that living energy, and the energy which is time, were neither accidental nor fortuitous. They were bestowed. Living energy is intelligent energy. . . .
>
> I cannot say finally, for nothing is final, but the last enormous experience was that of seeing the source of this bestowal. For many years of my life I had, instinctively as I supposed, rejected the notion of an identifiable God, for I felt there to be a Force of incomprehensible power in existence, and there were times in my life when I had actually seen evidence of this Force. I did not believe that this Force could be described in human bodily terms. I do not now believe it. What I have seen is beyond my powers to describe, for truly the dimensions of this Force are beyond description. All I say, and I say this with my life, is that this Force exists, and it is of equally incomprehensible intelligence. It is Mind.

Lorraine experiences a Void, something that was apparently outside her experience, for she "commenced to learn more of this experience," discovering in the process that the notion of a Void is common to the East. Thus, since she was unfamiliar with the notion, we may suppose that she did not desire to experience a Void. She mentions that at the time of her first experience she "had no formal religious convictions." What she means by this is that she did not belong to any "sect, or creed, or party"; she had little interest in or sympathy for institutional religion, and still is of the same frame of mind. She states that she had drifted from the notion of an "identifiable God" to the notion of a Force, a notion which she finally (fourth experience) seems to connect with the Void but which in the first experience she did not.

In fact, we seem to see the following progression in her experiences: first experience—she experiences a Void; second experience—she experience her soul as living energy, an all pervasive energy, an energy which is the essential nature of the Void; third experience—the energy is intelligent and bestowed; fourth experience—the source of the bestowal is the Force, which she had thought about previously and which she now sees to be essentially Mind. What I wish to emphasize is that the experiences seem to lead her thoughts rather than *vice versa*. In other words, the experiences do not seem to represent where she was in her thoughts about God; rather, her thoughts about God developed out of her experiences. If her experiences had followed her thoughts, then she should have had the experience of a Force first, for she had thought about this notion, and it seemed to be her received view of the basic Reality of the universe. Yet the experience of the Force comes last. The first experience is of the Void, a notion she was unfamiliar with, a notion which she does not describe, but which at the time of the first experience she apparently did not think of as either energy, force, or Mind. These thoughts came later with the other three experiences. Moreover, she gives no indication of desiring to experience the Void in these further ways. Since she experienced the Void as ecstasy and felt intense joy after the experience, she would hardly have a desire for anything other than a repeat of that experience. Why look for anything more? How improve on ecstasy and joy? Yet the second experience was not a repeat of the first. Thus, desire was certainly not a sufficient condition for the second experience, and probably not a necessary condition—I doubt that anyone wants to say that desiring to experience the Void is a necessary condition for experiencing living energy as the nature of the universe, or that it was a necessary condition in Lorraine, if not in anyone else.

Lorraine also mentions several precognitive experiences of a traumatic nature, traumatic because they concerned the deaths of two of her children and her father, resulting in "the lacerating griefs of living the deaths of my family before their deaths occurred." These experiences obviously did not prepare her in any way for the experience of a Void and definitely did not place within her the conscious desire to experience a Void. Supposing that the desire was on the level of the unconscious is a violation of *Socrates*. Just as a reminder, I shall make explicit the constraints of *Socrates*. Traveling down to the unconscious does not relieve us of the burden of explaining where the notion of the Void came from or why Lorraine would be desiring to experience a Void. Further, postulating, without evidence, an unconscious desire to experience a Void, a desire which is unconnected with other desires or impulses in the unconscious, is *ad hoc*—a hypothesis designed to account for the experience of a Void but nothing else.

But perhaps the experience of the Void arose from an unconscious desire to return to the womb. This suggestion fares no better than the attempt to install an unconscious desire to experience a Void. Lorraine was apparently unhappy at the time of her experience, so that supposing a desire to escape from unhappiness, from the griefs and pains of her existence, would not be unreasonable. Indeed, we may very well grant that she desired this, desired it consciously! And we may also grant that on the unconscious level she desired to resolve her unhappiness by a return to the womb. Why, then, was the experience of a Void an experience of ecstasy, followed by the feeling of intense joy, feelings hardly representative of a womb-like existence, which at best might be pictured as peaceful, although I have indicated that it might be very stressful or at least a mixture—some peace, some stress. In fact, a womblike state is necessarily not peaceful in any common usage of the term, for the term 'peaceful' refers to a conscious state, which, as far as anyone can tell, is not the state of a fetus. We might think of a Void as similar to an unconscious state, but Lorraine's experience seems anything but similar to an unconscious state, for she knows that she was in a Void, is aware when she emerges from it, says it was an ecstasy, and later identifies it as energy and light. Further, a womb-like state is a state of dependency, but Lorraine does not seem to have feelings of dependency—hers is a feeling of joy. Finally, why the additional experiences? Having experienced the security of the womb, did she then wish to come to birth, experiences two through four representing this birth? I shall let the reader play with this suggestion.

An appeal to unconscious guilt is also a non-starter. One way of resolving guilt would be by way of an Impersonal Reality, like a Void, because no moral rules, moral condemnation, moral judgment, or anything of the like can issue from a Void. Why, then, go for Mind? This does not make sense, unless we suppose that guilt is not the issue, as it does not appear to be. Her experiences seem devoid of any sense of guilt or resolution thereof. Therefore, I do not see any grounds for appealing to unconscious guilt.

Before ending the discussion of Lorraine, I wish to note a point which will be significant for the discussion in Chapter Nine. Lorraine sees no inconsistency between her experiences of the Divine as Void, as Energy, as Intelligence, and as Mind. To be sure, she does not elaborate on the nature of the Void, but then she does not for the same reason that Buddhists do not try to elaborate on the nature of Nirvana—viz., that It is indescribable, beyond words. However, we may note several points about the Void in Lorraine's experiences. First, Lorraine comes up with the term 'void' on her own. Somehow she sees this term as capturing her experience. We should not think that she uses the term in exactly the same way as do Buddhists, but then we should remember that not all Buddhists use the term in exactly the same way. There are various schools of Buddhism, with many giving different slants on the nature of the Void, and some saying things about the Void which others would deny. She certainly sees her experience within a Buddhist framework, the framework of "Ultimate Enlightenment." Second, Lorraine said that she was impelled into the Void. How she was impelled I cannot say because she does not say; yet it is almost as if this Reality reached out and gave her a strong shove, rather than her reaching out to It. She certainly was not (and had not been) reaching out to It by way of prayer, meditation, the elimination of desire, or other religious practices. In this respect her experience is at least not characteristic of the Eastern path to experiencing the Void. If Lorraine had been what we might call "a typical Buddhist," she would have set herself on the course of progressively eliminating desire, a course involving study of Buddhist Scriptures, meditation, and perhaps guidance by a guru, a course on which one unparalleled day she simply pauses, finding herself, apart from any effort or decision on her part or any intrusion from without, in the Void. Third, she does not mention a loss of individuality or selfhood and her description of the experience seems to involve awareness of her subjective state— joy and ecstasy (if the latter term applies to her; it could apply to the Void). Her experience at this point may be uncharacteristic of Buddhist experiences of the Void, but I think I must add 'some Buddhist experiences'. In any case, I should maintain that for a Buddhist to describe a state as one without distinctions, as a stillness, and as peace, is at least to assume self-awareness and individuality. Fourth, the experience, although not egoless, seems to be free from desire, similar in this respect to the experience of Nirvana. Her focus is on the Void, with the resulting experience being one of joy. Joy is a far more positive state than peace or total stillness (terms more commonly used to describe Nirvana), yet it is clearly a state relatively free from desire, at least any of the normal desires of life.

Given these various characteristics of her experience of the Void, I wish to return to my main point, viz., that Lorraine does not see inconsistency between her experiences; therefore, going with her sense on this point, I think that we must say that whatever the Void was, it was a Reality not incompatible with development, finally, into Mind. We certainly must not say that the Void was the final, normative experience for her. All the experiences were normative in a sense, but the last experience is surely considered by her as most insightful.

How to work out the consistency between the Void and Mind is not something I can do much better than did Lorraine. I can point again to the pope's words, already quoted,

> You are the Calm, the great Silence,
> free me then from the voice;

or a further quote:

> Locked in such an embrace,
> a gentle touch against my face:
> then amazement falls,
> and silence, the silence without a word,
> which comprehends nothing, and the balance is
>   nil. (Wojytla, 1979, 8)

If we met these words without knowing their source, I daresay that we should consider them to be of Eastern origin. However, the pope also clearly believes that the Silence is the same Reality that "spoke to our fathers by the prophets," and "in these last days has spoken to us by a Son." (Heb. 1:1-2) Why not? Why may not God meet us in both ways? In human relationships we may at one time sit in silence with a spouse or a good friend, feeling close, whereas at another time we may be deeply involved in conversation—without ever getting the slightest idea that we or they are different persons at these different times. I shall, as I said, pursue these matters further in Chapter Nine.

Clark (4139)

Clark was thirty four and happily married (so he thought) when one fine morning his wife announced her love for another man and her desire for a divorce. Clark was devastated, first turning to alcohol "to alleviate the anguish" but then quickly deciding that he needed to get himself physically fit, hitting on a program of walking at high speed, six miles per weekday and ten miles or more on weekends. He reports that toward the end of one of these hikes, as he was approaching the summit of a hill, he had the following experience.

> I became suddenly 'aware' of a figure on top of this hill in a feather outfit with arms outstretched, rotating slowly on one leg! I don't think I actually 'saw' the figure with my eyes but I became aware of him. He resembled a shaman and before I could question what was happening the following happened simultaneously:
> 1) I felt an incredible joy;
> 2) I felt an absolute one-ness with everything (a one-ness which subsequent research has led me to believe is quintessentially Taoist).
> 3) The words of the Beatles' 'Fool on the Hill' flooded into my mind—every one relevant to the way I was at that point in time.

The words to the Beatles' song go as follows.

> Day after day
> Alone on the hill
> The man with the foolish grin
> Is keeping perfectly still.
> Nobody wants to see him
> They can see that he's just a fool,
> And he never gives an answer.
>
> Well on his way
> His head in a cloud
> The man of a thousand voices
> Talking perfectly loud
> But nobody ever hears him
> Or the sound he appears to make
> And he never seems to notice.

> Nobody seems to like him
> They can tell what he wants to do
> And he never shows his feelings
> He never listens to them
> He knows that they're fools
> And they don't like him
>
> Chorus
>
> But the fool on the hill
> Sees the sun going down
> And the eyes in his head
> See the world turning 'round.

Obviously, since Clark categorized the experience of oneness as Taoist only after further investigation, we may be fairly certain that at the time of the experience he was not familiar with Taoist or other notions of oneness. Clark states that he had always been interested in the esoteric and in the study of pre-history, remarks which he directs to the "vision" of the shaman figure, not the experience of oneness. Thus, Clark was hardly likely to be desiring an experience of oneness, and perhaps was not even conversant with the notion. If he was conversant with the notion, he was not conversant enough to know the origins of it, and thus we may say that the notion was certainly not central to his thinking. It may have been somewhere in his memory banks, but that is the most we can say. We have no reason for thinking that on the unconscious level the notion had a more salient position.

As for the shaman figure, Clark was conscious that he did not visually *see* the shaman figure but was "aware" of it. Thus, among other things, we may note that the experience did not rob Clark of his critical capacities, a fact which seems to have escaped a psychiatrist who told Clark that the experience was a psychotic attack and that Clark was lucky not to have experienced its full effects, namely, getting "tipped . . . into temporary insanity." Of the psychiatrist's interpretation, Clark says, "I remain unconvinced . . . despite my clearly erratic mental condition at that time." A major reason to be unconvinced about the psychiatrist's interpretation is that the shaman figure is not at all a bizarre, abnormal item in the experience, representative of a confused mental state, or a state simply out of touch with reality. Just the opposite, for although the shaman figure is peripheral to the experience in the sense of not carrying the main content or feeling of the experience, the figure is clearly representative of the meaning of the experience, viz., that it was an experience of supernatural insight or illumination. Clark seems to place this interpretation on the figure, for he immediately makes the connection with "The Fool on the Hill." All this apparently escaped the psychiatrist.

Clearly, though, the core of the experience for him is the sense of "incredible joy" and of "absolute one-ness with everything." In speaking of the lasting effects of the experience he does not mention the shaman figure; instead, he says:

> The knowledge of the experience is still with me: I still feel the oneness; I have a heightened reverence for life (and indeed can see 'life' or, rather, the force of the Universe in rocks, in the earth itself); I can picture myself in the whole 'plan' far more clearly. . . . I feel psychologically enhanced by the whole thing.

Edna (505)

Edna gives the following account of her religious journey.

> I come from a family of vaguely anti-clerical Roman Catholics and up to the age of ten was educated in a convent school, in an atmosphere of piety and religious sentiment. At ten I was moved to a secular school. . . . Until about the age of 14 I was conventionally religious, trying to be 'good.' At 14 I rebelled against the authoritarian elderly priest who was in charge of religious instruction and who refused to answer any questions, however well-intentioned. Since asking 'Why?' is part of my nature, and also because at that time my yearning for God was becoming very strong, I became friendly with some Protestant girls whose brand of Christianity seemed more generous and less stultifying than the Roman version, and I started reading the New Testament.
>
> It was then that I first discovered the feeling of religious belonging which, through many changes and variations, has been with me ever since—although not continuously. The feeling had nothing to do with organized religion; in fact, I finally stopped practising as a Roman Catholic at the age of 20, and have never regretted it. The essence of the feeling is a very deep belonging to a huge, ineffable, perfect Reality which exists both immediately below the surface of everyday life and also infinitely removed from it. Sometimes I call it God, but more often 'the All' seems to describe it more accurately. My consciousness of this Reality explains the fact that at all times, even in difficult conditions or great personal distress, I have always felt that basically,

and at the level where things really matter, all is well and exactly as it ought to be. (I should add that I am not a passive or indifferent person, and therefore this basic acceptance cannot be the result of weakness or apathy.)

Since Edna had been brought up on conventional notions, her experience, which started at approximately age fourteen, is not to be explained in terms of the ideas familiar to her. We might suppose that she had run various alternative ideas about God by her mind's eye, but she certainly gives no indication of having focused on the notion of God as a "huge, ineffable, perfect Reality which exists both immediately below the surface of everyday life and also infinitely removed from it." Moreover, she may not have run any alternative ideas by her mind's eye at all, for her questioning may well have been less of an intellectual blossoming than sheer teenage rebellion against authority. It almost looks more like the latter. Further, if we suppose that Edna felt alienated from parents (something which we have no evidence for), we shall have to explain why her alienation is met by sensing that she belongs to an essentially impersonal, rather than personal, Reality, and the explanation will not be made any easier by moving to the level of the unconscious. She does say that she was yearning for God, but since she was attending church with Protestant girls and reading the New Testament, we should expect the yearning to be for the received God of Christianity, a clearly personal God. Indeed, her reluctance to label her experienced Reality 'God' indicates that the God of her yearnings was not the God she experienced. Moreover, we have no evidence to make us think that we should expect different yearnings on the unconscious level. Thus, Edna's experience does not seem to be a function at all of any yearnings—desires—for God which were present, unless we wish to say that yearnings for a God of any sort are a condition for the experience of a God of any sort. I think that we have enough evidence to quickly do-in that possibility.

Vivian (897)

Vivian remarks that her "parents say that they believe in God but religion was never discussed much" when she was young. All the same, she took communion and was confirmed in the C/E. When she was sixteen, the illness of a friend was the occasion for her to kneel before a small cross in her room and "say a quick prayer." The quick prayer turned into a full-length experience of God's reality.

I seemed to find myself in a great hall without walls or a roof. I was kneeling down . . . and yet I was not conscious of a floor. I had a feeling of great rushing winds and yet everything was quite still and silent. Everything was gray like a summer morning early shrouded in mist waiting to burst into life. Before me was a presence clothed in mist. Omnipotent. I was not conscious of good or evil, joy or pain, fear or relief. Somehow in a still small voice that penetrated my being like the loudest noise in the universe, I was told that 'everything is going to be all right.' To say that this presence was totally responsible for our lives and all powerful throughout the universe and eternity would limit the concept I have of this presence. I was in the presence of God. I did not feel that he was good or bad, loving or vengeful, the lion or the lamb, and yet he was all these things to different people, different generations, different races, different worlds. The 'message' that I received was not meant for my friend or me or even the whole world, it wasn't reassurance, it was a statement of fact. Good and bad, right and wrong, love and hate, peace and war are all part of a balance which is 'God,' which he created and which is only a small part of this "presence" which I experienced. . . .

I don't believe in God; I know that he exists as surely as I can know that this is paper that I am writing on. . . . There is not much further I can say—the experience defies words, they limit to concepts that are too small. The description of the experience is difficult enough; the conviction and knowledge that it leaves behind is virtually impossible to describe.

Vivian's experience clearly breaks out of the mold of her received religion. The hall without roof or walls symbolizes this fact, as does the rushing winds, for rushing winds are wild, incapable of being contained or captured. The notion of rushing winds is surely a Christian symbol, although we cannot be certain that Vivian, at age sixteen, was aware of its meaning. At any rate, her experience of God takes her to a Presence that is really beyond attributes. She says that the Presence was omnipotent, yet goes on to say that calling the Presence all-powerful would be to limit her concept of the Presence. Again, the Presence is really beyond attributes, beyond good and evil, right and wrong, love and hate, and so on. The notion of a God that is beyond attributes may be found within Christianity but is more characteristic of Eastern religion. One is immediately reminded of the Hindu characterization of Brahman as, *neti, neti*— not this, not that. God is a mist—mysterious, beyond our attempts to capture It in some religious box or other.

As for the notion of the world as a balance of opposites, that is a notion firmly imbedded in ancient Greek philosophy but hardly a notion customary in Christian philosophy, not to mention common Christian instruction and worship. Yet again, she qualifies her assertions concerning the balance, saying that the balance "which is 'God', which he created," was only a small part of the presence she experienced, the Mist. The opposites seem to represent her inability to express this ultimate Reality, a Reality that may be conceived of as a Unity—indeed, is often so experienced. We might say that trying to get the Unity into the molds of thought and speech always ends in paradox. The Unity is ineffable in the sense that verbal expression can never totally capture the full nature of It—but then, this is true even of something as mundane as sensory experience. Our words for sense experience can never capture the full nature of the experience. The words, as in the case of the Divine, simply point to or remind us of our experience.

Thus, we may say that Vivian's concepts of God are beyond anything one would attribute to a sixteen year old, especially a sixteen year old brought up within the C/E. Saying that she desired an experience of the sort she received seems just plainly false. Moreover, we do not have any evidence to direct us to the unconscious level. Why concern for an ill friend should issue in the experience she had is anything but clear. Her concern would likely have been alleviated by the Voice saying that "everything is going to be all right." Indeed, even a Voice is too much, for if the Voice is the unconscious speaking, the question is why the unconscious comes by way of a Voice rather than by way of a strong conviction that everything is going to be all right. The conviction is what counts, anyway, and that an unconscious carrying the conviction by way of a Voice could not carry the conviction without a Voice does not seem reasonable.

Here we meet again the deceptive unconscious, along with the theoretical problems of that unconscious. I note again one of the major problems, viz., that the alleged deception of the unconscious in religious experience is *ad hoc*, unlike the normal workings of the unconscious, the workings we find in other cases. When we meet deception, say, in the form of delusions and hallucinations, we meet it in a pathological setting, and the results are pathological, unhealthy. Yet Vivian's Voice is not part of an acute or chronic pathology; it is part of the experience of a young girl who does not seem in the least pathological, a girl who incorporates the experience into her life, again apparently with healthy rather than pathological results. Vivian states that her family is without a history of mental illness and that she considers herself something of a "down to earth" person. When she wrote her account, she was married and apparently functioning in a normal way. Thus, in Vivian's case, as well as many other cases of religious experience, the deceptive unconscious functions apart from a pathological setting and has healthy consequences, whereas the normal functioning of the deceptive unconscious is within a pathological setting and with unhealthy consequences. (I note that many religious experiences are delusional—some voices, e.g., are clearly of a pathological sort. In other words, some religious experience may be defeated, overridden. I shall consider this matter in more detail in Chapter Eight.)

The problems that I have just raised are intensified tenfold by the rest of the experience. If explaining the turn of the unconscious to a Voice is problematic, how much more problematic is the turn of the unconscious to a God that breaks the molds of Vivian's traditional C/E conceptions. Vivian, by the way, apparently remained a practicing C/E member.

Because Vivian does not spell out what she means by her various statements about God, they could spell trouble. E.g., if she meant that God is truly both loving and vengeful, rather than that God is seen as vengeful by some people, some generations, some races, as loving by others, then her statement about God would be internally inconsistent. (How could God be both vengeful and loving?) However, her remarks may be interpreted so as to avoid inconsistency; indeed, the most plausible interpretation seems to be one which takes this route. The essence of the experience seems to be that those qualities which appear to us as opposites in God, as conflicts within God and His world, are, in the end, expressions of a deeper unity, a unity we may not be able to get into our conceptual molds. Vivian clearly articulates that God is ultimately beyond any concepts, at least in the sense that no concept or set of concepts adequately captures the reality of God. I think that we should have to agree with Vivian to a considerable extent. Even saying that God is love must be said with a degree of tentativeness, if for no other reason than that we do not fully comprehend the nature of love (Christians regularly say that God's suffering for us in Christ is beyond our abilities to comprehend.), and we often do not see how some events or actions fit into love.

The viewpoint that our concepts of God are ultimately inadequate and limited is shared probably by all people who have ever encountered God. St. Thomas, for example, towards the end of his life, after having written the *Summa*, a book in which he conceptualizes God on a level few have been able to approach, encountered the Reality he was talking about, saying, as a result, that all his writings about God were nothing but straw. A fairly extended account of this occurrence goes as follows.

> On Wednesday morning, December 6 [1273], the feast of St. Nicholas, Thomas arose early as usual to celebrate the Mass of the feast in the chapel of St. Nicholas. During Mass, Thomas was suddenly struck (*commotus*) by something that profoundly affected and changed him (*mira mutatione*). After this mass he never wrote or dictated anything. . . . When Reginald [Thomas' chief scribe and companion priest] realized that St. Thomas had altered entirely his routine of more than fifteen years, he asked him, 'Father, why have you put aside such a great work which you began for the praise of God and the enlightenment of the world?' To which Thomas answered simply, 'Reginald, I cannot.' But Reginald, afraid that Thomas was mentally unbalanced from so much study, insisted that he continue his writing and return to his former routine, at least at a slower pace. But the more Reginald insisted, the more impatient Thomas became until he replied, 'Reginald, I cannot because all that I have written seems to me like straw.' Reginald was mystified at this reply. But Thomas was serious; he could not go on. He was physically and mentally unable to do so. The only recourse he had was to prayer for himself, and acceptance of his inability to work. (Weisheipl, 1974, 321)

Later in December or in early January Reginald, becoming ever more disturbed at the oddity of Thomas' behavior, pressed him

> to tell him why he refused to write and why he was so constantly dazed (*stupefactus*). After much urgent questioning and insisting, Thomas at last said to Reginald, 'Promise me, by the living God Almighty and by your loyalty to our Order and by the love you bear me, that you will never reveal, as long as I live, what I shall tell you. All that I have written seems to me like straw compared to what has now been revealed to me.' (Weisheipl, 321-22)

Various explanations for Thomas' radical change have been offered, including that of stroke and that of the breakdown of his constitution. Weisheipl inclines to the latter explanation, saying that the breakdown was not "caused by mental disturbance, but it would have been a physical breakdown resulting in mental disturbance, anxiety, and a change in emotional values wherein the *Summa* and the Aristotelian commentaries no longer seemed important." (323) That Thomas was affected physically ("there was impaired speech and a loss of manual dexterity and gait") seems unquestionable, but that Thomas' experience resulted in mental disturbance and anxiety seems highly questionable. Reginald seemed very anxious about Thomas, as did others, but Thomas did not seem anxious about Thomas—at least Weisheipl does not present clear evidence of anxiety, not to mention mental disturbance, unless a radical change of lifestyle and values is invariably a sign of anxiety and mental disturbance, a position we could make out, I think, only by begging the question. Certainly, Thomas' conversations with Reginald appear very sensible. I grant that his words could come as a shock to those who tended to view his writings as closely approximating the truth about God, with the result that these people would have a strong motive for trying to downplay his experience and its significance. This is a bit of an *ad hominem* swipe, and yet it is not useless if it serves as a means for examining possible biases. *Ad hominem* swipes aside, the evidence fails to show, I think, that the December 6th experience most likely knocked Thomas into an unbalanced mental or emotional state. What I read seems to indicate that Thomas was in full possession of his senses. He had a radical change of values, but he gave a sufficient reason—a revelation. Isaiah, too, among many others, had a revelation of God—"I saw the Lord, high and lifted up"— with the result that he had a radical change of heart—"Woe is me, for I am a man of unclean lips."

A further point is that Thomas' words are really not very different from those of Plato concerning the Good, words no one has attempted to say arose from Plato when he was not fully in his senses. Plato certainly does not state the essence of the Good and does not even describe the Good with any sort of completeness. Indeed, Plato says that the Good exceeds essence: "The good may be said to be not only the author of knowledge to all things known, but of their being and essence, and yet the good is not essence, but far exceeds essence in dignity and power." (*Republic*, Bk. VI:509). He seems to leave knowledge of the Good to experience of the Good, to the "beatific vision." (Bk. VII: 517) Words just will not convey the nature of the Good--they are like straw! A final point is that Thomas' words also express the fundamental view of Scripture, viz., that our attempts to capture the reality of God are always truncated. We are like Moses, forever seeing only the backside of God.

Thus, Vivian's paradoxical statements are part of a strong tradition within the literature of religious experience. She obviously is not to be compared with Thomas in the attempt to achieve clarity and consistency, yet she stands in the same mist as Thomas ultimately does—God's reality cannot be captured in words but only in the gift of His revelation to us.

Therefore, our words always appear like straw in relation to the rocklike Reality, and our words always threaten to blow away in the winds of meaninglessness and inconsistency.

Leanna (388)

Leanna writes that in her late twenties and early thirties she had fairly regular bouts of depression.

> I bore it in silence.... But at the age of thirty three this state was so intensified that I felt I must be going mad. I felt to be shut up in a cocoon in complete isolation and could not get into touch with anyone (although outwardly I carried on my normal life and occupation).... Things came to such a pass and I was so tired of fighting that I said, 'I can do no more. Let Nature, or whatever is behind the universe, look after me now.'
>
> Within a few days I passed from a hell to a heaven. It was as if the cocoon had burst and my eyes were opened and I saw.
>
> The world was infinitely beautiful, full of light as if from an inner radiance. Everything was alive and God was present in all things, in fact the earth, all plants and animals and people seemed to be made of God. All things were one, and I was one with all creation and held safe within deep love. I was filled with peace and joy and with a deep humility, and could only bow down in the holiness of the presence of God. At one time a more personal Presence seemed to be near me in the room where I was. I felt a great urge to serve mankind in any lowly way.... How had I lived for 33 years and been so blind? This was the secret of the world, yet it all seemed so obvious and natural that I had no idea that I should not always see it so.... Gradually, however, I felt the vision retreating....
>
> Psychologically, and for my own peace of mind, the effect has been of the greatest importance. In times of bereavement and suffering I have been able to turn to the memory of that which has brought peace and comfort. It has also given me understanding in reading the Bible and other scriptures and mystical writings.... I also feel that the world is good, and remember ... that the divine is within the common.

Elsewhere in her writing Leanna mentions that prior to her experience she "had never heard of the mystical experience" but afterwards she read about it in various books. Clearly, then, she thinks of her experience as mystical, essentially, I suppose, because of her sense of oneness with all. Since she was not aware of this sort of experience prior to having it, we can be certain that she was not desiring it, either consciously or unconsciously.

What strikes us immediately is that the experience comes after she just gives up. The term 'surrender' might be used, but I think 'gives up' more adequately characterizes what she did, although the giving up did involve a readiness to receive healing from Whatever is behind the universe. On a Freudian model we might see her action as some sort of submission to parental authority. The fact that she was depressed may indicate a deep sense of guilt, stemming from childhood conflicts with parents. Yet the Reality she experiences is not clearly personal, although she does use language which may allude to parents—"being held safe within deep love." She mentions that at one time the Presence was more personal—more personal, i.e., than in the original experience, a remark which only serves to underscore that she takes her original experience to be of an essentially impersonal Being, albeit a Being that was love and hence a Being which logically had to be personal in some sense. Nevertheless, the fact that she sees God as essentially impersonal is not what one would expect from dynamics supposedly arising from personal relations (with parents) and normally resolved in personal relations (insight and transference in psychotherapy). What we may say, then, is that Leanna, if submitting to parental authority, is submitting to a Reality very unlike parents, for It is not clearly either personal or an authority figure and is certainly not a Reality with demands or threats. Moreover, the Reality did not straightway recognize her submission, for passing "from a hell to a heaven" took a few days. Why the delay, if the experience had its origin in the unconscious?

If we suppose that Leanna deeply desired a loving Being, aside from any connections to unresolved parental conflicts, the first point to notice is that, as a matter of fact, she probably was not desiring anything besides simple release from the pain of depression. In this respect she was probably like Tim, the drug addict—his desires, conscious or unconscious, were not even close to being on God; they were focused on not dying. Further, what Leanna really seemed to desire was the *working*, the healing effects, of Whatever was behind everything, something that can be accomplished apart from a sense of union with a Presence. Why, then, the sense of union?

I also note that her image of being in a cocoon has strong associations with the womb. She is cut off from outside communication, travails in her desperate depression, and then bursts forth into the light, as in birth. I mention this because her womblike associations are anything but pleasant, peaceful, or comforting. For her the womb is a place to exit, to leave at the earliest opportunity. I do not wish to generalize from what she says or to draw any conclusions concerning existence in the womb, except to remark once more that the idea of life in the womb as a universally halcyon existence seems to have as much in its favor as the thesis that the existence of primitive humans was universally halcyon.

Joy (3046)

Joy's experience was not so much the experience of that which she knew nothing about, an experience outside her conceptual molds, as an experience which filled those molds with life and meaning, making them seem as if previously they had been contentless.

Joy says that at the time of the experience she was not a member of any church and considered herself an agnostic. She says that

> although at present I am not working I am a fully qualified clinical psychologist, with a B. Sc. (special) and have a distinction in my diploma in Abnormal Psychology. I mention this, that you may. . . understand that I have some experience in observation and report. I think it may also be relevant, that immediately prior to the experience, I had been concentrating with considerable effort for one or two hours each day on drawing. I had also stopped smoking at that time and had also undertaken a rather drastic diet. I was not during any part of this time, taking any drugs, pills or medicines of any sort.

> One quite unremarkable morning, having finished the dreary housework, I sat down on my own to drink a cup of coffee. I was of a sudden struck by the thought that my mind was overloaded with acquired knowledge. I had the feeling that this was acting as a barrier, to what I did not know. Upon this very thought it was as if everything I had ever known was spontaneously deleted from my mind. I felt my reason to be held suspended. My mind felt to be, at the same time, both non-operative and yet supremely existent. For the description of the experiences one struggles with the limitations of language. Even with the greatest care the common meaning of words cannot be made to convey adequately the quality, which is so *extra* ordinary as to be felt to be, beyond question, on quite another dimension from ordinary experience, however intense that may be.

With my mind in this strange state, I became aware that both time and space had somehow been obliterated as relevant dimensions. I only knew that I had ever had such concepts, by this direct experience of their absence. At the same time all the polar opposites with which we habitually tease our minds, flew together to merge into one another. Common needs and values shrank to such an extent in order to come into proportion with the immensity of this new realm of experience, that they totally disappeared, dissolved utterly and became totally irrelevant.

Subjectively, there was a duality of consciousness, awareness had two aspects, both whole in themselves. One part of me was totally submerged in the experience—the blissful tensionlessness of it all—the incredible ecstasy. The other part, equally whole, with the utmost acuteness of awareness, was observing the whole process, testing its quality. Whilst I was suspended thus out of time and space, all the impossible statements which I had heard in connection with Buddhist enlightenment became understandable. The meaning of Nirvana was directly apprehended through the experience, which thus embodied its own validity for me as experiencer. . . .

Thereupon my mind seemed to race again, and I felt as if I spun-off again beyond space and time. In a totally indescribable way I felt myself to be lifted up and placed upon the Cross. I did not feel in any way holy, but . . . I knew directly inside myself every tiny tension of muscle, and every excruciating agony of mind which it must cause an aware consciousness to suffer crucifixion, as Christ had done for His expressed purpose. . . . The entire teaching of the Gospels felt as if they flipped over in my mind to reveal their true meaning which, I felt at the time I had never glimpsed properly before. I experienced most profoundly a sense of rebirth. . . .

Even while I was still submerged in the experience, I was able, with that strangely watching part of myself, to test the common ground of the Nirvana and the Kingdom of Heaven experience, by directing my conscious awareness to an assessment of the quality, of which I was directly aware as experiencer. In searching for a description of its true character the Source of all Creation was the phrase which rang clear as a bell. Even now some six months later it still has that same feeling of truth form.

I find myself in a most anomalous position of having come round from the experience with a faith I had not before. But it is no orthodox faith, in fact I feel more strongly than ever that the established Church is far from helping man towards an achievement of his potential as regards religious experience. . . . I have not gained a faith in God as conventionally conceived, but I have come through this experience to believe that there is some form of underlying process to which on occasion we may become transparent.

We see in the case of Joy what we have seen in numerous cases, viz., that the experience of another dimension of reality intrudes on ordinary experience, indeed, the most ordinary of experiences, such as drinking a cup of coffee. The notion of intrusion points up the fact that the experience comes without conscious desire. Joy was not consciously desiring any experience of the sort she had, and given *Socrates*, we may say that she was also not unconsciously desiring the experience. The fact that the experience presents her with the significance and meaning of both Nirvana and the Kingdom of God underscores the fact that she grasped neither of these realities prior to the experience. Only the experience brought her understanding. Exactly what the understanding was is not clear, except that we may pick up on several items. First, the experience was in a dimension beyond space and time ("My kingdom is not of this world." Jn. 18:36); second, in this dimension opposites merged; third, the dimension is of such unsurpassed value that the values of this world become irrelevant; fourth, the dimension is a dimension of ecstasy and bliss; fifth, it is a dimension of knowing the agony and the meaning of Christ's suffering on the cross. Apparently, none of these items was understood by Joy prior to the experience and thus she could not have desired them. One cannot desire what one does not understand. One may desire to understand, but that is an entirely different matter.

Of course, what we see is that the experience is one of enlightenment, an experience in which reason is alive, active. Her mind, "with the utmost acuteness of awareness, was observing the whole process, testing its quality." Again, I emphasize what I did at the start, viz., that religious experience does not reduce to an experience of ecstasy or bliss (many people do not have these feelings or anything like them) but is essentially a perception or apprehension of a Reality transcending normal space-time reality. Repeating this point is not without purpose, for the idea that religious experience is strictly some kind of feeling state is such a pervasive prejudice that the reports of the experience as cognitive often are treated as if they did not exist.

In trying to explain the experience, we shall find little help in the Freudian unconscious. We might try to relate the merging of opposites to the resolution of childhood conflicts with parents, but that seems to get us nowhere. Joy, a woman who prides herself on her careful observation and her understanding of abnormal psychology, says not one word about conflict or about guilt or about forgiveness. Perhaps her abandoning smoking and taking on a dietary regimen indicate guilt in some way, but she apparently does not think so, and I see no reason why we should think so. Besides, the Reality she enters into is certainly not clearly personal, and thus there is nothing even vaguely like reversion to a parental figure. Indeed, we might even have trouble classifying the experience as religious, for there seems to be no clear sense of presence. Yet her description of the dimension she entered into as outside space and time, as being value laden, as having meaning (the true meaning of the Cross), and as being described best by the phrase 'Source of all Creation' seems to clearly place her experience in the category of the religious, of the experience of a Divine reality.

Appealing to a mixed unconscious makes more sense than appealing to a Freudian unconscious, although doing so does not get us much further. We might suppose that Joy was working on joining notions East and West, although she does not mention that she was. Supposing that all the work was being done on the unconscious level is to go beyond the mixed model and suppose that for which we have no evidence. We have evidence (Winson's, e.g.), or at least we have material which may be interpreted as evidence, for an unconscious which works with the conscious self to resolve the problems of our existence. We do not have evidence of an unconscious which works on intellectual issues which are not perceived or treated as problems of our existence. Joy speaks about the problem of polar opposites as one which "teases our minds," hardly an indication that the problem was a pressing one of her existence, a problem which, e.g., caused tension, anxiety, or the disruption of behavior, as did the anxiety over meaning in the case of Jason (Chapter Three).

Moreover, supposing that somehow the conflict of religions East and West was a serious issue for Joy, was a felt conflict, we still do not get very far. Since Joy does not clarify any of the notions she uses (the dimension beyond space and time, Nirvana, the merging of polar opposites, and so on) we might say that the unconscious resolves the conflict apart from any content. I have noted that the unconscious could resolve conflicts without any appeal to God, could resolve, e.g., anxiety over life's meaning (as in the case of Jason) without presenting some divine Reality to consciousness. Therefore, if we say that the unconscious resolved Joy's conflict without presenting any kind of content, then we have double reason to ask why the unconscious went for a divine Reality at all.

Yet I think that there is content, content which Joy, like Buddhists or Hindus or Christians, simply cannot adequately express. If so, then the unconscious is presenting as real that which either is not or may not be real, and we are back to the deceptive unconscious. More problematically, the unconscious is creating experiences for which there is no background in Joy, coming up with content which is outside of Joy's experience. Further, if, as seems to be the case, religious conflicts East and West were not a serious problem for Joy, then we have the unconscious working out intellectual problems on its own, something that we do not find the unconscious doing elsewhere. In addition, we then have to explain why the resolution the unconscious worked out comes with ecstasy and bliss, as well as a sense of value, when the resolution simply could have come as the common experience expressed by, "Aha, I've got it." E.g., Kekule did not have anything close to an experience of ecstasy or bliss accompanying his experiences of insight about benzene.

Ned (1986)

Turning now to Ned, we find him reporting that at the time of his experience he could not have felt better about his life, about every major aspect of his life—his mental state, his marriage, his career (he was a professor of psychology and clinical psychologist). A colleague in psychology, who knew Ned in his last teaching position, writes: "Accounts from his earlier days as a professor [the time of his experience] . . . seem to suggest that he was always a person who was immensely supportive and fatherly. I certainly experienced him so." Thus, Ned's account of himself as feeling positive about life is paralleled by at least one account from a colleague that he was a positive, healthy person. We shall see a further account of Ned which indicates that he was a secure person, one without a personal agenda.

At any rate, Ned was listening to a sermon in an evangelical church and says that

> never, not at the time or since, have I felt manipulated by anyone or anything in the church. I was not told how to feel and there were no models anywhere around for me to follow. No one else gave any

observable signs whatever of having feelings like mine. And never since then have I learned of anyone in the church having a transcendental experience at that time or at any subsequent time. May I repeat the point then that my responses were strikingly out of proportion to the occasion of their appearance. Certainly auditory and visual stimuli were present. Certainly they carried meaning and value. But my point is that seemingly they could not be considered capable of producing such profound and lasting changes as occurred in my life. . . .

While participating in the service, listening to the prayers and songs and following the minister's sermon, I floated in and out of a rich and turbulent internal world of feelings and sensations. I could not breath. My breath would not come. It had gone astray; it had been taken away. Was I dying, or was I dead already? I observed my body in which I found myself incarnated. I was not frightened by its loose hold on me and I felt that I could go on and on from world to world. . . . Paradoxically, I had no feeling of weakness or of losing consciousness. But still in some sense had I died and returned anew. There was the physiological event of faltering respiration; the psychological event of utter dependency and helplessness; the social event of the church service; and the transcendental event of a unitive bond with *Being itself*. I did not focus on any one of these levels of the experience. I considered it a single, new event. I was left with no feeling of exhaustion or weakness, but rather with a sense of transformation. This latter feeling carried in turn, feelings of surrender, gratefulness for my life, and unselfish love for others. I felt a sobbing gladness that life would win; that it would not end. It has always been here and it would always remain. . . . Never before had I experienced such heightened self-awareness. I was crystal clear to myself, yet completely dispersed. I was here and everywhere else simultaneously. At once there was both an amplification and a diminution of individuality. I was alone and yet with all else. The universal had been enmanned in me. . . . Meaning and yet meaninglessness were both here and therein lay the despair as well as the hope of my vision.

Ned was totally surprised by the experience. In his stylistically quaint and understated way he indicates that the experience lacked any natural source he could think of. He talks about having no model for the experience, meaning, primarily, that the church did not provide a model and meaning also, probably, that he did not have a model from his past experiences. Although he focuses on possible sources of the experience in the present, the assumption seems to be that if the present provided no explanation, the past certainly did no better. He clearly would not—and did not—find in an evangelical church any mention or allusion to the kind of "transcendental experience" he had, an experience of "a unitive bond with Being Itself," a personal, yet impersonal, experience in which, he says, "I was crystal clear to myself, yet completely dispersed." That is language one simply does not find in evangelical preaching, teaching, or literature. Thus, Ned had an experience which was outside the molds of the religion he had contact with and also probably outside the molds of his learning and background. We may suppose that a man of his profession would have heard or read about mystical experiences, yet what he had heard or read apparently carried nothing relevant for the content of his experience—he makes absolutely no mention of anything he had come across in the past concerning mysticism. The colleague quoted above writes: "He never dabbled in or pursued an interest in eastern religions of any kind of which I am aware." All that he had learned was, apparently, like an empty abstraction rather than a model providing substance for his experience. Whatever the truth about his past, the truth about the present was that he definitely was not consciously thinking about or desiring an experience of the sort he had—and, given *Socrates*, we should say the same for the unconscious.

Ned says that not only did he lack a model for his experience but there was nothing else in the situation that could account for his experience. He was clearly not being manipulated, for to be manipulated would have required at least that the minister talk about the experience, hold it up as something desirable, and so on—things which obviously were not happening. Ned also sees nothing in the sensory stimuli present that could conceivably account for the experience. In short, the experience was, in his words, "strikingly out of proportion to the occasion" of it; i.e., there was nothing present in the setting or in him which could account for the experience.

Ned's experience consisted of sensing a unity with Being, but it also consisted of sensing opposites, something that we have found in many of the people who had Eastern-oriented experiences. Experiencing opposite states seems unproblematic to Ned; the opposites seem to come through to him as not finally opposite but as part of the deeper unity of Being. One lesson to draw from his experience is that we need to go slowly with any claim that opposite experiences—e.g., of God as impersonal Unity, on the one hand, as personal Agent, on the other—reveal irremediable inconsistencies in views of God. Another lesson is that we do not need to compare Christian and Hindu, e.g., to find experiential paradox or conflict; we can find paradox and conflict within the experience of a single individual, a Christian.

Although Ned's experience seems opposite to what is customarily experienced within Christian contexts, he did not abandon either his belief in the personal nature of God or his Christian faith or the evangelical church he attended. In fact, he ended his teaching career in an evangelical seminary. Ned is, in a way, another example of the Thomistic sense that all our words are straw in relation to the Reality experienced. His colleague writes:

> The after-effects of the experience were that he became increasingly evangelical in his associations but never ceased to become a kind of unique individual in his theology. He kept telling [his colleagues] . . . that he didn't know any theology and that he would trust them for it. His own experience was very mystical and somewhat incomprehensible. . . . He went along with all of the folderol that goes into an evangelical theological seminary and never challenged any of the basic assumptions underlying Protestant orthodoxy. Nevertheless he certainly would not have been seen by those of us here as a person to whom the public should look for orthodox statements.

The fact that Ned was in a state of well-being at the time of the experience makes appeals to the unconscious particularly weak. The appeal to a Freudian unconscious seems without merit because we simply do not find any evidence of Freudian dynamics; moreover, the impersonal nature of the Reality (Being itself, the Universal) underscores once more the total inadequacy of Freud's analysis of religion as a regression to infantile dependence on a parental figure. Appeal to some kind of egoless state (the oceanic feeling) is no more adequate. The appeal to a mixed unconscious makes more sense, particularly if we think of the unconscious as always pressing for further levels of growth and integration. I shall focus on the notion of integration, noting that any problems attending it also attend the notion of growth.

Integration: Jung

Integration is a central notion in the theory of Carl Jung, with the idea of God having the potential for integration of the self. One of the powerful impulses on the level of the collective unconscious is the religious impulse, the idea of God being an archetypal notion with all the power of the religious impulse. The proper pursuit of the religious impulse and the associated idea of God can be healthy and self-enhancing, i.e., can provide for high-level integration of the self. Whereas Freud saw religion as regressive, an unhealthy turn of the self, Jung sees religion as having healthy, self-enhancing possibilities.

However, Jung's theory does not seem any better than Freud's for explaining religious experience. Jung's theory certainly does not provide an explanation of Ned's experience, for Ned already exhibited a high level of integration, with his evangelical view of God apparently playing an important role in this integration. More generally, Jung's approach does not provide an explanation of religious experience for two reasons: 1) the work of integration can be accomplished apart from religious experience; 2) the unconscious would still be deceptive, presenting as real that which either is not real or only possibly real.

Integration: Another Possibility

But perhaps the unconscious seeks integration about that notion providing for as comprehensive an integration of the self as any of the other notions available to the unconscious.

The self can, of course, find integration on a variety of levels. E.g., the self could be integrated on the level of strictly physical needs. This sort of integration would ignore other aspects of the self, such as intellectual and aesthetic capacities. Thus, the thesis is that the unconscious would select integration about intellectual or aesthetic capacities (assuming that these notions were in the repertoire of the unconscious) over the physical because the intellectual or aesthetic is more comprehensive than the physical—integration about the intellectual, e.g., includes fulfilling physical needs but not *vice versa*. In Ned's case, then, the unconscious moves for integration about the notion of Being because that notion provides for a more comprehensive integration than is present in Ned's life.

As far as I can tell, the thesis I have just developed is false. I do not find any evidence that the self, conscious or unconscious, consistently selects from the notions available to it the one providing for as broad an integration of the self as possible. In fact, one could easily make out a case for the opposite. Plato's "Parable of the Cave," as well as the New Testament, emphasizes the penchant of humans to choose darkness rather than light, thus reminding us that a considerable array of evidence can be marshalled against any thesis to the effect that the self has a tendency to choose ever broader forms of integration (or growth or any similar goal). As for Ned, his Christian notion of God (his God was Ultimate Being and the source—creator—of all other being) seems at least as comprehensive an integrating notion as Being. Indeed, the latter is highly abstract and vague, so that its integrative capacity is suspect. Additionally, even if the notion of Being is more comprehensive than Ned's notion of God, why should Ned have an experience of unity with Being? One can grasp the comprehensiveness of the notion of Being, apart from the experience of unity. If the reply is that the notion was not in Ned's consciousness, the counter is that the notion could have been presented apart from the experience of unity—e.g., memories of what Ned had read or heard, say, in a class on Hegel, could have been unpacked. If the notion is not in Ned's repertoire of concepts at all, then the unconscious will not likely produce an experience having to do with that concept.

Aside from these objections, I note the following. First, the notion of 'comprehensive integration' is anything but clear and adequate. What makes one sort of integration more comprehensive than another? Do we have clear, adequate, non-controversial criteria? I think not. What criteria, then, does the unconscious employ? I think the best approach would be simply to suppose that the unconscious adopts the criteria of the conscious. Second, whatever the unconscious actually does, why should we think that comprehensive integration of the self is an adequate goal? Why not weight intellect, e.g., above the physical, apart from the notion of comprehensiveness, so that the intellectual life would be pursued even to the relative neglect of the physical, as in the case of Socrates? I think that any adequate measure of integration will have to take into account not only quantity but quality. We must concern ourselves not only with the number of values brought together but also with the weight of the values. Thus, integration of a few weighty or high-level values would be more desirable than integration of many low-level values. Third, does the unconscious present notions apart from any reality evaluation, just as long as the notions provide for the most comprehensive integration? This question arises because the appeal to the unconscious is supposed to explain Ned's sense of unity with Being; i.e., his sense of unity is supposed to be strictly a product of the unconscious. In that case the unconscious is ignoring reality criteria, with the result that we have a recipe for disaster in the long-term, for if the individual comes to find no support, or finds counterevidence, for the integrating notion, the beautiful structure of integration will come crashing down. This sort of appeal to the unconscious is unattractive, if for no other reason than that it introduces incoherency into the self—the unconscious merrily ignores the rational criteria of the self. Why take this approach? Why not have the conscious and unconscious working in concert, as the notion of the mixed unconscious really presumes? I shall dwell further on this objection in the next chapter.

Contra Maslow

Because of what I have said in the previous two sections, I must take serious exception to the thesis of Maslow that

> the human being has within him a pressure (among other pressures) toward unity of personality, toward spontaneous expressiveness, toward full individuality and identity, toward seeing the truth rather than being blind, toward being creative, toward being good, and a lot else. That is, the human being is so constructed that he presses toward fuller and fuller being and this means pressing toward what most people would call good values, toward serenity, kindness, courage, knowledge, honesty, love, unselfishness, and goodness. (Maslow, 1959, 126.)

I believe that Maslow is just wrong in what he says here. Somehow this very capable theorist fell prey to that most common of fallacies—neglecting half the evidence. Or perhaps Maslow would have defended his thesis by saying that all humans do, indeed, run toward the goal of "fuller and fuller being," most of them, however, getting tackled, piled on, and injured by society so that their progress toward the goal is halted.

I do not consider this sort of defense very convincing, but will leave detailed criticism to others. I shall simply make two points. First, I do not see all humans at some time attempting to run to the goal. When do we see this? In infancy? What are the marks in an infant of pressing toward fuller and fuller being--crying for a bottle, crying for a change of diapers, reaching out with the hands, crawling, learning how to walk? I do not think that any of these activities, or others we could list, are marks of pressing towards fuller and fuller being, at least as fuller and fuller being relates to truth, goodness, and the other values Maslow lists. Is infant exploring or learning how to walk linked to Maslow's values? Why? What evidence establishes the link? Thus, the main question is: What marks do we find—and at what stage or stages of life do we find them—which are linked by clear evidence to pressing towards fuller and fuller being in the sense of pressing towards fuller and fuller realization of the values Maslow lists? Second, granting that at some stage all humans do press towards fuller and fuller being, most humans must be utter weaklings, for they fall down at the mere touch of a finger. In short, the pressing towards fuller being is so easily and consistently thwarted by society that it almost looks as if there is no pressing in most cases. That some individuals press for fuller and fuller being, I grant; however, they are a remnant, an exception to the rule. Moreover, I do not know of any evidence showing that their pressing for fuller and fuller being is a result of an inborn internal pressure towards growth, towards realization of full humanity.

Summary

In this chapter we have considered people who had experiences we would not expect them to have, given their knowledge and experience at the time. More particularly, we have considered people who, without knowledge of or interest in Eastern religion had experiences of an Eastern cast, experiences in which they felt themselves to be one with a Reality of a largely impersonal nature. We found that many of the experiences were mixed in the sense that the Reality encountered was often felt to be in some sense personal, as well as impersonal. The main point is that the experiences do not seem to be accounted for in terms of desire, conscious or unconscious, or by any other unconscious motivation or work. I note that some of Ned's colleagues in psychology realized the futility of psychological explanations, with the result that "he was accused of having a minor stroke." So, a minor stroke, one for which no one can find evidence other than the experience, is sufficient to produce a major religious experience. We seem to have a Thomistic rerun here, about as effective in Ned's case as in Thomas'.

Chapter Six

The Notion of the Unconscious

1. Results So Far

What I should like to do in this chapter is concentrate further on the notion of the unconscious. I have already discussed the notion in a number of cases, showing, I think, that for the cases examined the appeal to the unconscious—Freudian or mixed—is not strong enough to defeat the *prima facie* status of religious experience. The cases I have discussed do not represent any selective bias that I know of, such as being strictly cases of people with college degrees. Even if all the persons I considered were college-educated (or not college educated, or wealthy, or poor, or any like characteristic), I could still say that for these cases, the unconscious is not a defeater. Moreover, we would not have any reason to presume that other cases would be different. The fact is that the cases cutthrough economic, educational, and other criteria of social class—not that each group is equally represented. The most serious deficiency of the material I have, at least as I see things, is its cultural provincialism. I do not have significant data from other cultures.

Thus, my claim is that so far we have no reason to think that the unconscious, as well as the other factors I have considered, is a general defeater for religious experience as *prima facie* justification for religious belief. The unconscious might be shown to be a defeater for religious experience among certain classes of people, say, schizophrenics; even so, the important point is that we have no more reason to dismiss the general cognitive nature of religious experience because of some cases of cognitive failure than we have to dismiss the general cognitive nature of sensory perception because of some cases of cognitive failure, as in color-blindness or hallucination. In fact, focusing on schizophrenics for the moment, we might ask whether their religious apprehensions are any more off the mark than their sensory perceptions. I suspect that their failures in religious apprehension are far less extensive than their failures in sensory perception (e.g., having hallucinations and not distinguishing between them and accurate perceptions). I imagine that for every divine Voice "heard" by schizophrenics there are scores of other non-divine voices "heard" and non-divine states of affairs "perceived." Be this as it may, the essential point is this: We do not write-off sensory perception as generally non-cognitive because of its failure on occasion, even fairly regularly among certain classes of people (e.g., schizophrenics). I see no reason for doing otherwise with religious experience; or if we do, we shall certainly need to engage in further argumentation. Actually, in the case of schizophrenics, we do not even write off all their perceptions as non-cognitive just because some are; e.g., they are likely to describe accurately the landscape they are looking at, the interior of the building they are in, and so on. Likewise, I do not see any reason why schizophrenics may not have cognitive, as well as non-cognitive, religious experiences. I do not consider myself an expert on much of anything, certainly not on the religious experiences of schizophrenics; therefore, I shall leave this subject for others.

So far, then, what I think I have shown concerning the unconscious is, first of all, the inadequacy of the Freudian unconscious as an explanation for religion or religious experience. Second, I have shown that the appeal to a mixed unconscious is subject to three general criticisms: 1) the appeal tends to be *ad hoc* and thus non-parsimonious; 2) the appeal leaves us with as much mystery as we began with; and 3) the appeal makes the unconscious deceptive. As a result, I think that I have already said sufficient to undercut any claim for the unconscious as a general defeater of religious experience. The appeal to the unconscious may very well—and does, I believe— defeat in any number of specific cases, but, as I have argued, that is not sufficient to provide a general defeater of religious experience. I consider the appeal to the unconscious an appeal to the most powerful naturalistic defeater of religious experience now available; hence, if I have done what I think I have, I have accomplished a considerable task.

2. The Aim of This Chapter

In this chapter I wish to focus further on the unconscious, considering its status as an explanatory concept. In the previous chapters I did not raise any questions on this point, at least in any systematic way. My procedure was, in effect, as follows: Assuming that the unconscious functions as theory says it does, can it account for the religious experiences presented? Now I wish to questions the adequacy of unconscious theory. My claim will be that we have little reason to put much stock in any psychoanalytic theory of the unconscious, so that appealing to such theory in order to explain religious experience is at the start a very weak appeal.

I shall focus on a specific theory, one that I have already said is theoretically inadequate to account for religious experience, viz., Freudian theory. The reason for focusing on the theory of Freud is that the questions I shall raise are essentially methodological, and Freudian theory has been examined more extensively on methodological grounds than other similar theories; moreover, some theorists have maintained that Freudian theory does or may (with further development) meet at least some of the methodological requirements of the natural sciences. In addition, none of the other similar theories does any better than Freudian theory methodologically, or so I contend. By 'other similar theories' I refer to theories normally classed as ego psychologies, including the theories of Anna Freud, Hartmann, Adler, Jung, Erikson, Horney, Fromm, Sullivan, and Rogers. I shall class the Freudian theory and the theories of ego psychology as psychoanalytic theories, probably a broader use of 'psychoanalytic theory' than is normal. I shall also class my mixed unconscious in this group of theories. I note that I do not discuss notions of the unconscious developed from cognitive psychology, a major reason being that so far, at least to my knowledge, no attempt has been made to employ any cognitive theory for explanation within the field of religion.

I shall raise two questions concerning the theory of Freud: 1) What is its scientific status? and 2) What is its status as a naturalistic alternative to a theistic explanation?

3. The Scientific Status of Freudian Theory

Freud's Claims

Freud claimed that psychoanalysis, because of its appeal to the unconscious, made possible a kind of physics of the self. Psychoanalysis, by holding

> that the psychical is unconscious in itself, enabled psychology to take its place as a natural science like any other. The processes with which it is concerned are in themselves just as unknowable as those dealt with by other sciences, by chemistry or physics, for example; but it is possible to establish the laws which they obey and to follow their mutual relations and interdependences unbroken over long stretches—in short, to arrive at what is described as an 'understanding' of the field of natural phenomena in question. . . . [The hypotheses and concepts of psychoanalysis] can lay claim to the same value as approximations that belongs to the corresponding intellectual scaffolding found in other natural sciences, and we look forward to their being modified, corrected and more precisely determined as further experience is accumulated and sifted. So too it will be entirely in accordance with our expectations if the basic concepts and principles of the new science (instinct, nervous energy, etc.) remain for a considerable time no less indeterminate than those of the older sciences (force, mass, attraction, etc.). (Freud, 1970, 15-16)

Since Freud wrote all this shortly before his death (in fact, the work, *An Outline*, is considered incomplete), his claims for psychoanalysis seem a bit astonishing. Already a number of inadequacies with his position had surfaced, inadequacies which he himself recognized. I shall not engage in a detailed criticism of his claim that psychoanalysis falls in the same class as the natural sciences but will simply note two important respects in which it does not measure-up to the rigors of the natural sciences.

However, I shall first note that I may be entirely wrong in my reading of Freud, i.e., in reading him to say that he is after a science along the lines of a natural science. Bruno Bettelheim has criticized this sort of reading of Freud, maintaining that the term translated 'mind' should really be translated 'soul' (from the German 'Seele'), and that the term 'science' when related to the soul does not refer to natural science (Naturwissenschaft) but science of the spirit (Geisteswissenschaft), both sciences in German culture being spheres of knowledge but not knowledge achieved in the same way, i.e., exclusively by the methods of the natural sciences. Thus, according to Bettelheim,

> Psychoanalysis is plainly an idiographic science [a science concerned with the singular event, as in history, the unrepeatable], utilizing unique historical occurrences to provide a view of man's development and behavior. Whether Freud analyzes his dreams, which are unique to him, or establishes the past history of patients, or discusses what constitutes the essence of a work of art and how it relates to the life and personality of the artist, or analyzes the origin of religion or rituals, the psychology of masses, or the basis of society or of monotheism, he is working within the framework of the *Geisteswissenschaften*, applying the methods appropriate to an idiographic science. (Bettelheim, 1984, 43)

If Bettelheim is correct, then Freud did not mean for his theory to be comparable to a theory from the natural sciences. In that case we shall have to ask what his theory is comparable to. What sort of status does it have? I shall consider this question in the next section. For the present, though, I wish to address the question of how Freud's theory, whatever his intentions for it, measures up to the requirements of the natural sciences called "laboratory." This will be important to do in order to determine the explanatory power of the theory.

Control and Quantification in the Laboratory Sciences

The laboratory sciences are characterized essentially by controlled experimentation, physics being the paradigm case of a laboratory science. Of course, not all sciences referred to as laboratory exercise the same degree of control over conditions. In astronomy, e.g., we obviously cannot control the motions of the heavens or even the conditions of the nighttime sky. We can, however, closely control and monitor the conditions under which we observe the heavens (using, e.g., carefully crafted and controlled telescopes with spectral or radiation receptors and recorders), and the theoretical framework of astronomy is physics; thus, we still consider astronomy a form of laboratory science. We might note that one of the crucial tests for Einstein's theory of general relativity was an astronomical test— observation of light from the distant stars, an experiment certainly considered to have been controlled. As for geology, I think that we would probably not consider it a laboratory science. I should say that it is more a field than laboratory science, although various types of laboratory experiments are carried out (e.g., chemical analysis of rocks).

Control

When Pascal wished to test the hypothesis that air pressure varies with altitude, he sent his brother-in-law out, barometer in hand, to climb the Puy-de-Dome, a mountain in central France, a procedure which could not control accurately for temperature, which, obviously enough, could vary at the same altitude at the same time of day. Boyle, on the other hand, when testing for the relation between pressure and the volume of air in a tube, performed his test in a laboratory, a setting in which he could control the temperature, as well as other relevant conditions, and consequently could be certain that he was getting the relation between pressure and volume, not the relation between pressure, volume, and something else.

Quantification

"Mathematics plays a many-splendored role in physics, from the coding of experimental results in terms of numbers to the formulation of physical laws in terms of equations." (Pais, 1991, 176) A laboratory science not only controls conditions, but the hypothesis or theory is quantified, so that a quantified result is obtained. E.g., Boyle quantified both pressure and volume, coming up with quantified results, conforming to the equation, known as Boyle's Law, $PV=K$. The requirement of quantification translates into a general requirement that scientific hypotheses (or theories) be such that quantified deductions may be made from them. E.g., Toricelli, having developed the hypothesis that air is like a sea and thus exerts pressure, deduced that mercury would rise in a vacuum tube two and three-sevenths feet. Similarly, Einstein, in working out the consequences of his theory of general relativity, deduced the degrees, minutes, and seconds that light from the distant stars would bend as it passed through the field of the sun. (His deduction, as it turned out, was not quite correct.)

Control and Quantification in Freudian Theory

Control and quantification are characteristic of a laboratory science. What, then, about the unconscious—has unconscious theory met the requirements of control and quantification present in the laboratory sciences?

Quantification

This question really answers itself. The unconscious, as understood within the framework of Freudian psychology or the larger framework of psychoanalytic theory, neither is nor has been the subject of controlled, quantified experimentation. In the section quoted above Freud said that the hypotheses and concepts of psychoanalysis "can lay claim to the same value as approximations" that belongs to the hypotheses and concepts of the natural sciences. He added that "it will be entirely in accordance with our expectations if the basic concepts of the new science remain for a considerable time no less indeterminate than those of the older sciences." However, the concepts of the older sciences did not long remain indeterminate, so that we soon had equations for force ($F=ma$), momentum ($p=mv$), gravitational attraction ($F=G$), and so on. Neither Freud nor any other psychoanalytic theorist even attempted equations for basic concepts or for the theory of the unconscious. An interesting comparison, especially since the theoretical work was at generally the same time, is between Freud's theory of the unconscious and Bohr's theory of the hydrogen atom (1913). Bohr articulated his bold new theory by way of a series of equations, whereas Freud did not produce a single equation; indeed, the unconscious and its associated concepts do not look as if they are capable even in principle of quantification, unless we can develop a correspondence with or reduction to neurological activity.

Marshall Edelson, who has made the most rigorous attempt I know of to show what would have to be done to get Freudian theory in scientific form and who thinks that the task can be done, does not think that the task requires making a link to the neurological. According to him, we may stay entirely within the psychological domain. Even if he is correct, I certainly do not find his words on quantification reassuring. What he says is the following.

> Perceptions, fantasies, or thoughts . . . may be more or less vivid . . . or more or less definite. . . . Affects, feelings or emotions may involve more or less physiological arousal. . . . They may be more or less intense or peremptory, may involve more or less of a tendency . . . to remove, to avoid, or to prevent a state of affairs. A subject may be more or less confident of his competence or ability to bring about, to remove, to avoid. . . . (1984, 90)

I need say only that "more or less" is not quantification in any sense employed by any of the natural sciences. Toricelli could have said that mercury will rise less in a vacuum tube than will water, but he did not—he quantified. Einstein could have said that light from the distant stars bends more in the gravitational field of the sun than outside that field, but he did not—he quantified in terms of degrees, minutes, and seconds. Moreover, I note that Tim, similar to others we have considered, said that his midnight experience was more intense than the experience with his parents—a statement I never considered to be within the realm of the quantitative. I have no strong, principled objections to considering the more and less as quantitative; I only note the difference between this sort of "quantification" and the quantification of the natural sciences.

Thus, I continue to maintain that the unconscious, along with its related concepts, lacks quantifiable form, and Edelson has not shown us how to alter this situation. Some further remarks on this subject may be useful. Suppose that we form the following hypothesis concerning Lefty, a man subject to acute episodes of guilt: Lefty's guilt is a consequence of his childhood wish for his father's death, a wish arising because his father thwarted Lefty's sexual desires for his mother; in short, Lefty's problem is repressed guilt over his desire for his mother and his desire for his father's death. This hypothesis is clearly not in quantified form, so that deductions from it will not be in quantified form. The absence of quantification leaves us with the inability to answer a number of crucial questions, such as: How much repressed guilt must there be or how intense must it be for Lefty's conscious life and behavior to be affected? What will he feel guilty about and when, and what forms of behavior will he exhibit and when?

Although Edelson does not provide for quantification beyond the level of the more and less, he still employs some concepts which seem capable of providing an answer at least to the first of the questions just asked. For example, he employs the concept of threshold intensity, saying that "a psychological entity is produced only if some instinctual wish or impulse is above threshold intensity." (102) Thus the answer to how intense Lefty's repressed guilt must be before it produces a psychological entity (felt guilt) is: Threshold intensity. Yet this answer is highly problematic, as can be seen by the following considerations.

To begin with, What is the threshold intensity in the case of Lefty? We would never get an answer in terms of units, such as degrees of intensity. The concepts of instinctual wish and impulse, concepts which refer to something ostensibly like physical forces, have nothing of the definiteness of physical forces, a fact underlined by the absence of any equations for the concepts. The failure to provide a quantified answer to the question about threshold intensity is indicative of a deeper problem: The point just above threshold intensity is determined strictly by Lefty's felt guilt. In the case of a physical system--say, a heating system set on a thermostat—we have independent measures, measures other than the heating system kicking in, for the point above threshold. E.g., we can look at a thermometer. In the case of unconscious guilt we do not have any independent measures—nothing other than felt guilt. And we might also note that with the thermostat we can manipulate the threshold, meaning that we can manipulate the degrees of heat, something that we cannot do with the unconscious guilt. The absence of any independent measure of the point above threshold intensity means that we cannot be certain that Lefty's felt guilt is the product of unconscious guilt, and specifically unconscious oedipal guilt. Perhaps Lefty's felt guilt has its origin in the recent event of cheating on an exam or a more distant event of cheating on his wife.

In saying what I have so far, I do not intend to deny that we can, and already have, quantified guilt to some extent by way of psychological tests. What we are measuring, I think, is felt guilt; certainly, the connection to unconscious guilt is anything but clear. Yet we do have some tests, and better tests could undoubtedly be developed. Of course, therapists in the psychoanalytic tradition are not inclined to use present tests and may not be inclined to use better-developed tests.

Returning now to Edelson, I note that the whole list of his psychological entities is outside the realm of the quantifiable. The list includes wishes, beliefs, thoughts, memories, perceptions, and feelings. (87) Just as problematic as the psychological entities are what Edelson refers to as the pretheoretic concepts of psychoanalysis, concepts such as 'making sense' and 'conflict'. I am not certain what these concepts are supposed to be comparable to in the natural sciences, but conflict, e.g., would seem comparable to the opposition of forces. As we have seen, forces in physics are capable of being specified in numerical terms so that the result of one force meeting another also can be put in numerical terms. However, Edelson's pretheoretic concepts are no more quantifiable than any of his other psychological terms; moreover, they partake of a vagueness which easily spells trouble. I shall focus briefly on the concept of making sense.

Edelson says that "a psychological entity or structure makes sense when it is apparent that it is *purposive*" and rational and intentional and appropriate and logical and reality-adapted. (94-96) In order to simplify my discussion I shall ignore the phrase 'it is apparent that'. What is immediately obvious, I think, is that neither 'making sense' nor any of the terms clarifying this phrase partake of precision, not to mention quantifiable precision. Yet the concept of making sense is central to what Edelson sees as the core theoretical ideas (stated as theses) of psychoanalysis. The first thesis is that senseless mental content requires an explanation. I take this to mean that some mental content only appears senseless but really is not, so that the thesis amounts to saying that all mental content makes sense. The second thesis is that all mental processes are purposive, the apparent assumption here being that all mental content is a result of mental processes. We may note that thesis one does not follow necessarily from the assumption and thesis two.

Assumption: All mental content is a result of mental processes.
Thesis 2: All mental processes are purposive.

These two premises do not yield

Thesis 1: All mental content makes sense.

The reason is, as we have seen above, that something makes sense if it is purposive *and* rational *and* intentional, and so on; or perhaps Edelson means that something makes sense only if it is purposive and rational, and so on. Either way, the argument does not yield that all mental content makes sense. Perhaps, then, no logical development is desired, the theses being logically independent, each based on evidence from analysis. However, another thesis, Thesis 3, seems to play a logical role in getting to Thesis 1: *"There can be no senseless mental content (which is unrelated to any conscious purpose) without unconscious purposes."* (80) I take this statement to say: Any mental content unrelated to a conscious purpose is related to an unconscious purpose. We still cannot logically get to Thesis 1.

Of course, I may be misinterpreting Edelson's theses, a problem which would not be present if I had equations, such as Bohr's equations for the hydrogen atom. Whether I am misinterpreting or not, the main point is that we need considerable tidying-up before we can know exactly how the principles are to be stated and exactly what the logical relations between them are. (I have not stated all of Edelson's principles.) Edelson says, in effect, the same, noting that an adequate psychoanalytic theory would require, among other things, carefully defined theoretical predicates, as well as psychological laws. (84) Thus, I do not believe that my criticisms indicate that I am really very far removed from Edelson. My main contention is that even with all necessary tidying-up, we should still be far removed from the precision and definiteness of quantified predicates and quantified psychological laws.

Control

The upshot is that the theory of the unconscious is not put in quantifiable form. Lack of quantification means a serious slippage of control, as one would gather from my remarks on threshold intensity. Of course, Freud did not see controlled experimentation as the test of his theory, maintaining instead that psychoanalytic procedure is the means of testing psychoanalytic theory.

> Every science is based on observations and experiences arrived at through the medium of our psychical apparatus.... We make our observations through the medium of the ... perceptual apparatus, precisely with the help of the breaks in the sequence of 'psychical' events: we fill in what is omitted by making plausible inferences and translating it into conscious material. In this way we construct, as it were, a sequence of conscious events complementary to the unconscious psychical processes. The relative certainty of our psychical science is based on the binding force of these inferences. Anyone who enters deeply into our work will find that our technique holds its ground against any criticism. (Freud, 1970, 16)

The last sentence certainly represents Freud's judgment, not that of his critics; or better, the remark in his hands and those of his followers simply begs the question. Those who do not think that Freudian "technique holds its ground against any criticism" are those who simply have not entered deeply enough "into our work." Further, the relative certainty of his science is belied by all those psychoanalytic theorists who have departed substantially from his theory. These points aside, though, the fact is that Freudian technique is not a technique of controlled experimentation. He says not one word about controlling variables or about ruling out alternative hypotheses. Obviously, his statement is summary, and we do find Freud, on occasion, employing what we normally take to be controls. (See below on Freud's application of Mill's method of agreement and difference.) However, in a section comparing psychoanalysis with the natural sciences we would at least expect some mention of control.

Again, a comparison with Bohr is useful. Bohr's theory agreed with the data from controlled spectroscopic tests, and it predicted a spectrum, experimentally verified a year after he developed his theory. (Humphreys and Beringer, 1950, 275) Over the next decade further tests showed the theory to be inadequate as a general account of the atom, the result being the development of quantum mechanics. Freud's theory did not agree with data derived from controlled tests (there were no such data!), it did not successfully predict a novel phenomenon, and it was not modified in a decade (or two, or three) because of further tests. Freud's theory simply lacks quantified precision and his methodology is not that of controlled experimentation. I shall mention three points at which adequate control is not present.

First, the therapist does not control for the emotional state of the patient or of himself—aside from gross observation or self-awareness—yet the emotional states of both can significantly influence what goes on in the session. A patient could be angry at a therapist and thus be in a mood to mislead or withhold information; or a therapist could be angry at the patient and thus be in a mood to give slanted, painful interpretations of dreams or to dominate the patient. Perhaps in the long-run truth will out in the therapy session—a very debatable contention—but the point is that nothing along the lines of a reliable test is administered in individual sessions in order to control for emotional state. Of course, I would maintain that there is not any emotional test that is reliable to the extent, say, of the test for the temperature of a laboratory room. Consistent monitoring by independent observers would be another way of introducing control for emotions, a way which immediately raises the difficult problem of selecting the observers (selecting only Freudian observers would beg the question) and of determining how they shall monitor—viewing through a one-way window, video tapes, audio tapes, written reports, or oral reports. I should think that nothing short of a video would be adequate because of the importance of visual cues.

Second, in the counseling situation little is done to control for memory, memory of dreams and of childhood experiences. Many dreams, including important ones, ones which might be crucial in therapy, cannot be recalled upon awakening. (One is left knowing that there was a dream and feeling the importance of the dream but is unable to recall what the dream was about.) Also dreams may easily be distorted, consciously or unconsciously. As for childhood memory, confabulation remains a constant threat, but it is not consistently controlled for. Generally speaking, the therapist does not spend time checking out childhood memories. (Among other things, the therapist would likely lose the patient because fees would go out of sight as a result of hiring additional staff.) Moreover, some memories cannot be checked because of the absence of records, the deaths of witnesses, and so on.

Third, in the counseling situation little is done to control for patient domination by the therapist. The idea that since the therapist has been through analysis, the therapist is aware of all tendencies to direct, guide, or manipulate is simply without foundation; or, at least, is highly problematic. We must appeal to the adequacy of the therapist's analysis, yet the therapist went through analysis with another Freudian, who, the accusation goes, is subject to being directive and thus likely to overlook the directive tendencies of the therapist, at least those which fit Freudian theory. Since the same problem arises for the analyst's analyst, we are in an *ad infinitum* series, from which we can rescue ourselves by begging the question—or by developing independent measures for being directive or manipulative, i.e., measures independent of Freudian theory.

At any rate, the very essence of the psychoanalytic session seems to be to guide—e.g., to encourage further free association where emotional blockage is perceived, or to stop when insight

(measured by Freudian theory) is achieved. I shall have more to say on this point later. For now I wish to note that I, contrary to Edelson, have not come across philosophers of science who either say or give the impression that analysts generally guide by making direct suggestions like: "You have an oedipal complex." (130) Philosophers of science, unless also analysts, certainly do not have a detailed awareness of the therapy process, but they are generally aware that analysts employ indirect procedures. Yet I also note that analysts are not generally so indirect that they consistently ask questions along the line, "Well, what do you make of all this?" or "What inferences would you draw from what you are saying and doing?" These sorts of questions, although directive in a sense, are not directive in the way of suggesting a particular conclusion.

In sum, psychoanalysis is not comparable to the natural sciences with respect to quantification and controlled experimentation. Exactly the same may be said for the other psychoanalytic theories, as well as my mixed theory of the unconscious.

A More Generous Approach

Perhaps we can loosen up the scientific requirements, thereby finding space for the unconscious as at least a broadly scientific notion. If Toricelli had said that mercury would rise far less than water in a vacuum tube, and if Einstein had said that light rays from the distant stars would bend some in the field of the sun, we would still probably be impressed with their theories. Or perhaps we could simply follow the suggestion of Bettelheim, thinking of Freud's theory as more comparable to history than physics—more of a social science than a natural science. Whatever Freud's theory is comparable to, we should still want to know its epistemic status. What argument or arguments can we offer for the theory? Are they valid? What evidence can we produce for some of the major concepts? And again, what level of science does it or can it achieve? These are questions which I shall focus on.

The Tally Argument

I shall accept Grünbaum's criticism of Karl Popper that Freud's psychoanalytic theory is, contrary to Popper's contention, a falsifiable theory and thus a theory which at least meets a necessary condition for a scientific theory. (Grünbaum, 1984, 104-126) The next question is whether Freud's theory passes the falsifiability tests to which we may subject it. Grünbaum's answer to this question is negative.

Grünbaum first directs his attention to what he sees as Freud's basic argument for his theory (an argument Grünbaum calls "The Tally Argument"), the argument from therapeutic success. But this argument is unsound. The specifics of Grünbaum's analysis are as follows.

According to Grünbaum, Freud considered therapeutic success to consist "in an adaptive restructuring of the introspected personality dispositions such that there is concomitant lasting overt symptom relief without symptom substitution." (139) Two obvious questions about this criterion of therapeutic success (I shall consider it Freud's criterion) concern symptom relief and symptom substitution: How long must one be free of a symptom to be free of it, and how does one tell that some new symptom is related to a new neurosis, not the old neurosis? In addition, the criterion itself may be inadequate. E.g., Edelson develops the following three criteria of therapeutic success: 1) there is a decreased propensity for symptom formation; 2) there is a decreased propensity for automatic reactions; and 3) there is an increased propensity for love and work. One and two look very much as if they express what is expressed by Freud's criterion, and three, although an addition, is consistent with Freud's criterion. However, each of the therapeutic achievements mentioned by Edelson is a function of the "altered and expanded set of interpretations and appraisals of himself and his world" that the patient makes, interpretations and appraisals which must be veridical. In short, Edelson takes veridical insight as crucial for measuring therapeutic success. (40-42) I am inclined to say that for him therapeutic success is measured simply by the increased propensity to employ veridical interpretations and appraisals in guiding one's life. I shall have more to say on veridical insight later on. For now I want to emphasize that if veridical insight is determined by insight according to Freudian theory, then no alternative theoretical approach can ever match the therapeutic success of the Freudian. Of course, we would also have a slight case of begging the question with respect to therapeutic criteria. I am sympathetic to Edelson's approach, as long as we do not restrict veridical insight to Freudian theory. However, I shall stick to Freud's criterion of therapeutic success, if for no other reason than that comparative studies focus on symptom relief, not veridical insight.

Turning now to Grünbaum's statement of the Tally Argument, we have the following: 1) therapeutic success is impossible apart from correct patient insight into the unconscious dynamics of the patient's pathology; 2) only the Freudian approach provides correct insight into unconscious dynamics; 3) therefore, only the Freudian approach can achieve therapeutic success. (139)

The obvious way to defeat this argument is to show that therapeutic success is or might have been achieved by other approaches. This defeater works apart from anything said concerning psychoanalysts. The suggestion that therapeutic success might not be achieved within psychoanalysis because of the inadequacy of psychoanalysts is irrelevant to the argument, aside from the fact that at least Freud would be considered a first-rate psychoanalyst—if by no one else, then certainly by Freud! The argument says that true insight, which must be Freudian insight (based on Freudian theory), is a necessary condition for therapeutic success; therefore, if therapeutic success is achieved apart from Freudian insight, then the conclusion is false, and it is false regardless of the adequacy or inadequacy of psychoanalysts. If therapeutic success is achieved apart from Freudian insight (the denial of the conclusion), then either true insight is not necessary (premise one) or true insight may be achieved outside Freudian theory (premise two). If premise one is false, then so is Freudian theory, for premise one is an essential aspect of Freudian theory. If premise two is false, then obviously Freudian theory is not the only route to therapeutic insight.

Therapeutic Success with Alternative Theories

What, then, about the counterexamples? Numerous studies have shown that therapeutic success for the various major psychological approaches (with different theories of the self and the unconscious) is equivalent—no particular approach has a monopoly on success. (Vanderbos and Pino, 1980, 33-36; Stiles, Shapiro, and Elliott, 1980, 165-67) Actually, a thesis that psychoanalysis is no more successful than other therapies is far stronger than we need to defeat the conclusion of the Tally Argument. All we need is a thesis stating that other therapies are sometimes successful. The various studies conducted (reviewed in Vanderbos) indicate that non-Freudian approaches achieve therapeutic success. I shall cite one example (which, theoretically, is enough to do-in the Tally Argument) related by Hans Eysenck.

Eysenck states that obsessive-compulsive hand-washing behavior is very resistant to treatment by psychoanalysis. However, Eysenck and Rachman treated the disorder by employing classical conditioning, more specifically by employing a method of emotional flooding and response prevention, the results being 80 to 90 percent cure rate for the cases treated. Whether or not this high cure rate would hold is, of course, not the issue; the issue is simply whether or not the approach of Eysenck and Rachman brought any cures. (Eysenck, 1986, 379-80).

Freud would have a way out of this kind of counterexample, although he did not take it in the case of obsessive-compulsive hand-washing behavior. The way would be to eliminate certain neuroses—e.g., obsessive-compulsive handwashing—from the class of psychoneuroses, the class of neuroses with dynamics in the unconscious, the class treatable by psychoanalysis. Freud did adopt this general approach, calling the other neuroses "actual neuroses," one of which was anxiety neurosis. According to Freud, anxiety neurosis is not a psychoneurosis, i.e., a neurosis, the origin of which is in the unconscious (more specifically, repression plays a role). Instead, it is a neurosis which is caused strictly by *coitus interruptus*. Yet how is this determined—by the analysis of dreams, free association, and so on? Apparently not, but simply by the employment of Mill's methods of agreement and difference. (Grünbaum, 169-70) What this means, then, is that Freud must subject all neuroses to the same sort of analysis, i.e., an analysis using Mill's methods. And he cannot resort to therapeutic success to support psychoanalysis, unless he shows that therapeutic success was not and could not have been achieved in any other way, something which he could not do without employing Mill's methods. In the case of the disorder treated by Eysenck psychoanalysts do not take the tack of relegating it to an actual neurosis. Therefore, they must face the reality of an alternative successful therapy. Even if obsessive-compulsive handwashing were classed as actual, the question would be why, and the answer would have to be something other than that it cannot be treated by the psychoanalytic approach.

The fact is that other psychological approaches are employed on the neuroses called "psychoneuroses," with the other approaches meeting with as much success as the psychoanalytic. The studies employed may be deficient in that they lack stringent standards of success, but if so, psychoanalytic theory will not benefit, for it will, the same as the other approaches, have been measured by the same inadequate standards. Obviously, we shall not wish to measure psychoanalysis by any set of strictly psychoanalytic measures of success, for in that case we shall be begging the question.

Another successful approach to psychoneurosis which certainly needs to be mentioned in this book is religious experience. Numerous people are cured of neurotic symptoms by a religious experience. We have already come across some people who were either clearly neurotic or close to being so (had severe depression, e.g.). Obviously, if religious experience effected the cure for them, then the Tally Argument does not go. Moreover, if the unconscious is supposed to be the explanation for their experience, some argument other than the Tally Argument will have to be found.

Instead of showing that therapeutic success is achieved by other approaches, we could do the simpler task of showing that therapeutic success may plausibly be considered a result of other factors than psychoanalysis. E.g., we might claim that therapeutic success is a consequence of patient compliance with therapist suggestions. In short, since the therapy session is one in which the therapist functions as an authority figure, any therapeutic success is a consequence of patient compliance to the therapist's desires (the patient accepts the therapist's interpretations or the therapist's measures of therapeutic success) not insight into dynamical truth. This possibility takes issue with premise one. Neither Freud nor his followers have ruled out the possibility, and certainly cannot do so by an appeal to therapeutic success, except on pain of begging the question. What Freud and his followers must produce are controlled studies showing that patients are responding not to the authority of the therapist but to insight into dynamical truth. The studies have yet to be produced.

Or therapeutic success might be a result of spontaneous remission. By spontaneous remission I do not mean immediate recovery but recovery apart from psychoanalysis, recovery taking place, say, over a period of time equivalent to that of psychoanalytic treatment. Psychoanalytic treatment is very lengthy, lasting normally from three to five years, a period of time which, we might reasonably suppose, would bring therapeutic success to most anybody who is working with family and friends— especially supportive family and friends—to resolve psychological problems and to achieve growth, or perhaps to most anybody who is just trying to relieve psychological distress. Time, as we all know, is said to be the great healer. In 1952 Hans Eysenck presented the thesis that there was no firm evidence indicating the superiority of psychotherapy to no treatment at all in the case of psychoneurosis. The weight of the evidence now seems to indicate that psychotherapy is superior, but the evidence does not deny spontaneous remissions. Indeed, it recognizes them. (Vanderbos, 1980, 33-36) Since the only thesis necessary to defeat the Freudian argument is that spontaneous remissions occur, a thesis which Freud himself accepted (Grünbaum, 160), we again have reason to abandon the Tally Argument as an argument for Freud's position.

Enough, then, for the Tally Argument, except to say that any other psychological approach using a similar type of argument (i.e., appealing to therapeutic success) does not fare any better than psychoanalysis.

Causal Relationships

The Tally Argument may be fallacious, yet Freud's theory may still be true, for Freud may just not have hit upon the proper argument for his theory. Perhaps, then, his theory has support which he did not articulate or which others have developed in later years. Perhaps we can defend the theory by deducing consequences from it which prove to be true or by spinning off sub-hypotheses from it which prove to be true. What I should like to do now is focus on several specific areas of research which are designed to test Freudian theory but which either raise doubts about the theory or leave the theory untested.

One area of research in recent years has focused on the general notion of defense, of which repression is the most notable example. According to Freud, repression consists of excluding from consciousness certain distressing or painful experiences, intentions, or ideas in order to avoid the distress or pain associated with them. (Erdelyi, 1985, 220) Erdelyi has developed a defense-process model, along the lines of an information-processing flowchart. (241) I shall quote from his analysis of the flowchart.

> If the level of anxiety [x] that the information would provoke in consciousness matches or exceeds the unbearability criterion [m], the information-processing is aborted ('Stop processing/accessing information'), without it being transferred to Pcs. (a preconscious information buffer). Note that the value of m may actually vary, so that when the individual feels in a particularly vulnerable state the criterion value, m, may be set very low, whereas under more auspicious circumstances, it might be set much higher (allowing for the possibility of consciousness for the painful material that is excluded from consciousness in other circumstances). Also, any agent (such as hypnosis or sodium pentothal) that would lower the level of anxiety, x, associated with the information, would necessarily result in greater potential consciousness for the material. (p. 240)

In this quotation we find Erdelyi doing what Edelson does: He employs concepts with the appearance of quantification but not the reality. We would almost think that anxiety is like temperature in a room, so that when the anxiety reaches a certain level (determined by the unbearability criterion, m, with its value)—in short, becomes too hot to handle—the system cycles it out of consciousness, just as when temperature in a room reaches a certain degree, the cooling system cycles on, lowering the temperature. My remarks on Edelson's notion of threshold intensity apply here, so that I shall not say anything further.

Actually, speaking about anxiety level and unbearability criterion, as well as a state of vulnerability, is little more than a diversion. The real question is whether material can be excluded from consciousness apart from any anxiety at all. Items might well be cycled out of, or remain out of consciousness, for a variety of other reasons, such as intense concentration on something else, a flood of stimuli blocking out the item, an immediate strong desire doing the blocking, or a number of other factors. Further—and this is the crucial consideration—even if anxiety is associated with some material excluded from consciousness, the question is whether the material is excluded because of the anxiety associated with it, because it is too painful for consciousness—or for some other reason. Anxiety-laden material may be excluded from consciousness for a variety of reasons: attention is focused on some other matter of immediate concern, not necessarily important, such as solving an engineering problem from work (a condition which could well occur within a therapeutic setting); preoccupation with a value-laden matter, such as the terminal illness of a spouse; the dominance of other feelings, such as grief or anger or joy, feelings which must be considered anxiety laden only by begging the question; the presence of some anxiety-laden material other than the item excluded from consciousness . . . the list of reasons could continue. Has Freud, Erdelyi, or anybody else shown, or does anybody even have a way of showing, that some material is repressed *because* it is too painful for consciousness? Not that I know of.

In order to underline what I have just said, I shall consider investigations of two items: selective perception and intentional forgetting.

Selective perception, viz., the process of a subject filtering out material from perception, may be taken as a given. Of course, one may filter out material which is not emotionally charged, as well as material which is charged. I may be thoroughly concentrating on one aspect of my environment (e.g., looking for sanddollars along the seashore), with the result that I neglect other obvious aspects of the environment (e.g., a closely-matched two-person volleyball game, or a lifeguard tower), aspects which I find at least as difficult to get into consciousness as any emotionally charged material. This point aside, we may still admit that there is emotionally charged material which is filtered out. But is it filtered out because there is a defensive intention to do so? Erdelyi puts the question this way: "Does lowered sensitivity necessarily imply a defensive intention not to see, as opposed to a general disruption of processing by emotionality?" He maintains, on the basis of a study conducted by him, that there is evidence for disruption resulting from emotionality rather than defensive intention. His conclusion on the issue of selective perception is as follows.

> It has been experimentally shown that (a) emotional stimuli may yield impaired perception and (b) that the perceiver can intentionally and selectively reject perceptual inputs. What has *not* been demonstrated

in the laboratory, however, is the conjoint fact that the perception of emotional stimuli is disrupted *because* of intentional rejection by the perceiver. (256)

Surprisingly, Erdelyi considers the conjoint fact to be highly plausible, even though the conjoint fact was not demonstrated by his study; in fact, his study, according to him, casts suspicion on the fact.

Turning to intentional forgetting (or more exactly, to the recall of material supposedly forgotten intentionally), Erdelyi says that

> we find, for example, that a subject (in therapy, hypnosis, or with just the passage of time) manages to remember some heretofore inaccessible painful idea, including in many instances the original resolve to reject the material from consciousness. (244)

Two problems are associated with this finding. The first of these is confabulation or false recollection. According to Erdelyi, subjects under hypnosis, e.g., can recover memories not only from early childhood but from a previous existence or from the future! (67-68) Of course, records and relatives may help check memories from childhood, although access to either one is not always possible and is usually not pursued in therapy because of therapeutic irrelevance or lack of time or other resources to do the checking. The second problem has to do with trying to determine whether subjects are presenting material previously excised from consciousness or whether they are simply reporting material which, although in consciousness, was not previously reported. Erdelyi says that the resolution of this problem does not seem to be forthcoming. (71-72, 247-48)

An Analysis of Free Association

These two instances, then, underline what I said: We do not have clear evidence—and we do not presently know how to get it—that the cause of certain material being excluded from consciousness is the defensive intention to avoid anxiety. Yet a psychoanalyst might say that anyone involved in the therapeutic setting, employing the methods of psychotherapy, will find all the evidence that is needed. If the epistemic validity of what goes on in the therapy session really rests ultimately on the Tally Argument, then I need say nothing more. However, perhaps the major procedures of the analytic setting have an epistemic worth independent of the Tally Argument, so that they need to be evaluated apart from the argument. I believe that the procedures have epistemic worth only in so far as they meet the rigor's of Mill's method of agreement and difference, a method which is not systematically applied in the therapeutic setting. However, for the sake of the argument I shall consider the possibility that the procedures of the therapeutic setting have epistemic worth in themselves. I do not wish to cover all the major procedures of the analytic setting, for Grünbaum has done so, and I cannot improve on what he has said. (190-245) However, for illustrative purposes I shall briefly consider free association.

Free association is of crucial importance because it is a means of arriving at the correct interpretation of dreams, as well as the correct interpretation of slips (of memory, tongue, pen, and ear). Therefore, if free association is problematic, so is the interpretation of dreams and slips. I shall focus on a case considered by Grünbaum, a case reported by Freud, of a young man Grünbaum dubs "AJ". (190)

AJ, venting to Freud his frustration over the social and career handicaps which have come to him because he is a Jew, quotes a line from Virgil's *Aeneid*, doing so inaccurately, inverting word order and leaving out a noun. AJ asks Freud to explain the memory lapse, whereupon Freud asks AJ to free associate. He starts with the noun he left out, continues until he reaches something "intimate," continues once more when Freud urges him on, and stops after relating that he was fearful of having impregnated his paramour. At this point Freud stops the free association. And at this point we may raise the first question, viz., Why stop with the intimate story? Where would AJ have gone if free association had continued? Perhaps he would have ended up with something even more anxiety laden, or perhaps his associations would have revealed some other reason for the forgetting, or perhaps there were other reasons for the forgetting, independently of what free association might reveal, such as the whole list of strictly linguistic reasons, or perhaps he never learned the particular line of the *Aeneid* well. These suggestions—a few of many that could be made—are indicative of the alternatives Freud did not check out but absolutely had to check out in order to support any claim of superiority for his theory.

The suggestions are also indicative of the serious probative deficiencies of free association. In other words, Freud, to one degree or another, directed and controlled free association; in fact, free association is anything but free. Naturally, I take Freud to be representative of the best of therapists at free association. What is obviously happening in the case of AJ is that Freud is directing the association in harmony with his theory of the unconscious, a marvelous way to achieve support of one's theory! In short, by stopping when he wants (Read: Stopping when the data fit his theory.), he is effectively selecting his data to fit his theory—the very item at issue. Actually, we might suggest that as long as Freud was directing, he could have directed AJ to free associate on the inverted word order. I think that if AJ had done so, he still would have ended up with his fears about his paramour. More on this below.

Various studies support the thesis that what happens in free association is a function, to one degree or another, of the therapist. What I have said above is really enough to support the thesis, but J. Marmour summarizes the findings by saying: "'Clinical experience has demonstrated that . . . "free" associations of the patient are strongly influenced by the values and expectations of the therapist.'" (Grünbaum, 211) He goes on to maintain that

> depending on the point of view of the psychoanalyst, patients of every psychoanalytic school tend, *under free association,* 'to bring up precisely the kind of phenomenological data which confirm the theories and interpretations of their analysts! Thus each theory tends to be self-validating. (Grünbaum, 211)

Given that reflecting on the noun, which allegedly was anxiety laden, led to AJ's fears of an impregnated paramour, we are not justified in moving from association or affinity of ideas to causal influence. Actually, one suggestion would be that whatever term he reflected on—a term, say, that he remembered accurately—he would have ended up with his fears about his paramour, simply because these fears were foremost in his thinking. Further, Freud has not even shown that the forgotten noun was anxiety laden; all that he showed was that reflecting on it led to an anxiety laden item. A more serious deficiency, is that the example of AJ is not a good example of getting to repressed material by way of free association because the fears of AJ were apparently not repressed. This point aside, though, the other points I have made still stand.

I especially wish to underscore the point that associative relationship between ideas does not in any way demonstrate causal influence. I repeat: The fact that AJ moved from the forgotten noun to his fears regarding his paramour does not show that he forgot the word because of his fears about his paramour. Therefore, even dismissing the criticisms concerning a therapist's directing and influencing free association, we do not have assurance that free association provides us with anything causal. Some other procedure will have to be employed, a controlled experimental procedure, I should think, the very kind of procedure generally eschewed by psychoanalysts.

Obviously, if free association has the problems I have noted in the case of slips, it will have the same problems in dream interpretation. Thus, to the extent that free association is essential to the proper analysis of dreams, to that extent the epistemic inadequacies of free association color the interpretation of dreams. Moreover, to the extent that other theories of the unconscious rely on free association to validate the notion of the unconscious, to that extent they partake of the epistemic weaknesses associated with free association. In fact, I should say more generally (relying on Grünbaum for the more general critique) that to the extent that other theories of the unconscious rely for the validation of the unconscious on the major clinical techniques of the Freudians (free association, slips, dreams), to that extent they partake of the epistemic weaknesses of those techniques.

Erdelyi on Freudian Theory As Science

Before concluding this section on the scientific status of the psychoanalytic method, I wish to do two things. First of all, I shall focus on a remark of Erdelyi. He says that the difference between a Freudian clinical approach and the approach of the natural sciences may be summed up as follows. "The problem of interpretation is not that it is in principle unscientific (unruleful) but rather that we do not as yet have a science of interpretation that goes substantially beyond intuitive understanding." (95) Erdelyi seems to be saying that clinical interpretation is scientific in one sense but not in another (the most important, I should say); i.e., clinical interpretations are in principle scientific—they are capable of ruleful development— but as of now they are not ruleful but intuitive. Why he believes that the interpretations are in principle ruleful, I do not know because he presents no reasons. However, if the interpretation I have given his words is correct, I am satisfied to let the matter stand there. According to his own admission, the interpretations of the clinical approach are not scientific, as long as science involves the explicit articulation and elaboration of experimentally confirmed rules (laws). To date the major interpretations of psychoanalysis have not been subjected to controlled testing, testing of such a sort that a process of weeding out takes place so that some interpretations— in rule form— come to be preferred over others, i.e., come to be confirmed. In short, the interpretations are not, as I said, scientific in the most important sense.

However Erdelyi seems to undercut the reading I gave of his statement by saying that "we demonstrably apply ruleful processes to the extraction of deep meanings from deep stimuli—otherwise there would be no consensus." (95) He is referring here to specific advertisements and cartoons in which a penis interpretation is simply undeniable. Determining the meaning of certain symbols, commonly used in society, such as sexual symbols, is very easy, as easy for the lay person as the clinician; thus, for these common social symbols I do not see that the meanings are deep or that the stimuli are deep. The same goes for dreams—some of the symbolism within dreams is simply a carryover of symbolism from our conscious life. Saying that we apply ruleful processes to extract the meaning of common symbols seems highly overstated, unless Erdelyi simply means that we apply what we have learned or that learning is in some sense ruleful. The problem with dream symbolism comes at the point that provincial theoretical interpretations are imposed on the symbolism, interpretations which, indeed, are ruleful—they follow the rules of the particular theory, say, Freud's—but not ruleful in any sense similar to the rulefulness of the natural sciences.

The main point, though, is that Erdelyi says that we employ ruleful processes to extract deep meanings from deep stimuli, and thus intuitive understanding is apparently not the means of arriving at the interpretation, unless 'intuitive understanding' is now taken to be inclusive of ruleful processes. Be this as it may, the proof of the application of ruleful processes is supposed to be consensus. Consensus among whom? Hopefully, not just among those who agree on the meaning of the symbols! The fact is that consensus is limited on the interpretation of dreams and even on common social symbols—some people never get adequately socialized. Further, consensus on the meaning of symbols does not necessarily represent the application of ruleful processes, i.e., the application—implicitly, I suppose, if not explicitly—of some rule in the extraction of meaning. E.g., having learned the meaning of certain symbols, we immediately grasp the meaning when we see the symbol, without employing any kind of ruleful process. More generally, we can be conditioned to respond immediately to certain stimuli, without applying some rule to get to the response from the stimuli. Or in the case of jokes, an example also used by Erdelyi of intuitive understanding, consensus of laughter may arise because some people get the joke and others laugh because they do not want to appear ignorant. Other reasons for consensus can certainly be enumerated. The consequence is that Erdelyi has at best—and the best is, as I have noted, questionable—made a case that clinical interpretations are scientific only in principle.

Edelson and the Miss X Case

The second thing I wish to do is focus on an example Edelson uses to show that psychoanalytic hypotheses can be tested within the psychoanalytic session, i.e., tested using what he calls a "single subject research design." The case is that of a Miss X, who manifested thirteen instances of momentary forgetting during some three hundred sessions of psychoanalysis. In Freudian theory "momentary forgetting is an instance of a neurotic symptom or parapraxis," and a neurotic symptom cannot appear (or increase in severity) apart from "an increase in the intensity of a focal conflict." (145) These are two theoretical hypotheses to be tested, the latter hypothesis being less than adequately stated because of the vague phrase 'increase in intensity'. Given Edelson's previous remarks about the threshold intensity of an instinctual wish or impulse, I should think that he would at least make reference to a threshold intensity, for a very slight increase in intensity would not likely issue in a symptom (if we could have a scale of one to ten, a rise of one-half a degree would seem unlikely to produce any symptom), unless the intensity was just below the threshold to begin with. In any case, we have no idea of the degree of increase required for the appearance (or increase in severity) of a neurotic symptom.

Another theoretical hypothesis included in the test is the Freudian view of transference, which leads to the further hypothesis that an increase in the intensity of a focal conflict in the psychoanalytic situation will issue in an intensified emotional involvement with the analyst. The same remarks I just made about 'increase in intensity' would also apply here. The hypotheses, along with the facts concerning Miss X, lead to the following prediction: "The degree of emotional involvement of Miss X with her psychoanalyst is much greater in those contexts in which momentary forgetting occurs than it is in those contexts in which momentary forgetting does not occur." (145)

The statement of the predicted outcome is inadequate for at least two reasons. First, Edelson certainly does not want to say that the degree of emotional involvement is greater when forgetting is present than when it is absent, even though when it is absent, some other neurotic symptom (say, obsessive behavior) is present. Thus, he should say, "in contexts in which neither forgetting nor other neurotic symptoms occur." Second, the phrase 'in those contexts' is vague in that it does not spell out causal relationships, so that, among other things, we do not know whether forgetting follows greater emotional involvement or *vice versa*, or whether greater emotional involvement and forgetting appear at the same time, both being effects of the focal conflict.

Yet vagueness moves to possible confusion when Edelson speaks of the test's outcome. He says: "The null hypothesis that the outcome might be expected to occur by extraneous influences alone, acting randomly (not all in one direction), even in the absence of any relation between emotional involvement with the psychoanalyst (resulting in intensification of conflict) and momentary forgetting, is eliminated by statistical test." (146) I shall examine this claim below, but for now I simply focus on the words 'emotional involvement with the psychoanalyst (resulting in intensification of conflict)'. The hypothesis following from Freudian transference theory was that intensification of a focal conflict leads to intensification of emotional involvement with the analyst. Perhaps Edelson means that intensification of a focal conflict results in intensification of emotional involvement, which, in turn, further intensifies the focal conflict. Or perhaps he means 'intensification of conflict with the therapist', although he has not used the term 'conflict' in that way. His hypotheses seem to require a causal sequence going from 1) intensification of focal conflict to 2) increased emotional involvement with the psychoanalyst to 3) momentary forgetting. If I am wrong about this, we may still be certain that the predicted outcome concerns the association between forgetting and intensified emotional involvement, whatever the sequence of the two.

I leave aside any comments on the notion 'degree of emotional involvement' and will go straight to what Edelson presents as the control situation or context. He says: "A control context is a matched passage, of similar length and the same amount of time into the session, from a nearly contiguous session in which no symptom occurred." (145) Since the predicted outcome compares a situation of forgetting to one in which forgetting does not occur, 'no symptom' here must refer to forgetting. However, I simply reiterate what I said above: If the matched passage contained another neurotic symptom, then according to Freudian theory we should clearly also have an increase in emotional involvement, so that Edelson should be looking for passages without any symptom at all. Perhaps this is what he meant, but since I cannot be certain, I shall pass on to another control issue.

Since the test is trying to determine the association between forgetting and increased emotional involvement, we must be able to determine the latter. I left aside any comments on 'degree of emotional involvement', but now I must say something, viz., that a slight increase in emotional involvement would not seem likely to produce a neurotic symptom. Thus, how much of an increase in emotional involvement must we see? Edelson does not discuss this issue. What he discusses is how to get an objective evaluation of emotional involvement. He says that we must have judges who make their evaluations without knowing the passages in which the symptom occurred. I add that the judges must also be independent, unbiased judges, meaning at least that they must come from a variety of theoretical backgrounds. To say that only Freudian psychoanalysts can be proper judges is to beg the question. At any rate, the experiment concerning Miss X apparently did not employ any judges, for Edelson remarks that "in an ideal execution of this research design" the judges would be necessary. (145-46) What Edelson calls "an ideal execution" I call "a normal test execution."

According to Edelson, the result of the actual test for Miss X is positive: We "observe" the predicted outcome, which, as we saw above, is: "The null hypothesis that the outcome might be expected to occur by extraneous influences alone, acting randomly (not all in one direction), even in the absence of any relation between emotional involvement with the psychoanalyst (resulting in an intensification of conflict) and momentary forgetting, is eliminated by statistical test." (146) 'Observation' here means, then, 'statistically supported'. However, testing for random influences is testing simply for one alternative hypothesis, which I shall assume is eliminated. However, there are numerous other alternative hypotheses, and since the predicted outcome specifies merely an association between forgetting and increased emotional involvement, without specifying anything about the sequence or causal relations between the two, the alternative hypotheses are more numerous than if causal relations were carefully specified.

As for alternative hypotheses, we should certainly have to consider non-psychoanalytic theories of forgetting. One theory was mentioned above when we were discussing Erdelyi, viz., sheer emotionality; i.e., if the sequence is from forgetting to increased emotional involvement, then momentary forgetting could produce an emotional state—apart from any focal conflict—which affects the relationship with the therapist. E.g., forgetting the name of a good friend when an introduction is required generally produces some emotionality. Or if the sequence is from increased emotional involvement to forgetting, then we may very well get increased emotional involvement without any increase in the intensity of a focal conflict. One way would be by a form of the Clever Hans Phenomenon, by Miss X cueing on the psychiatrist; i.e., the psychiatrist could react when content he sees as related to focal conflicts arises (e.g., he pulls on his beard), Miss X cueing on his reactions and becoming emotional, then forgetting. Another possibility would be that the memory lapses occurred when the psychiatrist questioned or pressed on some subject, whereas apart from questioning or pressing memory did not lapse. I leave other possibilities to the experts.

In sum, the test of Miss X is a weak test, not employing adequate controls and not eliminating an array of major alternative hypotheses (only a few of which I have mentioned). In addition, we have the very serious deficiency of a single subject design, viz., generalizing from it. What was true for Miss X may not be true for Mr. Z or Mrs. Q. or . . . Ms. N.

Scientific Status of Freudian and Theistic Theories

I am of the opinion that the sort of confirmation achieved in the Miss X example does not exceed the sort of confirmation achieved by a theistic theory of religious experience. My study is an attempt to provide some control for natural circumstances which might give rise to religious experience. The controls are primitive, but that is just the state of the art now. Yet we can, e.g., more easily eliminate the Clever Hans Phenomenon in the case of religious experience than in the case of therapy, essentially because numerous individuals have experiences in private. We should have to consider alternative cues, cues in the environment or perhaps internal cues, but at least we should not have the Clever Hans Phenomenon to consider as a general explanation. When some other person is present, we should have to control for the Phenomenon, but that would not be much more difficult than in the case of the therapeutic session. In principle I do not know why we cannot improve controls significantly.

Coming at this from a different angle, I would say that Edelson has shown nothing more in the Miss X case than that the Freudian hypotheses are not falsified. I believe that the same may be said for many theistic hypotheses concerning religious experience. What this means is that I consider many theistic hypotheses for religious experience to be falsifiable, with some not being falsified. The approach of this book is that if naturalistic alternatives for explaining religious experience function as overriders, then at least one type of theistic thesis (God meets us in our experience) is falsified. My argument is that the theistic thesis is not falsified.

Edelson presents another case, a case of what he calls "the bootstrap method." (147-53) I do not think that the case improves his position at all, but I shall leave the case for others to discuss.

If, as I hope, most of what I have said to this point is in order, then the Freudian case for the unconscious, if not falsified, is at best only weakly confirmed. At some points— e.g., as an account of the turn to religion or of religious experience—it is falsified, or so I think I have shown. Be this as it may, other psychoanalytic theories of the unconscious do not seem to fare any better than Freudian theory. Certainly, other theories do not outscore Freudian theory on their capacity to certify causal mechanisms of the unconscious; e.g., the two problems of selective perception and intentional forgetting are not, as far as I can tell, resolved better by any other theory of the unconscious than by Freudian theory, and no other psychoanalytic theory provides for better controls in testing than does Freudian theory. Additionally, no other group of psychoanalytic theorists actually implement better controls than do Freudian theorists. My mixed theory fares no better than the Freudian theories.

3. Is Freudian Theory a Naturalistic Alternative to Theism?

I should now like to return to what I said above, viz., that Freudian theory does not look much better, scientifically, than a theistic theory. In fact, I think that the Freudian notion of the unconscious is, in many respects, like the notion of God. And here, I should say, I am picking up on Bettelheim's characterization of psychoanalysis as "the science of the soul." In other words, if Freud's theory is not meant to be scientific in the sense of a rigorous natural science, then how does it stand *vis a vis* a theistic theory? Of course, whatever Bettelheim says, my point is that Freudian theory does not measure up to the demands of quantification and control found in the natural sciences and also found to a significant degree in the behavioral sciences. The question, then, is: What is the status of the theory *vis a vis* a theistic theory?

If the unconscious is such that it can intrude into a person's life unexpectedly, can bring about immediate character transformations, can produce a sense of the Divine in people with radically different parental backgrounds, can present the Divine as a reality which our best critical efforts endorse as real, can present a Divine which is outside of the molds of culture or of any thoughts that a person has had, and can intrude as a Presence independently of any particular set of environmental or physiological conditions, then not only has the unconscious moved out of the sphere of the lawlike but it seems fairly obviously to be functioning very much as God is said to function. In other words—and this is the main point I wish to make here—if, in the case of religious experience, the unconscious is given the same function as God, then we seem to be confronted with little more than a semantical difference, so that whether we call the Reality of religious experience "God" or "The Unconscious" is of little consequence. I shall briefly examine this possibility.

Lawlike Statements

First of all, the Freudian theory does not provide us with any lawlike statements to account for religious experience. I emphasize here the notion of the lawlike, or what Erdelyi called "the ruleful." These notions characterize science—a major effort of science is to discover lawlike relationships in nature, which may be expressed fairly narrowly as laws (e.g., the law of gravity) or more comprehensively as theories (e.g., the theory of relativity). In fact, the assumption is that nature is lawlike, so that if we enter a realm in which we do not discover or do not think that we shall discover the lawlike, we have departed the realm of the natural. A non-natural realm may have its own laws, but as of now I do not think that we can state anything concerning the realm of the paranormal or of religious experience that is lawlike along the lines of the natural sciences. If we do develop spiritual laws, then obviously they will not be natural regularities or natural laws, i.e., laws applying to strictly space-time realities. Thus, perhaps I should say that Freudian theory does not provide us with any natural lawlike statements for religious experience.

The chasm between the lawlike and Freudian theory is very obvious in the case of religious experience. We have seen that Freud tries to explain only our turn to religion—not religious experience—by his theory of regression to the infantile. At any rate, the hypothesis does not even explain the turn to religion, for we have seen that the hypothesis is easily falsified. Thus, the Freudian theory of the unconscious does not provide us with any lawlike statement—not to mention a confirmed lawlike statement—to the effect that when the unconscious state of people is of a certain sort, they will have a religious experience. No other psychoanalytic theory of the unconscious does any better—neither does any reinforcement theory (along Skinnerian lines) or physiological theory.

I shall not maintain that theories of the unconscious are unable to provide us with a lawlike statement which might be confirmed, only that none has yet done so. I maintain, though, that any lawlike statements offered are likely to be tendency statements of the sort: People with a certain unconscious state will tend to have religious experience of a certain kind (Western, Eastern, and so on). Perhaps the statements will be put in statistical form. Whether in statistical form or not, the question is: What is the significance of the statements as naturalistic challenges to the view that religious experience is a rational ground for religious belief or to the view that the God hypothesis is a rational account (at least as rational as any other) of religious experience? To discover that people with an unconscious state of a certain sort tend to have religious experience is much like learning that people with college education tend to have religious experience or that people who fast and pray tend to have religious experience. In fact, I think that we are likely to find a higher correlation between fasting and praying and religious experience than between some unconscious state and religious experience. Obviously, I do not have any kind of systematically developed evidence for my thinking here. My main point, though, concerns not what I think the correlations are but what the significance of tendency or statistical statements is. I shall say that tendency statements provide only for weak naturalistic explanations. A strong naturalistic explanation would be one appealing to laws stating necessary and sufficient natural conditions for religious experience. In-between would be a gradation of explanations: e.g., explanations employing laws stating either a necessary or a sufficient condition, but not both; explanations employing statistical laws stating a high correlation (such as in the case of smoking and lung cancer) between natural conditions and religious experience; and so on.

My contention, then, is that theistic theories and theories of the unconscious are similar in that presently neither provides us with lawlike statements accounting for religious experience. (Obviously, in the case of theistic theories we do not expect lawlike statements.) Moreover, if tendency statements are developed for the unconscious, the same can be developed for the Divine: e.g., people who seriously seek the Divine tend to encounter the Divine. If 'seriously seek' is supposed to be a problem, I do not see that it is any more of a problem than specifying, say, degree of emotionality.

Spirituality

Yet if theistic theories and theories of the unconscious are similar with respect to lawlike statements, are they not different in that the Divine is spiritual, whereas the unconscious is non-spiritual? Freud said that "'psychical topography has *for the present* nothing to do with anatomy; it has reference not to anatomical localities, but to regions in the mental apparatus, wherever they may be situated in the body.'" (Erdelyi, 135) This quotation is ambiguous, and in being so mirrors Freud's ambivalence on the issue of the association of mental and physical structure. He says that psychical topography, as regions of the mental apparatus, has nothing to do with anatomy, yet the regions of the mental apparatus are apparently situated somewhere in the body. Thus, the mental does and does not have something to do with the body. Perhaps he meant to say that at present the mental is associated with the body, viz., the brain, but not with any specific locale of the brain. In fact, Freud did say previously in the same passage that "mental activity is bound up with the function of the brain as it is with no other organ." Hence, we should expect him to say something along the lines of, "although psychical topography has to do with the brain, at the present it cannot be tied down to specific locales of the brain."

Since Freud did not say this, we must again ask what he meant. He at least seems to be thinking of the mental as something distinct from the anatomical, the physical. Even if he had said that mental structures and mental activity are *associated with* anatomical structures and activities, e.g., with specific sorts of neural activity in specific areas of the brain, he would obviously not be reducing the mental to the physical but would be thinking of the mental and physical as distinct from one another; for if he thought that the mental is some aspect of the physical, then he would not talk of the mental being *associated with* neural activity in the brain but of the mental *being* neural activity (say, of a special sort) in the brain. As a result, Freud's unconscious cannot be compared to theoretical particles in physics, such as electrons, protons, and quarks. These particles are irreducibly physical, always, e.g., occupying some locale of space (even when they are considered spread-out in some form or as existing only when tested for). If the unconscious is not a physical sort of structure, activity, or functioning, then it seems to be of a sort similar to what we have in mind when we speak of the spiritual. Whatever Freud thought, his theory of the unconscious, as well as other psychoanalytic theories, has neither been reduced to anything physical (say, some aspect or set of processes of the brain) nor has it been shown to be entirely causally dependent on anything physical. Hence, the Freudian unconscious looks as if it is a kind of spiritual reality.

Self-Transcendence

A further reason for considering the two notions semantically similar is that the unconscious, like the Divine, functions so as to transcend the individual self, if in no other case, then certainly in the case of religious experience. What, then, are some of the self-transcending aspects of religious experience?

Physical objects transcend the individual in that their appearing and the way they appear are not a function of the oedipal experiences, educational background, financial status, or other similar conditions of the individual. Likewise, religious experience—its occurrence and its content—is not a function of the oedipal experiences, educational background, financial status, or other similar conditions of an individual. Further, physical objects transcend the individual in that they appear independently of the desires or wishes of the individual. Religious experience, as we have seen, is also independent of the desires or wishes of an individual, at least in the sense that they are neither a necessary nor a sufficient condition for the experience. And religious experience is not at all like obsessions or hallucinations, experiences which are independent of conscious desire or wish, yet not independent, according to psychoanalytic theory, of desire or feeling. Some desire (such as for a forbidden object) or feeling (such as guilt) was pushed down (repressed) into the unconscious, only to make an appearance later as an obsession or hallucination, an appearance which is not healthy, and not healthy on the grounds of psychoanalytic theory. Additionally, physical objects transcend the individual in that they take us where we could never take ourselves by our own powers. A large wave may take us at high speed either where we do or do not want to go (depending on whether we are or are not expert body or board surfers). Religious experience takes people to a new level of experience, and often to a radically changed course of life, with the people saying that they could never have accomplished any of this by themselves, some of them having tried very hard to do so. Finally, a physical object transcends the individual in that it is recognized as an independently existing reality, and recognized so even after our best critical thinking is applied to it. Religious experience also presents people with an Object that they cannot dismiss as merely an object of their own consciousness, even after their best critical thinking is applied to It. Thus, the unconscious, if it is the explanation for religious experience, seems to function in all these self-transcending ways, i.e., in the very ways that a divine Object would.

At this point I shall remark that Carl Jung, with his Collective Unconscious, introduces another component to the unconscious which has to be considered self-transcending. I leave a detailed, systematic discussion of this issue to others.

Psychoanalytic theorists would generally insist, I grant, that the unconscious is individual and natural. What I am saying in this section is that their insistence is less than convincing. If the unconscious has the self-transcending functions just mentioned, then it is not the strictly individual reality of traditional theory. Further, if it functions outside a lawlike framework, then it is not natural. The only sense in which it is natural is that those who theorize about it hope that their theories will become more lawlike. If the theories become more lawlike, then I predict (without prophetic credentials or a Voice) that the unconscious will account for spheres of life which are on the hither side (to use James's terminology) of our experience, rather than the farther side, the mystical dimension or the dimension of Mystery.

A Rebuttal

Suppose, though, that we defend the natural status of the unconscious along the following lines. We are not able to say why a particular hallucination or a particular dream arose at a given time. Our explanation for the phenomena is not lawlike, or at least not lawlike enough to permit us to predict precisely when a particular hallucination or dream will occur. (E.g., "Tonight you will dream of Jeanie with the light brown hair, who will represent etc.") All the same, we know that there is a cause for these mental phenomena and that the cause is natural, residing somewhere in the unconscious or semi-conscious. In addition, hallucinations appear in our consciousness with a certain self-transcendence—they do not come upon conscious invitation. But we again resort to strictly natural causes of an unconscious sort for an explanation. In other words, we can no more predict (or place within a lawful system) a dream or hallucination than we can religious experiences, and we can no more explain precisely the self-transcendence of hallucinations than we can religious experience; yet we do not resort to an explanation by way of the Divine for the phenomena of dreams and hallucinations, so why do so for religious experience?

Dreams

To explore dreams adequately requires an excursion into dream theory, an excursion into very controversial territory. I cannot make the excursion (as I noted, this is not a book about everything); thus, my remarks will be superficial and oversimplified but indicative, I hope, of some of the basic features of dreams.

Dreams are related to life issues and events, at least in the sense that they tie in to our fears, hopes, frustrations, anxieties, wishes, desires, and so on. I shall not suppose that dreams have a common origin, that all are expressions of the sexual impulse or the impulse to power or the impulse to meaning or anything of the like. Nothing in my argument here will hinge on dreams having a single origin or multiple origins.

Suppose, then, that one day I am especially frustrated at my work, and that night I have a frustration dream: I am running a 400 meter race but just cannot seem to get my legs going properly, so that people I normally would beat are passing me with the greatest of ease. My dream is accounted for by appealing to the frustration of the day or perhaps my anxieties about the race I shall run on the weekend in the Masters Track meet. Even if the dream shows a deeper frustration or fear than what I have mentioned, viz., a chronic sexual frustration or fear, the dream still ties in to the reality of my sexual life. If I do maintain that the dream has sexual roots, I shall require evidence, besides the dream, that I am sexually frustrated or fearful; otherwise, I shall be begging the question.

Now suppose that I have a religious experience, which someone explains by saying that I had a desire for God. I did not know that I had a desire for God because I was an agnostic— not the militant type but just indifferent about questions of God, doubting that they could be answered. Anyone looking at my life, including my dreams, would have been unlikely to come up with evidence that I had a desire for God, conscious or unconscious. So already we are off to a bad start, bad because the explanation from desire will have to go down to the unconscious, and in my case the argument looks as if it is going to beg the question.

Yet even if there is desire on the unconscious level, then like my other desires, impulses, and so on—the really important ones—it would likely have surfaced in my dreams. Yet instead of dreams, I had a religious experience. Whatever this experience may or may not be, it is not a dream or like a dream, even the most vivid dream. The religious experience presented a divine Being as real, as so real that after much critical reflection I continue to maintain the reality of the Being. To explain my experience on the grounds of the unconscious, I must resort either to mystery or *ad hoc* hypotheses. I shall not review what I have already said on these points. The sum of the matter is that appealing to natural causes in one case, the case of my frustration or fear dream, makes excellent sense—does not require explanatory head-stands, whereas in the case of my religious experience it does .

Hallucinations

Now for a few remarks about hallucinations, hallucinations which are not chemically induced. Since I lack expertise in the case of hallucinations even more than in the case of dreams, my remarks will necessarily be superficial and oversimplified but, hopefully, indicative. I note that theory of hallucination is no more settled than dream theory.

Hallucinations are normally embedded in a broad pathology, a pathology revealed in dream material, various obsessions or compulsions, a general social disfunction, and the conscious life. The cases I have presented in chapters two through five are of people who, as far as the evidence goes, were not pathological in any received sense of the term. Some of them were in crisis or had serious problems, with a few even having gone through therapy or been institutionalized (e.g., perhaps Jason). Yet none seemed pathological at the time of the experience, at least none was institutionalized and none was in long-term therapy. There are numerous cases of pathological people who have had experiences of a religious sort, and I have looked at a few cases, without including any in this book. Someone else will have to do a serious, systematic study of the subject. All that I wish to claim now is that the cases I have presented (along with the overwhelming majority I have not presented) are of non-pathological people. Indeed, most are healthy in one or several of the following ways: they are socially functional, carrying on the normal routines of life; they are satisfied with their lives, or not deeply dissatisfied; they have sound reality perception. All are healthy in the last respect, and almost all are healthy in the first respect (Tim, e.g., was not), although a few were carrying on their daily routines with difficulty. Prior to their religious experience they had no record of hallucination (except for Tim, who had drug-induced hallucinations) or any pathology associated with hallucination, during the experience many of them were very aware that they were not dreaming or hallucinating, and after the experience their reality perception continued to be on target, with the people often becoming more healthy and more growth-oriented than prior to the experience, something that we certainly do not generally find among hallucinating people. In this sense, then, religious experience is very different from hallucination: The states prior, during, and after religious experiences are very different from the states prior, during, and after hallucinations. Or put slightly differently, we do not in religious experience find the pathological web in which hallucination normally is found. Further, if the two were similar, then we should expect religious experience to be more along the lines of hallucinations, that is, consistently involving sensory imagery. As we have seen, though, visionary or auditory experience is only occasionally present in religious experience, the visions usually being marginal, functioning more as attention-getters than anything else.

Religious experience is also not like hallucinations in that we may discriminate hallucinations, particularly if we are in a normal frame of mind. I have spoken to several people who hallucinated copiously under the influence of LSD; yet they insist that during the experience they knew what material was hallucinatory and what was not. I shall certainly not try to form a general principle on the basis of a couple of reports I have come across. Instead, I simply say that anyone hallucinating can in a minute discover what is going on: A few reality tests, such as trying to touch a hallucinated being, will help a person decisively discover what is going on. Spots before our eyes are a form of hallucination, but we can tell in an instant that the spots are "before our eyes," i.e., not really in the physical world. But religious experience regularly passes the reality tests people apply, tests which are as stringent as they know of. On the one hand, then, people who have had hallucinations but are in a normal state of mind when speaking about them are likely to say very simply: "Yes, I sure did hallucinate." They recognize that their reality perception was off. On the other hand, people who have had religious experience normally look back and say: "I felt the very presence of the Divine. I can't explain it. I definitely wasn't dreaming or hallucinating. I just experienced this other Reality."

Thus, religious experience is not like hallucination, so that in order to get it into the same category we either appeal to mystery or go *ad hoc*. The conclusion, as in the case of dreams, is that appealing to natural causes makes sense in the case of hallucinations, but not in the case of religious experience. I have not covered other phenomena like obsessions or compulsions, but I am of the opinion that they would not alter the conclusion I have reached for dreams and hallucinations.

In sum, my main contention in the present section is that the concepts of the unconscious and of God are semantically similar in crucial ways: neither provides us with statements which are anything more than marginally lawlike, and of the marginally lawlike statements, none is strongly confirmed; both refer to a reality spiritual in nature; and both are transcendent of the individual self in crucial ways. These similarities do not make the two concepts equivalent, mainly because the concept of God has many expressions. The standard Western view is that God is omnipotent, omniscient, and morally perfect. So far I have done nothing to show that the unconscious has any of these characteristics. I could begin to do so by engaging in a course of reasoning along the following lines: Insofar as the unconscious generates religious experience which brings positive, radical changes to people, we could infer that the unconscious is very powerful, knowledgeable, and loving; insofar as these results are far beyond the capacity of the conscious self, we are talking about effects from a Reality which at least has a family resemblance to the Divine; and so on. I shall not attempt to develop this course of reasoning any further or to consider other possible courses of reasoning.

4. *Epistemological Conclusions*

I should now like to see what we can say about my general thesis that religious experience is a rational ground for religious belief. I have been working with a specific form of this thesis, viz., that religious experience is *prima facie* justification for religious belief. I shall call this the strong thesis (ST). I believe that I have made a fairly strong case for saying that appeal to a psychoanalytic unconscious cannot defeat ST. Another development of the general thesis is this: Religious experience justifies religious belief in that a theistic hypothesis—a God-hypothesis, to use the terminology of William James—is at least as adequate as any alternative naturalistic hypothesis. I shall call this the weak thesis (WT).

Evaluation of WT

The contention I wish to make now is that the unconscious is a less adequate hypothesis than the God-hypothesis for explaining religious experience; in other words, WT holds in the case of the unconscious. The detailed objections I have made in individual cases to explanations from the unconscious serve as a partial justification for WT, just as they serve to eliminate the unconscious as a defeater. The further point is that if there is anything to my statements about semantical similarity, then the unconscious—at least in its expression as an explanation for religious experience—looks very much like a God-hypothesis. In other words, we do not really have much of an alternative hypothesis, particularly if we accept a Jamesian view of a limited God, limited at least in power. I shall attempt to clarify this further by enlarging on one point I already made, the point concerning lawfulness.

A major reason for lumping the unconscious together with a God-hypothesis is that both are capable of only marginal or weak lawlike statements. Religious experience does not seem to follow any pattern. Whatever generates the experience does not seem to do so according to any naturalistic pattern, any pattern which fits into a strictly spatio-temporal universe. According to the God-hypothesis, or at least major versions of it, this is exactly what should be expected, for God is not a Being that can be manipulated, that can be called in at will, that can be produced on demand. One way of describing this aspect of God is to say that God is free. God intrudes in human life and affairs at will, often in thoroughly inexplicable ways. The pattern, if we may call it that, is the pattern of positive or loving energy, a pattern which does not fit a natural or space-time model. By saying that the pattern is that of positive or loving energy, I mean that God intervenes in ways positive for humans, positive in their immediate and long-term experience, i.e., their long-term health, wholeness, growth, development, and state of mind. I shall not comment on the notions of health, wholeness, and so on because they are terms employed both by those who appeal to the unconscious and those who appeal to God. If the terms are problematic, they are problematic for both. To be sure, we recognize that some experiences— e.g., the experiences of those who felt abandoned by God—do not nicely fit the concept of a loving God. The experiences also do not nicely fit the concept of the unconscious, whether of the Freudian or mixed model. However, the religious explanations for problematic experiences— say, for the dark night of the soul—make more sense, I think, than some sort of explanation from the unconscious. Thus, the God-hypothesis, by incorporating the notion of a free, loving Energy, accounts for religious experience better than a hypothesis about the unconscious. Indeed, insofar as a hypothesis about the unconscious resorts to explanations of the sort "It happens, I know not why!" it is resorting to an explanation similar to the God-hypothesis. I.e., insofar as the hypothesis of the unconscious does not explain religious experience by an appeal to the lawlike operation of natural factors but by an appeal to an unconscious which freely (i.e., we resort to the know-not-why explanation; the unconscious just does what it does) applies positive energy to the self for an experience of felt Presence, immediate joy, peace, or ecstasy, with long-term consequences of health, wholeness, and so on, the hypothesis about the unconscious takes on the characteristics of the God-hypothesis.

A Coherent View of the Self

A further point is that the God-hypothesis leaves us with a more coherent notion of the self than does the explanation of religious experience by way of the unconscious. The notion of the unconscious was introduced in psychology to explain a whole range of natural phenomena concerning people, including the phenomena of dreams, phobias, hysteria, obsessive-compulsive behavior, certain types of anxiety, and so on. The form that the unconscious takes in Freudian theory for explaining these phenomena is not a form which makes it capable of explaining religious experience, so that we have to introduce what I have called a "mixed unconscious." Yet the mixed unconscious offers little more hope than the Freudian unconscious, since it requires *ad hoc* (non-parsimonious) hypotheses in order to account for religious experience. I have already discussed this point in detail and will not repeat what I have said. We may say, then, that although the unconscious is a weak hypothesis in the case of the phenomena it was originally designed to account for (the present chapter has been stressing this point, among others), it becomes even weaker in the case of religious experience.

If we take the approach that religious experience is cognitive, getting us in contact with the Divine, then we end up, as I have maintained, with a more coherent view of the self than in the case of unconscious explanations of religious experience. The self is not misled in taking the experience of the Divine as real; rather, the conscious and unconscious are in harmony with respect to reality evaluation, so that the sense of validity, reality, or truth—standard for religious experience—expresses the agreement of both conscious and unconscious in judging the experience. We do not suppose an unconscious which imposes on consciousness an experience in violation of conscious standards of truth and reality.

The Cognitive Nature of Peak Experiences

My approach here is similar to that of Maslow in his treatment of peak-experiences. Maslow's peak-experience is not on all fours with religious experience, inasmuch as peak experiences include aesthetic experiences and experiences of human love. Yet some peak experiences are, according to Maslow, religious experiences. The main point is that peak-experiences are experiences of the self at its healthiest, with health conceived in terms of self-realization. Since some religious experiences are peak experiences in Maslow's sense, these religious experiences are also expressions of the self at its healthiest. Although there is some ambiguity about what Maslow would recognize as religious experience, I think that he would accept Ned's experience, say, as a religious experience of a peak nature. Further, I maintain that the religious experiences I have considered generally express the self in a healthy mode, the self either as self-realizing or as experiencing a strong impulse toward self-realization. I shall add some further remarks on this topic in Chapter Seven. What I want to emphasize now is Maslow's basic epistemological point: How odd if the self in a healthy mode should be consistently misleading! Maslow is worth quoting on the point.

> All peak-experiences feel like Being-cognition, but not all are truly so. And yet, we dare not neglect the clear hints that, sometimes at least, greater perspicuity and greater efficiency of cognition can be found in healthier people and in healthier moments, i.e., some peak-experiences *are* B-cognitions [cognitions of Being]. I once suggested the principle that if self-actualizing people can and do perceive reality more efficiently, fully and with less motivational contamination than we others do, then we may possibly use them as biological assays. Through their greater sensitivity and perception, we may get a better report of what reality is like, than through our own eyes, just as canaries can be used to detect gas in mines before less sensitive creatures can. As a second string to this same bow, we may use ourselves in our most perceptive moments, in our peak-experiences, when, for the moment, *we* are self-actualizing, to give us a report of the nature of reality that is truer than we can ordinarily manage. (Maslow, 1968, 100)

I note that Maslow does not in any wholesale fashion accept peak-experiences as cognitive. The context of the above paragraph makes very clear that peak-experiences are to be subjected to critical analysis. Yet "some peak-experiences are B-cognitive." I do not know for certain how close Maslow and I are here. He sees some peak-experiences as B-cognitive. Does he intend to say that the presumption is: They are cognitive? I think he should say this, especially given what he says about the experiences being healthy expressions of the self. The same, then, would be said for religious experience: The presumption is that religious experience is cognitive because it is generally a healthy expression of the self. The assumed epistemological thesis is that a healthy self is a truth-realizing self, and *vice versa*. This thesis fits with what I term "the Greek view of the self," a view I accept, a view summed up in the Socratic words: "The unexamined life is not worth living."

I take the Greek view to say at least the following: The proper guiding principle of the self is the rational principle, a principle operative in aesthetic, value, moral, and religious judgments, as well as judgments about the physical world, a principle which also guides feeling. As for feeling, I note that the Greeks did not see the examined life as excluding feelings. In Plato's parable of the charioteer ("Phaedrus," 246-57) the unruly horse (desire) is not speared; rather, it is disciplined until it "follows the will of the charioteer." Actually, the Greek treatment of desire may well have deep ties to the psychoanalytic treatment of the self, particularly to the id as a cauldron of irrational impulses. The epistemological development of the Greek view is that living rationally, as opposed to living otherwise, tends to get us in touch with the truth; moreover, health is nothing other than self-realization, i.e., the realization of our rational capacity.

To deny the Greek approach is, in effect, to say that a healthy self does not tend to get us in touch with the truth, or is as likely to misperceive the truth as an unhealthy self. This view of the self is incoherent in the sense that a chasm runs through the self, with health being on one side of the chasm, truth-seeking on the other. On my approach and that of Maslow, the self is coherent in the sense that the notions of health and truth-seeking are in harmony. Since the view is coherent, it is also parsimonious, i.e., more parsimonious than the view of the divided self.

Coherence and Therapy

However, there is a deeper incoherence in the view that health and truth-seeking are disunited, that a healthy self is at least as likely to be misled as an unhealthy self. I think that the assumptions of therapy are radically contrary to this view. People accepted into therapy because they have serious problems, people considered neurotic, people afflicted with chronic anxiety, obsessions, compulsions, and so on, are certainly viewed as unhealthy, and unhealthy because they are not in touch with the reality of themselves—something which is not the case with the therapist, or at least not to the degree of the patient. I cannot imagine Freud saying that he was no more healthy than the Rat Man, or any of his other patients, including therapists who were analyzed by him in preparation for their therapeutic role. The basic therapeutic claim, I think, is this: I am aware of vitiating unconscious motives within myself and therefore able to guard against them in order to give true interpretations to the patient; in this sense I am a healthier person than anyone who is not aware of vitiating unconscious motives. If the therapist does not make this claim, then I do not see how claims to correct interpretation are anything but arbitrary. The essence of what I am saying here is that epistemology must be consistent with therapeutic commitments. If I am thoroughly incorrect about the therapeutic claim, I wait to be informed. In that case I would return to the first point about incoherency.

However, I do not think that I am off target on the therapeutic claim; or if I am, then so is Edelson, who is a strong ally on the matter of truth. His views come through very clearly in the section on the therapeutic goals of psychoanalysis. (139-42) I encourage the reader to look at the entire section because I cannot reproduce the impression of what he says. However, just noting the times that he uses the phrase 'veridical insight' or the times that he talks about getting the patient off the track of fantasy is enough to realize the centrality of getting to the truth in the therapeutic process. In fact, I am inclined to say that according to Edelson people are healthy just to the extent that they achieve veridical insight into themselves and guide their lives according to this insight. Such guidance may not make life easier for them, for as Edelson wisely notes, life circumstances may be such as to make a pleasant or happy life impossible. And here I must quote him. Clearly, there is no guarantee that an analysand will end up pleased or happy with himself, others, or the world he lives in— only that his discontent and misery are now determined by intransigent obstacles in the world impinging upon him, and by the unavoidable chasm yawning between his wish and his power to gratify it—and not by unconscious fantasies or conflicts. (140)

The upshot of these remarks is that the God-hypothesis provides for a more coherent view of the self in the case of religious experience than does the notion of the unconscious. If we do not proceed in a Jamesian way but proceed by way of PC, we arrive at the same conclusion.

General Coherence

At this point I wish to note that not only does the notion of the Divine provide for a more coherent view of the self than does the unconscious in the case of religious experience but it provides for coherency over a wide range of phenomena—the creation of the universe, the regular functioning of the universe, morality, mystery, events apparently outside the realm of natural law, religious experience, and a number of other phenomena. Interpreting the Divine as, say, loving Energy, we note that the notion of loving Energy is no less able to account for religious experience than for creation or the lawful functioning of the universe. Or put differently, one does not tack on a new hypothesis about God when moving from the creation or lawfulness of the universe to religious experience. This is not to say that the notion of the Divine easily accounts for everything, without any *ad hoc* hypotheses. The lawfulness of nature, e.g., fits the notion of loving Energy in some respects, but in others it does not seem to fit. Disease, e.g., is part of the lawfulness of nature, but it is not quickly or easily adjusted to the notion of love. Adjustments may be made, but in some cases the adjustment is an appeal to ignorance. E.g., free-will consistency defenses of God's goodness need say no more than that there is not necessarily any inconsistency between God's love and a nature in which we find disease. That is not an explanation but an appeal to mystery. I think that we can go beyond a consistency defense in most cases and come up with plausible accounts of how disease fits in with God's love or benevolence. (Wall, 1984) All the same, we must admit that the notion of the Divine, whatever form it takes, is not without its *ad hoc* hypotheses and appeals to mystery. The same is true, of course, for any alternative notion (or set of notions) introduced to account for the same range of phenomena the notion of the Divine attempts to account for. My view, clearly beyond the scope of this book, is that appealing to the Divine fares at least as well as any alternative appeal.

For the purposes of this chapter I make no such general claim. Instead, my primary claim is that the unconscious is not a naturalistic general defeater of religious experience as *prima facie* justification for religious belief. Further, I think I have also shown that, taking a Jamesian approach (WT), the God-hypothesis does a better job accounting for religious experience than does the unconscious.

6. Other Naturalistic Accounts

Admittedly, the data I have do not provide much information about a whole list of circumstances or background factors, including the factor of the family and its child-rearing practices, so that I cannot provide adequate counterexamples to a whole list of possibilities which might be raised by those adhering to a naturalistic approach to religious experience. Specifically, my material is very light on early family life, including child-rearing practices, conflict in the home, divorce, and so on. However, I do not know of data which provide better information on these issues. This entire book is a matter of doing the best I can with the data I have, and of noting in the process what other data must be discovered in order to develop a stronger position. Yet given the wide variety of backgrounds and circumstances my data provide, I think we have reasonable grounds for positing the thesis that no background or circumstantial item, or combination of items, determines the nature of religious experience in the sense of being either a necessary or sufficient condition for the experience.

Thus, if someone suggests that having at least one affectionate parent—a parent who, among other things, did a lot of touching and holding and playing with—in the first years of life is a necessary condition for a religious experience of a loving God, I shall respond with a tentative denial, even though in most cases I do not have any data at all about the first few years of life. What I do have are some data which permit reasonable inferences about some child-rearing practices. For example, if a person, like Alice (Chpt. 2), says that she had loving parents, we could reasonably infer that parents who were loving from the earliest memories of childhood would also have been loving during the first several years of life and that probably, then, there was considerable touching and holding and playing with. (Alice, we may remember, had an experience of a "vast, timeless benevolence," an experience which would support the thesis that affectionate parents during the first year of life are a necessary condition for the experience of a loving God.) Or suppose that someone suggests that Ron (Chpt. I), who felt as if arms went around him, had parents who put their arms around him. Yet Ron says enough for us at least to have doubts about the claim. Ron mentioned that his dad would take out a dollar bill and say, "This is God." Usually people who say of a dollar bill, "This is God," are the kind of people who are pursuing their god, and they do not have much time to hold, play with, and enjoy children at any stage of life. If Ron's parents were distinguished by acceptance and closeness, we should expect Ron to say something along the lines of: "Although my dad was very materialistic, he really was a warm, loving guy"; or, "Even though dad was pretty materialistic, mom etc."

Although I generally lack data concerning early childhood, I do have some data in several cases, cases which turn out, I think, to be counterexamples to the thesis under consideration. Terri seems to have had a fairly secure first several years of life. Her mother breast-fed her and seemed to dote on her, not working until problems arose in the family. The problems arose when Terri was around age four, with alcohol entering the home, giving rise to conflict, followed by divorce, and then the shuttling from one relative to another. According to Walter, Terri's childhood memories were exclusively of the fragmenting home and the post-divorce period of an insecure home life. She never mentioned pre-divorce or pre-conflict situations of closeness and affection. Thus, at least in her consciousness, the feelings of unhappiness and insecurity held a monopoly. Yet the God she experienced was a God of love—among other things, she had the assurance that this God would accompany her through death.

Her husband, Walter, also came from a home in which there was not much touching, as far back as he can remember. Perhaps he was held and touched considerably in the first year of life (he was breast fed), but the evidence is lacking on this point. His parents cared for him and conscientiously carried out their responsibilities as parents, yet they were not touchers; moreover, their view of God had a harshness to it, the harshness of a hell for all who did not believe. Yet Walter's experience was of a supportive, caring, loving God.

Tim also did not have a home distinguished by strong affection. His father was something of a distant figure, with his mother carrying the major load of caring for and providing affection. Tim characterizes her as a loving mother, but he also notes that her love was mixed with demands and conditions. In addition, the God of his parents was a God, like the God of Walter's parents, that sent unbelievers to an eternity of punishment. All the same, Tim met a God of total love.

Finally, Marie felt great guilt at age ten but had an experience of profound forgiveness and the assurance of a divine plan for her life. The fact of her extreme guilt, along with the fact that her parents were Scottish Presbyterian and that she could not communicate with them about her experience, would indicate parents who were not especially warm and loving in her early years.

Obviously, what I have just said about the early childhood years of Ron, Terri, Tim, and Marie is inadequate and speculative. However, I do not rest my case on these counterexamples. More important, I should say, is the consideration already mentioned: Since the wide variety of factors for which we do have information provides us with neither necessary nor sufficient conditions for religious experience, there seems to be no strong reason to think that other factors for which we do not have information should be either necessary or sufficient conditions. Moreover, I should think that something like love in early home life will influence religious experience only if love gets translated into desire, desire for a loving Being. Insofar as I have shown that desire for a religious Object is not a necessary or sufficient condition for the experience of the Object, I have shown that any kind of influence which has to get translated into desire in order to be operative cannot be a condition for the experience of a religious Object. Of course, childhood influences may operate independently of desire. I certainly cannot definitively deny that they do. I welcome any investigation of the topic.

A final point is that approaches allegedly more scientific in nature than psychoanalytic approaches—e.g., a Skinnerian approach—fare no better at this time than psychoanalytic approaches. Skinner, e.g., would say that religious experience is a direct consequence of the whole process of past reinforcement—only this is just a grand promissory note rather than a confirmed hypothesis concerning the specific processes of reinforcement which issue in specific kinds of religious experience. Thus, I am still of the opinion that no naturalistic alternative on the scene today provides a stronger account of religious experience than the unconscious, an account, though, which I think I have shown is thoroughly inadequate.

Chapter Seven

The Effects of Religious Experience

I shall now move on to consider some general defeaters other than defeaters in the general category of naturalistic explanations.

1. The Defeater from Effects

Earlier, when considering Angelique's story, we came across some criteria mentioned by her as criteria for the validity of religious experience. These criteria concern the effects of religious experience. On the basic epistemic approach I have taken, viz., that religious experience provides *prima facie* justification for religious belief, one general defeater might be that religious experience does not have the effects we should expect from a genuine encounter with the Divine.

The first question is, What effects should we expect from a genuine meeting of the Divine? For the sake of simplicity I shall note two types of effect: short term-and long-term. Short-term effects are those associated with the experience itself; long-term effects those associated with the course of life after the experience. I think that the objection— viz., that religious experience does not have the effects expected—focuses mainly on the long-term effects; however, I do not believe that short-term effects may be ignored. If we are looking for effects of the Divine, then we need to look at the trail-head, as well as further down the trail.

Again, though, what effects should we expect? I think that the objection we are considering trades on the notion—and rightly so—that experiencing the Divine puts us in contact with an immense Source of positive energy, energy for reconstructing a shattered life and going on to live a whole, healthy life. Do those who encounter the Divine give evidence of effects consistent with what we should expect from contact with an immense Source of positive energy? And do those who continue in the pursuit of the Divine give evidence of the growth we should expect from contact with an immense Source of positive energy? The answer in both cases is affirmative for the great majority of cases I have looked at. In saying this, I do not presume that there is any single, non-debatable set of criteria for a whole and healthy life. All the same, I shall stick with the concepts, employing criteria which are fairly commonly adopted in our society, as well as in a number of other societies. Moreover, I think that perhaps the concepts may be avoided, at least to an extent, by simply concentrating on the effects, letting people classify them as they will. E.g., if, following a religious experience, someone becomes more peaceful, I shall simply note this fact, letting others classify a sense of peace as they will. I, for one, classify it as *prima facie* healthy. The main thing, though, is to note the effects.

2. Freedom and the Effects from Religious Experience

In saying that the data I have strongly support the positive effects of religious experience, I do not mean to imply that the effects follow in any automatic way. I do not see any necessary connection between encounter with the Divine and positive effects in life, particularly long-term effects. If we assume that we are free, as I do, then the long-term effects of an experience will depend on how a person chooses to respond to it, on whether or not the person commits to a spiritual way of life. Generally speaking, I should say that we expect religious experience followed by commitment to a spiritual way of life to result in long-term growth toward wholeness and health.

As for people who have a religious experience but do nothing with it, i.e., do not commit themselves to some way of proceeding further with the experience, we have come across people who did not respond to their religious experience: e.g., Pam, who had an experience in childhood, and who considered childhood a phase of life discontinuous with adulthood; and Nina, who expected her religious experience to be repeated, was frustrated in her expectations, with the result that she felt abandoned and never discovered the plan which she was assured of in her experience. I shall mention two further individuals.

Cecil (3133)

Cecil had little use for religion in general and church in particular, but he attended church at the insistence of his son. While worshiping, he experienced a sense of Presence and was filled with a deep feeling of love for mankind and a need to express the love. He reflected on the experience, realized that following it up with a life of loving mankind would require radical changes in his life, changes he was unwilling to make, and simply turned from the experience, acting as if it never occurred. Cecil certainly experienced a short-term effect of encounter with the Divine (feeling love for mankind and the need to express it), but he rejected commitment to any religious way which would take him to development and expression of this love.

Wanda (803)

Wanda had an experience of God's power which left her amazed and disturbed. She visited her doctor, who told her that she had to stop thinking about God. She writes: "This was invaluable advice, and I haven't done any thinking since, i.e. for the last thirty years." What I want to say immediately is: "She just has to be joking." I surely hope so, but she gives the impression of trying to be serious. The death of Socrates becomes easier to understand all the time.

3. Review of the Cases

Turning now to the material we have looked at so far, we can say that people respond to their religious experiences in a variety of ways, some taking 180 degree turns, others taking less complete turns, still others turning not at all. As I have noted, though, we may say, generally, that the overwhelming majority of people responded positively. Of course, I do not claim that my sample is representative; indeed, it is probably biased in favor of those who experienced positive effects. For the interviews I obtained I can say that I did not seek people with positive effects from their experiences; however, the people selecting the interviewees for me (clergy or leaders of religious communities) selected on the ground that the interviewees had experienced significant positive change in life. I shall simply note that I had access to most of my interviewees only through the leaders of religious communities. As for the cases from the Alister Hardy Research Centre, the people writing in would likely be those positively affected by the experience and probably affected in the long-run. They would write because of the continuing importance of the experience. Those who were not affected, those for whom the experience meant little, would probably not take the trouble to write in. Or so I shall suppose. Thus, I make no claims of adequate sampling and hence shall not claim, e.g., that the great majority of people having religious experience respond positively to it and give evidence in their lives of contact with a powerful Source of energy.

I shall also mention that the reports of the effects come mainly from the subjects of the experience, so that there may be exaggeration or distortion. In the case of the interviews I obtained, I had the general report of the clergy or leaders of the religious community that the interviewees had had a religious experience which produced significant changes. As for Tim, Terri, and Walter, I have personal knowledge of the effects in their lives. I consider the reports submitted to the Alister Hardy Research Centre to be generally accurate. In this chapter, then, I shall review some of the cases I have already introduced.

Tim

I shall begin with Tim because his case is about as spectacular as any. Tim experienced an essentially loving Being, the Creator of heaven and earth, reaching out to him, saying, "This is Me," and graciously inviting Tim to turn to the Me. The immediate results were that Tim felt love and understanding for his parents, felt love even for drug dealers with whom he was in conflict, felt elated, and forthwith lost all desire for drugs. Since his experience, Tim has never again touched drugs, has married and become a father, has resolved feelings of resentment toward his father, feelings which surfaced when Tim took on the role of father, has been a minister for almost twenty years, and has in recent years begun to expand his intellectual horizons significantly, a point of some consequence because Tim's intellectual background was very limited, the religion of his family and his early ministry being little less than anti-intellectual. Thus, I should say that not only was Tim's experience spectacular but the effects—short-term and long-term— have been equally spectacular. Certainly, the effects are consistent with what we would expect from encountering and responding positively to a loving Being that created heaven and earth.

Terri

Terri experienced union with God—"I was in God." The immediate result was mental coherency, coherency which lasted not for an hour, not for a day, not for a week, but for over six weeks, coherency in a woman who had been getting progressively more incoherent and was not expected to live over a week or two. In addition, there was immediate peace and joy in a woman who had been agitated, angry. Even when incoherency set in again Terri did not exhibit the general agitation and anger which had become constants in her prior to her experience. Further, she accepted her death in the sense that she was confident of not being alone, of not walking the valley of the shadow by herself. Her union with God assured her of the reality of God's enduring presence. Moreover, the experience was not simply pasted on, scissors and paste style, at the end of her life. It was an almost natural culmination of a commitment to the Christian Way. In other words, the experience may be seen as fitting-in to a life of spiritual development in which the final challenge to spiritual growth was the passage through death.

Walter

Walter experienced God's sufficiency, the result being steady, unwavering support of Terri through two more years of battling cancer, support which did not leave him with signs of physical or emotional exhaustion. He says that at times he was physically exhausted, particularly when Terri was in the hospital for chemo treatments or surgery, times when he would drive round trips daily to and from work, approximately 180 miles. On the way back to the hospital in the evening he would often have to stop at a roadside park for a nap. And he sometimes became emotionally drained, but never, according to him, did he sense any chronic emotional exhaustion. Never did he have trouble sleeping, even in the hospital when he slept on an eighteen inch wide fold-out bed, with nurses making their regular nightly checks—i.e., with nurses doing everything in their power to keep patient and spouse from sleeping soundly. Never did he have an appetite loss or a weight loss. Never was he on tranquilizers or sleeping pills. In short, he did not have any chronic physical signs of emotional exhaustion.

And after her death? He never lost the zest for life. Checking with some of Walter's friends reveals that they never thought of him as having opted out of life. Further, he never felt or manifested signs of anger, but felt the closeness of God. Walter gets angry, and admits that he does; however, he is anything but an angry person and in the case of his wife's death he says that he experienced the love of God several times with a strength approaching that of his experience of God's sufficiency, so that he says, "I simply felt very taken-care-of." He reports that about a year after Terri's death a counselor friend of his engaged him in counseling for approximately three months. The counselor maintained that Walter's grief over the loss of Terri was really rooted in anger—anger at her for dying, anger at God, and anger at his parents—and that until his anger was resolved he would never be able to say "Goodbye" and get on with life. Yet Walter says that he was never able to work-up any anger toward any of the persons he was supposed to be angry with, even though he followed the counselor's instructions for getting at the anger. Either, then, the counselor's theory of grief was wanting, or Walter has rock-solid defenses. Walter simply repeats, "I had powerful experiences of God's love, so how could I be angry?" What we again seem to see is an individual who manifests spiritual development, spiritual development consistent with the reality of the sufficient Presence he encountered.

Mark

Mark said that over a period of nine months he experienced a "personalized sustaining power," the result of which was that he became "infinitely more concerned with and aware of people and my environment. Mental perception and originality of thought were heightened. Living reached undreamed of levels of sheer joy."

Juan

Juan found himself in a failing marriage, a condition which caused him to turn in desperation to God, the result being that he immediately felt peace and hope, as well as that he was loved by Jesus. He immediately took full responsibility for the failure of his marriage and then did everything in his power to save it. His marriage was, indeed, saved and is, as I observed, blossoming at the time I write this (twelve years after the turnaround), with both Juan and his wife being committed to a path of spiritual growth.

Ron

Ron was also in a failing marriage and, like Juan, turned to God. The immediate result was a feeling of God's love—"I could feel arms go around me." Then his loneliness and guilt left him. His marriage was not saved (in contrast to Carlos, he was already in the process of divorce), but he ended up with his two children. He says that people who know him have noticed a significant change, some of them saying, "You're happy—are you on something?" He grants that he is, most assuredly, on something—in his words, "Jesus"—and has been on the Something now for two years.

Cindy

Cindy, although aware of God as a child, did not follow up on her childhood experience, ending up in her adult life as an alcoholic, singing in a nightclub and practicing occultism in her home—reading palms and cards, conducting seances, engaging in necromancy. She had been under treatment by a psychiatrist, but she says that he simply threw up his hands, considering her a hopeless case. She had also come in contact with several Christian people who impressed her with their manner of living. Finally, in desperation she turned to Christ. She said that she immediately experienced elation; then she went to her apartment and threw out every bottle of alcohol and every piece of occult literature and material. She said that the people in the apartment quickly noticed a complete change in her. At the time that she related these things—fourteen years after her conversion—she was seriously involved in growing spiritually and in the secular world was managing a law firm.

Meg

Meg notes that at the time of her experience her "mind was immediately stilled," and yet she felt "ALIVE for the first time." The experience initiated in her a life of spiritual growth in which her objective was for "love . . . to permeate my every thought and emotion." She was fully aware of how demanding the objective was and how far she was from it, yet further experiences "of being immersed in an ocean of PERFECT LOVE," kept her going and brought to her life increments in love.

Angelique

Angelique, the psychiatrist, speaks of her spiritual experience as leading to "enhanced sensitivity and maturity, and . . . to growth in all areas of the personality." She had her ups and downs in spiritual growth but, along with further religious experiences, which she sees as the means "by which the Spirit calls my attention and then works on me," she continued on a path of growth. One essential goal in her growth was being sensitive to and serving others. An experience in her life which derailed her for a number of years was the realization of how uncaring she was, a realization brought about by a small act of cruelty. Yet she got back on track and was at the time of relating her experiences continuing to let the Spirit work on her.

Marie

Marie, experiencing at ten a sense of guilt and hopelessness, heard a voice assuring her of forgiveness, with the result that she could say of the next day, "my burden had fallen away, I was free, I was new-born." In addition, she experienced a voice assuring her of a plan for her life. Sixty years later she could write that the experience "proved to be the mainspring to the whole of the rest of my life. . . . I have remained deeply committed to God and to the idea of steadily unfolding Purpose in my life."

Jason

Jason had a nervous breakdown, but his religious experience produced in him immediately the feelings of joy and ecstasy. Jason says that the experience occurred when he was on the way to recovery, but the experience seemed to expedite recovery. He downplays the effects on his life by saying, "No outward difference. I got over my nervous breakdown, got married, served in the army throughout the War. Had children. Lived a normal life. The main difference I suppose is that I no longer looked for any intellectual answer to the problem of existence." At first glance his statement seems disappointing in that it seems to represent a cessation of critical reflection on a very significant human issue. However, we must remember that Jason was "taken over by something outside" himself. In short, Jason considered that he had experienced the meaning of existence, so he did not have to go on searching as if there were something else or as if he could get the Something into an intellectual box. That he did not shut down his reason is clear, for his very next words are:

> I didn't become religious. I am still sceptical of most claims of extra-sensory experience. The kind of people whose reasoning processes I respect are those like Richie Calder, Jargenhita Laski, Bertrand Russell, who I suppose would find some rational explanation for the kind of experience I had.

The main point is that Jason's experience was the catalyst for removing the question concerning the problem of existence from being obsessive and emotionally destructive—a very positive result, I should say.

Elizabeth

Elizabeth had an experience which "was as though my mind broke bounds and went on expanding until it merged with the universe." She says that the experience "was, and still is as a continuing influence, the most overwhelming thing that has ever happened to me.... It affected me in a very real way, reoriented my outlook and enriched and enlarged consciousness in many ways." These statements do not spell out details, but they certainly reveal that Elizabeth thought that something momentous occurred, something that affected her so as to enrich and enlarge her consciousness, a result apparently still present in her life.

Linda

Linda's first experience occurred when she was with her son in church, attending just to hear him sing. The priest said, "'The Lord be with you,' and to my great astonishment I suddenly knew that He was." She had another experience of presence about two years later, following which she "was filled with a deep sense of blessing and joy which has been renewed countless times since." Of the other long-term effects of her experiences and of following the Christian way, she says,

> life has become more livable. Formerly I was not a particularly happy person and did not value my life highly. Now that I know we are 'rooted and grounded in love' I have acquired a new confidence and serenity, a heightened appreciation ... of music and natural beauty, and a new sense of responsibility. Previously I had regarded each

man as an island, responsible only to himself; now I feel myself to be at one with all mankind and this has obviously affected my tolerance of 'difficult' people and my attitude toward such issues as euthanasia and abortion. It has also brought an uneasiness about our comfortable middle-class standard of living.

She also mentions that she spends most of her spare time helping the people in her village church and that she is learning to cope with trouble much better.

Will

Will, the electrical engineer from Purdue University, was knocked flat on the floor as he felt the "rush of the presence of God." The result, according to him was that he stopped living for himself; he accepted God's morality, and received the motivation to start living up to it.

Lorraine

Lorraine spoke of her experience of a Void, a Void which in later experiences was also identified as Energy and Mind. The immediate results of the experience were ecstasy and joy. Also immediate was the movement of her life to a new level: The experience "changed my life. I began to be happy." Her experiences also gave her strength to cope at a later date with the deaths of her two sons and her father.

Edna

Edna felt "a very deep belonging to a huge, ineffable, perfect Reality which exists both immediately below the surface of everyday life and also infinitely removed from it." And the effects? Edna says that "my consciousness of this Reality explains the fact that at all times, even in difficult conditions or great personal distress, I have always felt that basically, and at the level where things really matter, all is well and exactly as it ought to be. (I should add that I am not a passive or indifferent person, and therefore this basic acceptance cannot be the result of weakness or apathy.)" Later she had another experience of "the invisible presence of 'God'... which greatly helped to remove some of my remaining fears and apprehensions."

Clark

Clark, devastated by a divorce, had an experience of oneness with everything, an experience associated with the vision of an Indian shaman-like figure. The immediate result was joy. The lasting after-effects (he describes the experience a year after having had it) were as follows.

> The knowledge of that experience is still with me; I still feel the oneness; I have a heightened reverence for life (and indeed can see 'life' or, rather, the force of the Universe in rocks, in the earth itself); I can picture myself in the whole 'plan' far more clearly.... I Know ... that I am 'different'.... I feel psychologically enhanced by the whole thing.

Leanna

Leanna, in a state of intense depression at age thirty three, had the sense that "all things were one, and I was one with all creation and held safe within a deep love." The immediate results were peace and joy and humility in the sense that I "could only bow down in the holiness of the presence of God." Also her depression lifted. Further effects she describes as follows.

> Psychologically, and for my own peace of mind, the effect has been of the greatest importance. In times of bereavement and suffering I have been able to turn to the memory of that which has brought peace and comfort. It has also given me understanding in reading the bible and other scriptures and mystical writings.... I also feel that the world is good, and remember (although I no longer see) that the divine is within the common....

> But I doubt whether it has made me a better person, for many people who have had no such experience are much more self-giving than I am and more devoted to the service of mankind. Whatever 'good' I do is done from a sense of duty rather than by inspiration.

Leanna's last remarks are significant in that they show honesty and show also that the humility originally inspired by the experience still holds.

Ned

Ned, while sitting in church and feeling perfectly content with life, experienced "the transcendental event of a unitive bond with Being Itself." The effects he mentions were those he immediately experienced.

> I was filled with infinite compassion punctuated with the wonder of worshipfulness. I would observe, understand and identify in order that I might forgive and serve. I experienced a shift from a view of others being entirely and only my extension to a view of another having his own identity. I experienced a shift from the view that I must save my own life at all costs to the view that I must lose it, certainly at first, to save it at all.

Summary

The people I have considered in this chapter exhibit effects, including religious development, we should expect if they really encountered the Divine. Some, like Tim, experienced immediate, radical change, change which I would certainly class as positive, change, moreover, which has persisted and enlarged. Others experienced immediate effects, such as joy and peace, and lasting effects that were gradual in development, effects such as a developing thirst for God, more care and sensitivity for others, strength to cope with crises, effects which I would again classify as positive signs of spiritual development. As I said at the beginning of the chapter, I cannot say that the majority of people encountering the Divine experience effects, particularly long-term effects, which I would class as positive. Whatever the answer on that point, I think that the cases I have cited, representative of the vast majority of cases I studied, are sufficient to cast doubt on any attempted general defeater stating that the effects of religious experience are not consistent with what we should expect from a genuine encounter with the Divine.

Chapter Eight

The Religious Overrider System

1. The Necessity of an Overrider System

Recently the papers carried a kind of news item which appears fairly regularly. The item was about a cult leader who said that he helped Christ by killing a family of five. The father and mother in the family had opposed his teaching. He claimed that he had seen a vision to the effect that he helped take Christ off the cross by killing the family. I shall refer to this case as Case One.

This sort of case is often cited as a decisive defeater of religious experience generally, the idea being that a religious doxastic practice has no way of eliminating the case. In other words, a religious overrider system does not really have defeaters for this or other similar experiences, so that the lack of defeaters is in itself a defeater of religious experience in general. Or to be more exact, we observe that religious experience is the ground for a grab-bag of beliefs about God—a vengeful God, a loving God, a God commanding bizarre things (such as to repeat meaningless phrases), a God communicating falsehoods (such as that the world would end in 1985), and so on. Obviously, God cannot be everything that people experience God to be: thoroughly loving, vengeful, omnipotent, communicator of falsehoods, Shepherd of His creatures, Issuer of nonsense commands, and so on. However, there is no way of eliminating some religious experience or other so that we can even hope to gain consistency, no way of distinguishing between the genuine and the non-genuine. The result is inconsistency in beliefs, massive, uneliminable inconsistency, so that by the criterion of internal consistency, one of the three criteria for a doxastic practice, we show that no religious doxastic practice is adequate. PC cannot apply to religious experience.

To begin with, I think that we can see without much thought that the criticism goes too far. Just about any Christian doxastic practice we could mention, certainly the CMP of Alston, would eliminate Case One; moreover, the grounds on which the elimination would take place are, I maintain, grounds likely to be shared by Muslims, Hindus, and Buddhists—in short, the grounds function not merely as a part of CMP but as a part of URP. More on this below. However, I do agree that wholesale inability to distinguish between the genuine and the non-genuine in religious experience, wholesale absence of any defeater system, would do-in the appeal to religious experience, for it would leave us with massive, persistent inconsistency, a fatal internal infirmity to a doxastic practice. My view, though, is that we can make the distinction between genuine and non-genuine in the vast majority of cases—perhaps not with the same decisiveness or to the same extent as in the sensory realm, yet with enough decisiveness and to an extent sufficient for religious experience to remain under the general canopy of PC. In short, I believe that there is a sufficient overrider system for religious experience. Perhaps I am more sanguine than I should be on this matter; however, all I can do is go to the cases.

2. Elements of the Religious Overrider System

Case One

We should note, to begin with, that the cult leader may not have been telling the truth about his vision. I am inclined to think that this is the case, and will give my reason later on. However, for the sake of the argument, I shall assume that he was telling the truth and that his experience essentially amounted to a sense of Christ communicating to him.

The vision conveyed that the cult leader was helping Christ. If one is helping Christ, then one must be acting consistently with the life and teachings of Jesus. However, the man, who accepted the New Testament as Scripture, acted thoroughly inconsistently with the New Testament, particularly the Gospel, picture of Jesus. The Gospels certainly permit a wide range of views concerning Jesus, as does the New Testament in general; yet the range is not so wide that we can reject either the teaching of Jesus or the entire teaching of the New Testament about neighbor love. Jesus taught that his followers should pray for their enemies, turn the other cheek, go a second mile, not harbor any evil thoughts about an opponent, be peacemakers, and so on. He told stories about wayward people— the lost sheep, the prodigal son—stories in which God perseveres in seeking or waiting for the wayward. If there is judgment, as there is, the judgment is always for the last time, the end of the world, and God does the judging with justice. Moreover, Jesus never took any action to destroy his opponents; instead, he wept over them and forgave them. Jesus treated even Judas with great tenderness and sensitivity, at least according to the stories in John 13:1-11, 21-30. Thus, the cult leader acted inconsistently with the teachings he considered as authoritative. Given what we know about Jesus, we have to say that the cult leader did not help Jesus down from the cross but drove more spikes into his hands.

Jesus and the Authority of the New Testament.

A general point I shall make here is that I take the New Testament to be more authoritative about Jesus than religious experience, something that any standard CMP does. In short, the New Testament picture is part of a Christian overrider system, whether that be the overrider system of Roman Catholics or Southern Baptists. I do not believe that the New Testament leaves us with a Jesus who is nothing more than a historical cipher, at best nothing more than a reflection of the faith of the early church. Indeed, even if Jesus is largely the reflection of the faith of the early church, this faith would likely reflect, to a relatively high degree of accuracy, the essential teachings of Jesus. Thus, I believe that on historical grounds we can know some things about Jesus, a few of which I have mentioned above.

Even if I am wrong on this point, the more important point is that my belief is based on an appeal to evidence and argument. In other words, in order to support my belief, I should have to appeal to the evidence from New Testament studies (largely, I should have to appeal to authorities in the field) and inferences from the evidence. In noting this, I am noting methodology, a methodology which Muslims, Jews, Hindus, Buddhists, Taoists, or whoever would have to engage in and which, in fact, they do engage in. I do not, e.g., find Hindu Biblical scholars using different methods from Christian scholars. They may come up with different conclusions but no more different than the conclusions among Christian scholars. I cannot think of a much greater difference, e.g., than the difference between F. F. Bruce and Rudolph Bultmann on the historical Jesus. The point, then, is that we seem to find a common method, a method which functions, or could function, as a part of URP.

Returning now to Case One, I said that the cult leader acted inconsistently with the Biblical teachings concerning Jesus, teachings which are more authoritative about the character of Jesus than religious experience, something the cult leader recognized insofar as he viewed the New Testament as Scripture. I wish to dwell further on the notion of inconsistency, and in order to do so more adequately, I shall introduce another case, which will be Case Two.

Case Two

The case is from 1 Samuel, 15. Samuel comes to Saul, announcing what he takes to be the word of the Lord, viz., that Saul is to go off on a revenge extermination raid against the Amalekites. I shall assume that Samuel "heard" a Voice, much in the same manner as Socrates "heard" a Voice or St. Paul heard a Voice. The problem is that the Voice commands an egregious injustice, yet the God of Israel is a just God.

Consistency

What we see in both Case One and Case Two is that people must have consistency in their systems of beliefs. If the cult leader holds that Jesus is the Lord of love, he may not at the same time hold that he experienced Jesus commanding him to eliminate his opponents. Similarly, if Samuel holds that God is just, a teaching he considers authoritative, weightier than the experience of any single person, then he may not at the same time hold that he experienced God commanding unjust acts. People with contradictory beliefs know that at least one of their beliefs is false. They may not as yet know which is false, but they at least have a strong reason to go slow with belief until they resolve the contradiction.

And at this point I shall note that the rejection of contradiction is not peculiar to some particular religion but is universal to religion, a criterion which is universally valid and seems to be recognized across the board, at least among major world religions. The fact that religious beliefs often leave us with conflict, the conflict perhaps seeming beyond resolution, does not mean that we, with a smile of equanimity, accept the conflict, that we are unmoved by contradiction. No, we use the term 'paradox' or 'mystery', thereby indicating that contradiction is not, and cannot be, the final story. Thus, we seem to have a methodological criterion which functions, or could function, as a part of URP.

The question now is, Knowing that belief is in conflict, how may we resolve the conflict? In cases One and Two, How may we defeat one set of beliefs? I have already shown one way; however, I wish to come at the question in broader terms and thus will try to answer the question by way of a journey through sensory perception.

Some Defeaters for Sensory Perception

We all know that our perceptions sometimes come to us in ways such that beliefs based on them would lead to inconsistency: E.g., I see a pier piling in the water as bent, and so would believe that it is bent if I followed this perception; yet I run my hand up and down the piling and it feels straight, and so would believe that it is straight if I followed this perception. The perceptual inconsistency here is, of course, only one of many kinds of perceptual inconsistency. The question is: How do we sort things out perceptually so as to eliminate inconsistency? I shall mention four principles which we employ (four sorts of defeaters), not assuming that these principles are in the least exhaustive.

1) We may give more weight to one perception than another—e.g., more weight to touch than seeing or any other sense, and more weight to a carefully attended perception than to a glance. 2) We may discount, or at least seriously doubt (I shall not rule out miracles), a perception because it conflicts with a mass of regular, persistent perceptions over time—e.g., I may see the sun dancing in the sky, but this perception conflicts with the great mass of regular, persistent perceptions I have had, as well as those which others have had throughout the history of humans, not to mention the controlled perceptions within science. If I am to believe my eyes about some exceptional event, I must make very certain that I am seeing what I think I am and that my seeing is not just a vision or a hallucination, neither of which presents some state of the physical universe, say, the state of the sun. 3) We may determine a perception to be misleading by coming up with some highly probable statement explaining why the perception should be considered misleading—e.g., visual perception of a piling in water as bent is

explained by way of a statement concerning what light does when it enters another medium. Or put otherwise, we may determine a perception to be misleading by providing a theoretical explanation more adequate than any explanation to the effect that the perception is veridical. 4)We may discount perceptions because they are the result of some irregular physical or psychological state—e.g., we discount the perceptions of a person on LSD or someone who is psychotic, regularly subject to hallucinations. Similar criteria are present, I think, in the sphere of religious experience.

Parallel Defeaters for Religious Experience

First of all, some perceptions of the Divine are given far more weight than others. Cases One and Two do not provide examples of this fact, although the cases I have already discussed in previous chapters provide ample examples. Many of the people whom I have considered relate experiences which are salient in their thinking, experiences which they take as normative, some saying that the experiences were self-validating or the source of knowledge, not belief, and some reversing course in life because of the experiences. In short, some religious experience is rated above not only other religious experience but above sensory experience or reasoning. Jim is an excellent example. Jim gives great weight to Scripture, but listening to him conveys the impression that Scripture is being interpreted in the light of his experience. What he highlights in Scripture—God's love—is clearly a consequence of the extraordinary experiences of that night and morning. Nothing like the experiences has ever taken place again in Jim's life, yet the experiences carry a weight unparalleled to other experiences. Moreover, of the three experiences, the midnight one was weightiest—it was a "face to face" experience. In short, just as we give certain senses greater weight than others—our sense of touch is primary, vision has priority over hearing, and so on—so in religious experience we give greater weight to some experiences than others. When people say something along the line of, "The experience was completely self-authenticating," I think that part of what they are saying is, "Nothing is weightier than the experience. We use it to judge other experiences, not *vice versa*." Indeed, a number of people say explicitly just that.

We also judge one perception better than another because we are more attentive in one case than in another, or we do a double-take, noticing that what we thought we perceived we really did not. We thought our friend waved to us on the street, but a second look reveals a stranger hailing a taxi. In his account of the visit to Medjugorje Mr. Jackson conveys the impression that the people seeing the unusual phenomena are not having visions but are simply seeing what they want to. One way to check this would be to say something along the following lines: "Wait a minute! Let's look at that rosary again—let's take a closer look at it." In religious experience people also do double-takes, checking on whether they are dreaming, hallucinating, feeling the effects of drugs, and so on. Jim, e.g., thought at first that his experience was drug induced but quickly concluded that it was nothing like any drug experience he had ever had. Sheila rejects the notion that her experience of the One was anything like a hallucination. We have also come across other people who have done double-takes during the experience, rejecting the notion that the experience was a dream or a hallucination.

A second consideration in the sensory sphere is the number, regularity, and persistence of our experiences. If at Medjugorje I see the sun dancing in the sky, one important reason for hesitating to give credence to the perception is that it conflicts with the mass of perceptions to the contrary. In fact, I doubt that any person who has "seen" the solar phenomena at Medjugorje thinks that the sun actually behaved aberrantly. I have a friend who has been to Medjugorje a number of times, not merely as a pilgrim but also as a tour leader. He says that he has seen the solar phenomena, but he does not begin to think that either the earth or the sun was wobbling in its orbit. He maintains that his views parallel those of the other pilgrims. For him the phenomena were miraculous, not in the sense that the sun moved abnormally but in the sense that God gave many people the visual experience of the sun moving out of its path. (I shall restrict the term 'vision' to this sort of experience, viz., a sensory experience which the subject takes to be produced neither by his or her psyche nor by any natural objects but by some supernatural source.) I shall simply note at this point, without attempting to produce the evidence, that there are numerous reports of visions experienced by a number of people at the same time.

As for the rosaries turning into gold, again I should say that no one seems to be claiming that the rosaries are really gold, for if they are really gold, then anybody looking at them should see them as gold at the time that they are gold, not just a select group of the observers; or the rosaries should be able to pass chemical tests during the time that they are gold. Thus, if I am correct about what people are claiming to see at Medjugorje (if they are, in effect, claiming to have visions), then one important reason for that claim would be that they are taking into account all the other sensory experiences establishing the regularity of nature.

In cases One and Two the criterion of number, regularity, and persistence of religious experiences definitely comes into play. In both cases the experience must be tested against other experience which is relevant. In Case One the immediately relevant experience is that which people have of Jesus or the God of Christianity. The overwhelming mass of this experience is of a loving, caring, non-vengeful God, and the experience, because of its mass and persistence, is more authoritative epistemically than the experience of the cult leader or the small coterie of others like him.

And here I pause to say a word about those experiencing the dark night of the soul. The state cannot be considered a religious experience, for it is, in effect, the felt absence of God's presence. The Lover simply does not show up. All this is very much of an oversimplification, but the point is that the people having the experience usually come down, and come down strongly, on the side of God's love. In doing so they are resorting, at least in part, to explanation—in other words to finding as parsimonious an explanation as possible both for the presence and absence of God. I think that they are also resorting to the weight of their experience of God's love. At any rate, they usually end up being strong believers in God's love—some of the strongest that one could imagine. One need mention only St. John of the Cross and St. Theresa of Avila.

Returning now to experiences of God as loving, we should also mention experience from other religions in which God is personal and has moral characteristics, religions like Judaism, Islam, and Krishna Consciousness. Here again, the mass of experience is of a merciful or loving Deity. If the experience of the Divine as impersonal is relevant, I think that this experience also comes down on the side of love, non-vengefulness, non-retaliation. Those who experience God as impersonal—say, in the way of union or merger with an All— typically experience Something non-reactive and thus also non-violent or vengeful; they regularly report feeling peace and bliss in conjunction with their experience, feelings hardly connected with violence and vengeance. Also in experiencing union or merger they are experiencing Something that is receiving (accepting), as receiving as the ocean is of rain drops. We might note that Eastern mystics and holy people are typically non-violent, the experience of the Something apparently inspiring non-violence in them. In sum, the mass of experience East and West generally seems to be against the sect leader.

In Case Two, I shall say much the same thing. What Samuel believed about God's justice or what the Hebrew community at the time of Samuel believed about God's justice, I cannot say for certain. They may have held that God's justice was provincial, or since God was the God of creation, the God of heaven and earth, they may have grasped, however obscurely, that God was a God of universal justice. I think that the latter alternative is more likely, so that we should say the following: Samuel and other Israelites on occasion simply acted inconsistently with their notion of God as just (a notion based at least in part on a considerable amount of experience of God in the Hebrew community), doing so, perhaps, because they had not clearly thought-out the implications of universal justice, or because they simply fell into old and common habits of thinking and behaving. Be this as it may, the overwhelming experience of the Jewish community, particularly as the experience was expressed in the prophetic literature and in later literature such as the Talmud, was of a universally just God. I take the epistemic weight of this experience to be far superior to the experience of Samuel and those others who experienced a vengeful God. As in Case One, I could also appeal to non-Jewish experiences of a personal God, as well as experiences of an impersonal sort. The conclusion in Case Two parallels that of Case One: The mass of experience East and West seems to be against Samuel.

We saw that in sensory experiences we rule out some experiences as misleading by finding highly probable statements or theories explaining why they are misleading. In Case One an explanation for the cult leader's vision is that he wanted to maintain his position of power. The newspaper reported that he "manipulated his scriptural interpretations to persuade his followers to help kill" the family of five. His entire plan of action, including the report of a vision, seems to be nothing but a ploy to maintain his position of authority and leadership, a ploy used by many cult leaders throughout history. One depressing story from the Reformation era is that of the Munster millenarian rebellion under John of Leyden, who maintained the loyalty of his followers largely by way of reported visions, to the utter ruin of his followers—they were massacred by the Roman Catholic forces. As for the contemporary cult leader, the explanation that his report of a visionary experience is either just a false report (I am more inclined to this view, although in my discussion I have dismissed it as a possibility) or a true report of a vision produced by his desire to maintain his authority (nothing I have·said so far is a denial that desire can sometimes and in some circumstances produce visions or bogus religious experience) seems far more parsimonious than an explanation of his experience as a genuine supernatural visitation. If we say that the experience was a genuine supernatural visitation, then we shall have to discount his desires and fears about his authority (doing so will require, I believe, *ad hoc* hypotheses), as well as the forcefulness, number, and persistence of the experiences in which Jesus and God are perceived as loving, not to mention the evidence concerning Jesus from the New Testament.

As for Samuel, we may say the following. If we are to accept Samuel's revenge announcement as really from God, we must come up with hypotheses to account for the mass of experiences to the contrary. We must, as in the case of the cult leader, have hypotheses to explain away not only the forcefulness of these experiences but their number and persistence. Someone might suggest that a covering hypothesis of the sort 'All the other experiences are deceptive' would be as simple as the hypothesis 'The revenge experience is deceptive'; however, this gambit is what I should call "merely formal." The simplicity of the hypothesis 'All the other experiences are deceptive' is in the simplicity of the sentence alone. The question is, Why should we believe that the other experiences are deceptive? We must offer some reason for ignoring or discounting them rather than the revenge experience. E.g., we should have to say something along the lines, "Although the experiences of God's unchanging justice are at least as forceful as the experience of his revenge command, I discount the former because. . . ." Or, "Although the experiences of God's unchanging justice are more numerous and persistent, they are to be discounted because. . . ." In each case we need a hypothesis which will explain the discounting, a hypothesis, moreover, which will not come in conflict with other religious experiences.

Thus, we should not want a hypothesis saying that we are to discount all the other experiences (the experience of God as just and merciful) because people desire a God of holiness, justice, and mercy, with the result that they manufacture the experiences of a holy, just, and merciful God. In the first place we are here putting far more weight on desire than it will bear—the evidence I have produced shows that desire is hardly as effective as the hypothesis assumes. We may well expect desire on occasion--i.e., in conjunction with some set of circumstances—to be sufficient for a religious experience, but to be regularly sufficient is expecting far too much. Yet the experiences of God's holiness, justice, and mercy have regularly occurred in great number. Besides, the ancient Hebrew penchant for gods lacking justice and mercy (e.g., the Baals) is really, I should think, a decisive counterexample to any hypothesis of a strong, general desire on their part for a God of justice and mercy. In addition, I am not convinced that people through the centuries and up to today generally desire a God of mercy, a God that is non-retaliatory, if not vengeful. I should say that the God people normally go for is One that punishes and acts conditionally. In our society the reason is obvious: Our society conditions people to think in terms of earning their way, of no free lunches, of getting what they deserve, of deserving punishment for foul-ups, of being OK by performing adequately, and so on. The idea of a generous, no-strings-attached, graciously forgiving God is, although on the lips of many of the religious, not deeply in the psyche of people—it is not deeply believed and thus not deeply desired because considered impossible. In short, people might wish that God were thoroughly loving, but this wish, because it is thought to be—or deeply felt as—unrealistic, does not get translated into desires, certainly not strong, deeply-rooted desires.

Even in the religious sphere God often comes through as wrathful and judgmental, someone we have to plead with or prove our remorse to in order to receive forgiveness. I simply quote a brief passage from the Episcopalian Prayer Book, a book which is a regular part of my worship experience.

> We acknowledge and bewail our manifold sins and wickedness,
> which we from time to time most grievously have committed . . .
> against thy divine Majesty,
> provoking most justly thy wrath and indignation against us.
> We do earnestly repent,
> and are heartily sorry for these our misdoings;
> the remembrance of them is grievous unto us,
> the burden of them is intolerable.
> Have mercy upon us,
> Have mercy upon us, most merciful Father.

The New Testament says nothing about bewailing sins—but much about asking forgiveness. Further, the predominant portrait of God painted by Jesus is not of a God that is like a King, provoked to indignation and wrath by our sins, but of a God that is like a loving father, hurt and deeply grieved over our sins, waiting for us to return from living with the pigs. And when we return, even while we are so far away that he can barely see us, he runs to us, embraces us, forgives us before we can get a word out of our mouths, and then makes us a feast of the fatted calf, of wine on the lees, a feast with dancing and singing. Jesus' portrait of

God is a portrait which, because of the countervailing conditioning of our culture, we just have great trouble purchasing.

The upshot on the issue of simplicity is that although we can construct a simple sentence accounting for the genuineness of Samuel's experience, a sentence which looks as simple as one denying the genuineness of the experience, the simplicity is in the sentence alone, for the sentence really calls on us to introduce a number of sub-sentences (that is, sub-hypotheses).

A more parsimonious hypothesis would be that Samuel's experience of a vengeful God was just an expression of cultural influences. Samuel's world was one in which revenge against enemies was the norm, not the exception. For him to articulate a command in harmony with his world would not be surprising. In fact, accepting the experience as genuine calls for some reason to dispense with the presumption of cultural influence. In other words, we should need a hypothesis to explain why we are not to suppose the influence of culture when what comes forth is strictly in accordance with culture. Our explanatory hypothesis may well explain, but I suggest that it will explain only this particular instance—i.e., the hypothesis will be *ad hoc* and thus non-parsimonious. In brief, the hypothesis is likely to turn out to be something like: In this particular instance Samuel did not speak just out of cultural influences, although it looks exactly as if he did. Obviously, only the particular instance is explained, and explained without an appeal to evidence supportive of the hypothesis; i.e., the hypothesis actually amounts to saying: In this particular instance Samuel spoke independently of his culture, although we have no evidence to think so. My conclusion, then, is that Samuel's experience, at least what Samuel has to say about revenge, is probably not of God, but a projection of his cultural beliefs. I emphasize the phrase 'at least what Samuel has to say about revenge' because we need not maintain that the entire experience was manufactured. God may well have appeared to Samuel, speaking of His judgment on the wicked, a word which Samuel translated into revenge on the Amalekites. All that I am claiming is that the word about revenge was not likely from God. We have sufficient defeaters for it.

The final consideration I shall mention is that we must take into account the state of a person. If a person has been subject to hallucinations—say, the person has been suffering psychotic attacks—or has taken a hallucinatory drug, we should be on guard for claims about what the person experienced. A disturbed physical or psychological state could well generate the experience. Of course, we may not use the experience under question as a judge of a person's psychological condition; i.e., we may not say, e.g., that because Socrates hears a Voice he takes to be divine, he is unbalanced. We need evidence from another source, evidence which is not forthcoming in Socrates' case, with the result that we have every reason to look more seriously at Socrates' claim of a Voice.

We have to say the same, I think, about Muhammad. The standard story is that at age forty, while meditating in a cave on Mt. Hira, a mountain a few miles north of Mecca, he saw a vision of a heavenly being and heard the command, "Recite!" He was frightened by the being and did not know what to recite, but finally he heard the words:

> Proclaim!
> In the name
> Of thy Lord and Cherisher,
> Who created—
> Created man out of
> A (mere) clot
> Of congealed blood:
> Proclaim! And thy Lord
> Is Most Bountiful,—
> He Who taught
> (the use of) the Pen,—
> Taught man that
> Which he knew not.
> (*The Holy Quran*, S. XCVI:1-5)

Muhammad definitely did not know what was going on. He departed from the cave, thinking that he was either possessed or mad. Some accounts say that on that occasion or on later occasions he attempted to kill himself but was dissuaded by the voice of the heavenly being assuring him that he was a messenger of God. Moreover, his wife, Khadija, assured him that he was neither possessed nor mad but was the recipient of a divine message. Indeed, she was his first convert. (Watt, 1961, 14-22, 34) We may imagine her saying something along the following lines:

> You, Muhammad, Mad? Impossible! What about the caravan you led back to Mecca last week? and all the caravans before that? Where did we get our wealth? How did you get the reputation for shrewdness and resourcefulness? By being mad? And why are you worrying about madness now? Is such worrying typical of madmen? Never let the thought cross your mind that you are mad!

In short, Muhammed exhibited no signs of madness elsewhere in his life, and thus we may not judge him mad on the basis of his cave experience alone. Just the opposite: We have every reason to look more seriously at his claim of hearing a heavenly messenger. (I note that Watt, in his attempt to explain Muhammad's experience, makes the standard move of appealing to the unconscious, 17, 236-40.) This experience was apparently first taken by Muhammad as an experience of Allah, although later he identified it as of the angel Gabriel. (Watt, 15) I shall go with Muhammad's first impression, although nothing would really change by taking the message as from Gabriel, a heavenly messenger. The main point is that nothing in the original experiences of Muhammad indicates anything other than a man of sound mind. Because we have every reason to believe that Muhammad was of sound mind, we cannot defeat his belief that a heavenly messenger appeared to him by resorting to claims of madness.

As for the cult leader and Samuel, we do not have evidence showing that they were in any sort of disturbed state. Their experiences cannot be eliminated on this ground. However, the other criteria we have considered are sufficient to eliminate both experiences as genuine experiences of God. We have provided defeaters to the proposition that their religious experience was a good ground for their religious beliefs.

Other Defeaters

The criteria I have used as defeaters so far are criteria developed in parallel to four criteria employed in the case of sensory perception. But there are other criteria. We have a whole class of other sources of knowledge (other doxastic practices) which may counter or defeat religious experience. Since our religious doxastic practice must meet the condition of external consistency, it must be consistent with other doxastic practices.

One important doxastic practice which is highly relevant for religion is our moral practice. I shall assume, without argument, that we have a moral doxastic practice (e.g., we are thoroughly justified in believing that sadistic behavior is wrong) and that it is at least as authoritative as our religious doxastic practice. If what we believe morally comes into conflict with religious belief based on religious experience, then the former is at least a counter to the latter. I am inclined to believe that as a general rule moral belief, at least basic moral belief (belief we do not infer from other beliefs), can provide defeaters to religious experience.

Whatever position we take—whether we see moral beliefs as epistemically equal to or more weighty than belief based on religious experience—we must say that killing one's opponents, as well as revenge extermination raids, is inconsistent both with love and justice and thus inconsistent with our basic moral beliefs. If for strong reasons God has already been accepted as morally good—as God is in both Hebrew and Christian communities—then any experience of God as commanding the immoral must be rejected because of our moral perceptions. Thus, on moral grounds we have reason to reject the experiences of the cult leader and of Samuel. I am assuming that both would declare that God is morally good. I am not assuming, though, that either had thought out the implications of this position; therefore, I do not deny that Samuel may have held that God's command was for justice to be practiced only with respect to Israelites, outsiders being fair game for revenge. However, another alternative is that both Samuel and the cult leader knew very well what moral goodness implied; other factors simply overrode—cultural habits, in the case of Samuel, and the desire to maintain authority, in the case of the cult leader.

A still further doxastic practice is SP (sensory doxastic practice), a practice generally of greater epistemic weight than our religious doxastic practice. I say "generally" because there may be instances when SP comes up with an unclear answer (e.g., we are not certain what we saw because of distance) I have noted that I take the New Testament picture of Jesus to carry more weight than any conflicting picture from religious experience. My view about the authority of the New Testament picture of Jesus is a result, among other things, of numerous perceptual judgments about New Testament literature, about the history of New Testament times, and about the early church. (The perceptual judgments are those of the scholars seeing the manuscripts, viewing the artifacts, and so on. I accept their authority.) I note, in addition, that any prophetic material, material announced as being the Word of the Lord to the prophet, must square with archeological findings, i.e., must square with all the perceptions used to determine what occurred in history. If a prophet announced that Nebuchadnezzar, king of Babylon, would invade and defeat Egypt, so that the country would lie desolate afterward for forty years, then we should expect to discover evidence of the Babylonian invasion. Lacking such evidence, we would declare that the prophet did not really hear the Word of the Lord. A present day example may further underscore this point. This example will be Case Three.

Case Three (3748)

Paula says that she had a vision of Jesus, with Jesus telling her that He would return in 1985. Paula seems to take these words literally. I do not have any further information on Paula, so I shall assume that she was perfectly normal. Of course, if she were emotionally disturbed, having, say, hallucinations of a variety of sorts, we would have strong grounds for concluding that what she took as a vision of Jesus was really a hallucination. Assuming, though, that she was normal, we may say that since she accepts the return of Jesus, she also apparently accepts the authority of the Gospel picture of Jesus. It would be odd, then, for her to reject Jesus' statement that no one knows the date of His return, not even He Himself—only the Father. Thus, first of all, we may discount her experience by reason of the authority of the New Testament picture of Jesus.

The *coup de grace*, however, is administered by the events of history: Jesus did not return in 1985. Or put in perceptual terms, what Paula took to be a vision conflicts with all the sensory experiences everybody—including Paula—had in 1985, viz., that Jesus did not return. Therefore, what Paula had was a hallucination, not a vision.

If the words Paula heard are not to be interpreted literally, we may seem to be stymied in any judgment about her experience. However, I do not believe that we are. The non-literal senses in which Jesus could come in 1985, as opposed to, say, 1984, are not I suggest, going to fare better than a literal rendition of the words. E.g., if Jesus began some new program in the world in 1985, such a program is without authority in the New Testament and without the perception of anything programmatically different occurring in the world. The differences between 1985 and before are differences of the normal order of history. If the words meant that Jesus would come in 1985 in the same way that He comes every year, viz., as gracious, active Lord of life, the question is why the year 1985 was singled out. Things just do not look good for Paula's "vision," whatever the interpretation.

3. Remarks about URP

Having specified some of the basic criteria for judging religious experience, including other doxastic practices, I shall note that I have not taken any of the criteria as peculiar to CMP. The criteria have been methodological criteria, universal in scope and in actual practice. Thus, I believe that we have an operative URP, consisting essentially of methodology—not merely the specifically religious methodology but the methodology of the other doxastic practices with which our religious practice must be consistent. Actually, the specifically religious methodology is a fraction of the whole practice, most of the rest of it consisting of methods (practices) employed in other domains (sensory, moral, and so on). We might think, then, of URP as the whole panoply of methods (or practices) used in judging religious belief. In any case, URP is essentially methodological, so that belief content is secondary to methodological content. This is true for any doxastic practice, I should say. The real questions in a doxastic practice are always how beliefs were arrived at, what their *prima facie* status is, and whether on methodological grounds they have suitable status to be counters to or defeaters of other beliefs. If I should be told that, e.g., many Hindus and Buddhists do not employ the methodologies noted (along with others I should have to note in a complete listing), my counter would be that many do, and that, in any case, many Christians do not use them either. I have met ever so many Christians who, e.g., sluff off the Samuel experience as totally unproblematic. Indeed, I am not about to maintain that I consistently use the methodologies myself. I only set them forth as valid methodologies, which we try to live up to when we are working at our best.

Spelling out all the criteria for judging religious experience, along with the relationships between them, is an important task which must be carried out for my argument to be complete but a task which is beyond the scope of this book. The only point I note here is that we have criteria, methodological criteria, universal in scope and adhered to interreligiously, criteria for providing defeaters of beliefs based on religious experience. In short, I begin by granting that we can have experiences which have all the marks of an encounter with the Divine but which are not true encounters with the Divine, just as I grant that we can have sensory experiences which have all the marks of genuine perception but which do not represent anything in the physical world (i.e., the experiences are hallucinatory). We may not know how to account for the latter experiences any better than the former, and it may turn out that we can account for both in the same way; however, whatever the account of the experiences, the non-veridical experiences of the Divine no more discredit the appeal to religious experience as *prima facie* justification for religious belief than hallucinations discredit the appeal to sensory experience as *prima facie* justification for beliefs about the physical world. We would have accreditation problems with the Divine if we could not come up with defeaters of religious experience; but we can—or so I think I have shown. The system of defeaters may not be as strong or decisive as in the case of sensory perception, but the system seems strong enough for us to make distinctions between veridical and non-veridical religious experience in most cases. In the remainder of this chapter I shall present further problematic cases from the material I have gathered in order to see how well we can provide defeaters.

Case Four (1141)

Les was praying alone in a secluded spot when he felt a presence and "saw" a man in an overcoat just standing in front of him. He opened his eyes and the figure disappeared, with the result that Les asked himself: What does a man in an overcoat have to do with my praying to Christ? He never figured out the answer to this question.

Les does not seem to have considered the options. E.g., the man could represent Les, the coat representing the fact that Les was covering up something, hiding something, not really being honest in his prayer or elsewhere in his life. (A clinician could undoubtedly come up with better interpretations than this.) Thus, the image could very well have something to do with his prayer and could be, in a broad sense, Christ's response to his prayer. In this case the Divine could by employing a fairly natural working of the unconscious or semi-conscious (as in dreams) in order to convey truth to Les. Receiving something in consciousness may be more effective than receiving something in dreams, particularly if one is inclined to write-off dreams as unreal. All this is fairly speculative, the only point necessary for our consideration being that Les's experience is not a religious experience, an experience with a sense of divine Presence.

Case Five (447)

Earl reports that a divine spirit told him to say "X 10." He did, with no consequence. He does not say in what manner the divine Spirit spoke to him or how he identified the Spirit as a divine Spirit, but for the sake of the argument I shall assume that the divine Spirit presented Itself to his consciousness as a Presence telling him something. Earl does not say enough to let us know how he was functioning elsewhere in life or whether he was under treatment for an emotional disorder of some sort. I shall assume that he was a perfectly normal individual.

I classify Earl's experience as a religious experience because of the sense of a divine Spirit, a divine Spirit telling him something. I cannot tell whether or not the Voice came as an external, audible Voice, or as an internal Voice. The distinction does not matter, though, for the claims in both cases seem to be essentially the same in the sense that people who think that they audibly hear a divine voice or visually see a divine figure (such as Jesus or the Virgin Mary) usually are no more inclined to think that someone in their vicinity would hear or see what they do than they are inclined to think that someone would hear or see a strictly internal voice or figure. In other words, subjects who think that they have visions do not normally think of the visions as intersubjective. Ezekiel, e.g., had many visions in the presence of others (See the vision reported in Ez. 1.) but gives no indication that others also had them; in fact, he relates the visions to his fellow exiles, including, apparently, those who were with him at the time of the visions. (Ez. 8:1 with 11:25; 14:1-5; 20:1-3) All the same, visions may, as I mentioned, be intersubjective; we certainly have reports that some are. St. Paul's conversion experience would be an example, for the people with him on the Damascus Road apparently experienced some of the features of his visionary experience.

Since Earl received a message, we are clearly in the realm of a personal God. The immediate impression of the message to Earl is that it is meaningless and pointless, the kind of message we should not expect from a loving God. As I have noted, we have considerable experiential evidence for a loving God. I shall not presume, taking Jesus as a parallel, that a vision or some kind of message from God has to be in a form such that the person receiving it interprets or understands it, although I shall presume that it is in a form such that a thoughtful person would be able fairly readily to figure it out. Actually, a genuine vision or a message from God might very well be clothed in ambiguity, such as the words of the oracle at Delphi, the result being that we might need considerable time, as well as help from others, to figure it out. I do not know how long it took Socrates to figure out the oracle's words that he was the wisest of men, but it took more than a day or a week. In any case, if someone sees symbolic communication or messages clothed in ambiguity as inconsistent with a good, loving God, then I shall ask for the arguments demonstrating the inconsistency. What does seem presumptively inconsistent with a loving God is a sheerly meaningless or purposeless vision or message, a vision or message which thoughtful people would not be likely to figure out (a criterion which is anything but precise but which I shall not attempt to improve on).

The more deliberate consideration of the message to Earl also leaves us thinking that it is meaningless. Perhaps X10 has some relation to X9 of Kurt Vonnegut's *Cat's Cradle*, but we have no evidence for that connection; moreover, even if we did, we still could probably not work out any purpose for the message. Hence, the term 'X10' looks nonsensical, and repeating it seems to have no purpose other than, perhaps, just being obedient to God. Repeating the term will neither benefit others nor ourselves, for the term provides no information, no incentive for self-growth, no moral insight or instruction for others, and so on. Repeating it would be, at best, strictly an act of obedience to God. Focusing just on Biblical literature, I should say that the God of the Bible certainly does not seem to be in the habit of issuing commands for no other reason than obedience. Certainly the great commands of Scripture (Love God, love your neighbor, and love yourself) are value or moral commands, and thus have point beyond sheer obedience. Whatever questionable commands we may find here or there in the Bible, the fundamental commands are clearly commands to do good and loving things. ("Do justice, love mercy, and walk humbly with your God." Mic. 6:8) The reason is obvious: Since a good and loving God would presumably desire people to pursue goodness and love, his commands would be for people to do good and loving things, not things which are empty of good or loving content (repeating meaningless phrases, performing meaningless acts, such as blinking one's right eye seven times). In desiring people to pursue goodness and love, God would want people to see any commands coming from Him as rooted in goodness and love. Arbitrary, pointless commands obscure God's goodness and love. I shall not say that a command which fails to command good or loving action, its only purpose being obedience to God, is inconsistent with the goodness and love of God. What I shall say, though, is that the presumption is against God's issuing such a command, and if we find such a command, we should look for special circumstances which make the command functional. We do not have any special circumstances in Earl's case, so that the command looks pointless and therefore not likely from a loving God.

A further consideration is that people fairly commonly have compulsions and obsessions, which sometimes come to them as voices to do something or other. These compulsions and obsessions are pointless by way of doing something beneficial to the person or others, aside, perhaps, from temporarily relieving the person's guilt or anxiety. Indeed, the behavior is often, if not usually, disruptive of a person's normal activities or of relations with others. Usually, other features of a person's life (e.g., strong guilt feelings) or certain features of the experience (the regularity and frequency of the compulsions) provide evidence that we are likely looking at a compulsion or obsession. Lacking any further evidence in Earl's case, we could simply note the purposelessness of the command and thus its likeness to obsessions. This consideration would be enough, I think, to counter the experience, if not to provide an overrider.

Case Six (4256)

Ray says that he had an experience similar to that of A. J. P. Taylor, recounted in "The Observer," May 15, 1983. Taylor's account was as follows.

> I was sitting in the art room and looking through its big window across to the Minster when I had a revelation just like Saul's on the road to Damascus. A voice said: 'There is no God.' I had never thought about religion before; I had taken it for granted. From that moment Christian's burden fell from my back for ever. What a relief. I have had many troubles in life, but religion has never been one of them.

The experience related by Taylor is, of course, similar to an experience we have already come across, viz., the experience of Barbara (Chapter Three), who, upon asking, "Is there anyone to pray to?" received the answer, "No!" She, as Taylor, jettisoned belief in God, and probably with more excuse than Taylor, since she was a child, whereas Taylor was an adult, capable of a higher level of reasoning.

Now an experience like Taylor's is obviously not religious; however, such an experience is worth looking at, if for no other reason than determining what we are to do with the voice, whether, e.g., we should give it some sort of transcendent status, such as of an other-worldly messenger.

We recall that accepting at face value a voice like the one coming to Taylor is a course with formidable pitfalls. The immediate, obvious question is: Whose voice is it? If it is God's, then the game is up. No question about God's reality. And why shouldn't it be God's voice? The fact that God denies his own existence? If God did that, then God would be speaking ironically, something which we find prophets and angels doing in Biblical literature. An amusing story concerns the prophet Micaiah, who, upon entering the court of king Ahab, tells the king exactly the opposite of what he took the word of the Lord to be; in other words, Micaiah told Ahab exactly what the king wanted to hear. (1 K 22:13-23) At any rate, we should not casually dismiss the possibility of God speaking ironically or humorously. Barbara does, Taylor does, and so does Ray, as we shall see—naively so, I shall say.

In contrast to the literally-minded Barbara, Taylor, and Ray, I cite Alex (unnnumbered account, but taken from the Alister hardy Research Centre), who, while meditating on the serious pursuit of God and the consequences of experiencing God's presence, came to the realization that anyone really serious about God could very well be a public danger. What, then, should he tell people about God—that if they got serious, they would likely become public dangers? He continues his account as follows.

> The Person I had come to know in my life as the Holy Ghost intervened—delicately ironic as always. 'You are quite right,' was the remark, 'it is better to tell them to be atheists. Their love for Us can then proceed behind the scene of their minds—the only level at which it matters, and the only level at which it will continue.'

Thus, the voice to Taylor might have been God's, with God speaking ironically. But now it is time to turn to Ray. His story is as follows.

> My wife fell ill with a serious depression and had to go into a mental hospital. I was torn apart by her undeserved suffering and by the loneliness which besets one when anyone close to oneself is cut off.... A Baptist friend told me that there was 'One Above' on whom I could cast my suffering. Pondering on this one day as I drove to visit my wife at the hospital, I felt a powerful, imperious voice say 'No! You do NOT need a God!' I *felt*—but could not put it into words—that I *understood why* I didn't need a God; people attempting to describe a mystical illumination seem to me to be talking about something very like my experience. Talking about it the next day, I found the nearest I could get to it was to say 'I seemed to crash right *through* religion and come out into a calm sea and clear sky on the other side.' More frivolously, I compared it to crashing through the sound-barrier. Anyway, since that moment I have never experienced any temptation to hold any religious belief or to envy people who have such beliefs.

First of all the words which come to Ray are not a denial of God's existence. They are that Ray does not need a God. I underline 'a' because its presence in the statement introduces some likely meanings of the statement. Among other things, the Baptist's statement about God ("There is One Above on whom you can cast your suffering") may indicate a very limited view of God, viz., the view that God more or less waves His magic-wand over us, relieving us of our sufferings and putting things right in our lives—no struggling or searching or growing required. Ray himself may have held this view of God. Thus, perhaps the statement amounts to: "No, indeed, you don't need that kind of God!" Or perhaps it means, "No, you don't need *a* god; you need Me, the true and living God!" A statement with a meaning along these lines would not be too distant from the message conveyed to Alex, viz., that it is better to tell people to be atheists; or in Ray's words the message would be, "We need to crash through the sound barrier of religion because otherwise we will never find God." I think that Meister Eckhart put the whole matter in the best possible way: "I have given up God in order to find God."

The voice, then, might have been God's; but if not, then whose? Perhaps it was some transcendent being, at least a being transcending human limitations. Why, then, should anyone believe the being? Why should it have better knowledge of God than anyone on earth? How would the being have privileged access to anything about God? Did the being never experience God? Why would that be any more relevant or weighty than the fact that numerous humans never experience God? In a word, why should some being—say, in the afterlife—have any privileged access to knowledge of God's existence? Perhaps in the afterlife God's presence is no more or less evident than here. What puts such a being in a privileged epistemic state? I cannot think of anything that necessarily does. In any case, if transcendent beings exist, some of whom go about telling people that God does not exist, even though they do not know this, then Barbara, Taylor, Ray, and everybody else better have their intellectual eyes peeled for the beings. Indeed, we probably all need a twenty-four hour lookout, for the beings could just be evil deceivers, not merely playful or bored creatures from the beyond.

The fact that Ray experienced an "imperious" Voice should have alerted him to some of the negative possibilities of the being. But what we see about Ray, Taylor, and Barbara is that they simply do not react critically to their experience, something exactly the opposite of many, if not the overwhelming majority, of those we have considered. We have seen people who consider the possibility that their religious experience is a dream or hallucination (Jim, at the beginning of his midnight experience—"At first I thought that this [the inner Voice] was just part of the drug too, part of my trip."); people who consider the possibility that in prayer they were just talking to themselves (Ron, after five hours on the hill—"Well, now I talked to myself, and nothing happened."); people who try to figure out what went on, often remaining puzzled and troubled after the experience, the main point being that they devote considerable energy to trying to figure out what went on or what it all meant (Viola, almost forty years after her experience—"I am still astonished sometimes. Why should there be a God? I can think of no convincing reasons. And a personal God at that! It all seems so unlikely! Then I am astonished all over again."); and people who have a sense that the experience was self-authenticating (Angelique, reflecting on her experiences, says that they are "not only self-authenticating but" are "the ground or standard by which everything else in my subjective experience can be, and is judged."). But Ray, Taylor, and Barbara simply seem to dismiss critical reflection on their experience, immediately taking the voice to communicate that they should abandon God. I shall not say that they represent all the people who have experiences like theirs. That I do not know. I am talking simply about them.

If the words are not from God or from some transcendent being, then they must be from the self. Ray actually comes to the conclusion that his experience was from the self, saying: "It seems better sense to say that a conclusion which is produced by one's own 'internal computer' can present itself exactly as if it were a command from outside by a supernatural power." Ray does not say why "it seems better sense" to attribute the voice to himself, but he might have taken the following path.

Given PC, we may say that a voice seeming to come from outside is *prima facie* justification for believing that the voice is from outside, i.e., is not from one's self alone. Ray, then, has a *prima facie* case for saying that the voice is not from him. Since Ray seems to be a balanced individual, he does not have reason straight off to go for a defeater appealing to an abnormal state. The first question, then, for Ray is, Whose voice is this, if not mine? The previous considerations show, I think, that Ray should have at least as much reason to say that the voice is from God as from another being that denies God's existence—or if Ray has more reason to say the latter, he has no reason to believe the being. But what does Ray do? With lightning speed he jumps to the conclusion that God does not exist. He just seems to anesthetize his critical capacities, a strong indication that he did not want to believe in God—very much did not want to believe. Or better, perhaps we should say that he very strongly wanted to give up on religion, having illicitly identified God with institutionalized religion. We do know that Ray was bothered by the issue of unmerited suffering; he may have been bothered enough to want to give up on religion and God. I do not wish to appear judgmental about this, only evaluative from an epistemological standpoint. Who knows the trauma of Ray or of Taylor or of Barbara? Deep anguish often overwhelms us. At any rate, Ray certainly seems relieved about giving up on religion. The same goes for Taylor.

Of course, I am, again, not saying that strong desire always brings about what desire wants. However, as I have noted, nothing that I have said denies that sometimes strong desire (linked to anger or other strong feelings), in conjunction with other circumstances, can create its object or create an experience endorsing or giving authority to what it desires. In any case, Ray's initial jump to the conclusion that God does not exist and his relief at giving up on God should alert us to what he was probably desiring. Thus, if we do not have strong enough evidence to defeat belief in a voice from the outside, we certainly have strong enough evidence to counter it. Whatever the case on this score, I repeat that Ray certainly does not know whether the voice, if from outside, was from God or from some other being, an untruthful being, and therefore does not on the basis of his experience have a reason to dispense with belief in God.

Case Seven (191)

Judy was minding her own business when "suddenly it was as if God had spoken to me—'You must work for the Unitarian cause.'" Judy, a rock-solid theist, takes the message as from God and commits herself to working in the Unitarian church.

The information in this case is again very limited, so that any judgment is going to be fairly speculative. However, all that I wish to emphasize is that I do not have any good reason to question Judy's judgment that she received a message from God. The message looks sectarian, yet it is not necessarily so. The message is not that Unitarianism holds the only truth but that Judy is to work for the Unitarian cause. I can see how working in a particular expression of religion would be appropriate for an individual, even though that expression of religion might be deficient in some way or other. My view is that every particular expression of religion is deficient in some way or other, a view which is not equivalent to saying that all expressions of religion are equally deficient. At any rate, the main point is that a person may very well be "directed" into an expression of religion which is less adequate in some ways than some other expression, something which even the person involved might recognize. Many of the people writing in to the Sir Alister Hardy Research Centre were saying, I think, something along the following lines: "I could easily participate in the C/E if there were any life there. As it is, I've got to go somewhere else." Somewhere else could mean the Cotswold area, the Lake Country, a hill some starry night, or some group which may be a little offbeat but which is at least alive.

Many of the Hare Krishna people I met had become thoroughly alienated from Christianity because of the cultural compromise they saw throughout the church. In other words, they agreed with Whitehead's characterization of Western religion that "it was tending to become a decent formula wherewith to embellish a comfortable life." The Hare Krishna folk seemed to grasp intuitively the words of Jesus that the "gate is narrow and the way is hard that leads to life." They were not finding this truth accepted and lived in any of the Christian groups they were familiar with. The situation was almost as if either they found some group which took religion seriously or they were out of the religious game altogether. The Hare Krishna faith is very demanding, so that it certainly seems to take the religious search seriously—up at four in the morning, two hours of chanting and study of religious books, then out in parks propagating the faith, and so on. Supposing, for the sake of the argument, that Christianity is closer to the truth about God than Krishna Consciousness, I have no trouble accepting that God would speak to some person, saying, "Devote yourself to Krishna consciousness." Indeed, perhaps in our culture most people would discover more about the reality of God by taking the path of Krishna Consciousness than by taking the path represented by the institutional church. That does not seem to be a preposterous proposition, especially given the statements of many of our subjects about the thorough deadness of the church as they knew it. And that is also why the message that Alex received is not absurd, viz., the message that perhaps the best thing to do is to tell everyone to become atheists!

Thus, I do not have any good reason to say that Judy did not receive a message from God. If I knew more about her and her situation, I might have reason to judge otherwise; or I might not.

Case Eight (1037)

Ellen states that she experienced a being of light, saying, "I am Father, Son, and Holy Spirit." Information about Ellen is sparse, so again judgment about her experience is speculative. In this case all I want to say is that the experience need not be taken as an endorsement of any particular creedal expression of the Trinity. One translation of the statement could be: "I am the total God, encompassing all your conceptions of Me." Or, "I am the God that is Father (loving Father), Son (God come to seek and to save) and Holy Spirit (God as Presence with you)." Again, my main point is that I do not see any particular creedal endorsement in the statement. Moreover, I believe that the statement is not necessarily inconsistent with Ellen saying also that at some other time she experienced God as Brahman. But now I am anticipating the next chapter. All that I shall say for now is that I again have no reason to say that Ellen did not receive a message from God.

Case Nine (4709)

A final case is that of Kevin. Kevin was an atheist, who, having quit his job because he could not tolerate the unethical practices of the firm where he worked, found himself with some financial anxieties. One day while walking his dog in the field, "worried sick" over his financial condition, he had the following extraordinary experience.

> I heard words not of my choice—but like another voice within me saying my name. 'Kevin—none of this matters. You will always have what you need.' I remember it was a short initial statement that left me thinking—'what the hell'—then 'let's have more'—Then although now I cannot remember word for word I remember the way it went; it was something like: 'This is but a moment in the passage of time and it is for a purpose. It will bring you to what matters for you even if it matters not to the world. What is right for you will happen if you will only listen to your inner self.'

Kevin relates that he received many messages, which he has been reluctant to share with others for fear they would consider him mad. Indeed, he himself had doubts about his sanity. However, he put enough stock in his experiences to abandon his atheism, accepting the Reality speaking to him as a Universal Intelligence. Given the limited evidence I have on Kevin, I do not know whether he sensed the presence of a

Universal Intelligence or inferred it from the givenness of the words, as well as from their meaning and significance. For the sake of the argument, I shall take the former view.

The main reason to refer to Kevin is not to note that he traveled the route from atheism to belief but to concentrate on a message he received. At one time he asked about the many religions in the world, receiving the reply that "they are all equally valid but due to man's practice of listening to himself and others there are errors—but again that's because we can't hope to fully grasp the non-physical knowledge."

First of all, Kevin does not elaborate on this message, which is not altogether clear. What does he mean by 'the many religions of the world'? Does he mean the religions of the Amazon Basin or the interior of Africa, along with the religions the religions we refer to as "world religions"? I cannot say for certain, but normally when a Western person speaks of the religions of the world, the person is referring to the recognized world religions—Judaism, Christianity, Islam, Hinduism, Buddhism, perhaps Taoism. Kevin undoubtedly meant at least these religions. As for the errors in the religions, he does not spell them out, but he does not seem to distinguish one religion as having more errors than another. What, then, shall we make of this message to Kevin? Is it likely to have been from a Universal Intelligence?

The message to Kevin is too abbreviated to know exactly what it meant, and Kevin did not probe for a more precise meaning. I should think that a natural response to the message would be: "What do you mean, 'equally valid'? You mean that no religion is superior to another? No religion gives a more adequate picture of You?" Yet Kevin does not report asking any questions. (The Hebrew prophets continually questioned God, challenged God! Moses is an excellent example.) However, the coherency of Kevin's account requires that some limitations be placed on the notion that all religions are equally valid. Obviously, if Kevin is, as he says, experiencing a Universal Intelligence, one that can and does communicate with humans, then he may not say that a religion denying a communicating Universal Intelligence is equally valid. However, neither the Void of major forms of Buddhism nor the Brahman of major forms of Hinduism nor the Tao of Taoism may be considered a Universal Intelligence that communicates. Of course, if these religions are not taken as expressing the essential nature of the Divine, then coherency may be saved, as long as God's essential nature may be such that it can accommodate these varying expressions of the Divine—i.e., as long as the experience of a Void, e.g., may be made compatible with the notion of a Being essentially such that it may also manifest Itself in experience as a Universal Intelligence. I am assuming compatibility at this point. Thus, we could say that the various world religions give authentic glimpses of the Divine, and in that sense may be said to be equally valid. To say this, though, does not necessarily mean that each glimpse is equally adequate. One glimpse may get us closer to the essential nature of the Divine than another.

Since neither Kevin nor I know what the statement about equal validity means, and since it might meant something along the lines of what I have suggested, the statement may have been from a Universal Intelligence. I do not see any decisive defeater to the statement, given the interpretation I have just placed on it. Moreover, the ambiguity of the situation here is not unlike the ambiguity of some sensory perception. I may have perceived some phenomenon in the sky but did not get a clear enough or long enough glimpse to figure out what it was. It may have been a reflection from an airplane or from something on the ground. I do not know, and cannot determine for certain.

If the interpretation of the message to Kevin is as I have suggested, we do not learn a great deal. Major questions of validity are still undecided because the statement is ambiguous.

But let us consider some other interpretations of the message. Another interpretation of the message might be that all religions are equally valid in the sense that they equally bring us into the experience of God's reality and power. In other words, although some religions may be closer to the truth about God, they are so distorted by erroneous trappings, especially in their institutional expressions, that they end up doing no better in getting people on the way to God than religions which are more distant from the truth about God. Thus, the real saints of one religion (not necessarily those officially recognized as saints) measure up to the real saints of another. This interpretation takes us close to what I said above when speaking of Krishna Consciousness. In other words, taking religions as a whole— their views of God, along with their ability to get people going on the path of sainthood (i.e., the path of genuine religious growth)—they all stand about the same height. One might be more insightful than another yet be weaker in getting people on the path to sainthood or *vice versa*. I find this interpretation attractive and will say more about it in the next chapter. Moreover, it is an interpretation consistent with saying that the message to Kevin was from a Universal Intelligence. No decisive defeater, then, to this view, as far as I can tell.

Summary

In this chapter I have tried to confront the objection, posed as a defeater to religious experience generally, that experiences of the sort, "God spoke to me and told me to kill the first person whom I laid eyes on," vitiate the whole program of appealing to religious experience because the experiences cannot be eliminated, defeated. More generally, the objection is that there are no criteria for distinguishing between genuine and non-genuine religious experience, so that we are left with a mass of conflict in belief, conflict which, without distinguishing criteria, we cannot resolve. My response has been that we do have criteria, methodological criteria. Moreover, these criteria are not tied to CMP or any other particular religion but are universal in scope and are practiced interreligiously. The criteria do not permit us to achieve 100 percent quality in the case of religious experience, any more than sensory criteria permit us to achieve 100 percent quality in the case of sensory experience. There are always borderline sensory cases which we cannot decide because we did not get a good look or the evidence is incomplete and we cannot get a rerun, or for some other reason. Yet we do not for lack of 100 percent quality jettison our confidence in the epistemic worth of sensory perception, i.e., its worth as *prima facie* justification for beliefs about the physical world. Likewise, the fact that we do not know what to make of some religious experience is no reason to jettison our confidence in the general epistemic worth of religious experience.

The main message of this chapter is that we do have principled ways, universal in scope and practiced interreligiously, for distinguishing the good from the poor in the sphere of religious experience. We do not have to accept just any experience coming through the human medium.

Chapter Nine

Two Conflicts in Religious Belief

In the last chapter I think that I made a case for our having principled ways of distinguishing poor from good quality religious experience—i.e., we have an overrider system. Indeed, I think that I made a case for our having URP—universally valid and universally operative principled ways of evaluating beliefs based on religious experience. I do not claim to have listed every criterion of URP or to have stated all of them adequately. However, I think that the case I have made is strong enough to think that we do have URP; or at least I think that we have as much reason to believe in URP as CMP. Indeed, I have suggested that in spelling out URP I could also be viewed as spelling out CMP; in other words, what I take to be the methodological requirements within CMP I also take to be the methodological requirements in URP. If I make a distinction, it is one of convenience for discussions within the Christian community. Thus, when speaking with fellow Christians, I accept certain beliefs which Christians generally (with some exceptions) see as meeting methodological requirements but those in other religions (along with some Christians) do not, beliefs such as creation out of nothing or the belief that Jesus is divine Savior and Lord.

Assuming, then, that we have URP, we may still be left with massive, unresolvable conflict between beliefs based on genuine religious experiences, experiences which pass muster under URP. If so, we should still be in an untenable position, for we should have failed the requirement of internal consistency, and thus there would be a general defeater for the appeal to religious experience. I do not believe that URP leaves us with massive, unresolvable conflict in belief. In order to support my view I shall focus on two conflicts which are often used as examples of pervasive, unresolvable conflict.

The first is the conflict over whether God is personal or impersonal, a paradigm case of the conflict being the Christian and the Buddhist. On the one hand, the Christian says that God is a Being that, among other things, communicates (e.g., his word to Isaiah), communes (e.g., with the writer of the twenty-third psalm), makes decisions (e.g., to make Abraham a blessing to all nations), and engages in various intentional actions (e.g., reconciles mankind to Himself in His Son). On the other hand, the Buddhist speaks of Ultimate Reality as a Void, a contentless Void, in which one experiences no communication or communion or action but a bliss which is essentially a bliss of peace.

The other conflict is over the superiority of some religion or other, a paradigm case of the conflict being the Christian and the Muslim. On the one hand, the Christian declares that Jesus is the highest revelation of God; on the other hand, the Muslim declares that Muhammad is.

The first question concerning these conflicts is the extent to which they rest on religious experience. The second question is the extent to which they are intractable. I shall begin with some general considerations related to the second question, viz., considerations of why some conflicts are very difficult to handle, not to mention resolve.

1. The Barriers of Language and Culture

The Problem of Language

Perhaps much, if not most, of the indecision, confusion, and debate over the conflicts we are considering, as well as other conflicts, is a consequence of the weakness and inadequacy of language, along with a simple failure of many of those relating their experiences to go as far as they can in describing and clarifying. Yet these people often— probably usually—do not go as far as they can because they just do not think that language can bear the reality of their experience—and they say so. They say that the experience is beyond description, and although they may offer descriptions which we think are clarifying to some extent, I think that we must take what they say seriously, viz., that the words just do not capture the experience. Vivian's statement concerning her experience of a Presence beyond attributes was that "the experience defies words, they limit to concepts that are too small"; Terri said concerning her experience of being in God, "It's beyond description," and that from a highly articulate woman; and St. Thomas, a philosopher of no mean competence, said after his experience: "All that I have written is as straw."

In a sense the claim that some experience is beyond words is not peculiar to religious experience but is common to experience generally, including perception. Indescribability is a feature of all experience which we might call "primitive," i.e., experience which is not reducible to other experience, such as our sense experience, pleasure, pain, feelings, and so on. E.g., the taste of frog legs is commonly said to be like chicken—but it is not. It has a unique flavor, not transferable by words. The main reason, I should say, that frog legs are said to taste like chicken is that frog legs are usually served deep-fried, the result being that the distinctive flavor has been fried into oblivion, as with deep-fried chicken. Perception of the color blue is likewise not something transferable by words to someone who has never seen the color. In trying to get across the nature of color I can make connections with other experiences; e.g., if I am speaking of a particular shade of blue, I can say that it is close to some other shade that a person is familiar with. However, if someone is going to understand exactly what I have in mind, the person must see the color. Or if I speak of being awed at the storm surf of southern California and am talking to people in the interior of Africa, I might refer to the storms they have experienced, although their experience might have been essentially fear, not awe. Thus, I might have to try another sort of experience, such as looking at the starry skies. I could probably find some experience the people had which was of the nature of awe, with the result that they would have some idea of what I was talking about. Yet if the people simply went through life totally preoccupied with the chase, never raising their eyes in contemplation of the starry skies above, never standing to watch the early morning colors turn brighter and brighter until the sun in its full splendor breaks over the horizon, they would likely listen to my story of awe with glazed eyes. In short, religious experience is not the only experience which is beyond words, not the only experience which we cannot convey adequately by words apart from the actual experience itself.

Although people regularly claim that religious experience is beyond words, they still, just as regularly, try to convey their experience by words, often turning to imprecise modes of expression, such as poetry, parable, and art. One reason for using artistic forms is that they are less focused, more open ended, being like many small beams of light rather than a single beam. Another reason for using artistic forms is that they tend to recreate in the sensitive person something of the nature of the religious experience, perhaps some of the emotions, and the emotions can then be the guide to the intellect, directing it into the interpretative paths which are most enlightening. In any case, the weakness of words in carrying the content of religious experience does not mean that words, along with other forms of expression, cannot be used to bring us closer to the experience, closer by way of creating in us a general sense of the experience, inducing in us some of the feelings of the experience, perhaps inspiring in us an openness to and a desire to search for the experience. A portrait of Terri in radiant stillness might be the very best way to convey the nature of her experience, the feelings surrounding it, and the desire to seek something like it, a desire which, if fulfilled, would be the final solution to the communication problem. To be sure, for the naive, for the literalistic, for the emotionally cramped, employing artistic modes of expression will be no more useful, perhaps less so, than complete silence.

Language, Concepts, and Culture: Steven Katz.

Whatever our means of communicating or creating, we find them immensely complicated when we turn to another language setting and culture. In our own society things are difficult enough, becoming far more difficult when we move into another society, with another language and culture. In addition, the language of religious description arises out of particular religious traditions, so that attempts to discover what people are really saying require careful investigation of the meanings peculiar to the traditions. Also, the language of description is normally infused with religious dogma and presuppositions. These points have been developed at length by Steven T. Katz. (Katz, 1978) I wish to consider a few of the things he says.

The basic thesis of Katz is as follows.

> **There are NO pure (i.e. unmediated) experiences**. Neither mystical experience nor more ordinary forms of experience give any indication, or any grounds for believing, that they are unmediated. That is to say, *all* experience is processed through, organized by, and makes itself available to us in extremely complex epistemological ways. ... A proper evaluation of this fact leads to the recognition that in order to understand mysticism it is *not* just a question of studying the reports of the mystic after the experiential event but of acknowledging that

the experience itself as well as the form in which it is reported is shaped by concepts which the mystic brings to, and which shape, his experience. To flesh this out, straightforwardly, what is being argued is that, for example, the Hindu mystic does not have an experience of *x* which he then describes in the, to him, familiar language and symbols of Hinduism, but rather he has a Hindu experience, i.e. his experience is not an unmediated experience of *x* but is itself the, at least partially, pre-formed anticipated Hindu experience of Brahman. (26)

What Katz says is directed specifically to mystic experience, but it also applies to religious experience as I have conceived it.

First of all, Katz's statement about the mediation of all experience is subject, I believe, to the following little game, which is worth playing just to open up some of the issues. I call the game the "Self-Application Game." The basic move of the game is to say that Katz's thesis about the mediation of all experience is itself necessarily mediated—mediated by the concepts Katz brings to the business of interpreting experience. In looking at the whole range of experience and reports on experience, Katz interprets the data by his pre-formed concepts about experience. Indeed, what may be pre-formed is Katz's notion that concepts pre-form experience.

A further move in the game is to ask how we can even understand Katz's thesis apart from being a participant in his conceptual context, i.e., the context of his culture? Since our society is an agglomeration of many sub-cultures, there is no reason to think that I can understand him, even though we may use the same language. His words will be infused with different meaning. If I had been brought up as a Quaker, and he as a humanist, our sub-cultures would be radically different, with radically different concepts. The differences would be greater, I suspect, than the differences between me, the Quaker, and a person from a Muslim culture. The question is whether I could ever become a participant in Katz's conceptual context.

A negative answer would land us in what we may call "radical cultural relativism," according to which we can never understand at all the concepts of another culture, a culture in which we were not reared. Radical cultural relativism is self-defeating, at least in the sense that relativists could not determine that there were other cultures, the concepts of which they did not understand. Since concepts are an essential part of any culture, radical relativists would have to know that they had come across a system of different concepts in order to know that they were in a different culture, the concepts of which they could not understand at all. Obviously, to know that the concepts were different would require understanding the concepts. E.g., I cannot comprehend that a square is different from a circle unless I comprehend both concepts. I shall say no more on the thesis of radical cultural relativism, if for no other reason than that I do not consider Katz to hold any form of the thesis.

Now playing the Self Application Game with Katz's statement that all experience is mediated shows us at least what interpretations of the statement to avoid. The fact is that the statement may be given innocuous interpretations, i.e., epistemologically innocuous. That we process experience need not mean that the processing vitiates reality, for the processing may be in accordance with reality. We could say, e.g., that human beings have certain rational categories, forms, or rules for processing experience. This rational equipment, with its ways of processing experience, can be affected negatively or positively by subjective or cultural factors, but when it functions properly, it can achieve knowledge of reality.

The idea that the mind, with it ways of processing, can achieve knowledge of reality, may be spelled out in terms of a number of theses, two of which I shall mention. One thesis could be that the mind is God's handiwork, and is such that when the processing is going properly, we can come to knowledge of reality. Another thesis could be that our universe is impersonal, our mind having developed out of a strictly space-time evolutionary development, a development which has so constituted our mind that when its processing is going properly, we are able to come to knowledge of reality. Obviously, each thesis would have to be worked out in detail, a work I have not done and cannot now engage in. However, without having worked out the details, I presently see no reason to trade either of these theses for a skeptical thesis which denies that our mind can achieve knowledge of reality. (I see Kant as within the skeptical tradition.) I also note that strictly learned concepts or ways of thinking need not be out of tune with reality, for they may have been formed under the tutelage of a properly functioning mind.

The question, though, is what Katz is really maintaining. Exactly what is his thesis? Speaking of the Jewish mystic, he says that the images, beliefs, symbols, and rituals in the background of the mystic "define, *in advance*, what the experience *he wants to have*, and which he then does have, will be like." (33) Again we could play our little Self-Application Game and say that Katz provides an explanation for mystical experience which his background conditions him to have. However, we may leave that game aside, for the real question is what Katz is maintaining.

His thesis might be that religious experience is completely created by the pre-existing conditions. I shall call this the "Strong Conditioning Thesis." This thesis must become self-defeating, I think, for I do not see any rational grounds for restricting it to religious experience. As a result, one would hold to the thesis because of pre-existing conditions, the same reason that one would hold to the denial of the thesis. In addition, the thesis trades on two explanations of religious experience which we have considered: the explanation from background (with special emphasis on Thesis C); and the explanation from desire (Katz's statement seems to assume that wanting—desiring—brings about the experience of the mystic). I think that I have provided sufficient counterexamples to falsify both explanations and thus to falsify the Strong Conditioning Thesis.

Yet I do not think that Katz holds to the Strong Conditioning Thesis but to what I should call the "Weak Conditioning Thesis," the thesis that pre-existing conditions shape or form religious experience to some extent. What he says is as follows.

> Mystics and students of mysticism have to recognize that mystical experience is not (putatively) solely the product of the conditioned act of experience as constituted from the side of the experiencer, but is also constituted and conditioned by what the *object* or 'state of affairs' is that the mystic (believes he) 'encounters' or experiences. To say, 'Smith experiences x' is also to recognize that this experience is in part dependent on what x is. But here is the rub—this recognition also requires the additional awareness of the complexity of the situation in that what 'x is' is itself, at least partly, determined by a contextual consciousness. (64)

Obviously, the Weak Conditioning Thesis can take a variety of forms, ranging from the thesis that pre-existing conditions show up very little to the thesis that they permeate and dominate the experience. I think that Katz's position is along the following lines: Religious experience tends (or strongly tends) to be permeated and dominated by pre-existing conditions. I have no objections to this thesis, although neither I nor Katz has any good statistical evidence to support it. Consistent with the position is the emphasis I should like to make, viz., that some religious experience seems to bear very little imprint from pre-existing conditions, whereas other religious experience (perhaps most) looks as if it were largely engraved by the pre-existing conditions. E.g., many Christians experience Jesus or God in a very standard form, experiencing God, say, as loving, forgiving Father. I am inclined to think that standard-form experiences are fewer than most people think, for many people have experiences which are highly individualistic or at least incorporate highly individualistic elements; e.g., some, without sensing forgiveness (forgiveness is simply not in the experience, although afterward the people may feel forgiven), feel the arms of God wrapped around them; others sense Jesus' love gradually coming into their body from head to toe or from toe to head; still others, after an experience of Jesus' love, go on to sense Love—now no longer connected directly with Jesus or God—in all creation, or they go on to sense an ocean of Love permeating the universe; and so on. In other words, many experience Jesus or God in ways not clearly derived from Scripture or from reports in the church or elsewhere (we may think of Ned, who, while in an evangelical church, had an experience with few, if any, marks of evangelical Christianity); or at one time they have a fairly standard experience of Jesus and at another have an Eastern form of experience (we may think of Joy, who first of all had a Nirvana-type experience, which then developed into an experience in which she felt herself to be a participant with Jesus on the cross, sensing the meaning of his death, as well as the meaning of the Kingdom of Heaven). And, of course, we should remember the childhood experiences we examined, most of which clearly broke out of the common religious and cultural molds of the children.

The upshot is that although many people tend to have religious experiences largely incorporating the pre-existing conditions of their religious culture, some people have religious experiences largely departing from the pre-existing conditions of their religious culture. The crucial question is, What is the epistemic significance of religious experience tracking culture? Does this fact cast suspicion on the experience as veridical apprehension of the Divine? The answer, I think, is, It all depends—depends on the concepts tracked and how they affect the total experience. Thus, a treatment of specific cases and specific religions is necessary. I shall, however, give a general treatment of the issue in the next section.

As a final word on Katz, I believe that he has done yeoman service in restraining any kind of facile assimilation of one experience to another. He has noted that we must have firm, specific evidence for saying that one experience is similar to another, evidence beyond very general categories, which may slop over important distinctions. E.g., if we say that a Christian and a Buddhist both experience Ultimate Reality, the category 'Ultimate Reality' is so broad that it slops over the enormous difference between the Ultimate Reality of the Christian and the Ultimate

Reality of the Buddhist, Ultimate Realities that might not even be consistent.

The Compatibility of Genuine Religious Experience with Cultural Forms of Experience

Granting that culture influences or shows-up in religious experience, we may ask the question, What is the epistemic significance of this fact? What if religious experience tracks culture, even fairly closely? My immediate answer is that I do not see why experience tracking culture is necessarily vitiated experience. To support this answer, I shall provide a small sample of explanations supporting the thesis that culturally conditioned religious experience may well be authentic religious experience.

Before getting to the explanations, though, we might ask, Could any single sort of experience wholly capture the Divine as It is? Actually, no single experience captures the whole of a physical object. Thus, given that the Divine is infinite Being, I should think that no single sort of experience, at least for a human without supernaturally enhanced powers (the allusion here is to Thomas and his views about the vision of God in the afterlife), could capture Its total reality. This consideration goes for a Divine that is not self-revealing as much as for a Divine that is self-revealing.

Getting now to the explanations, I shall assume, first of all, a self-revealing Divine. Even if such a Divine could reveal Itself wholly in a single experience, I do not see any reason why It should. I do not totally reveal myself to others on any given occasion, and to some I reveal more than to others. Why would not God, occasionally or as a general rule, follow the same procedure? I cannot think of any strong reason why God would not, and thus one explanation for a limited apprehension of the Divine is that the Divine functions in ways such as we do and for similar reasons.

The more general question here is, Why should the Divine not reveal Itself in a variety of ways, none totally adequate, some obviously complementing others, some appearing in conflict? Should we suppose that the Divine must reveal each aspect of Its reality to the same degree in each culture? If so, should we also suppose a Divine that must reveal each aspect of Its reality to the same degree in each individual? I see no persuasive reason for an affirmative answer to either question, so that we can come up with a variety of explanations for God's limited revelations, not the least of which is that God purposes that humans work in concert, as children working on a puzzle, to piece together an adequate picture of His reality. To date, humans have managed fairly well to frustrate God's purposes, but God may be very patient.

What we should remember at this point is that each major world culture (Eastern, Western, and so on) incorporates a tremendous breadth of religious experience; further, as we have seen, the same individual may have a considerable breadth of religious experience. The question for those who say that religious experience is created or dominated by cultural notions is, Why do we find variety within a culture and within the same individual, a variety which in many cases seems independent of sub-cultural or individual differences?

Another possible explanation is this. If people have seen only a photograph of me in a suit or have just heard descriptions of me as a professor, they will probably not recognize me if they see me in my back-packing or bike-riding regalia, or if they see me role-playing in Socratic garb. In short, we could say that God tends to meet people in forms they are familiar with and would easily recognize. In fact, the forms may be inadequate in some way or other, but why not fill the cups people present, even if they are chipped, cracked, or non-aesthetic? Jesus did not ask people to be in some ideal intellectual, moral, or spiritual state in order to receive healing. He just healed them the way they were. Perhaps God, then, tends to meet people in ways that they would recognize and respond to, not limiting His revelation to these ways necessarily, but using them as a foundation or as a point of departure. Admittedly, the ways in which people are ready to respond to God may be deficient or distorted in some way–as I said, our cups may be chipped or cracked. How chipped or cracked would be something that we should have to discover by analyzing our cultural concepts and working in concert with others to develop adequate conceptions of the Deity. Moreover, many people want to clutch their chipped and cracked cups, never trading them for something more adequate or aesthetic. In short, some people never move beyond a very truncated experience. But then some people, never spend time watching sunrises and sunsets.

I shall pursue a form of this explanation—the cracked-cup explanation—a little further, focusing on the idea that God meets us according to our openness. A constant refrain of world religions is that we must seek God with all the heart, that we must hunger and thirst for God, that we must be willing to take that path which is narrow, arduous, and lengthy. One way of hearing this refrain is as a call to openness, as a call to being receptive to God. Moreover, the assumption of the call seems to be that God will reward us according to our openness. God will meet us in the ways in which we are open to His reality. In short, God respects and responds to our freedom, to what we have freely chosen to be open to. Or we could say that God tends to respect the forms of His reality which people have discovered, meeting them in terms of their discoveries, and then leading them from there.

Still another explanation would be that on our own initiative we, like the woman who reached out and touched the hem of Jesus' garment, can reach out and touch the Garment. On our own initiative we can plunge into the infinite Ocean. On our own initiative we can get into the Laser Light. I visit people, and people visit me. Why not the same with God? Of course, our visiting the Divine will be according to who we are, with the concepts we have; yet why should we not grasp what is really there, at least to a considerable degree? Indeed, why think that we could not come away from our visit with the realization that Whatever we encountered, it was not like anything we encountered before—it simply broke out of our system of concepts? That Garment we touched was not like any garment we touched before! We would, then, be like many of the subjects of this study, left mute, saying merely, "It was beyond description."

We could continue with further explanations, but the ones offered give an idea of the possibilities within the framework of a self-revealing God.

Of course, the last explanation also applies if we assume that God is not self-revealing. Another explanation, applying either to a self-revealing or non-self-revealing Divine is this. We could take the approach that our cultural concepts of God may be analogous in several respects to sense perception and memory. We certainly do not possess all possible sense receptors–we could imagine ourselves having receptors for magnetism, for a range of chemicals which we cannot now perceive, and so on. Yet we hardly think that we do not, e.g., apprehend something of the reality of trees and mountains just because we do not have the fullest possible range of receptors. Moreover, given the receptors we have, we must perceive an object or a situation from many angles before we can think that we have the whole of it. Indeed, perceiving an object— e.g., a long rectangular building— from one angle only, would be distorting. Regardless of these limitations of sense perception, we still believe that we can, with suitable attention and care, apprehend the world as it is at least in some of its aspects; e.g., there may be more to the story of a magnolia tree than my present perception tells me, but the part told, although incomplete, is not for that reason necessarily incorrect.

Memory, likewise, may give us a selective or limited picture of things. I may remember the make, color, and year of the Buick which collided with my car, but I may not remember the name of the street on which the collision occurred, even though I played on that street as a small boy. Certainly, I would not say that my memory of the collision is incorrect just because I do not remember the street on which the collision occurred.

The Principle of Coherence

Similarly to sense perception and memory, we may selectively apprehend the Divine but not for that reason apprehend what is false. What we apprehend becomes false only if we make grandiose claims, such as that ultimate Reality is nothing more than what we apprehend It to be. We must proceed, I should think, with religious experience as we do with sense perception and memory, not taking as final or complete a single experience or set of experiences of the Divine. Thus, we could develop a principle of coherence along the following lines: One view of the Divine is more adequate than another if it brings together more simply a greater range of non-defeated religious experience than the other.

Religious Maps

Yet I shall not deny that what we work out may still be deficient or distorting, even after considering the full range of religious experience, in the same way that what we work out for the physical world may still be deficient or distorting even after considering the full range of sensory experience. Who can say what an additional sense would do to our map of the world? We may think of how different the world would look to a person who acquired sight after having been blind from birth, or to a person who acquired color receptors after having been color-blind from birth. With another sense receptor the map of the world would likely be altered considerably or filled in with details never imagined. Thus, I shall not claim full adequacy or lack of distortion even for our best maps of the Divine, any more than I would for maps of physical reality, including scientific ones. At the present stage of exploring, our maps are hardly likely to be accurate to the last detail but are more likely to be only rough and ready sketches, adequate to get us successfully from some destinations to others, with the scientific maps being more adequate than the religious maps.

All this business about maps is, of course, vague and amorphous and would have to be worked out in detail. Is one religious map better than another? I should think so, just as scientific maps are better than magic maps. But why is one religious map better than another? There are usually a number of reasons but a very important one is conformity to the coherence principle stated above; however, none of this will make much sense unless we look at individual maps and see specifically what one has that the other does not.

The conclusion concerning the role of cultural concepts in religious experience is that experiencing God according to cultural concepts does not necessarily mean that the map drawn on the basis of this experience is irrelevant to the divine landscape or necessarily even seriously deficient. What we say depends on specific cases, i.e., specific concepts or sets of concepts. If, e.g., we impose on God our cultural concept of revenge, then we shall be in trouble for the reasons enunciated in the last chapter.

Transcending Barriers of Culture and Language

I am now going to introduce a major qualification to what I have said. I think that we can magnify the language-culture problem beyond all proportion. What I mean is that the sense of understanding may leap over barriers of language and culture. I sit down in a pub in Oxford with a man whom I have met just a half hour ago, and I sense that I have met a soul-mate, an awareness which was not in the least present the night before when I had dinner with a ten year acquaintance from the United States. And as the evening progresses, the awareness intensifies, strengthens. Similarly, I listen to two Vietnamese Buddhist monks explain the nature of Buddhism. One is translating for the other, translating in heavily accented English. What I am impressed with is their peace and joy. They do not say that they have peace or claim that they have joy, but I know that they do, and I also know that these qualities in them are not different from the peace and joy I experience. I also sense that we are in contact with some deeper Reality—I am not just sensing contact at the level of peace and joy, but I am sensing contact on a deeper level. Likewise, I meet a Sufi, and although his words are different, I sense that he is my brother, and the more he talks, and the more he uses his words which are unusual to me, spoken with an unfamiliar accent, the more I sense that he is my brother, that his God is my God.

All this may be mere sentimental fluff—or it may be steel-hard intellectual insight. Do I begin epistemically with my sensed unity, or do I begin with the differences in language and culture? Actually, what I suggest is that we go back to PC: I will put stock in what I immediately sense, what seems to be the case, and wait for the defeaters to come. Thus, I shall not ignore differences in language and culture, but I shall not ignore what I sense when I am in person to person contact with another; in fact, I shall give greater weight to the latter. When spending an evening in China with my Chinese friend and his family, I sensed acceptance, I sensed genuineness, not mere politeness, I sensed common joy in the evening. I accepted my sense of the evening, although I was ready to let it be defeated by the hard reality of my friend's perceptions, for he speaks frankly to me. Yet he volunteered, no prompting on my part, that his family embraced me, enjoyed my presence. My sense of the evening was correct.

A major problem, I think, is that many of our contacts with other religions, particularly in the world of scholarship, are through the written word. Yet the written word is only a fragment of the total communication process, and perhaps not the most enlightening fragment. The essence of modern scholarship in the humanities seems to be to sit and read what other persons have said, or perhaps listen to some tape, apart from a description of the interview session, including the interviewer's impression of the openness and frankness of the interviewee, along with the interviewer's impression of the relation established between the two. Reading what other people have written or listening to truncated interviews may be a received form of scholarship, but it is not necessarily the best, or even an adequate, means of discovering the truth about another person and what the other person has experienced or believes.

Plato's seventh letter provides some useful hints on the subject of the written word.

> Thus much, at least, I can say about all writers, past or future, who say they know the things to which I devote myself, whether by hearing the teaching of me or of others, or by their own discoveries—that according to my view it is not possible for them to have any real skill in the matter. There neither is nor ever will be a treatise of mine on the subject. For it does not admit of exposition like other branches of knowledge; but after much converse about the matter itself and a life lived together, suddenly a light, as it were, is kindled in one soul by a flame that leaps to it from another, and thereafter sustains itself. (341 b-d)

From the context we gather that Plato (or someone else, if the letter is not genuine) is talking about skill in philosophy, skill which he links to what he had previously referred to as "the true philosophic spirit" and "the fire of philosophy." The written word cannot convey the exact nature of this fire or how to achieve it; rather one catches it. If we should use less dramatic language and say that the skill of philosophy is a matter of "catching on," of "getting the hang of it," we would have given ourselves away as a typical 20th century philosopher, not a philosopher of the Platonic school. Thus, some subjects are caught through the give and take of conversation and living with one another, not through the written word alone. My suggestion is that the experience of the Divine is a subject of this sort, or, at the very least, may be a subject of this sort. Certainly, when conversing over time about a religious experience, a person will often, if not always, use different words in repeating the description of the experience, and the listener will come up with different questions. Moreover, if the two see each other regularly, there will be opportunity to witness the effects of the experience or to see another experience occurring. To see Tim patting the ground and saying, "This is God," is to find out something about his experience which we cannot discover even through conversation—it is to see the glow of his eyes, the exuberance of his spirit, the surprise and astonishment of his mind.

Granting that much about religious experience cannot be conveyed just through the written word, I still maintain that some aspects of religious experience can be conveyed fairly easily by words. Perhaps the most accurate thing to say is that there is a range of communication, with some things being easily conveyed by words, others not very easily, some hardly at all. At any rate, some may be conveyed fairly easily by words. When Tim says that he heard a Voice, not anything audible but something internal, I think I have a fair grasp of what he means, even though I have not had any experience of the sort. I have had insights, I have had phrases come to mind, I have perceived in an instant matters which were previously obscure, but I have never had anything like an internal Voice experience, a voice saying, e.g., "This is me, George." I at least know that the experience is not any kind of sensory experience. I also know that it is not like my experience of having phrases come to mind. Positively, it seems to be the awareness of an exterior Consciousness communicating to a person, Consciousness to consciousness. That seems to be an understandable thought, even for one never having had the experience.

Similarly, when a person speaks of an experience in which the sense of self was lost, in which there was not a subject-Object dualism but in which there was a merging of subject and Object, I have some idea of the experience because I have had parallel experiences. Sometimes, when performing a task or when viewing the world—the starry skies above or a landscape of bluebonnets and evening primrose—I become so absorbed in what I am doing or perceiving that I lose contact with the sense of self; the self recedes into the background. Only after the experience, when reflecting on it, do I say that self was present, highly perceptive, and perhaps even making decisions to do this or that, particularly in the case of a task. At other times, though, self is right up front. "Ah yes, I remember that the last time I saw this field of bluebonnnets my wife was with me." Moreover—and now I go beyond the present point—I do not consider the two sorts of experience to require inconsistent views of the self; or put differently, I do not consider the former experience inconsistent with the notion of me as a person, even though the sense of self was absent. I shall come back to this point; however, the main point for now is that I have experiences—regularly—in which the sense of self is absent, and hence I think that I at least partially understand what someone says when talking about the loss of the sense of self.

Yet if someone says, after I have related my understanding of an experience without a subject-object dualism, "No, my experience of the Divine was nothing like that at all," then I shall be puzzled and will have to look for other parallels in my experience. Perhaps the other person will emphasize that loss of a sense of self is merely a negative notion, not conveying the sense of positive merger present in the experience of merger with the Divine. Yet the experiences I mentioned are also experiences of positive merger—merger in a task or in my perceptual surroundings. The denials may continue, though, the result being a communication impasse, bridgeable, perhaps, by much further conversation, or perhaps only by my having a similar experience. In the case of the latter alternative the best thing for the other person to do would be to give me clues as to how I might have the experience. From all that I have said up to now, I could be certain that whatever clues the person gave, they would not be necessary or sufficient for my having the experience.

2. The Personal-Impersonal Conflict

My major thesis in this section is that personal and impersonal experiences of the Divine do not necessarily lead to incompatible beliefs. I have been noting how language and culture could obscure or distort experience so that the gap between the personal and impersonal would seem unbridgeable, or far greater than it is. Yet the gap seems to be present, whatever the limitations of language and culture. Thus, I shall consider some ways in which we might bridge the gap.

Eliminating Non-Religious Experience

One move we could make—a powerful move—to break the impasse between Christians and some Buddhists would simply be to say that some experiences of a Void are not religious experiences at all. I have been looking at religious experience as essentially an awareness of divine Presence or a sense of contact with divine Reality. I noted that the term 'Presence' was not meant to beg any questions in favor of a personal Reality but was meant to point to some form of spiritual Reality with which a person senses contact. Thus, if the experience of the Buddhist is *just* an experience of peace or bliss, it probably should not be classed as a religious experience. However, if peace or bliss represents our encounter with the ultimate Buddha Nature, a kind of all encompassing spiritual Reality of which we feel ourselves a part or in which we feel ourselves immersed, then experiencing this Reality certainly constitutes a religious experience. I think that we find different sorts of experiences among Buddhists, just as we find different sorts of experiences among Christians.

Eliminating Incoherent Descriptions

Mystic writings, both East and West, emphasize that there is a merging of subject and Object, knower and Known in the mystic religious experience. If we are to take mystic language literally, then we have the problem of how mystics can even know—i.e., remember—that they had the experience they say they did. If merger is a state of non-self—i.e., absolutely no self—then the individual mystic did not really have the experience and therefore cannot remember the experience, or better, the happening or state. Moreover, not even an omnipotent God could instill the memory of the experience because a genuine memory must be of that which the individual experienced. But if in mystic experience there is no individual self to have an experience, then God cannot give the memory of the experience—any memory will be a distortion of the true experience. In brief, a literal interpretation of mystic language leaves us with a contradiction, an impossibility—the mystic experienced what cannot be experienced. Thus, mystics could not rightly say that they had a mystical experience. If they said that they had, at least in the sense of having the unshakeable conviction that they had the experience, they would not be saying anything meaningful, for the term 'experience' would lack content, i.e., would remain a contradictory notion and thus inconceivable. Moreover, my having the experience would not solve anything at all, for the contradiction remains regardless of who has the experience. The problem is with the experience, not the communication of it. We do not conceive anything in a contradiction—there is no meaning whatsoever.

A literal rendering of mystic language which leaves us with no-self in the mystic experience also leaves us with no appeal to PC. The essence of PC is that things are as we perceive or sense them; but if we do not perceive or sense, if we are not in an experiencing state, then there is nothing to justify belief.

The basic problem with any literal interpretation of mystic description is that it runs up against the reality of mystics reporting their experiences. Thus, the reasonable move is simply to back off of a literal interpretation, to say that the language is relative, that it admits and requires qualification. In other words, since mystics report their experiences, their experiences must meet the conditions for having experience. The minimal condition is, I suggest, that the self (or some aspect of the self) be in some sense aware, that it in some sense be an experiencing subject. I think that this condition is often recognized explicitly within mystic writings; i.e., we find both that the denials of self-awareness are qualified and that the language of the individual self is introduced into descriptions of mystic experience.

First of all, as for qualified denials of self-awareness, we may turn to the Kena Unpanishad, where we read the following.

> There the eye goes not;
> Speech goes not, nor the mind.
> We know not, we understand not
> How one would teach It.
> Other, indeed, is It than the known,
> And moreover above the unknown. (Radhakrishnan, 1957, 42)

If the distinction of knower and Known is totally absent in mystic experience, then we should have to say that nothing is known, nothing is grasped, nothing is in consciousness. Yet the Upanishad says that It, Brahman, the Reality we merge with and therefore the Reality we should not be conscious of and should not know, is above the unknown. In some sense, then, the absence of the knower-Known relationship is not total, not absolute.

Second, as for language of the self being used within descriptions of mystic experience, I look simply at one example from S. Radhakrishnan. After emphasizing that in mystic experience "thought and reality coalesce and a creative merging of subject and object results," and that "the distinction of the knower and the known disappears," he immediately goes on to say that in the experience "the privacy of the individual self is broken into and invaded by a universal self which the *individual feels as his own* [italics mine]." (617-18) I do not offer his statements as any kind of proof text or resolution of the self-awareness problem or even as an adequate statement of the mystic experience. Undoubtedly, some writers on mysticism would not consider his last statement a felicitous description of the mystic experience. Nevertheless, I think that a careful examination of writings on mysticism would reveal that often the language used belies any assertion that there is an absolute loss of self-awareness or that the Reality experienced is strictly impersonal. The loss of awareness is perhaps deeper than my loss of awareness when absorbed in this morning's sunrise, but it is not of a totally different order; and if it is, so that there is a total loss of individuality, then the question again is how the mystic can even claim to have had the experience.

I do not believe that what I have just said is going to resolve the conflicts between mystics and non-mystics or between those who see God as personal and those who see God as impersonal. However, I should like to stress that what I have said does not rely on considerations peculiar to CMP but on considerations I view as being universally applicable. In noting for Hindus, e.g., that the literal rendering of merger lands them in contradiction, they may say, "So what?" Only I do not usually hear them saying this; instead, they usually take the charge more seriously and start to introduce qualifications, perhaps along the lines quoted from the Upanishad. Perhaps qualifications will not ultimately avoid contradiction, but my point is that Hindus generally seem to be less than comfortable with contradiction and thus reveal that they operate with similar standards to Christians. (I have met Christians who, with perfect equanimity, say about contradictions in their faith, "So what?")

People who Experience God in Both Ways

As I have noted and as we have seen in a number of the cases considered so far, numerous people relate experiences of God as impersonal, the experiences varying from a sense of merger with the Divine in which subject-object distinctions disappear to a sense of simply being in contact with a spiritual Force. What the experiences have in common is that the Reality is not sensed as communicating or communing. In the words of the Chandogya Upanishad, God is experienced as the "unspeaking, the unconcerned." Other people relate experiences of God as personal, as speaking to, communicating with, caring for, communing with them. The question again is whether the two different sorts of experience necessarily require incompatible beliefs.

A major reason for being very hesitant about an affirmative answer is that often we find people (or different people within the same religious community) experiencing God in both personal and impersonal ways, yet they normally do not see any conflict. The mystical tradition of the church encompasses people, such as St. Theresa of Avila, who experienced God as personal, yet also had experiences in which they seemed to merge in a great divine Ocean. For a contemporary example I turn to Carl.

Carl (3614)

Carl, who describes himself as a pantheist, had an experience of unity, an experience which he describes as follows. "I was no longer a man separated from the natural world. I was a part of the whole," a whole which breathed life. At a later time, though, he had an experience of "God . . . leading me through the world by the hand." His experience of God at one time as personal, at another as impersonal, is really just a reminder of all those we have already met who experienced the Divine at one time as personal, at another as impersonal. I note especially those considered in the chapter on Eastern forms of experience.

A Personal Report

I imagine that the compatibility of the two sorts of experience seems relatively unproblematic to me because I have had both personal and impersonal religious experiences myself. I have had experiences of God's loving presence, experiences I could classify only as personal. Yet I have also had experiences which I classify as impersonal or largely impersonal. One sort of impersonal experience is a nature experience. When viewing a Pacific Coast storm surf, I have experienced the power of God, my sense being of impersonal Power, Power unconnected with any particular personal action or communication from God; i.e., I do not have any sense of God communicating some message to me or of being present to me, say, as my Shepherd, and I do not think of God either as directly involved in making the surf crash or even as Creator. Rather I simply sense God as the constant, never-ceasing flow of spiritual Power that upholds a world of crashing surf, howling winds, shaking earth, and rolling thunder. However, I do not see this experience as inconsistent with my experience of God as loving Shepherd.

The experience of peace has also come as an impersonal experience. E.g., I have had the experience of peace or rest in God—I am, as it were, immersed in God, the ocean of peace, where there is no movement, no disturbance, and I am not aware of God communicating anything or acting. God is the Silence; and I am silent, at rest, satisfied to remain in the state I am in, without desire. Yet I do not think of this experience as inconsistent with God's personal nature. Thus, if Nirvana is an experience of total peace associated with the absence of desire— and I certainly am not the person to give an adequate account of Nirvana, if any can be given—I have little difficulty seeing the experience as compatible with belief in God as personal.

Other times, the experience of peace is, as it were intrusive, taking over, coming as from without, a gift which surprises me. In this case I again find myself without desire; the desire to get something done, to fix a pressing problem or to keep an appointment, simply disappears. I do not need to do any of the so-called important things; or better, I do not have to be successful in doing them. I may continue in my activity, but I am no longer dominated by the desire to bring whatever I am doing to a successful conclusion. If it works, it works; if it does not, it does not. More importantly, though, the peace comes upon me; it is intrusive but lacks any sense of a personal Presence or any specific message. Yet the intrusive nature of the peace immediately makes me conscious of God—the experience is a catalyst for my becoming aware of God, aware of God as the Giver of the experience, almost as if I should say, "Oh yes, God of peace, I forgot that you were by my side." And when I do not become aware of God, I at least make the inference to God. In one sense, then, the experience is impersonal but in another, personal—it begins impersonally but ends up as personal.

I have experienced even God's love in a sort of quasi-impersonal way; i.e., God's love is just sort of "there," uninterrupted radiation and warmth, which I simply get into, stand in, relax in, get warmed by, and so on. John compares God to light (1 Jn. 1:5), alluding to the sun. Thus, I may have a kind of impersonal experience of God's love, even though, admittedly, the notion of some sort of personal relation—e.g., acceptance or care—constantly stands in the background.

I should note that in relating my experiences, I am not certain that I am getting things quite right. Moreover, the nature experiences remains a bit fuzzy to me. I should like to have a tape of the experiences, so that I might go back over them to make certain that my account is correct. The exact sense of God's presence, say, when viewing a storm surf is fuzzy to me. Is there a background sense of God's care and love? Perhaps, but it is far in the background, at least as I recall. Indeed, I think that thoughts of care and love intrude after the experience. The problem is that the experience is usually all-absorbing, so that I reflect on it only after it has occurred; moreover, if I do consciously reflect during the experience, I think that I import the notions of care and love by my reflection. Yet I am not certain, so the experience remains fuzzy. In short, regardless of how honest I try to be, I have trouble reporting exactly what went on. I hardly think that I am unique in this respect; instead, I am likely a paradigm of what happens with many others. I am not saying, of course, that all experiences are fuzzy—some experiences of God's reality are very sharp, say, an experience of God's love rolling over me as waves of the sea.

Ian Barbour on the Personal-Impersonal Conflict

I have maintained that the same individual, or persons within the same religious community, have experiences both personal and impersonal. For Barbour this fact does not seem to count for resolving differences between religions. He says:

> I do *not* suggest that the Hindu Brahman and the Christian God, or other models from *different* religious traditions, be considered complementary. But we could consider the use of personal and impersonal models *within* one paradigm community as *complementary*, paralleling the use of wave and particle models within quantum physics. (Barbour, 1990, 49)

To begin with, I am not clear as to exactly what Barbour is saying. The Copenhagen Interpretation of complementarity is that the wave-particle duality is a scientific finality, not resolvable by some more fundamental unity. Einstein hoped for unity, but during his long controversy with Neils Bohr over the issue he was never able to fault Bohr's position, i.e., come up with a decisive objection to it. (Pais, 1991, 425-433) If Barbour is following Bohr, then he is saying that even in the Christian community the personal-impersonal duality is final, without resolution at a more fundamental level.

I think that Barbour wants to say something as follows: Personal and impersonal experiences are commensurable in the Christian community but not from one religious tradition to another. Even if he does not mean to say this, I think that the position is worth examining briefly.

First, I note that the Christian community includes people from a *potpourri* of cultures, many of them converts from the dominant religion in their culture. The same goes for all the major world religions, so that many people are experienced in two religious paradigms.

Second, I think that if one says what Barbour does in another place, then one has opened the paradigm door sufficiently to avoid incommensurability. He says that

> beliefs are both brought to religious experience and derived form it. Religion, more than science, is influenced 'from the top down,' from paradigms, through interpretive beliefs, to experience. But the influence 'from the bottom up,' starting from experience, is not totally absent in religion. Although there is no neutral descriptive language, there are degrees of interpretation. Thus members of various religious traditions can communicate even though they are dependent on culturally formed languages. (p. 84)

But if we can communicate with, say, a Buddhist, then why may we not communicate sufficiently to determine whether or not the Buddhist's impersonal experience is similar to some Christian's impersonal experience? Certainly, the fact that Christian mystics have often been seen as on the border of heresy would indicate that they were traveling a considerable distance from the accepted Christian paradigm or model; in other words, the Christian paradigm (or any other paradigm for that matter) is hardly a conceptual or experiential prison.

Third, to make out incommensurability, I think that we have to accept an assumption along the lines of the Strong Conditioning Thesis (see p. 487), a thesis which seems simply to be false and which Barbour does not accept.

Finally, I note that considerable experience and belief (often of very thoughtful people) belie the notion of incommensurability. Some Westerners believe that they have had a Nirvana experience of the same order as Buddhist monks from Tibet and would argue very strongly that they have. Indeed, I think that many monks in Tibet would grant that a Western pilgrim could very well have a genuine Nirvana experience, and thus an experience very like that of a native Tibetan monk.

At any rate, I do not see why experiences from different cultures cannot be complementary—in Einstein's sense. Or if they cannot be, then we must say the same for sensory perception, so that whatever the description of an experiment by a Tibetan scientist, it is incommensurable with the description of a scientist from the Bronx.

Perhaps an analogical argument from complementarity would be a useful ending to this section. For me to talk about the Copenhagen Interpretation of comlementarity is, in a sense, amusing. The interpretation arises from and, I should say, is defined by the technical concepts of physics (e.g., the state of a system, as defined by position coordinates and the momenta of the parts), as well as the mathematical formalism which underlies any understanding of wave or particle behavior. Discussing Bohr's initial lecture on complementarity in 1927, Max Jammer says the following.

> Bohr . . . discussed, from the viewpoint of complementarity, Heisenberg's uncertainty relations and the meaning of measurement in quantum theory, and pointed out that an adequate tool for complementary modes of description is offered precisely by the new formalism of quantum mechanics. For this formalism, he contended, is essentially a purely symbolic scheme which permits only predictions, in accordance with the correspondence principle, of results obtainable under conditions in terms of classical concepts. (Jammer, 1966, 353)

I do not have the slightest competence to understand either many of the technical concepts of quantum physics or the mathematical formalism underlying the principle of complementarity. In other words, I am not conversant with the scientific paradigm in this case, a paradigm including a difficult mathematical formalism. Therefore, my understanding of the Copenhagen Interpretation is marginal at best. I come to the interpretation with the paradigm of perceptual objects, a paradigm appropriate only for describing experimental results, not for quantum particles and processes. However, am I unable ever to understand the paradigm of quantum physics? I should have to work very hard, but I surmise that I could achieve a moderate level of competence in the mathematical formalism of quantum physics. The same goes, I think, for my understanding of a religion very different from Christianity.

Hewing to Experience

Different experiences, whether of the same persons or of various persons, could lead to conflict of belief but need not. A major reason is PC, which says that we are justified in believing that the Divine is what It seems to us to be and also whatever is entailed by what It seems to us to be. Thus, I sense a spiritual Force in nature and am justified in believing that there is such a Force. Insofar as I experience a mere Force, i.e., a Force that does not communicate or commune with me, I am justified in believing that the Force is impersonal. Yet am I justified in claiming that the Force is nothing but what I perceive It to be, that It is not, say, also a creating Force or a shepherding and guiding Force? I am not justified, unless a Force permeating the natural universe could not also be a creating, shepherding, guiding Force. Since I do not see why a Force in nature could not also be creating, shepherding, and guiding, I must remain agnostic about the latter qualities until I experience them or have good reason on other grounds either to attribute them or deny them to the Force I experience. I am following here exactly the same procedure I follow when I see only one side of a physical object, say, the south side of a tree. PC requires that I say only that the side I have seen is as I see it. I cannot say that the other side will be the same, for it may be covered with moss.

So far, then, I do not find a reason for saying that incompatible beliefs necessarily result from the experience of God as personal and the experience of God as impersonal. Indeed, there are analogies for these experiences within our common experience. As I said, experiences of God, some personal and some impersonal, may be analogous to viewing an object from different sides. Or perhaps it is like viewing an object from different distances: From a distance we do not see the needles of a pine, but up close we do; yet regardless of the difference in the experiences, we do not begin to think that we have seen different trees.

Thus, we might say that "from a distance" we may see God as impersonal but "up close" as personal. Or experiences of God might be analogous to the different sorts of action we take. We can send people on an errand by way of computer-printed instructions, and we can also hug them when they return, yet we are the same person in both cases. Or we might simply stand in silence next to a person deep in grief, later putting our arms around the person and uttering a word of comfort or hope, yet again we are the same person in both cases.

On Experiencing the Essential Nature of God

Even though many, perhaps most, experiences of God as personal and impersonal are compatible, the experiences will be incompatible if one set is of God as essentially personal, whereas the other set is of God as essentially impersonal. God simply cannot be both. The question, though, is: What sort of experience must we have in order to justify belief in God as essentially personal or impersonal? PC says that we are justified in believing what seems to be the case; hence, on the basis of our experience we may form the belief that God is essentially personal or impersonal only if God seems to be essentially personal or impersonal. In short, using PC alone, we are not justified in believing that which is not presented in our experience or entailed by our experience, so that we may not leap from, say, the experience of God as personal to the belief that God is essentially personal. If, on the basis of PC, we are to believe that God is essentially personal, then we must be aware of God as essentially personal.

I do not know how our experience would present us with God as essentially this or that. I shall assume, though, that the experience is possible. The fact is that we rarely, if ever, run across claims to the effect that someone was aware of experiencing God's essential nature or some aspect of God as essential. In all the cases I collected or examined I found neither claim made. Obviously, I shall not deny that the claim is ever made. However, I should be very suspicious of the claim, largely because the notion of essential nature is a philosophic notion, more likely to be read into the experience than read out of it. People sometimes say of their awareness of God: "That's the way God really is!"; e.g., "God is really personal." The question is whether saying this is equivalent to saying, "I experienced God as essentially personal." People may just be saying, "God really did come to me as personal," a statement from which, as I already noted, we may not leap to the belief that God is essentially personal.

What we must say upon the basis of our experience of God as personal or impersonal is that God is essentially such that we may experience Him as personal or impersonal. My view is that we must then go on to say that God is essentially personal. The personal experiences of care, forgiveness, love, specific messages, and so on seem incompatible with an essentially impersonal Reality, One that is the "unspeaking, the unconcerned." However, impersonal experiences of God seem consistent with God as essentially personal. In brief, that an essentially personal God could come as, e.g., the Silence, seems unproblematic to me, but that an essential Silence could come as communicating words, care, love, and so on, seems very problematic. Further, the intrusiveness of certain experiences and their independence from anything that we have done (pray, be open, and so on) seems more compatible with a personal God (One that initiates action) than an impersonal God. Further still, I think that as we examine accounts of mystic experiences, experiences in which the sense of self is "lost" by way of immersion in an impersonal Reality, we always find traces of the self (I have argued that logically one could not even remember a mystic experience apart from the presence and activity of the self) and often find reports (such as Radhakrishnan's) which require the Reality to be personal to some degree. My preference for an essentially personal Reality is controversial, but I shall not pursue the issue further.

Conclusion

What we may say in conclusion is the following. Experiences of God as essentially personal or impersonal are at best extremely rare. In the case of people reporting the experience we should have to examine each account for its genuineness, i.e., run it through the gamut of possible defeaters. Some claims may well run the gamut, leaving us with a conflict in beliefs, which might, however, be resolvable. We might come up with some reasoning (my reasoning is an example of a possible line of reasoning) which we consider strong enough to override one form of experience or the other. At any rate, a very limited number of religious experiences giving rise to conflict in belief is far removed from having massive, unresolvable conflict. Moreover, if having a limited number of conflicts, be they unresolvable, is fatal to PC in its religious application, then it is fatal to PC in its other applications, including applications in the worlds of sense perception and science. One need spend only a brief time in traffic court in order to realize that people have conflicting perceptual beliefs about the same incident, many of them having seen the incident from the same position (two riders in the same car); moreover, the conflicts remain unresolvable. (A court opinion is not likely to change the opinion of witnesses about their testimony.) Of course, traffic accidents are only a small fragment of the class of events in which we find conflicting testimony. Presently, a case is before the courts to determine who shot down Admiral Yamamoto (the reluctant architect of the Pearl Harbor attack) in April of 1943. Reading the various accounts of the witnesses impresses the casual reader that either the witnesses were in different worlds or they have provided highly creative, imaginative accounts. However, each witness has stuck to his story, one of the principals having gone to the grave without any confession of fabrication, distortion, or falsehood. Thus, the world of sensory observation presents us with innumerable perceptual conflicts— unresolvable perceptual conflicts. As for the world of science, it is clearly not a world without conflicting beliefs. Some beliefs simply have to be patched on to our scientific systems or left hanging around to wait for a more inclusive system. The movement of the orbit of the planet mercury did not fit Newtonian mechanics, yet the Newtonian system was not abandoned—or it was not abandoned until the development of relativity physics. Yet relativity physics and quantum mechanics are hardly systems in which all data, with their associated beliefs, fit neatly and nicely. We simply do not get perfect fits in our attempts to understand our world— physical or spiritual. Plato's words by way of the character Timaeus are most instructive on this subject.

> If then, Socrates, amid the many opinions about the gods and the generation of the universe, we are not able to give notions which are altogether and in every respect exact and consistent with one another, do not be surprised. Enough, if we adduce probabilities as likely as any others; for we must remember that I who am the speaker, and you who are the judges, are only mortal men, and we ought to accept the tale which is probable and enquire no further. (*Timaeus*, 29)

3. The Conflict over the Superiority of Some Religion

The second conflict I wish to consider concerns the status of religions. In Christianity Jesus is viewed as the highest revelation of

God, in Islam Muhammad has that status, in Buddhism Gautama achieved enlightenment which Buddhists certainly do not think Jesus surpassed, and in Hinduism any number of great saints and thinkers are viewed as having achieved insights equal to anything Jesus achieved. What are we to make of these conflicts? Do they arise from religious experience? If so, what religious experience?

Religious Experience and the Superiority of Some Religion

A religious experience in which we sensed the presence of God and received words to the effect that Jesus was the highest revelation of God would be a religious experience unambiguously grounding belief in the superiority of Christianity. A similar experience concerning Muhammad would ground the superiority of Islam. Of course, experiences of an impersonal sort could not provide any message, so that we could not expect messages within the main forms of Buddhism and Hinduism.

The fact is that very few experiences announcing the superiority of Jesus or Muhammad show up. Of the 5000 plus accounts I have considered (many from within the Christian community, and almost all of people in the West), none is an account in which Jesus or God announces or provides an inner voice to the effect that Jesus is the highest revelation of God. I also do not find any accounts in which a voice from God comes denying Jesus, or any other figure, a superior status. (Kevin's account of a Voice saying that all religions are the same is, according to my interpretation, consistent with the claim that Jesus is the highest revelation of God.) I do not deny that there are those who have had this sort of experience. My point is that the conflict concerning the superiority of some religion does not seem to stem essentially from religious experience. It stems, I believe, from Scripture, religious teaching, theology, and philosophy. In short, religious experience alone seems to present us with relatively little which is necessarily in conflict between religions.

Experiences of Jesus

Yet what about the fact that people experience Jesus as Savior and Lord? Does not this show the superiority of Christ's revelation? First of all, we need to understand what 'experience Jesus as Savior and Lord' means. I cannot say for certain, but I venture the opinion that for most Christians the phrase means that because of their commitment to Jesus Christ, they experience forgiveness, guidance, peace, strength, growth, or other positive effects; i.e., they experience certain effects because of their commitment to Jesus Christ. What I want to note is that the effects are not necessarily linked to any experience of Jesus' presence; e.g., guidance may be strictly the guidance of being led by Jesus' teachings. I believe that many, if not most, Christians experience the effects not because of having a religious experience, a sense of Christ's presence, but because of following Jesus, i.e., because of committing themselves to Him and His way of life.

Let us narrow attention, then, to those who have an unambiguous experience of Jesus and, as a result, experience the effects, or who have the effects—some of them, anyway—as aspects of the experience of Jesus; e.g., they experience Jesus' presence as guiding, strengthening, and so on. Do their experiences necessarily imply the supremacy of Jesus' revelation? I think not, for people in other religions also experience significant effects, both as a result of commitment to their way of life and also as a result of religious experience— e.g., numerous people associated with Krishna Consciousness claim that they often experience Krishna's guiding presence, peace from Krishna, joy, and so on. In fact, some people in other religions seem much further down the path of growth than many Christians, the measures of growth being those that the Christian uses, including a sense of forgiveness or freedom from guilt, thirst for God or the Divine, detachment from things, inner peace or tranquility, joy, moral earnestness, service to others, and consistent use of spiritual disciplines such as study of the Scriptures, prayer, and meditation. I think that on the basis of effects alone we shall have great difficulty showing that an experience of Jesus or, more broadly, a Christian religious experience, issues generally in the highest level of spiritual life. At least, I should not like to take on the task of showing this. I find myself here in essential agreement with what John Hick has to say about sainthood in the major religious traditions.

> All that I myself feel able to venture at present is the impressionistic judgment that no one tradition stands out as more productive of sainthood than another. I suggest that so far as we can tell they constitute to about the same extent contexts within which the transformation of human existence from self-centredness to Reality-centredness is taking place. (1989, 307)

I have spoken of spiritual growth rather than of sainthood, and have listed a number of the specifics of spiritual growth rather than speaking more generally of moving from self-centredness to Reality-centredness; however, I am quite willing to place the specifics of spiritual growth under Hick's more general characterization of sainthood.

Before concluding this section I wish to briefly consider the following two questions: What about those who do not experience Jesus? (In short, what about the overwhelming majority of the earth's population?) What is the significance of their lack of experience?

Failure to have an experience of Jesus is obviously not in any necessary conflict with Jesus' status as the highest revelation of God, unless one wants to argue in the following specious manner.

> I, along with many others, have not experienced the presence of Christ.
> Therefore, Christ is not the highest revelation of God.

The argument does not improve with the conclusion that Jesus is not divine Lord and Savior. The fact is that ever so many Christians, true believers in both the superiority of Christ's revelation and in Christ's deity, have never had an experience of Christ's presence. As for why those within the Christian community are usually the ones having experiences of Christ, I refer back to the comments on language, culture, and religious experience. Those comments are hardly sufficient, but they do provide some useful leads.

Trinitarian Experiences

But what about the people who have a trinitarian experience? Does not this imply the superiority of Jesus, the Son, as the revelation of God? First of all, I note that the experience of the Trinity is rare. Second, we need to ask what those reporting the experience really apprehended. What particular form of trinitarian doctrine does the experience support? St. Teresa of Avila reports the following trinitarian experience.

> Our good God now desires to remove the scales from the eyes of the soul, so that it may see and understand . . . by means of an intellectual vision, in which, by a representation of the truth in a particular way, the Most Holy Trinity reveals itself, in all three Persons. . . . It [one's soul] sees these three Persons, individually, and yet, by a wonderful kind of knowledge which is given to it, the soul realizes that most certainly and truly all these three Persons are one Substance and one

Power and one Knowledge and one God alone, so that what we hold by faith the soul may be said here to grasp by sight. (*The Interior Castle*, VII:1)

St. Teresa seems to support an orthodox statement of the doctrine, yet she provides no clarification of the doctrine, i.e., no new insights concerning the nature of the unity in diversity, no insights, e.g., about the sense in which the three Persons are one in power and knowledge. Indeed, in discussing a later experience of the Trinity, she writes: "Well, how do we see that the three Persons are separate, and how did the Son take on human flesh and not the Father or the Holy Spirit? This I haven't understood." (St. Teresa, 1976, 335) In a still later experience, she seems to achieve understanding.

Once while with this presence of the three Persons that I carry about in my soul, I experienced so much light you couldn't doubt the living and true God was there. In this state He gave me understanding of things I didn't know how to speak of afterward. Among them was how the Person of the Son, and not the others, took flesh. As I say, I wouldn't know how to explain any of these things. (St. Teresa, 1976, 345-46)

Without an explanation of the unity in diversity, we are left wondering what St. Teresa really did experience. We are totally without enlightenment from her as to how the three Persons are distinct and yet one. Therefore, we are far from certain what belief her experience is really supporting. Moreover, for those who do not believe that the doctrine of the Trinity is coherent, St. Teresa's experience of the Trinity will be defeated by the incoherence of the doctrine.

Assuming, though, that the traditional notion of the Trinity is coherent, experiencing the three Persons of the Trinity does not necessarily tell us why what the Son revealed on earth is the highest revelation of God. We could admit that the Son in the unity of the Trinity would have the very best access to the nature of the godhead, but then not only do we have to connect the Son as experienced in the Trinity with the historical Jesus and His mission but we also have to spell out why the mission of the historical Jesus provided the highest revelation of God. I think that the answer of the church on the latter point is this: Jesus' mission on earth, especially as it is expressed by the cross, is most deeply revealing about God (viz., God's love) and is at the heart of any claim for the superiority of the Christian revelation. All we need to note at this point is that apprehending the Trinity is not necessarily a direct awareness of the Son and His redemptive work. (The first experience I report of St. Theresa does not seem to have any redemptive link; whereas the second and third experiences do.)

Furthermore, the essential message of the Son's redemptive work is derived from the New Testament. Indeed, conceiving the earthly Jesus as the Son depends on New Testament teaching, as well as the creedal statements of the church, so that both the New Testament message and the creedal statements are probably the implicit background framework of trinitarian experience. A parallel would be the birth of my daughters. The events of their birth are a background framework of who they are. Surely, though, I do not think of their birth events every time I think of them; moreover, I know the events of their birth on grounds other than my present experience of them. Similarly, in a trinitarian experience of the Son the notion of the Son as Redeemer may be strictly background framework, a framework resting on a foundation other than present experience, with the present experience not having any conscious thought about the Son as Redeemer. E.g., the content of the consciousness may be of the Son as the One through Whom all was created. The point is that a trinitarian experience is not necessarily an experience of the superiority of Christ's revelation because the content of Christ's redemptive work may either not be present or be present only as background framework, a framework established on a foundation other than the present experience. And, of course, what must be further established is that Christ's redemptive work is the highest revelation of God, i.e., of God as love.

A final note is that a trinitarian experience is not at all inconsistent with experiencing God without trinitarian distinctions—most of St. Theresa's experiences, particularly in her earlier life, were non-trinitarian, and most Christians, the overwhelming majority, do not have trinitarian experiences. Thus, Muhammad's experience of Allah is not necessarily in conflict with either trinitarian experience or orthodox doctrine. First of all, we may note that Muhammad probably did not understand trinitarian doctrine, at least as articulated by a church father of the competence of St. Augustine. Muhammad was reacting largely to popular conceptions of the Trinity, popular conceptions then being no better than popular conceptions now. Thus, his pronouncements concerning God's oneness do not necessarily stand in conflict with Christian teaching. If a Muslim or Jewish philosopher-theologian should deny trinitarian distinctions within God, then the denial rests, I should say, not on religious experience but on philosophical-theological analysis, or traditional teaching. Moreover, Muslim and Jewish thinkers talk about distinctions in God (e.g., God's justice and God's mercy), while asserting the unity of God, exactly what Christian theologians do. If Christian theologians are to be faulted, they must be faulted on the incoherency of trinitarian distinctions—a matter which is to be determined by rational analysis, not religious experience. The essential point is that if the distinctions are incoherent, then any experience of an orthodox trinitarian nature is overridden; if the distinctions are not incoherent, a trinitarian experience is not necessarily inconsistent with a non-trinitarian experience.

Messages: Complementary or Conflicting?

I underline again what I have already stated, viz., that claims of some religion being superior (i.e., the religion provides the highest revelation of or the deepest insight into God) do not seem to rest essentially on religious experience but on Scripture, religious teaching, theology, and philosophy. Religious experience directly justifying belief in the superiority of some religious revelation or insight is relatively rare.

Someone might claim, though, that St. Paul's conversion experience is an experience communicating the superiority of Christianity. Paul is chosen to be a messenger of the Gospel to Jew and Gentile, from which we might infer that the Gospel is superior to other messages—it is to go to all mankind. Muhammad, of course, was also instructed to proclaim a message to mankind, so that we might also infer that his message is superior to other messages. However, we could refrain from making both inferences, noting that the command to proclaim a message does not necessarily imply that the message is superior in all respects to some other message. One message may speak more adequately of God in certain respects, whereas another message may speak more adequately of God in other respects. Or one message may introduce or emphasize that which another message does not mention or barely stresses.

What we may say, though, is that the Koranic portrait of Jesus conflicts with the New Testament portrait—a point underscoring my contention that the conflict over the status of Jesus does not arise from religious experience. We may suppose, then, a Muslim who takes the Koran as absolutely normative and thus as an an overrider for any religious experience of Jesus. Of course, we may also find a Christian who sees the New Testament as absolutely normative and as authorizing only certain sorts of religious experience. E.g., such a person may not find any New Testament experience like that of Terri (we may recall that Terri's experience had a kind of Eastern cast), and thus may consider her experience inauthentic. With people of this sort, both Muslim and Christian, we should have to discuss methodology, including their methodology for interpreting their Scriptures. In speaking about URP or CMP or other religious doxastic practices I have not said that everybody, or everybody in a particular religious community, adheres to the practice. My contention concerning URP has been that a number of thinkers follow it and that it incorporates valid religious methodology.

Appeal to URP

Thus, I come back to my claim that the arguments of many people about religious belief do not appeal to considerations peculiar to CMP (or the doxastic practice of some other religion). Instead, they appeal to considerations considered universally valid. Suppose, e.g., that I am trying to make a case to a Buddhist for the superiority of Christ's revelation. First of all, I have to make a case for love as the supreme value, no simple task in the case of the Buddhist who holds that absence of desire is the highest value. I may find myself gravitating to those who hold forms of Buddhism (Mahayana) which recognize the high value of compassion or love. In any case, I should not employ methodology in my conversation which I did not think the Buddhist accepted. Thus, in trying to show that Jesus reveals love to a degree not revealed elsewhere, I would do something along the following lines: I would concentrate on what I take to be an important, if not essential, meaning of Jesus' mission, a meaning expressed most forcefully in his death on the cross, viz., suffering love. I would then appeal to the Mahayana notion of a Bodhisattva, noting that in my opinion no being has ever "out-bodhisattvaed" Jesus. (I would consider this understatement sufficient for my purposes.) In the case of other religions, I would try to find expressions of suffering love, points of contact with what Robert Farrar Capon calls "the presence of the Word in all victimization." (1971, 65) I do not think that I exhaust the meaning of Jesus' mission with the notion of suffering love; however, my point concerns not what exhausts the meaning of Jesus' mission but what the nature of my appeal would be, viz., to something which I consider to be universally valid, a value-moral notion which holds interreligiously and which I think people in other religions would buy-into. In short, I do not expect others to change to some special methodology peculiar to Christianity but to employ a methodology which I think that they already accept. My expectations about their accepting any of my notions may be unrealistic (although, perhaps not, since my expectations are relatively modest), but they also may not be. I have accepted a number of Eastern notions which years ago I never figured I would.

On What Does Not Follow from Claims of Superiority

Supposing that one accepts the superiority of Jesus as revealer of God, what follows? Certainly not that there is no truth or possibility of spiritual achievement in many other religions, such as Islam, Hinduism, or Buddhism. This does not follow logically, and, as far as I can tell, it is not a teaching of the Christian Scriptures. Indeed, I think that we may assert the superiority of Christ's revelation, while still asserting the higher spiritual development of numerous people in other religions, as well as clearer insights or emphases in the religions on a number of matters. E.g., I have found more help in Eastern religions than in Christianity on the matters of detachment and focusing on my own spiritual development. (Perhaps most of my deficiencies in Christianity were a result of my religious culture. Many were, but I have found nothing in Christianity quite as helpful, e.g., as the Taoist prescription, "Do nothing." The New Testament emphasis on proclamation often obscures the priority of self-growth and of letting others be drawn to the truth.)

Conclusion

The sum of the matter is that religious experience giving rise to conflict over the superiority of some religion is relatively rare. Moreover, the conflict is not necessarily unresolvable, for other considerations may outweigh whatever experience we have on the subject and may support the view that some religion or other is superior, or that no religion is superior, each presenting some important aspect of the Divine and of the religious life, while neglecting other aspects. In any case, we do not seem to have massive, unresolvable conflict arising from belief based on religious experience.

4. What May We Know about God? A Note on John Hick

What I wish to do in ending this chapter is note the difference between myself and John Hick—or what I take to be the difference—on conceiving the Divine. Essentially, I do not, as does Hick, adopt a Kantian model for thinking about the Divine. Instead, I adopt a model which I see as a takeoff from the Greek notion of the "spark of the Divine," as well as the Hebrew-Christian notion of the "Image of God," a model which provides for conceptualizing God in ways which approach the divine Reality. To think of the Divine as Noumemon risks traveling the road of non-sense, for if the Divine is beyond all conceptions, then we do not think anything when we think the Divine, and the term 'noumenon' is a mere mark on the page or sound in the air. I think that this road is as bad as the road of contradiction and therefore do not wish to travel it.

However, Hick, along with most everybody else, would also agree that the road is one to avoid, so that he makes various twists and turns, yet without abandoning the road, I maintain. Or to change the figure, I think that Hick engages in some fudges in order to stay in the God-game. According to him, the ultimately Real, the Real *an sich*, is unlimited and therefore may not be equated without remainder with anything that can be humanly experienced and defined. Unlimitedness, or infinity, is a negative concept, the denial of limitation. That this denial must be made of the Ultimate is a basic assumption of all the great traditions. It is a natural and reasonable assumption, for an ultimate that is limited in some mode would be limited by something other than itself, and this would entail its non-ultimacy. And with the assumption of the unlimitedness of God, Brahman, the Dharmakaya, goes the equally natural and reasonable assumption that the Ultimate, in its unlimitedness, exceeds all positive characterisations in human thought and language. (Hick, 1989, 237-38)

In reply, we may say the following. If all concepts are limiting, then even the concept 'the Unlimited' is limiting insofar as it takes the unlimited Reality out of the category of the limited. This is what I shall view as a small fudge. Of course, if no concept applies to the Unlimited, the term 'Unlimited' is a mere mark on the page, empty of meaning.

A further criticism is that the concept of a Real limited in some mode does not, as far as I can tell, logically require giving up the concept of the Real as ultimate. I shall not attempt to spell this out in any detail but will simply note two items. If we limit the Real by saying, e.g., that the ultimately Real is uncreated, then according to Hick we limit the Real by "something other than itself." Supposing that this is true, the reply is, "What of it?" Thinking of the Real along the lines of Western religion, we may say that the Real, being uncreated, is limited by the created, by what is other than Itself, say, rocks and trees. Does this mean that the Real is not ultimate, particularly if rocks and trees have a reality derived from the Real? Only if we define 'Ultimate' so that we may not have any limitation, including conceptual limitation, in which case we risk emptiness, for our definition requires that we not employ any concept, including 'unlimited'. The second item is this. We may simply deny that we need to limit the Real by "something other than itself." We may suppose a universe with only the Real, nothing of a created nature. In such a universe created realities would be strictly a set of possibilities in the mind of God and thus not different from God. If some should consider conceptualized possibilities in the Divine to be other than the Divine and thus limiting of the Divine, I shall grant the point but deny that any such limitation deprives the Real of ultimacy.

But now we come to a big fudge. Hick says that the Real, being unlimited, "exceeds all positive characterisations in human thought and language." Why positive characterisations? Indeed, how distinguish between positive and negative? E.g., we must say (or think) something of the Real; otherwise, we are in the realm of non-sense—literally, we are not thinking or saying anything at all. Thus, Hick does characterize the Real—to begin with, it is real, of the nature of being, as opposed to non-being. The Real is also causal.

> All that we are entitled to say about the noumenal source of this information is that it is the reality whose influence produces, in collaboration with the human mind, the phenomenal world of our experience. (243)

Why the concepts of being and cause are negative, as opposed to positive, is far from clear to me. Whatever the concepts are called, the fact is that they are no less limiting, as far as I can tell, than any positive concept, such as the concept of love.

Hick goes on to say that other concepts than being and cause may be applied to the Real, such as the purely formal concept of God found in St. Anselm. (246) Here is another fudge. Hick introduces the notion of a purely formal concept (his actual language is "formal statement"), leaving the notion unclarified. (We are not totally in the dark, for in contrast to the formal we have substantive concepts, such as love.) Whatever the clarification, I fail to see how the Anselmian notion of "that than which nothing greater can be conceived" is any less limiting of God than the notion, say, of love. Indeed, the Anselmian notion of God's greatness is, in effect, a notion of God's perfection, so that included within the notion of God is God's perfect love—or so I should say.

Having made the fudges on the different sorts of concepts (positive and negative, substantive and formal), Hick then goes on to deny a list of attributes to the Real.

> It cannot be said to be one or many, person or thing, substance or process, good or evil, purposive or non-purposive. None of the concrete descriptions that apply within the realm of human experience can apply literally to the unexperiencable ground of that realm. For whereas the phenomenal world is structured by our own conceptual frameworks, its noumenal ground is not. We cannot even speak of this as a thing or an entity. (246)

Immediately following this passage, he speaks of the propriety of making formal statements about the Real, such as St. Anselm's. I shall say no more on this point, and I shall simply note the Kantian assumption about the restriction of our concepts to the phenomenal world, a restriction which I do not see as necessary. What is the logical necessity of saying that none of our concepts can apply to the ultimately Real? If we are made in the image of God—but I shall not complete the question because the area of controversy here is far too large for me to do anything other than indicate what I see as a possibility.

The main point I wish to make is that denying the listed attributes to the Real trades on the fudges already made. In short, the denial seems arbitrary (the attributes are arbitrarily classed as substantive) and also antithetical to what I should say are the best religious impulses we have. One of our best impulses is to avoid non-sense, and I again maintain that a consistent adherence to the Kantian restriction leads to non-sense. Another of our best impulses is, I should say, to recognize the ultimately Real as loving. To say that we have a poor grasp of love, and thus do not as yet understand the full nature of divine love, is hardly to say that the Divine is neither good nor evil. It seems strange to me that Hick goes to some length to show that in one form of Buddhism the ultimate Dharmakaya expresses Itself on the human level as boundless Compassion, similar to, say, the Hebrew God (as portrayed, for example, by Hosea) and the God of Jesus Christ, and yet goes on to say that the Real is neither good nor evil. Moreover, in another passage he speaks of the experiences of a compassionate Reality as similar to "veridical hallucinations," i.e., hallucinations in which authentic information is conveyed. He says:

> On the option that we are now considering, this experience [the experience of being in God's presence] is not caused by a particular invisible person—Jahweh or Vishnu, for example. It does however constitute a transformation of authentic information of which the Real is the ultimate source. (273)

And here I am inclined to think that Hick and I, although using different words, may be on the same path of meaning. I do not wish to say that we as humans get the Divine correct in any literal fashion. But then, I do not wish to say the same for our scientific attempts at understanding the spatio-temporal real. I think that we have made and are making progress in science, but I do not think that our scientific stories, if their aim is the space-time real, are yet close to their target. I think the same for our religious stories, although they may be further from the target than the scientific stories—although in some respects, perhaps not. However, just as I think that quark or string theory is closer to the space-time real than the Aristotelian theory of elements, so I think that speaking of the Divine as love is closer to the ultimately Real than speaking of the Divine as vengeful or as without moral quality at all. Or to return to my map metaphor, I do not think that our maps of the Real are presently very adequate, but I do believe that some are better than others and that our maps can become better and better. Yet can we get any perfectly adequate map? The question here is beyond my reach. All that I feel inclined to say is that the Real functions as a kind of ideal Limit, to which our maps can conform more and more adequately. If Hick would say something along these lines, then we are, I think, on the same path.

However Hick and I may differ in conceiving the Divine, I wish to note that we both appeal to methods which we take to be universal in scope and thus we both seem to be employing a URP. We are not proceeding by way of a provincial CMP. Both of us, I think, stand ready to be corrected on all scores by Hindus, Christians, atheists, or whomever, and thus we are taking the viewpoint that people from other religions are employing methods similar to ours, that we are, in effect, working within a URP.

Summary

What I have done in this chapter is focus on two major conflicts between world religions, showing, I think, that the conflicts may have a basis in religious experience but usually do not. In other words, there is not massive conflict arising from religious experience either on the issue of God's personal or impersonal nature or on the issue of the superiority of some religion. Further, I think that what is true for the two issues I have chosen is also true for many other issues supposedly in conflict. In general, I think that conflicts arising strictly from religious experience may be reduced greatly by concentrating on two questions: 1) What are the beliefs immediately justified by religious experience—i.e., the beliefs about what we seem to sense or perceive—or what are the beliefs immediately entailed by our experience? 2) Are these beliefs necessarily in conflict with the beliefs immediately justified by some other religious experience?

One matter that I have not considered and will simply mention concerns the issue: When are differently named deities really the same? One person experiences Allah, another the God and Father of Jesus Christ. Are they really experiencing different realities, or the same Reality? First of all, the cases I have considered do not have the Presence coming, announcing its name. I am not claiming that this never happens, only that it is fairly infrequent. When the Hebrew prophets said, "The word of the Lord came to me," they do not necessarily imply that God came to them saying, "This is the Lord: Now hear this!" In addition, the question I am raising is: Whatever the name of the deity, are we really meeting the same, or a different, deity? As a matter of fact, we often think that we have the same deity, even though different names are used. When interviewing Mike I was saying to myself: "Why, what he calls 'Krishna' is really what I call 'Christ'." Certainly, many Muslims, Jews, and Christians consider themselves to be worshipping the same God, even though each has a different name for God. These facts, of course, do not resolve the question of when we have the same deity.

The question of this chapter has been, Can the alleged conflicts in religious experience really be made consistent, so that a single deity could be the source of the various experiences? The question I shall not consider is, When are two supposedly different deities, deities with different names, the same or essentially the same? Surely, since Allah is Creator of heaven and earth, as is the God and Father of Jesus Christ, Muslims and Christians seem to be referring to the same deity, as is indicated by saying, "I want to talk about the Creator of heaven and earth, whatever you wish to call this Being, and whatever the other properties of the Being." As I said, though, I shall not pursue this issue but will leave it for the hands of others, some of whom have already pursued it in considerable detail. My point would be that I do not see any insuperable problem in going for the thesis that many of the gods of different names have some essential properties in common, and for those properties not in common, we may show that the properties are complementary or that one is essential, the other not, or that some property is simply not the property of deity.

In conclusion, I do not find that using PC leads to massive, unresolvable conflict in religious belief. As a result, if we wish to jettison PC in the case of religious experience, we shall have to look for a general defeater other than massive, unresolvable conflict.

Conclusion

My thesis in this book has been that religious experience, viewed broadly as encounter with the Divine, is a rational ground for religious belief. Specifically, I have taken the view that religious experience is *prima facie* justification for religious experience. I have followed the approach of Richard Swinburne and William Alston, specifically using Swinburne's Principle of Credulity (PC), interpreting the principle in terms of Alston's doxastic practices.

My general objective has not been to show that religious experience, by itself, will justify some theism, such as Christianity, or even theism generally. Rather, my objective has been to show that certain proposed general defeaters—defeaters of religious experience as such, not just this or that religious experience—do not defeat. Considering the objective from the standpoint of PC, I could say: I have attempted to show that some common objections to applying PC in the sphere of religious experience do not hold. Or put in terms of a doxastic practice, I could say: I have attempted to show that some common objections to viewing a religious doxastic practice as adequate do not hold.

First of all, I considered the general defeater that religious experience does not provide a good ground for religious belief because religious experience may be explained naturalistically. I looked at several common naturalistic explanations for religious experience: religious background, conscious desire, unconscious desire, other unconscious motivation. Using the specific cases of religious experience I had examined, I found numerous counterexamples to each explanation. I have not considered every candidate for a naturalistic explanation, but I have considered what I see as the major candidates. I mentioned some other candidates, most notably early childhood experience, but I observed that this explanation may reduce to an explanation from desire; in any case, we do not presently have the case material to test the explanation.

I also considered the general defeater that religious experience does not have the kind of effects one would presume for encounter with the Divine. I noted that the long-term effects are dependent on the response of the person having the experience; however, the majority of people I looked at had both significant short-term and long-term effects.

Then I considered the general defeater that we do not have an overrider system for religious experience, with the result that we end up with massive, unresolvable conflict in belief. I showed that there is an overrider system, universal in scope. I used this overrider system to evaluate nine specific cases.

Finally, I considered the general defeater that even with an overrider system we are left with massive, unresolvable conflict. I focused on two conflicts, the personal-impersonal conflict and the conflict over the superiority of some religion or other. I noted that these conflicts do not seem to arise essentially from religious experience. Insofar as they have an experiential base, we do not end-up with massive conflict, and the conflict is not necessarily unresolvable.

Thus, I do not find any general defeater for religious experience. PC applies to the sphere of religious experience. I also maintain that the objections to the various general defeaters provide a basis for saying, following William James, that the God-hypothesis is a rational account of religious experience, preferable to other accounts.

Bibliography

Alston, William, *Perceiving God* (Ithica, New York: Cornell University Press, 1991)

Auden, W. H., *The Age of Anxiety: A Baroque Ecloque* (New York: Random House, 1946).

Barbour, Ian G., *Religion in an Age of Science* (San Francisco: Harper & Row, Publishers, 1990).

Bettelheim, Bruno, *Freud and Man's Soul* (New York: Vintage Books, 1984).

Capon, Robert Farrer, *The Third Peacock* (Garden City, N.Y.: Doubleday & Company, 1971).

Davis, Caroline Franks, *The Evidential Force of Religious Experience* (Oxford: Clarendon Press, 1989).

Edelson, Marshall, *Hypothesis and Evidence in Psychoanalysis* (Chicago: The University of Chicago Press, 1984).

Erdelyi, Matthew Hugh, *Psychoanalysis: Freud's Cognitive Psychology*, New York: W. H. Freeman and Company, 1985).

Eysenck, H. J., "Consensus and Controversy: Two Types of Science," in Modgil, Sohan, and Modgil, Celia, Eds., *HansEysenck: Consensus and Controversy* (Philadelphia: The Falmer Press, 1986.)

Freud, Sigmund, *Civilization and Its Discontents*, trans. by James Strachey (New York: W. W. Norton, 1962).

_____, *An Outline of Psychoanalysis*, trans. by James Strachey (New York: W. W. Norton, 1970).

Grünbaum, Adolf, *The Foundations of Psychoanalysis* (Berkeley: University of California Press, 1984).

Humphreys, Richard F. and Beringer, Robert, *First Principles of Atomic Physics* (New York: Harper & Brothers, 1950).

James, William, *The Varieties of Religious Experience* (New York: The Modern Library, 1902).

Hick, John, *An Interpretation of Religion* (London: Macmillan Press, 1989).

Jammer, Max, *The Conceptual Development of Quantum Mechanics* (New York: McGraw-Hill Book Company, 1966).

Katz, Steven T., "Language, Epistemology, and Mysticism," in Katz, Ed., *Mysticism and Philosophical Analysis*, (London: Sheldon Press, 1978), pp. 22-74.

Kazin, Alfred, Ed., *The Portable Blake* (New York: The Viking Press,1946).

Kreeft, Peter, *Heaven* (San Francisco: Ignatius Press, 1980).

Maslow, Abraham H., *New Knowledge in Human Values* (New York: Harper & Brothers, Publishers, 1959).

_____, *Toward a Psychology of Being*, 2nd Ed. (New York: Van Nostrand Reinhold Company, 1968).

Pais, Abraham, *Niels Bohr's Times* (Oxford: Clarendon Press, 1991).

Plantinga, Alvin, *The Nature of Necessity* (Oxford: Clarendon Press, 1978).

———, "Reason and Belief in God," in Plantinga, Alvin, and Wolterstorff, Nicholas, Eds., *Faith and Rationality* (Notre Dame: University of Notre Dame Press, 1983), pp. 16-93.

Radhakrishnan, Sarvepalli, and Moore, Charles A., Eds., *A Source Book in Indian Philosophy* (Princeton, New Jersey: Princeton University Press, 1957).

Stiles, William B., Shapiro, David A., and Elliott, Robert, "Are All Psychotherapies Equivalent," in Vanderbos, Gary R., Ed., *Psychotherapy: Practice, Research, Policy* (Beverly Hills: Sage Publications, 1980), pp. 165-80.

Swinburne, Richard, *The Existence of God* (Oxford: At the Clarendon Press, 1979).

St. Teresa of Avila, *Interior Castle*, trans. by E. Allision Peers (Garden City, N.Y.: Image Books, 1961).

———, Collected Works, Vol. I, trans. by Kieran Kavanaugh and Otilio Rodriguez (Washington, D.C.: ICS Publications, 1976).

Vanderbos, Gary R., and Pino, Christopher D., "Research on the Outcome of Psychotherapy," in Vanderbos, Gary R., Ed., *Psychotherapy: Practice, Research, Policy* (Beverly Hills: Sage Publications, 1980), pp. 23-69.

Wall, George, *Is God Really Good?* (Washington, D.C.: University Press of America, 1983)

Watt, W. Montgomery, *Muhammad: Prophet and Statesman* (London: Oxford University Press, 1961).

Winson, Jonathan, "*The Meaning of Dreams*," Scientific American, 263 (Nov., 1990), 86-96.

Weisheipl, O. P., *Friar Thomas D'Aquino: His Life, Thought, and Work* (Garden City, New York: Doubleday & Co., 1974).

Whitehead, Alfred North, "Religion and Science," in Johnson, A. H., Ed., *Interpretation of Science* (New York: Bobbs Merrill, 1961), pp. 170-183.

Wojytla, Karol, *Collected Poems*, trans. by Peter Kewicz (New York: Random House, 1979).